REVOLUTIONARY DISCOURSE
IN MAO'S REP

S.W.

REVOLUTIONARY DISCOURSE IN MAO'S REPUBLIC

David E. Apter

Tony Saich

HARVARD UNIVERSITY PRESS

Cambridge, Massachusetts
London, England
1994

Library of Congress Cataloging-in-Publication Data
Apter, David Ernest, 1924–
Revolutionary discourse in Mao's Republic / David E. Apter, Tony Saich.
p. cm.
Includes bibliographical references (p.) and index.
ISBN 0-674-76779-9 (cloth)
ISBN 0-674-76780-2 (paper)
1. Revolutions. 2. Revolutionary literature. 3. Discourse
analysis. 4. Social movements. 5. Revolutions—China. 6. China—
History—1937–1945. I. Saich, Tony.
JC491.A58 1994
320.5'323'0951—dc20
94-4421
CIP

For Ellie and Yinyin

CONTENTS

✳

PREFACE

※

What is the relationship between the power of radical ideas and the mobilization of political movements? "Les livres ont-ils fait la Révolution?"[1] Few would doubt the appropriateness of the question or that the French revolution was, among other things, an intellectual revolution. The ideas mobilized against the Old Regime were transformed from philosophical truths to political solutions—liberal monarchist, parliamentary, Jacobin—the most extremely radical versions of which (like the anarchism of Buonarotti or the communism of Babeuf) being the least intellectually nuanced. So important was the part played by ideas and more particularly books that Robert Darnton speculates that "by following the flow of literature outside the law, one can find an unfamiliar route that led to the Revolution from the Old Regime."[2]

However, the role played by books and pamphlets in the formation of new ideas ought not to be separated from the events leading up to and involved in the revolution itself. It is in the intertwining of events and ideas that people reinterpret their circumstances, and on occasion come to change them through revolutionary political action. In this regard the French revolution is by no means unique. Indeed, in all major revolutions a certain reciprocity will obtain between violent actions choreographed within master narratives and master narratives realized in the form of essential texts. In the interplay between them few events remain unexamined. Even spontaneous narration spoken on the spot before a crowd, especially when it represents itself as some higher voice (to be disembodied from the clothes, posture, gestures of the figuring agent), may anticipate textual transformation. Body acts become anchored in language acts. Then, in the peculiar alchemy of transcription, violent events become experiences, experiences become sequences, estrangements and intimacies become the marks of punctuation, and a surplus of signifiers becomes embodied in a logic of meaning. Endow a subversive text with a surplus of signifiers and it becomes important twice: the first time as an act of writing (text as a metaphor of freedom), the second as an interpretation (text as a metonym for a theory).

This double role of the subversive text applies particularly well to the Chinese revolution. Within the Chinese Communist Party, especially in Yan'an during the 1930s and 1940s, certain texts became both the instigators and the objects of struggles, the outcomes of which would define new rules and roles and impose presumptive obligations both on party members and followers. To show how this occurred we too will follow an unfamiliar route in tracing the flow of literature outside the law. Although the literature of that time and place is rough and ready, more like the radicalism of Buonarotti or Babeuf, and lacks the kind of intellectual pedigree Darnton's remark implies, we can nevertheless see how a surplus of signifiers came to be embodied in iconographic texts bound together in the form of an inversionary discourse containing both disjunctive ideas and a master narrative.

Many of the ideas in this discourse were home-grown translations and in key respects anti-intellectual. Yet even though the Chinese revolution was in many respects more different than similar to the French or the Russian, it nevertheless derived certain powerful intellectual antecedents from both (not to speak of German, English, American, and Japanese influences) in addition to adding those of its own, as Jonathan Spence, Benjamin Schwartz, Joseph Levenson, and others have described so well.

Indeed, perhaps no other major revolution relied more heavily on revolutionary discourse than the Chinese or took its ideas more seriously—so much so that, despite all the emphasis on class struggle and social contradiction, a good deal of the disposable power available to the communists was based on a logic of belief and a belief in logic.

A good many writers, artists, and journalists contributed to this discourse. In the Nym Wales archives at the Hoover Institution Library at Stanford University there is a list compiled by Mao Dun, one of the more important writers of the period, of some forty distinguished intellectuals who were imprisoned, tortured, and one way or another eliminated by the Guomindang (GMD, or Nationalist Party) in its struggle with the Chinese Communist Party (CCP). In its formative days the CCP was a party of intellectuals; and though the party changed radically after Mao Zedong came to power, it remained perhaps the supreme example of a party of the word—to the point where we can speak of the Yan'anites as a chosen people.

Mao belonged to a generation of politician-thinkers with cosmocratic impulses and a remarkable ability to use ideas as action. This tradition

included not only Lenin and Trotsky but also Gandhi, and subsequently
influenced Nkrumah, Nyerere, Ho Chi Minh, and Cabral. Each of these
revolutionary figures was, with varying degrees of sophistication, a producer of political discourse, inversionary in purpose, rupturing in intent,
and morally transformational. If the fate of their ideas was not a politically
noble one, it was not for lack of trying. Despite often bizarre consequences, their ideas embodied a good deal of the political yearning of the
twentieth century.

The Yan'an period in China is also worthy of study because it represents
political yearning transformed into both a discourse and a discourse community bound together by what can be called symbolic capital. It also tells
us something about the nature of personalized power cast in the form of
depersonalized principle. The framework we use to examine Yan'an can
apply to religious, ethnic, and other movements where people pore over
texts in search of truths that take the form of binding obligations.

Though Mao was no philosopher in the rigorous sense nor even a
qualified theorist in the Marxist tradition, no Gramsci, Lukács, or Lenin,
he nevertheless made theory the basis of a politics of principled ideas of
which he remained the consummate politician. Out of the terrible circumstances and conditions of life prevailing in China, Mao culled myths and
stories, texts and logical prescriptions. In short, he created a utopic republic, instructional as well as military, which, though it lasted only a short
while, from 1936 to 1947, came to represent the moral moment of the
Chinese revolution.

*

OUR WORK is situated within two general areas of research. The first is
comparative theory in political science/sociology/anthropology; the second is China studies. The empirical focus is on social movements and
revolutionary behavior; the analytical focus is on how people form morally
purposeful discourse communities—what we call political discourse analysis. Our concern is with how people interpret their experiences and create
languages to express their interpretations—that is, the codes, lexical systems, and symbolic structures that enable them not only to take greater
possession of their lives and circumstances but also to transcend what might
otherwise appear to be insurmountable difficulties.[3] In addition, conditions
are established for a "collective individualism." We discuss these and
similar ideas drawn from a variety of theorists in greater detail in Chapter
1. We also show explicitly how ideas and events become coded as both
myth and theory.

The disciplines of political science, sociology, and anthropology have been exposed, to some extent, to these and similar ideas less in the form of political discourse theory than in partial, fragmentary, and unsystematic ways. Even where discourse theory is recognized as such it is hardly considered respectable; there is a tendency to dismiss it as somehow vaguely belonging to "cultural studies."

Moreover, there is discourse theory and discourse theory. Some theorists rely heavily on literary analysis, the examination of texts and the search for hidden meanings. In such cases, the selection of which aspects of discourse theory to employ will depend on how well they decipher "hidden" meanings in "social texts." But if this is to reveal something important about the way in which people go about their lives in a context of its meanings, empirical examination will be required—and that means field-work.

Indeed, some of the ideas applied here to the study of revolution were first formulated in conjunction with a field study of extra-institutional protest in Japan.[4] Others were derived from a comparative analysis of violence using case materials. In the present discussion, we have tried to make discourse theory explicit and systematic in the context of a revolutionary movement that seeks the disjunctive moment, the radical break.[5]

In putting together the analytical framework employed here we became aware of the fact that some ideas are more beguiling at first glance than second. Many tire easily. Similarly, there is a problem of fit. Not a few of the theorists who interest us fail to derive or ground their ideas in empirical material. Bourdieu is an exception. So are Goody and Geertz. Others, such as Ricoeur, Baudrillard, and Barthes, deal with a different level of facticity, one that focuses on the linguistic representation of reality rather than the immediacy of political events. It is therefore not surprising that many social scientists are suspicious of theories that rely almost exclusively on mental exercises, no matter how brilliant or imaginative they may be. Though much of the criticism may be simply ill informed, some carries considerable weight: the genre is too often devoid of any reference to facts; it criticizes existing field studies without providing any of its own; it makes up in piety what it lacks in intellectual rigor.

For us, theories derived from texts constructed on texts are of little long-term interest in the social sciences unless they can offer insights obscured by conventional theories. We intend to use the ideas of writers, critics, and theoreticians against whom some of these criticisms have been levied where their ideas illuminate processes and principles obscured by professional orthodoxy. The real question is not one of pedigree, but whether or not such ideas, whatever their source, offer insightful ways to interpret empirical material. Furthermore, using them enables us to explode notions of ideology, nationalism, or culture, which (along with other commonly used and widely accepted terms) explain everything and therefore nothing. Our own preferred nomenclatures offer more nuanced ways of examining how and what people do when they use discourse politically, that is, as a form of action. In short, our interest in such ideas is not because they are unconventional but because they offer subject-centered vantage points for empirical work.

Our use of political discourse theory represents less a paradigmatic ambition than a paradigmatic consolidation. The intention is not to displace more conventional approaches but rather to enlarge conceptual competence. If the kinds of movements we seek to examine are simple in their objectives, they are anything but simple in their consequences.

More particularly, the Chinese revolution may be seen in the light of other major revolutions that constitute disjunctive moral moments. Such moments are rare. When they occur they pose deeply disturbing questions about the nature of political beliefs and their "truth values," especially when formed out of the raw materials of people's own experiences and the concrete events in which they have participated.

We also want to challenge simplistic notions of rationality and turn attention not only to economic but also noneconomic factors of transformational political experience. We are especially interested in how particular events take on new meanings, become coded, and serve as signifiers in a systematic and radical discursive practice. If, as we have said, the political emphasis embodied in the more inversionary forms of discourse theory is on people trying to transcend and overcome their current predicaments by reinterpreting them in ways that rupture conventional views and open up what they believe to be new truths, a case study enables one to understand how this process works. The problem, however, in every analytically ambitious case study is to find the right balance between the richness of the materials and the appropriateness of the analysis. At least for comparative purposes one wants a case neither drowned in its own uniqueness nor illustrative of only what is already known—a mere exercise in example. In this sense we consider the present work an argument for comparison.

Our inquiry has to do with how inversionary discourse generates power that in return helps form discourse communities with particular reference to certain neglected aspects of political power. Hence the emphasis on symbolic capital: how it is derived, how it is dispensed. That said, we want to make clear that it is not our intent to challenge received ideas about power as considered in established theories in political science or sociology (coalition theory, pluralist theory, configurationalism, functionalism, organizational theory, network analysis, and so on). The most we claim for discourse theory is that, used properly and with caution, it can add another lens to the camera, change the angle of view, and offer new perspectives. But it can do this only if the objective is needle sharp.

We are aware that our approach may disturb scholars steeped in the history and scholarship of China and for whom virtually any "outside" theories may be suspect. We have done enough specialized research ourselves to be sympathetic to such a reaction. It is in this context that we ought to make clear at the outset what our position is on Yan'an and Mao's role within it.

It is fair to say that we are both as cynical about Mao and his role as anyone in the China field—perhaps more than most, since we now know enough about him to have the best reasons for such a point of view. But we believe that simply debunking Mao is too easy. It begs questions rather than tries to answer them. After all, Mao's apotheosis was based on a good deal more than the ruthless and shrewd exercise of power. For one thing, he didn't have that much power at the start. For another, manipulative shrewdness, although obviously crucial at certain points (as we will see in Chapter 2), cannot by itself explain how Mao got as far as he did with so little and against such odds. In any case we are not interested in Mao per se but in the connection between power and belief. The real question is how it was that during the period under study so many came to believe in Mao and what he purported to represent. That Mao was inflated in his time by those overly impressed with him (such as Edgar Snow) is obvious. Nevertheless Mao's accomplishments were real enough. He was able to generate power under what appeared to be very unpromising conditions and by means of a complex, not a simple, process. This is why the Chinese revolution remains paradigmatic for movements that seek to change the world by reinterpreting it. More than any other, the Chinese revolution sought to make change irreversible. (Of course, it is always interesting when "irreversible" change turns out not to be irreversible after all.) In the Chinese case, trying to prevent reversibility is perhaps one way of explaining the periodic bouts of political madness that engulfed the regime after it came to power.

We consider Mao himself in terms of two universalized metaphorical prototypes. He can be seen as a kind of Odysseus: on two occasions during his long political life, Mao explicitly defined himself as an internal exile with redemptive intents. He can also be seen as a Socrates, uncovering the linguistic and logical structure underlying events, thereby establishing new truths and offering novel strategies of action. Of course, by putting Mao into such a Western context we run the risk of offending those purists who want to keep China for the Chinese.[6] But the Odysseus theme (and the Socratic role as well) is found in many cultural settings. It is representative of such universal phenomena as loss and the struggle to regain the patrimony through the wanderings of redemptive exiles and has become one of the more enduring political metaphors within colonial as well as revolutionary experiences.

We also elaborate somewhat on the idea of "revolutionary Platonism," which follows from the Socratic role and which we use with respect to the inversionary discourse that appeared in China. In using this term, we want to emphasize the extent to which the Yan'an experience was an exegetical creation, an express embodiment of a structure of ideas with its own hierarchy based on a dialectical epistemology. The revolutionaries' claim was that both the dialectic and the system of ideas were always there, an enduring authenticity waiting to be perceived, but disguised or obscured by conventional modes of thought and action. It is in this sense that Mao's role emerges as something akin to a Socratic agent. From on high and through relevant texts he reveals a coded language, a structure and hierarchy of ideas. Unlike Plato's, however, Mao's construct has no deontology, no reality independent from authentication from below.

In China none of the ingredients of classical Marxism was present. The revolution lacked a class with revolutionary brains. The proletariat was minuscule compared with the magnitude of the revolutionary task. Hence, in China even more than in Russia the party became the "weapon" of choice rather than a class as such.

Validating his ideas from below, or giving the appearance of doing so, was a persuasive trick by means of which Mao and his associates opened up a legitimized field of action for themselves within the Chinese Communist Party so that the party eventually came to serve as the collateral agent of the peasantry in the absence of a genuine revolutionary proletariat. Such validation also gave Mao leverage against his opponents within the party and also the authority to monitor, hector (in the name of teaching the teachers), and discipline the intellectuals (as we will see in considerable detail). So if indeed Mao tried to persuade people of what was assuredly an anti-Platonic assertion, that peasants and workers constitute a true fund of wisdom, evidence shows that neither he nor anyone else at the top in Yan'an believed it. The techniques of the mass and the mass line allowed Mao to serve up a conceptual stew that would be sufficiently appetizing to attract mass loyalty to him even more than to the party. This shrewdly manipulative strategy enabled the concepts of Maoism to be transformed into precepts. It is in the transformation of concept into precept that we find the notion of revolutionary Platonism useful.

That said, one should not lose sight of the fact that Yan'an was first, if not foremost, a military base. In this it had much in common with the other nineteen or so base areas, many of which also had some special quality of their own. None, however, so perfectly illustrated Plato's parable of the caves, or became so critically an instructional community. Certainly no other achieved Yan'an's symbolic stature. With the possible exception of the Jiangxi base, which was destroyed by the GMD and so triggered the Long March and from which Yan'an claimed putative descent, no other area could be considered the cradle of Mao's revolutionary ideology.

How then to consider Yan'an? For us it appears as a revolutionary simulacrum, a symbolically orchestrated tutelary regime, with Mao Zedong the self-anointed cosmocratic figure. As the agent for higher truths he, in concert with others, deliberately formed and fashioned an explicit inversionary discourse. Organized around universities, schools, and other instructional bodies, the course of study fashioned certain texts into a revolutionary syllabus. People were made to study these collectively in a process we call "exegetical bonding." Not only were certain ways of thinking taught, but a specific political language was learned. Embedded in the discourse were such themes as loss and recuperation, reenactment, retrieval and projection, narratives and texts, myths and logic, leading to the formation of symbolic capital (in the absence of the economic kind). We see Yan'an evolving into the moral center of the revolution from its origin as a military base with the Yan'anites coming to regard themselves as a chosen people.

In addition to being a consummate strategist, Mao is also a storyteller (who comes to figure in his own stories) and a cosmocratic agent (who claims to be the representative of higher truths). The Mao who emerges in our analysis is not only a master at stalking his opponents within the party but also at translating specific events into surrogates for his own mythologic.

Much of the material is based on lengthy interviews conducted between 1986 and 1989 with survivors of the Yan'an experience. Both of us also conducted extensive interviews with students in Tiananmen Square in April, May, and June 1989 and were present at the demise of the movement. In Tiananmen Square we came face to face with the irreversible reversal of irreversible change. There we could see in action what might be described as Foucault's paradox, the ruthlessness of an inversionary discourse that has become hegemonic.

ACKNOWLEDGMENTS

✳

We are indebted to many people, not a few of whom took risks on our behalf. The idea of this book and funding and support for the field research originated with a fellowship and then a research grant to David Apter from the Committee on Scholarly Exchange with the People's Republic of China. The analytical ground was prepared in the intellectually congenial environment of Magdalen College, Oxford, where Apter was a Visiting Fellow in 1988. The Institute for Advanced Study in the Humanities and Social Sciences, Wassenaar, provided exceptional facilities for writing up the research. We are particularly grateful to the Director, D. J. van de Kaa, and the staff of the Institute for their help and support. The Center for Chinese Studies under the International Studies and Overseas Program, UCLA, provided time and space for the final editing to be completed. Auspices in China included the Chinese Academy of Social Sciences, most particularly the Institute of Marxism-Leninism, Mao Zedong Thought, and the Department of History of Beijing University; and, respectively, Professors Su Shaozhi and Luo Rongqu. We are much indebted to them, to Yue Wei Li, and to Fang Shi of the Xinhua News Agency. Zhao Yi, Michelle Chua, Zhang Meng, and Song Xiaobing, members of our research team, labored mightily even under the watchful eyes of discomfited authorities.

Among the many people who gave us a great deal of their time and consideration were Tang Tsou, Stuart Schram, Roderick MacFarquhar, Merle Goldman, Edward Friedman, Robert Scalapino, and Michael Oksenberg. Part of the crew that inhabited the Haoyuan Hotel in the summer of 1986 and freely shared ideas with us included Jean Oi and Andrew Walder (who subsequently furnished comments on various parts of the manuscript), James L. Watson, and Ruby Watson. Helen Snow, who granted us many interviews, provided access to the Nym Wales archive at the Hoover Institution in Stanford. John Service helped us at the very preliminary stage of the study. We had lengthy and useful discussions in

China with Rewi Alley (now deceased), Israel Epstein, and Sol Adler, all of whom provided us with the unique perspectives of westerners who had thrown in their lot with the future of China. Michael Lindsay, who had been in and out of Yan'an during the period under discussion, provided us with background information. Eleanor S. Apter, who participated in all phases of this work, took careful notes during the interviews to supplement our tapes.

Among the many Chinese scholars who helped us from the start were Hu Hua (now deceased), Gong Yuzhi, Wen Jize, Li Rui, Feng Lanrui, Dai Qing, and Huang Hua. Needless to say none of these people is responsible for the ideas and observations (some of which would strike them as very odd indeed), and some, out of the goodness of their minds, tried to persuade us to work with more conventional interpretations.

The Royal Netherlands Academy of Arts and Sciences provided financing for two research visits to China, as did the International Institute of Social History, Amsterdam. We would also like to thank the staff of the Sinologisch Instituut, Leiden, for helping us locate materials.

Portions of Chapter 3 appeared in a different form in David E. Apter, "Yan'an and the Narrative Reconstruction of Reality," *Dædalus* (Spring 1993), pp. 207–232.

REVOLUTIONARY DISCOURSE
IN MAO'S REPUBLIC

1

TOWARD A DISCOURSE
THEORY OF POLITICS

✳

It seems to be a lesson of history that the commonplace
may be understood as a reduction of the exceptional, but
that the exceptional cannot be understood by amplifying
the commonplace. Both logically and causally the exceptional is crucial, because it introduces (however strange it
may sound) the more comprehensive category.

Edgar Wind, *Pagan Mysteries in the Renaissance*

One of the principal aims of this book is to lay out the terms and
relationships of a discourse theory of politics. Contextualized in a case
study, and elaborated by means of a logocentric model, the theory is in
part derived from fieldwork. Some of the categories applied here were
already in mind when the inquiry began.[1] However, it was in the course
of the research and in the analysis of the materials that the present version
of a discourse theory took shape, as well as the logocentric model with
which the discussion begins.

A certain perspective has been followed throughout that affirms the
value of ethnography in political studies, despite methodologists who
complain about the superior virtues of statistical and quantitative comparisons over contextual knowledge (often without realizing that the analytical
distancing produced by their instruments may distort the quality of their
interpretation). Ethnographic writing has become a subject in and of itself;
reconstructive criticism claiming to demonstrate the inadequacy of field
experience has presented interpretations that make dubious any claims to
authority.[2] As well, and especially in political science and sociology, case
studies, like area studies more generally, are often considered descriptive
and parochial and therefore not useful for more general comparative
analysis or construction of theory.

There is validity in all these points of view. They suggest what to avoid
and offer criteria for what needs to be done in the way of overcoming

some of the common limitations of the usual case study. Whether we have succeeded or not in overcoming these perceived limitations is up to others to decide.

Our case is a historical one although it has a certain residual impact on present Chinese politics insofar as the story remains within the living memory of some of its participants. Reconstructing it by means of interviews and documents is, of course, very different from direct observation and experience. Using a retrospective phenomenology to tease out of participants a reliving of an important piece of their lives is full of pitfalls. We therefore can make no claims to ethnographic authority. Yet we have been able to probe rather deeply into the events of what was certainly a heightened political moment. It was the point during the Chinese revolution when the discourse community was reformed and generated sufficient power to change the course of China's history. Indeed, our fundamental concern is with discourse and power. In Yan'an we can see how the one produced the other, deliberately, with great shrewdness, and with consequence.

Yan'an is our case. The categories are designed to apply to political movements more generally, especially of an inversionary kind where power is in part constituted through the use of interior languages, symbols, and interpretive networks. We will see in this case the curious but not uncommon role played by intellectuals as an anti-elite elite. We shall also see the dramatistic consequences of confrontation and conflict.

Within the larger framework of discourse theory, two model tendencies can be identified. One is logocentric; the other is econocentric. Long-term politics favors the second, but in any concrete system, and from time to time, tendencies towards the first may occur. The shifting tendencies between them constitute an uneven or bumpy dialectic of their own. As a discourse community Yan'an represents the logocentric model. Today the problem for China is how to transform the discourse according to the rules and practices of the econocentric model. That the transition will not be easy is suggested by the events in Tiananmen Square in the confrontation between students and state in 1989. But the long-term outcome is inevitable.

From a present-day standpoint, using Yan'an as a case study may seem odd. In its own time and to most Chinese it was so far from the main centers of China that it was hard to conceive of as more than a place of refuge. Even after its founding few believed it could become a powerful revolutionary center or morally privileged radical community. That underestimation was one of the major political errors of the century. The Chinese are still living with the consequences.

However, even if it became significant in its day, what about now, when to virtually all Chinese Yan'an is distant, remote, and too primitive to be relevant to contemporary concerns? Yan'an is just one of many episodes trivialized by history, and not even new information that is becoming available on the period seems of more than passing interest, except perhaps to historians of political movements and specialists in Chinese politics.

Moreover, even its historical relevance is disappearing. Yan'an no longer occupies its former position as the central legitimizing myth of Chinese communism. Few in China bother to pay it more than lip service despite occasional feeble efforts made by the authorities to prop it up. The Chinese have other concerns: the extension of a market economy, political reform, and the unfinished business of democratization, to name but a few. Finding a new discourse around which to rebuild society and state, and on principles embedded in the econocentric model—this is China's predicament today. Yan'an has nothing in common with such matters. In any case, with Edgar Snow's *Red Star over China,* Mark Selden's *The Yenan Way in Revolutionary China,* and more recent commentaries, surely enough has been written about it.[3]

Despite all this, we think Yan'an remains interesting both for general analytical purposes and for understanding the evolution and direction of contemporary China. Indeed, our final chapter explains why the Yan'an legacy is not to be entirely discounted if only as a potential source of nostalgia for the puritanism it represents in a more corrupt age. In addition, despite its preoccupation with the practical business of war and revolution Yan'an had in its logocentricism certain proto-religious characteristics intertwined in a secular theory of politics that identified logos with power. This was the opposite of more conventional notions of power found in "normal" bargaining and compromising forms of politics, where interests prevail over principles, and negotiation over confrontation.

One can, of course, examine Yan'an by means of theories of rational choice, methodological individualism, marketplace models, and bargaining processes. But this would reduce events to the flat plane or surface of normal politics while ignoring how and why Yan'an and equivalent movements are able to generate alternative modes of power. And, while it certainly is true that we live in an increasingly universalized econocentric world, that world is more than ever interrupted by powerful political movements that are inversionary in intent and easily influenced by ethnic, religious, and racial concerns. The goal, then, is to deepen our understanding of political movements by decentering rather than displacing more econocentric models, which tend to analyze "normal" politics and the character of bargaining, negotiating, compromising, and coalition forming.[4] Econocentric models emphasize how politics as a process objectifies private and individual wants and desires in the form of social needs and priorities according to distributive schedules and alternative possibilities.[5] At the center of the econocentric model is *methodological individualism.*[6] At the center of the logocentric is *collective individualism.* The logocentric model is concerned less with choice than with projections made on the basis of some doctrinal definition of necessity that specifies its own rules and theoretical principles and for which it provides its own logic. Deterministic rather than probabilistic, the logocentric model "works" when it persuades people to "convey" their private narratives and personal interpretations to the collectivity. For them to do this, however, no ordinary community will do.

Yan'an was no ordinary community. From the perspective of the survivors themselves, it was created by a small band of revolutionaries who gathered in Yan'an after surviving the famous Long March. Once there they deliberately and explicitly sought nothing less than to change the world by reinterpreting it. It remains remarkable that they were so successful in realizing this presumptuous ambition. So regarded, Yan'an remains a prime example of how power can be generated by an inversionary discourse community that, while constructing its own language of belief, bundles it together with ideological, ethnic, religious, and linguistic strands.

Hence we treat Yan'an as a case for the presentation of a logocentric model. A discourse community revolutionary in object and inversionary in goal, it embodied a radical, disjunctive, and transformational nationalism. As a place it represented the translation on the ground of passionate boundaries and totally demanding affiliations. Its immediate context, however, was not choice but conflict and chaos, war and revolution. Its central project was to reestablish order in the form of a redefined and projected equity. A politics of the "overcoming" variety Yan'an generated political yearning, shame to be overcome, guilt to be exorcised, loss to be regained.[7] Redemptive in character and transformational in consequence it also produced a cosmocratic figure who, although secular, might easily have been theocratic. In this respect, Mao Zedong rubs shoulders with such other cosmocrats, left or right, as Lenin, Hitler, Gandhi, Peron, and Nkrumah, to mention only a few. Despite enormous doctrinal differences, their common tools of the trade were an oracular vision and exegetical persuasiveness. They were all storytellers who treated the national vicissitudes as narratives of paradise lost and to be regained. The movements they headed were intended to be nuclei for societies yet to be built requiring commitments that took priority over any ordinary preference and elevated identity over normal affiliation, morality over practical relativism and, above all, "truth" over open-ended choice. They also agreed on the intrinsic importance of violence as the general condition and with it the politics of spectacle. Death and its rituals, funerals, parades, the body as a point of visceral departure for a larger and more theatrical frame, all were of special significance.[8] Such phenomena are endemic in modern politics. They go with the exceptionalist premises that can be shared by a particular membership or, better, brother- and sisterhood.

To one degree or another one can find similar efforts in many parts of the world today when certain political events suddenly become symbolically dense and loaded with interior meanings and participants begin to retrieve the past and project a future in ways both mythic and logical. Then, as in Yan'an, political discourses become boundaries that define and elevate difference, demarcating a fundamental separation between insiders and outsiders. They involve some form of exegetical bonding. Dignified rather than undermined by conflict, discourses of this nature refract between boundaries in the mind and on the ground, the violation of each making them more rather than less important. By seeking the moral moment in the cannon's mouth, inversionary discourse communities aim to alter fundamentally their relations to the state or with each other.

Such communities and the confrontational politics they pursue have become more rather than less frequent. This at a time when democratization has for the first time, or after many years of being thwarted, become an option for many countries. Clearly inversionary discourse movements may prejudice democratic prospects. The problem is that most are symptomatic of long-standing grievances, social circumstances long ignored and badly in need of rectification. It is not surprising that inversionary discourse communities form, converting a history of such grievances, real or imagined, into new forms of truth, and turning episodes and events into coded narratives and sacred texts. Playing on uncertainty, chaos, and frustrated hopes and ambitions, though they promise far more than they can deliver, they may accomplish a lot.

Which brings us close to the emotional roots of political power. How was it that a miscellany of individuals could be transformed into a chosen people and under entirely unpromising conditions? It is a question to be asked of many other political movements, emancipatory in character, that favor radical forms of nationalism and are redemptive in origin and transformational in ambition, that create republics of truth, real or imagined.[9] These movements generate symbolic capital in the absence of the economic kind. One can make comparisons with many "last shall be first" religious or theocratic movements, of which there is a long history.[10] The defining characteristic of the logocentric model is that it offers alternative truths on which to act and promises to those who accept such truths that acting on them will transform one's own condition by altering the conditions of society at large.

To join is not a matter of mere membership. Affiliation is commitment. In the most radical versions membership and affiliation result from an original act of choice that then becomes a permanent obligation. Boundaries become sacrosanct not only on the ground but also as principles and beliefs objectified by the terrain. Once one crosses the border and enters that terrain it becomes difficult to turn back or change one's mind. Opting out is betrayal. Insofar as discourse communities occupy a physical ground or terrain, the space itself is sacralized, endowed with meanings iconographic, mobilizational, symbolic. This "meaning-space" we will call a simulacrum.[11]

Such discourse communities constitute primary affiliations. They replace family and friends and offer an equivalent intimacy. At the beginning they are conceived as miniaturized versions of societies in the process of becoming. Obligations, orders, and powers take on a critical importance. Choosing, the original act of selecting among political alternatives, is like oath-taking. Once made, the commitment is to the organization, which, no matter how personalized the leadership, claims a higher truth and demands devotion.

The logocentric model is particularly useful in examining what might be called "the politics of the moral moment." Not that this cannot be studied by other means—rational choice theory, for example. We can also reverse the argument. "Normal" politics can be studied by means of discourse theory and a logocentric model. In doing so one would emphasize different aspects—symbolic coding, spectacle, the significance of rhetoric in the formation of political groups but also as employed by governments and the state.[12] Here, however, we prefer the logocentric model for analyzing a politics of "truth" rather than wants and a moral rather than a political economy, for it reveals principles of rationality that rely less on the market and individual rationality than symbolic capital and collective individualism. It shows how the functional relations between people based on exchange and a diversity of wants can be transformed into those based on cooperation and defined goals and objectives. It is in this context, one might even say (with a certain irony), that in Yan'an as a discourse community one can find something approximating Habermas's ideal speech situation, although not the sort he had in mind. Even better, perhaps, we can refer to it as a kind of revolutionary Platonism.[13] Whatever the preferred reference, however, the point is that logocentric models enable us to study how some discourse communities seek to establish conditions of truth and realize these conditions by means of collective action.[14]

The framework used for these purposes will seem at first glance more complex than it really is. Four key terms are employed throughout. These are *retrieval* as the creation of a mythic past, *projection* as the logical derivation of an identified future, *exegetical bonding* as means of discipline, and *symbolic capital* as a form of power.[15] These terms are applied in three contexts: structural, phenomenological, and hermeneutical.[16] The terms and contexts are connected by five paired analytic criteria: orality and writing, magic and logic, narrative and text, myth and theory, retrieval and projection.

We emphasize interpretation rather than choice. The dynamic factor is thinking one's way out of current predicaments. If the connection between choice and democracy is crucial in the econocentric model, with its emphasis on how to reconcile the principle of self-sustaining rules and institutions with the principle of perpetually open ends, the logocentric model deals with the relation between individual and collective *projects of overcoming*.[17] In Yan'an, people came to believe that as a consequence of their individual contributions to the collectivity each was able to draw down more than he or she put in. Hence the logocentric model remains individualistic but with collective consequences, the examination of which provides the rationale for what we call symbolic capital.[18]

The logocentric model enables the deployment of categories suggested above. To be useful these need to be applicable to concrete situations. We are not interested in theories theorizing about theories. We also want to explode such overused concepts as "culture" and "ideology" and "nationalism." These are terms all too often wheeled into place to serve either as residuals or supplements to econocentric models, picking up where such analyses leave off or their predictions go wrong, or turned into independent variables that result in simplistic explanations. Rather, we want to probe as deeply as possible into the minds and actions of ordinary people when, as followers and participants, they surprise even themselves.

There is, of course, nothing new or unique in talking about politics in terms of discourse. As for the logocentric model, it goes back to Plato's *Republic*. But by examining it in this way we hope to understand better the sense of interiority of revolutionary movements and the way in which these movements use knowledge as discipline and power, or truths as a condition for punishment. Nor is normal politics immune from such tendencies. In the most practical and econocentric groups where people understand the overriding "truth" of the market as a fundamental principle of political life, it is the losers who are the punished. When the losers become the clientele for political yearning, and an appropriate discourse is set out that challenges the conventional theoretical languages and articulates an alternative logic and practice, the stage is set for the kind of politics that concerns us here.[19]

Passionate Boundaries

Almost by definition a radical politics involves difficulties. For would-be adherents the road to follow is filled with dangers. The familiar is left behind. Uncertainty becomes the norm. In the beginning there are few clear signposts. One is attracted perhaps because of desperate circumstances. A chance encounter might result in an engaging connection. And the way is paved with unforeseen consequences. In the Chinese case, to join the Chinese Communist Party (CCP) meant opting for a life of clandestinity and secrecy and entering into a dangerous world of foreign settlement police, nationalist agents, warlord soldiers, and Japanese invaders. Even to come to Yan'an in the first place was no ordinary act. Those who made such a choice voluntarily left their homes, schools, workplaces, and farms, making their way with great difficulty through Guomindang territory and enemy lines in order to participate in what purported to be first and foremost a nationalist crusade, a war against the Japanese far more than a communist revolution; only later and within the framework of the former, did the movement reveal itself as primarily a revolution against the Guomindang (GMD).

If there are many reasons why some will decide to join such a movement when most will not, and why, at certain times, more will join than at other times, one common denominator underlies them all. To join in such a movement means trying to think one's way past current predicaments and arrive at fresh, new solutions at once comprehensive and radical, most importantly, in concert with others. To think in such a manner requires one to join not just a political movement but one that has at its disposal its own language, discourse, myths, and logic. One becomes found rather than lost, a decision-maker rather than a wanderer, and an activist rather than a victim.[20] As a member of a discourse community rejecting what is, and projecting what is to be realized, one is engaged in commitment to action that compels the abdication of previous judgments in the belief that by so doing one will move beyond the world as generally perceived toward some more powerful or revealed truth. Such insight distinguishes insiders from outsiders, with insiders impelled to impose and universalize their discourse. Thus, having left the old behind, they no longer consider themselves bound by the "ordinary" rules of the game. These rules, too, are left behind and with them the roles in which they were embodied. But to do these things requires acceptance of symbolically charged and ritually reinforced alternatives.

Of course such choosing is not decision-making in the conventional sense. Rather it represents the beginning of an exercise in interpretative action. The crucial ingredient is the narrative construction of reality. Logic becomes utopic, and myth provides the events of experience. The first defines a negative pole to be transcended. The second identifies a positive pole, a transformational end state, moral in scope and just in consequence—a utopic equilibrium. Together these constitute a complete project, inversionary in object and transformational in consequence. Individual experiences shared with others are bound together in the more general knowledge of principle. Moral boundaries superimposed on physical ones sacralize the terrain, turning it into a mobilization space.

However, Yan'an is also a good story. It is a story people told themselves while they lived it and provides an uncommonly interesting example of beliefs becoming so powerful that they changed the way people acted, thought of themselves, and responded to others, at least for a time. If Yan'an never did fit the description memorialized in Edgar Snow's classic, *Red Star over China* (with its unforgettable portrait of Mao Zedong), it nevertheless was the moral moment of modern Chinese history.

What struck Mark Selden, of course, as well as Edgar Snow a generation earlier (not to mention Agnes Smedley and Anna Louise Strong, who with Snow make up the pantheon called the "Three S Society"), was how Yan'an mobilized, representing to a remarkable degree discipline, selflessness, and commitment. Indeed for them so remarkable was the achievement that it came to represent the ethos of China's revolution. Snow, in particular, contrasted Yan'an with the corrupted and compromised regime of Chiang Kai-shek with its strange mixture of Methodism, Confucianism, comprador capitalism, landlordism, and fascism (with its German advisors). For Sidney Rittenberg, who came much later (in 1946) to work for the communists, the spartan conditions in Yan'an gave the place a simplicity and a purity that contrasted with the greed and corruption he had witnessed in the China outside.[21] Proximity to the nationalists produced a negative reaction from many foreign observers and Chinese intellectuals, which formed their starting-point for analyzing what they witnessed in, or read about, Yan'an.

But if Yan'an was remarkable in its own time in the way it presented a social and political environment totally different from that which prevailed in the China of its day it also represented the wishful thinking of a revolution. It stood for the positive in opposition to the negative, the China of faded grandeur and lost patrimonies. Yan'an contradicted all the metaphors of pollution, the sick China, the poisoned China, the diseased China, the China of coolies and Mandarins, the opium, the selling of children into slavery, and above all the internecine killing, warlordism, and domination by Japan and other countries. Yan'an was an alternative to all this, but it also embodied the heroism of survivors against repeated attempts to exterminate them. Even the CCP's defeats became tokens of what was to be done, each loss made into an instruction for the future. Hence, Yan'an was a center, a sanctuary, a mobilization space, a simulacrum of a utopic community. But more than anything it was an idea, complete in itself, whose time had come. By the same token Yan'an could never have served as the design for a modern industrial society. Rather, it offered a fresh start by deconstructing the China that was, transforming the main episodes of war and revolution into turning points for both a narrative of history and a projection of truth.

Those setting out for the first time for the city did not "go to Yan'an" *(qu Yan'an),* they "returned to Yan'an" *(hui Yan'an),* as if it were their "spiritual home."[22] For many, Yan'an was the home of the revolution, its moral center, giving it the quality of a New Jerusalem, its inhabitants a "chosen people."[23] These people had a moral agenda different from the rest of Chinese society, with their own language to go with it. To become an insider in the small world of Yan'an was to enter an order in every sense of the word. One in effect "took orders" and by doing so accepted the discipline that this implied, reinforced by the immediacy of fraternal experience and common intimacy. One entered into a totally different world, in which everything familiar was ready to be changed. It was a world looking inward to China and more immediately to Yan'an. By the same token, one also became a member of the larger communist fraternity, which included very different cultures, societies, and states. One became intensely aware, for example, of the struggle of the Spanish loyalists against fascism during the Spanish civil war, and one could link this with the CCP's struggle against Japanese fascism and Chiang Kai-shek's Blue Shirts.

It gave a broader meaning to life in the caves, linking the partisan resistance to a common enterprise shared by radical nationalists from India, Indonesia, and elsewhere in the colonial world and to the spread of communist parties in France and Europe. Above all, it put one on the same historical track as the Soviet Union, where the marching orders of communism as the next stage of history had already been given by Lenin and Stalin. The Bolshevik disjunction that had occurred with the October Revolution and the subsequent mobilization and organization of a party state were indisputable facts, surrogates for the superiority of Marxism as a method of truth and historical insight, independent of the reality of the relationship with Moscow at any given historical moment.

Part of that reality was the orchestration of knowledge by the CCP in what became the most intense instructional campaign ever attempted. The testimony of survivors and the reports of foreign witnesses make it clear that what took place in Yan'an was no ordinary experience. Not only did the participants frequently see themselves as unique and exceptional, they also found themselves capable of meeting demands placed on them, shouldering burdens, and realizing tasks that they had thought far beyond them. Participants came to believe that they could think their way past crises and predicaments. They believed that by interpreting their world they would change it.

Yan'an was both an instructional community and a revolutionary simulacrum throughout its short history, from 1936 to 1947. However, this was particularly the case during the period 1939–1943. During this time, insight and logic were so suitably articulated and explanatory theories so sufficiently absorbed that not only did participants convey to the collectivity their experiences and judgments, but something much more than a public interest was defined; a redemptive solution and a utopic project were developed which, although far from being realized became logically persuasive.

In this sense, people going to Yan'an got more than they bargained for. Caught up in a new discourse, each person became immediately complicit. In return all were provided with exceptional opportunities for their own individual enhancement through collective enterprise. Each person was explicitly shown "the way" to transcend him- or herself—the illiterates became literate, the intellectuals became knowledgeable through learning communist theory (the textual versions of Mao's "sinified Marxism" providing the educational corpus) in a series of projects the aim of which was to realize the ideal of the "good communist." Moreover, this theme of self-enhancement through collective attainment emphasized education as the key to power, a concept already widely accepted in China, as was the idea that knowledge was a form of truth. Mao's dialectical strategy emphasized that such singular notions of truth would enable each person to think his or her way out of difficult situations and predicaments and so overcome all obstacles, no matter how formidable, whether military, ideological, material, or economic. So if each person defined the revolution in his or her own terms, very quickly and firmly and by a systematic process of exegetical bonding, the scope of individual discretion was narrowed at the same time as one's understanding of the discourse was enlarged.

Required then was no mere revolutionary commitment or even a keeping of the faith but a sharing in a discourse that effectively turned one's politics upside down and one's personal life inside out. So upending and disjunctive was the consequence, that one became, in one's own as well as the eyes of one's peers, another person.[24]

We have suggested that most of those who went to Yan'an were animated by a desire to rid the country of the Japanese invader. However, they also despaired of the GMD, which not only lacked the ability and will to fight, but also was riddled with corruption. It represented the problem, not the solution. But whatever the mix of particular motives for joining the revolution, these quickly became irrelevant whether one liked it or not. By learning the new political language one became a "Yan'anite." That is, one became affiliated with a movement that was organized in such a way that it was capable of continuous cell reproduction and nucleation, re-forming itself in other base areas and behind enemy lines.[25] One could cut off pieces and they would simply divide and nucleate. Hence, the CCP could be defeated again and again and still survive, its defeats becoming ingredients of both a mythic narrative and a new theory composed of polarized positive and negative binaries, radical versus reactionary, idealist versus materialist, productive classes versus exploiting classes, each set serving as a basis for metaphorical comparisons and a logically connected link in a syntagmatic chain. Moreover, each polar opposite could be represented by political surrogates, parties, factions, leaders, and friends and enemies. The more one understood "objective" conditions, the more one could combine radical disassociation within a larger framework of association. This helps explain the curious relationship between the CCP and the GMD in which the communists joined the GMD in order to pursue more effectively the war against a common enemy, the Japanese invader, while thinly disguising their true hostility.

The Narrative Reconstruction of Reality

We have suggested that the analytical framework employed here can be useful in the comparative study of radical social and political movements. Certainly the logocentric model with its emphasis on inversionary discourse has affinities to religiously inspired revolutionary, separatist, or ethnic movements, indeed to all movements prone to discontinuous and ruptural moral moments.[26] Some, more violence-prone than others, use Maoism and Yan'an as their explicit model; Yan'an was attractive to a number of third world leaders.[27] At one time, too, there were plenty of aspiring militants in the West who displayed a marked predisposition to the Maoist version of inversionary discourse, to the point where Mao and Maoism occasionally reached cult-like status.[28]

In China, Yan'an was both a pause and a midpoint. Poised between survival and prosecution of both war and revolution it was also an instructional community. Organized around schools, training institutes, universities, academies of arts and literature, there was, running through it like a single filiation, the principle that truths and virtues were derivable by means of a correct application to situations and circumstances of dialectical method and a reconstructed Marxism.[29] Far from simply adapting Marxism, however, Mao invented his own form of inversionary discourse out of the immediacy of the Chinese experience, and in doing so assumed the role of a cosmocratic teacher, a kind of radical Socrates.

One of the most important ingredients of the mix was what we will call the narrative reconstruction of reality. Its consequence was the logical interpretation of myth.[30] We begin our analysis with narratives and show how logical interpretive processes were applied to them. The place to begin is narrative as myth, text as logic, and place as spectacle. Yan'an, which came out of a virtually biblical experience, the Long March, was also a creation of carefully composed social texts, magic realism, and dialectical logic. Narratives of an overcoming and inversionary variety, following lines of the original master-slave relationship of Hegel, portrayed Chinese society as having fallen into a condition of disintegration, a state of anarchy. By the same token, China had also come to represent a kind of linguistic and symbolic prison composed of dead or obsolete political languages (Chinese and foreign). The prevailing *doxa* stifled the imagination. Its keepers and guardians were embodied in the GMD. Only a revolution with its own language would allow China to be restored to health.[31] It was necessary not only to destroy the GMD but also to open

up the way for new principles containing new conditions of possibility for
a redeemed and transformed China. Required for this was a radically new
discourse that could provide for both the exorcising reenactment and a
transcendence through the interaction of words and deeds.[32] Required too
was an ethnologizing phenomenology that rooted words in deeds and
expressed them through orality, literacy, narrative, and texts.[33]

Size was an important consideration. China is huge, but Yan'an was
small. It served admirably as a primitive nucleus. It was a republic of the
caves. Most of the participants lived in caves hollowed out of loess and cut
into the sides of mountains. In the caves, instruction was carried out.
Within the core community an extraordinary intimacy prevailed. It was
in this setting that Mao's writings were shaped, first as speeches, then as
texts. Hearing Mao's words directly in such an intimate setting, the
listeners became complicit in the construction of the texts. One might say
that an "agora principle" was basic to the initial delivery. Only later, when
Mao's words were translated from the style of an original delivery at the
public forum and transcribed in written documents (a good many original
meanings being altered in the process), did they take on the properties of
*writ*uals.

In these respects Yan'an was never just another communist base area. It
was intended to reveal in an unusual and stark way the relationship
between ideas and actions, networks and structures, and the consequences
of thought in action.[34] It is possible to trace such relationships in terms of
particular events. One can mark the beginnings of hermeneutical power
in the events leading up to the Rectification Campaign, for example,
during which the authority of the text as embodied in the *Selected Works*
of Mao Zedong was made abundantly explicit.

It was explicit also in terms of concrete activities—fighting, growing
crops, making clothes, raising food—under conditions part siege and part
sanctuary. All such practical activities furnished the raw materials for
interpretation from below, in the construction of everyday life, and in the
casting of even the most mundane in the form of higher principle. But the
process begins with the narrativization of events and experiences.

The narratives themselves were made to fit inside each other like nesting
boxes. The first, the long story, is a tale of loss—loss of the national
patrimony to imperialists following the Opium Wars and the loss of the
peasant patrimony through economic marginalization. This narrative contains a double negative, loss as a result of external imperialism and loss as
a result of internal comprador feudal-capitalism.

The second narrative, the intermediate story, describes the world of chaos and violence that follows such losses. It is about the struggle for the inheritance of Sun Yat-sen's power between Mao Zedong and Chiang Kai-shek, and between the CCP and the GMD. The third is also about struggles, but within the CCP itself, over appropriate lines and strategies, and contending claims over whose dialectic leads to the higher truths. All three narratives culminate in Yan'an. There, embodied in both a core discourse community and a larger base area, they served as the basis for symbolic capital and the exercise of power.

By the same token the three narratives are also represented in crucial texts in which a logic and an instruction are embedded. The long story represents imperialism on a world scale, the intermediate one a struggle for power between contenders claiming history is on their side.[35] The third, or interior, narrative of struggles between party lines had as its subtext Stalin's *Official History of the Communist Party of the Soviet Union (Bolshevik)*, the lesson of which is the need for the ruthless exercise of power to obliterate factional struggle. It is in this context that Mao becomes the central figure in his own story, and the self-proclaimed inheritor of the Marxist tradition, the chief representative of dialectical wisdom and revolutionary praxis.

Thus each narrative occurs twice, the first time as myth and the second as logic, once as retrieval and then as projection. As one moves from the long to the short story Mao becomes more central as a figure in his own story, representing the unfinished task of the revolution. Taken together the narratives convert space into time (the end of history) and time into space (Yan'an). They also provide historical and contemporary "facts" that need to be interpreted by the theory.

Agency

Of course the principal agent was Mao Zedong. People describe Mao as a thinker and a dreamer, a person not given to organizational concerns. But they also recognize how practical, shrewd, ruthless, and manipulative he was. His attention to the details of organization and power was hidden behind a demeanor, given credibility by Snow, that portrayed his openness and accessibility. A good many of Mao's enemies discovered otherwise, to their great chagrin.

Nevertheless, aside from the fact that he worked until very late at night and slept until late in the day, which reduced his accessibility considerably, there was much about Mao that was endearing. One of his saving graces was his earthiness, his habit of scratching himself, his carelessness about clothes, his trousers full of burn holes from the cigarettes he constantly smoked. Those who knew him speak of his immediate and sympathetic responses to the needs of ordinary persons, his concern with individuals, his individual acts of kindness. But those who clashed with him and lost describe a very different Mao, more ruthless, always one step ahead of his opponents, preparing, sometimes with their own connivance, their downfall.

Mao himself appeared in two guises, first as an Odysseus wandering in exile, culminating in the Long March of 1934–1936. In Yan'an he becomes a Socratic Mao, the philosopher-king, the teacher cum cosmocrat. The transition is a particularly notable event, the Rectification Campaign. In it, Mao appears as an agent, the spokesman for Marxist truths. But there was also a real Mao, always a palpable presence, who touched everyone's life. In front of large audiences he always appeared modest, yet authoritative. But when the words faded away, the texts remained, and with them a hermetic language punctuated by earthy examples and classical allusions.

In this regard, writing constituted permanence. It locked authority into interpretation. Orality and writing, listening and reading, together they form a mutualism, a special form of sodality. We do not use the term "mutualism" lightly. It has a particular resonance—the mutualism of work and understanding that harks back to Mao's flirtation with anarchism, to Kropotkin and Proudhon, and to that more primitive radicalism which, no matter how much he later denied it, remained an element in Mao's own view of the world. Some of the themes Mao emphasized in his storytelling were anarchist more than Marxist: patrimonial marginalization, displacement, dispersion, and dispossession. One finds their counterparts in other transformational movements that use inversionary discourse, from the early Christians to the Levelers and the Diggers. Mao's stories run with the grain of oft-repeated tales of peasant rebellions in Europe as well as China, and so make universal the plight of peasants squeezed by rapacious landlords, themselves victims of a mandarinate that represents a corrupt dynasty, which is itself a victim of external imperialism and foreign domination.

The earliest period in Yan'an was closer to anarchism in spirit than any organized Marxism. But there was no mistaking its organizational power. The party center reigned supreme and the doctrine of democratic centralism, so short on democracy and long on centralism, prevailed.

The narratives were simultaneously general and particular. They expropriated as their own such past events as the Taiping Rebellion, with its curious mixture of nationalism, modernism, and antiforeign xenophobia (even though Christian inspired). It served as one of Mao's indigenizing prototypes for his own revolution. "Anarchist in substance, Marxist in form" would be too strong a way to describe the Yan'an principles, but as in anarchist doctrines, Yan'an's emphasis is on the marginalization of the peasants, the lumpen, and the disinherited in ways not found in classical Marxism. By the same token, the instrument of redemptive repossession was the party—a party derivative of both Leninism and Stalinism.

Such themes were real enough to the Chinese, many of whom had lived out the realities of poverty, submitted to the barbarism that accompanied the erosion and disintegration of central power, and found in social banditry the last hope for protection. During the long period before, and during, the civil war the Chinese had by their own reckoning become what Lu Xun, one of China's leading writers, called "maneaters."[36] From the fall of the Qing dynasty (the Manchus) in 1911 to 1949 when Mao took power on the balcony overlooking Tiananmen Square, atrocities were commonplace. As for the GMD, its leadership disgusted a good many foreigners who helped the nationalists in the war against Japan, such as General Stilwell. A shrewd and long-term China hand like Edgar Snow saw in Yan'an a totally different China, and in Mao's thinking a unique version of Marxism. A combination of dialectical thinking, Chinese in structure and tradition and liberally sprinkled with references to Lenin, Stalin, and others, it was a language in itself, coded with references to more universal revolutionary truths—truths that revealed what common sense and taken-for-granted assumptions hid. The sense of those who observed, as well as those who participated, was that they were sharing in a process as much revelation as revolution, but practical in consequence. Here they found the link between Chinese uniqueness and the larger epic struggles. They believed that the Chinese struggle was more open and democratic than the October Revolution in Russia, and in the long run more oriented to the needs of peasants. For out of Mao's version of Marxism, from the fall to the projected solution, one found a state of grace. He projected himself both as the translator of Marxism to Chinese conditions, and the creator of a generalized theory of third world Marxism.

Mao's role is critical. But no one, not even Mao himself, was able after taking power to figure out a way to retain the spirit of the revolution and institutionalize it within the structures of a developmental party. The leadership tried to have it both ways. They saw the discipline of Yan'an as a system of moral incentives rather than economic ones and a form of motivation uniquely appropriate to communism. But, as always, after the revolution, as collective individualism became unstuck, replaced by a methodologically individualist "socialist" system, state coercion and control resulted, minimizing the ability of individuals to act on their own and as their own principal agents.[37] Taken together, the texts outline a general evolutionary dialectic of stages or epochs, and a logic that projects an end state. So conceived, time, the long history of the revolutionary struggle, is converted into space; the immediate compass of Yan'an becomes a mobilizational space and a simulacrum of the revolution. In this sense, the Maoization of Marxism establishes noncontingent and timeless truths and the yearning to realize them as a way to recapture patrimony and negate loss.

Mao used his followers as sources of authentic information for narrative materials. He made texts and their study the basis of exegetical bonding. "Educational institutions" served as one of the major modes of organization. His aim was to create symbolic capital and translate it into economic capital by means of a mobilizing praxis. Yan'an as an instructional republic served as a decentered, recentered cosmological Archimedes point, a place to stand for making a transformational revolution, with Mao's ideological compass (the pragmatics of power) manifested in the four struggles, with Liu Zhidan, Zhang Guotao, Wang Ming, and Wang Shiwei (see Chapter 2).

If Mao used peasants as his chosen instruments rather than proletarian revolutionaries, it was partly a recognition of realities that more Stalinist ideologues chose to ignore (with disastrous consequences). But it was more than a matter of necessity. Mao's peasants were surrogates for a bigger process touching on long-standing grievances of the past. The double loss of a patrimony was represented by the heroic figure of the peasant dispossessed from his land and dispersed from his village, who became both marginal and proletarian, the long-suffering and brutalized signifier of a nation robbed of its patrimony by foreigners, the English first, then others, and finally the invading Japanese.

The central theme of Maoism is that of a state alienated from its society, and a society destroying its own people. Put all this in the double context of peasant rebellions on the one hand, and the overturning of ancient dynasties on the other, and it is clear how evocative the retrieving side of Chinese communism can become. And as for the Marxism of Chinese communism, its dialectical logic, and the inheritance of Leninism and Stalinism, Mao modified the shrewdness of Stalinism and added on to it. The dialectic took on peculiarly Chinese characteristics, and was a far cry from conventional theoretical Marxism.[38] Yet, by the same token, it was Marxism that gave to the Chinese experience a certain universality, a link to developed, underdeveloped, and colonial countries.

The Empirical Context

Virtually all in Yan'an were extremely young at the time they "joined the revolution." The "founders" were exhausted survivors of the Long March, a relatively small band compared to those who had started the march, all of whom had gone through one of the great ordeals of modern history. Thus, whatever their origins, they had been "purified" by danger, and had as a result come to feel exceptional. Those who came to Yan'an later entered this sacred place not only with reverence, but with an eagerness to share in its inheritance. So Yan'an became an instructional republic in which education and knowledge remolded individuals within the context of exceptionalism. Virtually every act—working, training for the military, being sent to the front, organizing underground or in areas controlled by the GMD—were touched by this exceptionalism. For some, Yan'an was an experience so total, so penetrating, so all-encompassing that no hindsight or later experience could quite eradicate it.

Much of the evidence for the above remarks and the discussion that follows derives from new and recently available documentary materials. Much of our empirical evidence was gathered by means of extensive interviews with survivors of the period who were members of the original discourse community. The value of such interviews of course varied considerably, particularly since they are screened through the distance of fifty or sixty years of turbulent memories. Nevertheless, they throw a very interesting light on some of the qualities and characteristics of Yan'an and radical political movements generally.

Approximately one hundred fifty people were interviewed intermittently from 1986 to 1989. They included peasants, workers, intellectuals, former Red Army soldiers, teachers, writers, poets, artists, playwrights, actors and actresses, filmmakers, underground workers, musicians, senior cadres, one of Mao's former secretaries, Mao's personal photographer, and members of research institutes and training centers in Yan'an. We also talked to some very angry widows, survivors of those whose faction, or unit, had been on the losing side in the internal struggles for power within the CCP. Survivors in every sense of the word, they were not like ordinary people reliving the past, nor were they inclined to be neutral about their past experiences. They knew very well that how they recounted their experiences of Yan'an to outsiders could one day come home to haunt them. All were already haunted by later experiences. Virtually all had been accused of and penalized for "crimes." Deviations to left or right, or both, were compounded by their earlier status as official heroes of the revolution. Very few of those interviewed had been exempt from physical abuse and verbal assault, if not before then during the Cultural Revolution. All had survived by learning how to keep their mouths shut, except to parrot the appropriate line and use the exact words, phrases, and expressions countenanced by the authorities.

The first round of interviews, which were made one on one with a translator, were at best ingenuous. It was a situation unfortunately aggravated by the somewhat precipitous and unforeseen way the present project was launched—unsolicited, unplanned, a chance that came out of the blue, with no time for the necessary preliminary preparation and research. But delay was dangerous: the survivors of Yan'an were old, and when they died Yan'an as an experience would disappear.

In the beginning the opportunity was greater than the reward. Our interviewees were underutilized. Our questions only occasionally stimulated them and failed to tap the kind of detailed knowledge we knew they had. It took repeated interviewing over several years to overcome these deficiencies.

There were some important exceptions. A few individuals were willing from the start to open a door to a profitable line of inquiry. A rich, and indeed large, resource for uncovering actual events rather than myths is the many widows. China is a country of angry widows. Each shift in the party line produced its own legacy of such widows whose husbands were pulled down, humiliated, subjected to trials, committed suicide or died of beatings, or were atrophied by long prison sentences.

In analyzing these interviews one confronts the problem of how to go from the small to the large, the personal to the social, the individual experience to the collective one, and how to account for the complex interaction between these in light of events that shook the world yet remained a mystery demanding resolution. One practical solution is to go back and re-interview some of the same people, and over several years. Another is to change the method of interviewing. The research became the joint effort of a small team, which worked together every day, gathering documents, mapping events, and above all engaging in joint or group interviewing. Key people were interviewed four or five times over several years, in their homes for the most part, with each member of the team participating, asking questions, getting behind the replies to elicit fuller responses. As more precise knowledge was built up it became possible to open up much fuller discussions of events than initially. Indeed, sometimes the earlier interviews were turned upside down as it became apparent that what was said in the first instance was often the opposite of what actually occurred. As our own information increased, people responded in kind.

Bit by bit the presence of a great myth disappeared. Retrospective fantasy was screened out. Linking events appeared, patterns formed, and interpretative hypotheses began to fall into place. Later interviews were more like mutual discussions. Many went on for hours, a whole morning, occasionally a whole day. Where originally the interviewees used the same examples, the same terminology, and recounted the same events despite great variations in origins, education, age, and subsequent experiences, later they shifted ground, changed level, began to plumb depths.

It was only after the first round of research was completed and more of the relevant literature was studied that subsequent interviewing would take on such an informative character. We began to see what might be called the pragmatics of mystery, the instrumental within what can be referred to as political religion. We could see how Yan'an looked to people in terms of their experiences, how they recognized it as something bigger than themselves. The ingredients of such understanding included events experienced and interpreted through a created, even artificial language, a symbolic system capable of endowing people and situations with a particular density, time transformed into space. After all, in the last analysis politics is about terrains, jurisdictions, and the power relations within them. The interviews allowed us to locate certain themes, code them, and show what happened in Yan'an. By the same token they help define a model applicable to situations elsewhere—other radical political, nationalist, or ethnic movements.

The interviews were also aimed at recapturing the more mundane aspects of daily life in Yan'an. The question was, how did the mundane, the ordinary terms of existence come to be linked with the romantic and heroic picture of Yan'an that the interviewees themselves portrayed? How was it that they gave themselves to the revolution on the one hand, each person vehemently decrying individualism, while at the same time telling stories of their own lives, which emphasized the personal, the idiosyncratic, and indeed, described a sense of individual overcoming, of accomplishment? We sought the record of subordination to the word and the text, to submission to the authority of interpretation. We found that they regarded both as acts of realization. For them word and text, far from being oppressive, became a form of unique knowledge and understanding. So what seemed to be polar opposites, the liberation of the individual and the collectivization of the self, instead of working against each other became complementary. (However, as we will show, there were some dramatic exceptions.)

Yet the more we interviewed the more difficult it became to understand in a precise way the mechanisms whereby these two opposite tendencies were brought together. To put it in more Maoist terms, how did the contradiction become resolved at a higher level? One answer was that those who favored individualism and liberalism were simply eliminated. But as it turns out, this happened to relatively few. Another answer is that they were indoctrinated. Of course this is the case, but indoctrination implies a kind of resentful passivity or at least an abdication of judgment. But interviewees described a quickening of intelligence, a sense of self-worth and accomplishment, something "oceanic" or like Barthes's *jouissance*.[39]

We decided that the best way to resolve at least some of the mystery was to let the interviews speak for themselves as much as possible. For example, when the interviewees described a certain process more or less frequently, we would identify and label it accordingly. Thus, the interviews pulled us towards the categories rather than the other way around, the insiders suggesting to us what from an ensemble of categories might be most useful and appropriate. In this way we hoped to avoid imposing a theory or terms from the outside. Many of the categories and ideas presented earlier in this chapter were to a considerable extent developed this way, out of the interviews.

As to the interviews themselves, while each is of intrinsic interest, it is their cumulative effect that is important. Each constitutes a story told by the interviewee about him- or herself: how each joined the party, made the transition to Yan'an, and how that person's individual experience became meshed with the collective one. One thing that emerges is a certain distancing from the votive Mao. The carefully expressed respect is particularly suspect. Virtually everyone we interviewed had first been treated as a Yan'anite "saint" before being cast down not once but many times as the party line shifted from left to right to center, the Cultural Revolution being especially traumatic. Nevertheless, one did not come away from these interviews with a sense of great discrepancy between the people being interviewed as they are today and as they were as participants in Yan'an. Yan'an was for them a stage, in which their roles and many parts were played in ways increasingly choreographed. Yet even when they resisted the choreography, they shared a sense of the drama. Yan'an was a theater in which everyone was touched with the exceptional. It was for the participants an exceptional moment in which they, as individuals, performed exceptionally, as they never again would in their lives. What also emerged in the interviews was their recognition of the discrepancies between what was attempted and what was realized. Indeed, at the time they were interviewed they had just begun to regain the capacity to make their own judgments about that.[40]

Of course, people's views of Yan'an differed greatly. To a local Red Army guerrilla commander who was constantly on the move, it was a sanctuary and a place of rest. It was more complicated for the "intellectuals."[41] For them, Yan'an was the place to become a communist revolutionary rather than a radical or a nationalist, or simply anti-Japanese. This meant intensifying their individualism while giving it up. It was this peculiar quality of appearing to gain in individuality while at the same time losing it, a kind of collective individualism, which makes Yan'an so relevant today.

Through the course of our interviews, each participant emerged as a distinct individual with particular memories and recollections of what had been lost and what gained in the events of the time. There was great variation in what it meant to be a party member in those days. We tried to stimulate recollections of the everyday life of Yan'an: we asked what people ate, what the sleeping arrangements were, how people coped with extremes of heat or cold, how they repaired their clothing, where the latrines were located, what books were available, how they were printed (coarseness of paper, for example), how people coped with minor illnesses or more serious wounds, and above all how those in Yan'an redefined themselves as "a good communist" and how such things as personal failures or disappointments in love and war affected their self-image. As long as we concentrated on the ordinary and the familiar, rather than the abstract and the rhetorical, considerable richness emerged from the interviews. We were shown a picture of life in Yan'an that, while romanticized, was also punctuated by flashes of bitterness, regret, a sense of lost opportunities.

Hidden, perhaps, is the role Mao played in orchestrating the individual and the collective, in integrating the individual stories and narratives into a larger collective experience. To see how he did this one must turn to the texts that were developed in Yan'an for specific instructional occasions; one must also examine the character of Yan'an as an instructional republic; and, within the structure of its "universities," one must uncover some sense of the frenetic activity that went on.[42]

Political Contexts

Yan'an suffered two temporary demises. The first came just after the CCP came to power on October 1, 1949, and the second after the Cultural Revolution. The "New Democracy" of Yan'an was replaced by bureaucratic structures in party and state. Hierarchy, total mobilization, and forced draft industrialization followed a more or less Stalinist pattern. However, Yan'an was not entirely forgotten. As Mao became disillusioned with the Soviet model of development and was disappointed by the response of his own intellectuals during the Hundred Flowers campaign, he turned back to the countryside to form the basis of his development strategy. Echoes of Yan'an could be detected in the commune system, a nostalgic rural base to sustain a moral superstructure. Nevertheless, when Mao left Yan'an in 1947 for the last time to escape the Nationalist forces (riding his famous white horse, now stuffed and on display in the Museum of the Revolution in Yan'an), neither he nor the revolution ever went back.

But Yan'an was revived as the moral center of the Cultural Revolution. The nostalgia for what Yan'an stood for became the "might have been" of the revolution that actually occurred. For the Red Guards it was the counterpoise to the corruption of party, state, and army, and the neofeudalism of those who replaced Mao at the center. It was then that Yan'an became the essential myth of the revolution. Thousands of young people reenacted the Long March. They made pilgrimages to the caves. Yan'an became a sacred place. Today, all this has vanished, virtually without a trace. Visiting Yan'an in the late 1980s, we saw few outsiders. The caves of important political leaders were clean and freshly whitewashed, the courtyards swept. Small signs barely suggested what had transpired there. It takes a great leap of imagination to recapture the intensity of movement, the sounds and smells of armies, horses, equipment, the echoing voices of commanders shouting orders to their troops, the frenetic activity involved in feeding, clothing, and educating the participants. Even Yan'an City, an ancient and then-beautiful walled city on the old Silk Route, has become, like virtually all others in China, a Soviet-style city of cement blocks, its monolithic buildings garnished with bits of Chinese architectural kitsch.

The present generation of leaders, some of whom (such as Li Peng, reportedly an adopted son of Zhou Enlai) have close links to the past, would like to retrieve the myth of Yan'an as a revolutionary parable. A good technocrat, Li Peng has little time for fables and sentimentality, but fears socialism in China will suffer the same fate as it did in the Soviet Union. To save socialism, and thereby to save their own privileged positions, these leaders have reactivated the myth of Yan'an to support a rigid political structure at odds with a liberalizing economic practice. Used in this way, Yan'an has disappeared for good.

This suggests that even as a good story there are enough puzzling ingredients to warrant a fresh evaluation of Yan'an. What has been the consequence of this place of public yearning, this moment of intense political desire where virtually everyone was imbricated and complicit in the revolutionary life? Today Yan'an represents the negative pole to the democratic movement which made its appearance in Tiananmen Square in spring 1989.[43] In the Square, albeit very briefly, Yan'an and Tiananmen were juxtaposed as opposites. Yan'an was seen to hold back historical development and the democratization China needs. Yan'an was opposed to liberalism and subjectivism. Tiananmen Square represents the yearning for just such notions.

Whatever else it was, Yan'an was also a system. Utopic in certain key ways, it was anything but a utopia. The critical moment, the fault-line crack in Yan'an, was the Rectification Campaign of 1942–1944. This crack widened, rather than narrowed, over time. Within the fault line was an even more serious flaw, a moment of vindictive retribution called the Rescue Campaign (1943), which involved forced confession and the enactment of false guilt. Orchestrated by Kang Sheng (Mao's "pistol"), the event was to be recapitulated in terrifying proportions during the Cultural Revolution.

Of particular interest to us is the way in which the Rectification Campaign represents "exegetical bonding." It established the rules that enabled Mao to control the agenda and totally restructure economic, social, military, and political life. Many still argue that in the context of the time, rectification was perhaps necessary for the effective prosecution of the anti-Japanese war and the sustaining of revolutionary momentum against the Nationalists; it also prevented Chiang Kai-shek from becoming totally supine in the face of the Japanese invasion.

The negative underside of Yan'an has been understated in the general literature. With the benefit of hindsight of Chinese politics after 1949 we can see how the methods developed in rectification occurred again and again to become the central disciplining mechanism of the party-state. While the spirit of Yan'an production campaigns could be detected in the Great Leap Forward, one could also argue that the Cultural Revolution is rectification gone mad. No doubt it is these and other parallels that impel the Central Committee of the party to prevent too much poking around in the Yan'an period. Yan'an is the heroic myth of the revolution, and no one wants it punctured. Nor do they want to reveal who did what to whom in the struggles for power, the battles between the First Front and the Fourth Front Armies, between the followers of Wang Ming and Mao. Nor do they want to expose what happened to the intellectuals, Wang Shiwei, Ding Ling, and many others.

If people want to talk at all about the actual events of rectification, it is to emphasize how necessary it was to root out spies and backsliders. Or they speak of the emphasis on literacy, the translation of major texts, the teaching and discussion, the insight, and the tempering of a sense of discovery about the world with a greater suspiciousness of potential enemies. Above all they will not admit that the goal of Yan'an was the relinquishing of autonomous judgment that is the "crime" of liberalism and subjectivism. After rectification, Yan'an was made to become one thing to all people—a single discourse community; prior to rectification it had been a framework that could mean many things to many people. Studying the transition of the meaning of Yan'an enables one to understand what might be called today the Yan'an mafia.

The Yan'an Legacy

What was the Yan'an legacy? On any scale of magnitude, Yan'an was an extraordinary transformational and revolutionary accomplishment. The claims it made were breathtaking, and its consequences far-reaching. Yan'an became ground zero for a movement that aimed to do nothing less than start the world all over again, far from the centers of civilization. Like some microscopic organism, Yan'an persisted despite efforts to stamp it out. It retained life and remained regenerative. This sense of new beginnings was enhanced by the rude setting, the primitive living. In their caves people pored over texts even as they pursued more practical activities. And within two years of being pushed out of Yan'an for the last time by Nationalist forces, the CCP proclaimed the People's Republic in Tiananmen Square in 1949.

For some orthodox party members the legacy of Yan'an remains the utopic moral standard. In their view China is perpetually in danger of succumbing to the virus of liberalism. They see today a dramatic erosion and corruption of revolutionary principle requiring the restoration of authority through a thorough, ongoing ideological training. For them it is anathema that the end point of the revolution should come to be represented by students whom they see as pampered, ignorant, and presumptuous, the ungrateful beneficiaries of untold suffering and previous sacrifices, whose "democracy" is little more than opportunism, whose self-interest is raised over principles, and who suffer from "spiritual pollution."

But what proponents of both views, liberal and reactionary, have in common is a deep concern, even despair, that the future is becoming ever more ambiguous and its outlines ever more blurred. Goals that once seemed definitive have disappeared. Even the old guard knows it is impossible to restore old political beliefs in a context totally at odds with the original conditions. Moreover, even if they call for something of the moral discipline of Yan'an, none would think the structures within which it was originally embedded would have any relevance today.

This brings us to a more general point. Everywhere former revolutionary regimes, whether nationalist, socialist, or even theocratic, discover that it is one thing to build up symbolic capital in movements against domination and hegemonic power, but it is another to use that capital as a basis for exercising such power. The loss of belief at the moment of triumph is something virtually every militant movement coming to power experiences. In other words, to be in opposition is one thing; to be in power is totally different, especially when party and state come together to transform society. What is lost is a previously privileged role as agent of the progressive forces in history. Revolutionary regimes exercising power from above define the public as an obstacle rather than a resource. To change society, the state confronts society itself. No matter how worthy its original intent and principles, the movement's structure becomes hierarchical and its politics coercive. At this point there begins the kind of struggle between society and the state in which, sooner or later, the state loses.

It loses because it becomes victimized by its own power. Where before movement leaders knew reality better than their opponents, now they know it only through information passed upward by subordinates. The more coercive the regime, the more what passes upward is what leaders want to hear. Negative information is suppressed and its agents repressed. Records are falsified (as production figures were in the Great Leap Forward),[44] and this leads to ever more extreme falsifications, which eventually create economic or political crisis. If at this point the regime tries to generate political reforms it runs the risk of inflaming those who, while appearing passive, wait only for the right moment. Underground movements flourish: revivalism, religious, linguistic and ethnic extremism, various kinds of nationalism, a return to past loyalties and identities. New grievances are quickly piled on top of old ones. What politics today demonstrates better than at any point in the past is that beyond a certain developmental point—that is, where the need for information becomes very great—it becomes extremely difficult to reduce coercion without inviting vast structural change. In the Soviet Union prolonged coercion and bureaucratization so deprived the state of the capacity to innovate that eventually it broke apart. What appeared at the top as rational public planning was based on a jerry-built system of deals and private negotiations.[45]

In the Soviet Union not only did little accurate information filter to the top, the top rejected and suppressed what little it got. Nor could the directors of such a highly centralized state system trust each other or their party representatives. Once the move was made to make the Soviet Union a high-information, low-coercion system, the entire organizational structure unraveled. This is precisely what the present leadership in China is so desperately trying to prevent. Political coerciveness has been applied in fits and starts and has been combined with growing economic liberalization. The effect is to divorce effectively state from society. The state does not listen to public opinion.

Today the specter that is haunting China is democratization. But as the need for new technological and scientific information, changes in design, and knowledge about society itself grows, and the need to modify prevailing institutions, modes of production, and methods of allocation becomes more pressing, political reform is inevitable. The main question is when.

The events of 1989 in Tiananmen Square suggest that democratization will be more and more essential if development is not to be penalized. The state is governed by a party that has lost the respect particularly of its own younger members. It interferes with economic and social reorganization. The present leadership recognizes that the old mechanisms of planning are too clumsy for modernization and development. It fears the economic and social effects of more market-oriented growth, yet without such growth the entire country will be in terrible trouble. For, despite all the progress in economic reforms over the last fifteen years, the danger is that China may well get the worst of both possible worlds: a market increasingly grey, if not black; and a planning mechanism that lacks critical information in a system still excessively centralized.[46]

Some among Mao's successors have promoted, by turns, neoauthoritarianism or neoconservatism. Now, instead of Marxism, the children of the Yan'anites use developmental arguments to justify authoritarian rule.[47] Citing the examples of Taiwan and South Korea, they argue that modernization requires a strong centralized political structure, especially in the early phases, in order to prevent social divisions leading to the kind of unrest that would undermine the drive for economic modernization. Put quite simply, they equate democratization with chaos. However, even this logic does not rule out entirely the case for political reform.

The above comments appear to take us far from Yan'an. Yet government policy continues to be directed by those old Yan'anites who remain alive. Surrounded by their family dynasties, divided by old conflicts as well as new, they still struggle among themselves while hanging on to power. They know each other intimately. Each has, over the years, been betrayed and has betrayed, not once but many times. They, the old men of the revolution, are survivors many times over. Locked into their historical memories they are plagued by guilty knowledge. For only they know what they have done to one another, both before Yan'an, when communist plotted against and killed communist as well as other enemies and when factions fought each other as surrogates for monopolistic truths, and afterwards, when they came to power. Reluctant to pass the reins to a younger generation, they recoil from those who would like to initiate the "process" of democratization rather than impose demands. Still thinking in terms of class struggle, they are frightened most of all of a war between civil society and the state.

China must evolve toward something new. It needs to evolve politically, not reimpose a coercive apparatus. It needs to normalize politics. These last-ditch efforts by a Yan'anite old guard to shore up a shaky system can only intensify dissatisfaction, something the old guard knows very well. But they know also that time is very short. They have settled for outward obedience. The population has retreated into its shell after the brief period of the 1989 China spring. Yet fears persist that what began in Tiananmen Square will continue under the surface of political life. Hence the old leaders' strenuous efforts to define the events in terms they understand. The official history is written to portray the student-led movement as a counterrevolutionary rebellion against their revolution. This not only justifies the repression but also enables the old guard to portray themselves as heroes who reemerged from a transparent retirement to protect the values and gains of their revolution.

All this suggests that the events of China today need to be considered from many different standpoints. Ours will focus on the revolutionary trajectory, its buildup and decline with Yan'an as the critical point of transition. Yan'an was the moment when the protagonists of Chinese communism came to believe that they were gifted with a unique political insight, an insight that drives a political generation still in power, one whose lifetime included the May Fourth Movement of 1919 and the anarchy of warlordism, and who, as the earliest members of the CCP, fought against the GMD, made war against the Japanese, and survived the deadly factionalism within the party. For them a diminished role for the party-state raises the specter of society out of control, a fear reinforced by their own experiences during the Cultural Revolution. They fear, as well they might, that behind each regional or provincial army command lurks the danger of a new warlord, and behind each prefectural deal with a Hong Kong multinational, a runaway capitalism.

Perhaps most of all, however, they fear generational change, unless power can be passed on safely to their own children. Every democratic poster on the billboards at Beijing University that pokes fun at socialism and its leaders infuriates those at the top. Mockery, humor, and contempt are the secret weapons of a democracy gone underground. This is all the more so because words like "democracy" and "freedom," although very differently understood, also mean something to the old guard. It is the difference that matters, and this we can only see clearly by looking back to the times and places and special circumstances that formed the generation still in power, a generation that believes that only its refusal to die keeps the revolution alive.

I

FICTIVE TRUTHS AND LOGICAL INFERENCES

✳

Metonymic logic is that of the unconscious. Hence it is perhaps in that direction that one would need to pursue the present study, to pursue the reading of the text—its dissemination, not its truth.

Roland Barthes, *The Struggle with the Angel*

2

FOUR STRUGGLES

✳

We begin our analysis with what might be called the "hard" Mao, the military tactician who expropriated as his own the structures of power and was able to link his concrete accomplishment to retrievals—that is, antecedents in Chinese history and culture—and projections of a millennial future with utopic implications. The qualities we discern here remained in place throughout Mao's career, sometimes less visible, sometimes shockingly pronounced, to the point of his being megalomaniacal. But even when disguised in the "softer" version of himself—the intellectual, the scholar, the calligrapher—there was no doubting Mao's sense of his own exceptionalism. However he chose to define the rules, he never doubted his claim to do so. He used his various roles to endow his shrewd manipulation of people with the prior authority of the analytical accomplishment. Out of these qualities, in the here and now of Chinese civil and national war, Mao and his associates were able to construct a universe of meaning hitherto foreign to both conventional Chinese ideas and classical Marxism. While this universe at times came close to Stalinism, it retained certain peculiarities. Mao's accomplishment was to generate what we, following Bourdieu have called, symbolic capital. The creation of that symbolic capital and with it the transformation of Yan'an from a military redoubt into the Tantric center of the Chinese revolution brings us directly to the analysis of political beliefs and how they form. In the case of China, such beliefs were both specific to the event and more general in their claims, but always had the image of Mao at the center.

Mao converted time into space (history as a telelogy of "here" as well as "now"), first as an endowment and second as a simulacrum, both as the moral moment of the revolution. By considering Yan'an as a semiotic space we will show how it became saturated with symbolic iconography, part military (in common with other base areas) and part tutelary, within an institutional framework. Yan'an became a unique instructional community that considered itself to be in possession of final truths. Such truths were also a reason of necessity. Mao's exercise of power would have otherwise remained precarious. No matter how much control and military force he might command it was insufficient to realize his grander ideas. It was to this end that he combined the construction of a larger cosmology of power with pursuit of his enemies on the ground, first and most particularly those within the Chinese Communist Party who challenged his monopoly.

The fight to control the party was the precondition to the larger task, but Mao made it appear the other way around. He sought the role of Chief Agent of history in a party in which agency was the main claim to authority. From the start, no augmentation of military force was undertaken without moral and logical infusions. Teaching and military training formed a dual and complementary mandate. Nor was the teaching ordinary. Rather, it aimed at a form of exegetical bonding designed to convert the revolutionary simulacrum from a community of lost souls into a chosen people and, if necessary, consign the rest to the historical scrap heap.

It was sleight of hand; but it was also much more than that. Capturing power in the CCP was an accomplishment that went hand in hand with reinventing palpable truths in a way no historical reconstruction can recapture. If one speaks of the republic of the caves, one must think of a body of mainly young men, sick, healthy, tired, rejuvenated, sweating, freezing, farting, cooking, learning, writing, firing off documents as well as weapons, being hectored or monitored while under siege conditions, and finding in all of this the materials of practical accomplishment and manumission from whatever slavery they described as their original condition. Such manumission required training in the disciplines of the military and the tutelary life, the latter a discursive enterprise that was part revolutionary praxis, part revelatory inversionary discourse. It was a revolutionary Platonism that appeared to derive its truths from below, from peasants, from the popular mass, but in fact only validated them in the name of the mass. It was in the strict construction of texts that Mao and his coterie embedded their discourse, and those who went to Yan'an were transformed into a people of the word and the text, their original selves virtually destroyed.

Indeed, word and text themselves came to have iconographic significance. They not only embodied the new meaning but also represented it as artifacts, as things in themselves, with the same force as the portrait of Buddha imprinted on a tanka. Moreover, by destroying the logic of the old order, Mao created in its place a superior one, more relevant to the immediate individual as well as collective experience, to the revolutionary tasks defined. Violence was the constant testing ground. Indeed one might say that Mao's constructions were designed in the face of a pragmatism of violence, whether internal to the party itself or between the CCP and the GMD or against the Japanese. It was in this threefold context of violent struggle for power that we can see Mao's initial coming to power as a fight for what might be called the four corners of the cosmos. Each had to be conquered, and each represented its own specific kind of power. Before attempting to realize the larger tasks of the revolution, Mao and his associates had first to monopolize intellectual, military, administrative, and ideological power. Each was embodied in a concrete struggle with a key and powerful opponent within the party, each of whom was a surrogate for that larger cosmology, and each of whom had an armed clientele. Hence it is with this more immediate struggle that we begin our analysis of Mao's ascent from the assumption of military power to the formation of symbolic capital.

Each of the four struggles ended in the death or exile of Mao's designated opponent. In each case, his victory was complete. Examining each in turn demonstrates Mao's sense of strategy and timing. He knew when and how to close with an opponent so that in the end that opponent destroyed himself.

By monopolizing power in this concrete way—that is, by demolishing anyone who dared to challenge him in any of the four dimensions—Mao was able to position himself not only as a locus of power within the party, but also as a source of power in and of himself and his immediate circle. He did not do this alone, of course. But these struggles positioned him for what we will call a cosmocratic role, where he redefined a moral space and endowed it with both meaning and discipline. How he was able to do that and what this meant in more concrete terms we discuss in the next few chapters. However, first we study the "hard" Mao, the Mao whose exercise of power was as ruthless as it was pragmatic.

Simple domination was not enough for Mao. In this sense he was closer to Lenin than to Stalin. After winning his four struggles and consolidating his intellectual, military, ideological, and administrative positions, his goal was nothing less than the generating of new modes of power: the power of discourse. His objective was to organize a special discourse community, a bounded group within which people abdicated their ordinary judgments in favor of alternatives inversionary in content and transformational in object. To do this, Mao became a kind of moral architect as well as a storyteller. He created stories that were mythic in character, and that were repeated again and again like incantations. From these stories, like a magician pulling rabbits out of a hat, Mao pulled logical inferences that enabled others to break through their conventional thinking. The stories, which reflected shared experiences, became the basis of a logic, adapted both from Chinese traditions and Marxism, that enabled Mao to transform his stories into a single line, a mytho-logic. Each narrative established the conditions for the next. Each defined revolutionary obligations to China as a nation and to the peasantry as its class representative, while the logic became a theory with an outcome both "correct" and projective. Indeed, without a theory to chart one through all the pitfalls and dangers, the class enemies within and the imperialists without, the redeeming band would splinter and be destroyed.

It is essential, however, not to be deluded by the emphasis on discourse. Yan'an was no theoretical playground. Actual events were key, and they can be revealing in several different ways. One can see, first, the actual mechanisms by means of which Mao consolidated power; second, how Mao's own conception of power is revealed in the strategies and tactics he employed; and third, how the four struggles redefined his mandate. Each of these struggles had profound consequences for Yan'an, and tragic ones for those against whom Mao fought.

In addition, each of the struggles has its own logic. It was Mao's genius to understand that logic better than his opponents. By this means, he was able to persuade those around him that necessity rather than personal power was the dominant motive governing his actions. But the logic of each situation involved larger and overlapping contexts: the mutual duplicities built into the united front, the military struggle against the Japanese, the production campaigns, the organization and control of the Border Region as a whole. Each of these contexts added a sense of urgency to the resolution of the fundamental questions of power, and each struggle contained its own logic and suggested how the larger crises ought to be handled. Hence the cosmological aspects of the struggles are about realities of power and its appropriate exercise.

For those at the center, power meant truths devoutly political in their consequences. With the exception of the struggle with Zhang Guotao over military power and legitimacy, in none were the conflicts with Mao personal. Between Mao and Zhang it was different. These two disliked each other from the start, although their conflict remained muted until it became a matter of military power and domination within the CCP. For the others, the nature of their struggles with Mao seem oddly asymmetrical. It probably did not occur to Wang Ming to place Mao in the category of an enemy, simply because Wang Ming was his own (and perhaps Stalin's) man. In the case of Wang Shiwei, such a notion would have been far from his mind. He resented what he considered to be the mindless and unnecessary subordination of the intellectuals to ideology. As for Liu Zhidan, he probably never knew that Mao saw in him the threat of "mountain-topism." As far as is known, Mao had played the role of Liu's defender, not his enemy. Yet Mao first rendered all four helpless and then effectively destroyed them.

For Mao the four struggles had to do with conflicts between the ideal and the actual. The real power he had in mind was discretion on how, when, and where to transform the "imagined community" into the real thing. He was good at turning defeats into lessons, and lessons into claims to truth. In one of his typical sleights of hand for which he was famous, Mao was even able to profit from the loss of the Jiangxi Soviet, the original communist discourse community, at the start of Chiang Kai-shek's Fifth Extermination Campaign. Others were blamed for the loss while Mao was presented as a heroic leader escaping the trap by means of the Long March, a miraculous event.[1] This does not mean that it was easy for him to emerge as the central figure, however, and certainly not as chief cosmocrat. Many could have claimed this latter role—Wang Ming, Ai Siqi, Zhang Wentian, Liu Shaoqi, Bo Gu. Mao strengthened his standing in the military and party apparatus by means of a slow and dangerous process, requiring him first to remove or render ineffectual those who challenged him. The hidden agenda of the four struggles was not only the elimination of contenders for power but also the prevention of any possible ridicule of Mao's ideas by those who regarded them as not good Marxism, or little more than Chinese traditional dialectics dressed up in Marxist terminology.

The actual events leading up to Mao's taking power are well known.[2] In January 1935, during a rest in flight from the Jiangxi Soviet, the Politburo met in Zunyi. The meeting, originally called to discuss the current situation and decide where the Red Army should go, turned into a major review of past military policy.[3] The meeting marked a decisive step in Mao's move to supreme power. He was appointed to the five-person Secretariat together with Zhang Wentian (General Secretary), Zhou Enlai, Chen Yun, and Bo Gu. Together with Zhou Enlai and Wang Jiaxiang, he was to serve on the CCP Central Military Leadership Group. While Zhou was to be chief decision maker, Mao was to be his chief assistant. This broke up Soviet returnee Bo Gu's and Soviet agent Braun's (Li De, the Comintern advisor) control over military affairs, allowing a sinification of military policy to begin. Mao did not become Chair of the

Military Council or of the Politburo, as some historians have suggested, but he did become one of the five top leaders of the party and had the right to be involved in all party and army decisions. He made shrewd use of this right.

It was the four struggles that made Mao into a cosmocratic figure. Each came to represent one of the four quarterings of a universe in which Mao himself sat at the center of his own pantheon, much like Buddha in his tantric circle, with the lesser gods (Liu Shaoqi, Zhou Enlai, Ren Bishi, Zhu De) around his head, and the enemies (Trotskyites, the Japanese, the GMD) in the lower regions.

Three figures tumbled from the upper to the lower regions of Mao's tantric pantheon: Zhang Guotao, who represents superior military power; Wang Ming, who represents superior Marxist theoretical knowledge; and Wang Shiwei, who represents the Lu Xun tradition of intellectualism. Elevated to a place among the "divinities" is Liu Zhidan, who, as an example of independent local authority challenging the Party Center, disappears from view, the hero who had to die.

What these struggles show is a Mao capturing the moral high ground of the revolution in order to create the utopic community. The coercive power he sought was well disguised. The struggle with Zhang Guotao was a life-and-death one for political and military control. Between Mao and Liu it was over centralized versus decentralized authority, which, if lost, would give rise to "mountain-topism," independent "red warlords" acting on their own authority. Between Mao and Wang, who was closely associated with the Comintern, it was a fight for ideological control. The struggle with Wang Shiwei, although not involving Mao directly, was for monopoly over intellectual life. These four struggles reveal that Mao did not create an order-producing discourse out of storytelling and logical construction alone. He plotted and built up personal networks of loyalties and obligations; and, though he used stories to represent such symbols as redemption, renewal, and transformation, underneath it all was a hard and shrewd political genius with a sense of the facts of revolutionary power.

Thus, these cases represent the four bases of Mao's authority: military power, centralized power, theoretical power, and intellectual power. They also show Mao at his hardest and most manipulative and ruthless, the Mao who not only recognized that power comes out of the barrel of a gun, but that you don't have to shoot in order to kill. The struggle with Zhang Guotao is virtually a game. Military power and party prestige are the trade-offs. Zhang Guotao, with his superior military power, challenges Mao, who has greater party prestige. The game ends with Zhang's army effectively destroyed, with Zhang going over to the GMD in 1938. With Wang Ming, who represents both the Comintern and the Russian Returned Students, the game is cat and mouse. It ends with the humiliation of Wang Ming, who eventually goes to Moscow accusing Mao of poisoning him.[4] Toward Wang Shiwei, the translator and intellectual who challenged Mao's clamp-down on the intellectuals, Mao showed both irritation and respect. He kept him in jail, but accessible. Wang Shiwei was killed after the abandonment of Yan'an to the GMD in 1947. As for Liu Zhidan, he was the local popular hero who died in battle under somewhat mysterious conditions. The town of Bao'an, where Edgar Snow interviewed Mao and Liu Zhidan in 1936, was named after him.

Military Power versus Legitimacy: The Entrapment of Zhang Guotao

Mao's conflict with Zhang Guotao provides an excellent example of how Mao uses the logic of a situation to entrap a shrewd, dangerous, and powerful political opponent. Zhang Guotao, a founding member of the CCP, chaired the party's first congress in Shanghai. An engineering graduate of Beijing University, Zhang had organizational experience among workers as well as soldiers. Many believed him to be a more able commander and a more sophisticated political leader than Mao. Moreover, Zhang had no regard for Mao either as a military strategist or as a leader. In his own words, he considered Mao "imaginative and sensitive; his thinking sometimes became quite bizarre, and he would make mythic utterances. He lacked the ability to organize and was reluctant to make precise calculations when dealing with difficult matters. Sometimes his ideas were not clearly expressed, and he often defended his 'opinions of a genius' in an emotional mood."[5]

To his later regret, Zhang underestimated Mao. While their differences were ostensibly over preferred strategies, their struggle was really a win-or-lose battle for power. Mao was the leading figure of the First Front Army, Zhang of the Fourth Front Army, a much more powerful force. While he argued with Mao over whether the Red Army should march north or south, Zhang's real problem was how to balance his predominant military strength with a subordinate political position. While Mao had only between 10,000 and 20,000 troops under his command to Zhang Guotao's 80,000, Mao and his supporters held the key positions in the Party Center and on the Military Council. Each pursued a double strategy, the ostensible one emerging out of the logic of the military situation involving the appropriate moves in terms of terrain and timing, the real one over control of the Central Committee and its Politburo, the final repository of legitimate authority in the party. Mao never lost control of the Politburo. He was thus always able to fix the limits within which Zhang could maneuver. This was crucial given Zhang's much greater military force.

In September 1932, well before Mao's departure from the Jiangxi Soviet, Zhang and his troops, the Fourth Front Army, had been driven out of the E-Yu-Wan (Hubei-Henan-Anhui) Soviet by Chiang Kai-shek, who had launched his Fourth "Anti-Communist Suppression Campaign" the previous May. Zhang thus made his own long march. After three months, he and his troops tried to settle in Sichuan.[6] On December 29, 1932, he founded the Revolutionary Committee of the Sichuan-Shaanxi Base Area. Zhang's decision to leave the E-Yu-Wan base and undertake the "western flight" was criticized by the Party Center in March 1933, but little blame was assigned to him.[7]

Sichuan's economic conditions were very backward and, as a result of decades of conflicts among the Sichuan warlords, local military forces were divided. These circumstances were beneficial to the Fourth Front Army, which experienced a rapid buildup in strength during the following two years. The policies Zhang pursued, such as land confiscation and redistribution, were even stricter and harsher than in the Jiangxi Central Soviet, which was noted for its hard line on such matters. Able-bodied peasants were drafted into the Red Army, while youngsters were organized into red guards. Such radical actions arose out of the Fourth Front Army's own practical needs and had little to do with the Party Center's mandate.

Forced to live on the margins, Zhang tried to impress his local audience by showing how the communists were part of a larger, and more successful, whole. He made reference to the international and domestic situations, but in terms that had less to do with Marxist doctrines than with the practical task of cheering up his audience.[8] So much did Zhang brag about the size and power of the Party Center and the importance of Jiangxi that the power of the Red Army in the Jiangxi Soviet must have seemed awesome to his men in the Fourth Front Army. Inadvertently, such tales also built up the prestige of Mao, who was the head of the Jiangxi base, a situation that undermined Zhang's position with his own men when the conflict with Mao broke out.

The conflict with Mao was precipitated when the Party Center required Zhang to evacuate his new base area. It was decided that the First Front Army should vacate northern Guizhou, cross to the north of the Yangtze, and establish a new Soviet base area in southern Sichuan. In late January 1935, the Red Army's headquarters issued orders to army corps commanders of the First Front Army to try to secure this objective. Also, the Central Military Council and the Politburo sent telegrams requesting active cooperation to Ren Bishi and, importantly, to Zhang Guotao. Ren was with the joint forces of the Second and Sixth Army Corps on the Hunan-Sichuan border, and Zhang was with his Fourth Front Army.[9] However, the Party Center underestimated the strength of the GMD forces. The First Front Army was defeated by the GMD Sichuan army at Tucheng. At the same time, the Party Center overestimated the loyalty of Ren and Zhang. Neither mobilized their troops to take effective action to help the central army achieve its objective.

The defeat meant that the First Front Army (Mao's army) had to abandon its original plan. During the next three months, the army roamed around Guizhou and Yunnan, unable either to create a new base area or to annihilate the enemy that was pursuing it. Its strength was further reduced by defeat in several battles. In late April, it made a detour through Yunnan to cross the Jinsha River, an upper tributary of the Yangtze, and entered southwest Sichuan. From there, it continued north to try to contact the Fourth Front Army in the Sichuan-Xikang area. Despite new leadership, the First Front Army's combat experience had been poor.[10]

Zhang Guotao had very good reasons for ignoring the January requests of the Party Center, as they called for his troops to make a sacrifice for the First Front Army by immediately engaging in offensive actions against the GMD Sichuan troops.[11] Instead of attacking south as requested, Zhang led his troops north to begin the "Southern Shaanxi Campaign," which lasted from late January until early March. He won a major victory over the Shaanxi Army. Only when his troops were blocked by Hu Zongnan's Central Army near Guanyuan did he withdraw to Sichuan. It was not until late March that the Fourth Front Army crossed the Jialing River, by which time the First Front Army was far away in Yunnan and Guizhou provinces. By this time, Zhang accepted that it was better to evacuate north Sichuan rather than be driven out. The area was, in any case, economically and physically exhausted from the continual warfare.

During late March to early June 1935, Zhang organized the withdrawal of the Fourth Front Army from north to west Sichuan and then to the Sichuan-Xikang border area. Here, in May 1935, Zhang set up the Northwest Special Committee of the CCP and proclaimed the establishment of the "Northwest Federal Government of the Chinese Soviet Republic."[12] The proclamation was made without prior approval from the Party Center.

Zhang's ideas diverged from central policy. Although the Northwest Federal Government was to form part of the Soviet Republic, its form was less radical than the governmental form envisaged by the Party Center. Zhang proposed policies that recognized the realities of the environment (for example, proposing unity with all minorities to fight against Japanese imperialism) and were thus less exclusive or destructive than those of the earlier period.

When in June 1935 the First and Fourth Front Armies unexpectedly met, there was suspicion and bad feeling between Zhang and Mao. The joy expressed at the rally held on June 14 to celebrate the reunion soon turned to suspicion; a bitter power struggle followed.

During the three-month reunion of the two armies, a number of Politburo meetings were held during which Zhang was outmaneuvered. The first meeting was held on June 26, 1935, and dealt with urgent military matters such as strategic policy, operational maneuvers, and army leadership.[13] Zhang differed with Mao and the Party Center over the direction in which the Red Armies should move. While Zhang proposed moving east, the Party Center had initially suggested moving west, but had now decided that it was best to move north. While Zhang desired better political positions for his Fourth Front Army leaders, Mao sought to prevent the Fourth Front Army from controlling the Red Army as a whole.

Two days after the meeting and after Zhang Guotao had left, Zhang Wentian drafted a resolution to summarize the discussions.[14] This resolution reflected the Party Center's decision to move north. However, a concession was made to Zhang by suggesting that a smaller part of the troops secure areas that would be beneficial for a push to the east. Compromise with Zhang was judicious, given that his troops outnumbered those of the Party Center by around five to one.

However, the meeting did not solve the issue of how to balance power between the better equipped and larger Fourth Front Army and the smaller but politically better placed First Front Army. This issue underlay deliberations at the Shawo Conference (August 5–6, 1935). Mao sought to use his majority in the Party Center to compel Zhang to go north, whereas Zhang wanted to use the defeat of the First Front Army in the Jiangxi Soviet to reform the Party Center leadership.[15]

On balance, the conference resolution favored Mao and the Party Center.[16] In fact, the resolution had been drafted before the meeting by Zhang Wentian, whose presentation on behalf of the Politburo caused a bitter argument with Zhang Guotao. The resolution was redrafted to omit personal criticisms. The final resolution still confirmed a march north to create a base area in the Sichuan-Shaanxi-Gansu area. Further, it reaffirmed that the political line of the Party Center had been correct during the Jiangxi period and that the rural revolution should be deepened to liberate the peasant masses. Party leadership over the Red Armies was to be tightened and "a very small number of comrades in the Red Army" who thought that the party's political line was incorrect were criticized. This, of course, was aimed at Zhang Guotao.

Although the political resolution favored the First Front Army and the Party Center, certain personnel changes recognized an increase in strength of Zhang's Fourth Front Army. The meeting confirmed Zhang Guotao as Political Commissar of the Red Army with Zhu De as Commander in Chief. Given the traditional predominance of commissars in the military system, this July 18 decision must have been pleasing to Zhang.[17] Mao's plan to march north was to be carried out through Zhang's command of the Army Headquarters. However, the appointment of Chen Changhao and Xu Xiangqian to Front headquarters was beneficial to Mao, as it brought two of Zhang's leading military figures closely under Mao's supervision, making them more likely to follow "party discipline" when required to do so.[18]

After the August meeting, the troops were divided in two for the move north: the left route army under General Headquarters (Zhu De, Zhang Guotao, and Liu Bocheng) and the right route army under Front Headquarters (Xu Xiangqian, Chen Changhao, and Ye Jianying).[19] The left route army was composed of five armies: two from the First Front Army and three from the Fourth Front Army. The right route army comprised four armies: two each from the First and Fourth Front Armies. The Politburo and Central Military Commission moved with the right route army. This separated Zhang from his two highest leaders, who were co-opted by their "promotions" and thus less liable to present a threat to Mao.

Frictions continued. On August 24, the Central Committee sent a telegram to Zhang and Zhu De calling on them to move northeast to Banyou and Banxi to link up with the right route army. On September 3, Zhang expressed his disagreement, calling for the left route army to move south. On September 8, Mao, with Zhou Enlai, Zhang Wentian, Bo Gu, Xu Xiangqian, Chen Changhao, and Wang Jiaxiang, repeated the calls for Zhang to go north, but Zhang resisted. On September 9, he sent a telegram to the left route army leaders arguing his viewpoint. While he accepted the idea of uniting the two armies, he proposed that it be on the basis of the right route army moving south and then the combined armies

continuing to move south. This was a direct challenge to Mao. Official
accounts refer to a second telegram sent by Zhang to Chen Changhao
ordering him to lead his troops south and "to launch a thorough inner
party struggle."[20] These accounts claim that Ye Jianying, who was Chief
of Staff at the Right Route Army Headquarters, learned of this telegram
and informed Mao. Finally, at midnight on September 9, Zhang sent a
third telegram to the Central Committee, explaining that the plan to go
north had many problems and strongly suggesting they give up the original
battle plan.

Whatever the precise details, Mao concluded that Zhang was a threat.
He slipped away to the camp of the Third Army, convened an Emergency
Politburo meeting on September 10, and got agreement for an immediate
move north.[21] Zhang was not present.

The Central Committee sent a telegram to Xu Xiangqian and Chen
Changhao, ordering them to bring their troops north to meet up once
again with Mao's. The combined forces were to be placed under Zhou
Enlai's command, perhaps causing some hesitation on the part of Xu and
Chen. Official CCP histories claim that Chen Changhao had toyed with
the idea of sending troops to intercept Mao, but that Xu Xiangqian had
vetoed the idea, remarking that it was unthinkable for one red army to
fight another.[22] Pressing his political advantage, Mao delivered a report at
a Central Committee meeting on September 12 at Ejie (Gansu) criticizing
Zhang Guotao. This presumably formed the basis for the decision on
Zhang's supposed mistakes.[23] Zhang was accused of opportunism and of
splitting the Red Army, thus displaying a "warlord" tendency.

Mao led his men in the First and Third Army to the north where they
eventually arrived in northern Shaanxi. Zhang and his troops turned south
to the Chengdu plain. After several inconclusive battles with GMD troops
in southwest Sichuan, the Fourth Front Army moved towards the Tibet-
Xikang border, where it would spend the winter of 1935. Through the
winter of 1935–36, the relationship between Mao in the north and Zhang
in the south remained poor. The secret flight of the First and Third Army
Corps under Mao from Baxi on September 11, 1935, angered Zhang, and
he convened a conference at Aba on September 13–14 that labeled Mao
Zedong, Zhou Enlai, Zhang Wentian, and Bo Gu as "right opportunists"
and criticized their northern march as "flightism and defeatism."[24]

In early October, Zhang convened a meeting to set up a new central
party apparatus in a direct challenge to the Party Center, which had moved
north.[25] A resolution was passed to dismiss Mao, Zhou, Zhang Wentian,

and Bo Gu from their posts, deprive them of their party membership, and order their arrest.

By December, Zhang thought he would be able to establish a firm base area on the Sichuan-Xikang borders. With this security, he sent a telegram on December 5 to party and army leaders with the First Front Army in north Shaanxi.[26] The telegram informed them of the establishment of the new party center and called on them to stop using the "false title of Party Center," that it was being demoted to the CCP Northern Bureau.

The Party Center in Shaanxi replied on January 22, 1936, in a resolution denouncing Zhang's false claims to power and instructing him to give up all his false titles.[27] Before this date, the Party Center had ignored the question of titles and simply communicated with Zhang over specific practical matters. It also announced that it was making public within the party the critical decision about Zhang Guotao taken on September 12 at Ejie. A major split was now evident, and it was clear that neither side would budge willingly. The standoff was eventually decided by the differing fortunes of the two army groups during 1936.

Things did not go well for Zhang Guotao in the south. In February 1936, his troops were defeated by the GMD Central Army, and he was forced to retreat westward. In March, the Fourth Front Army arrived at Ganzi on the Tibet-Xikang Border. While the GMD enemy had been left far behind, Zhang and his army found themselves in a nomadic region where the natural conditions were inhospitable and whose inhabitants were unfriendly. The southern expedition had failed. Against Zhang's wishes, his troops pushed for evacuation.

When the First and Fourth Front Armies originally left the south, the Second and Sixth Army Corps had remained behind in the Hunan-Hubei-Sichuan-Gansu border area, where they became the main target of GMD attacks. In early 1936, they also had to flee and began their own Long March. In early June 1936, after several months of fighting on the move, Ren Bishi and He Long led these troops to join the Fourth Front Army at Ganzi.

While the arrival of another Red Army group brought cheer to Zhang's beleaguered troops, it also led to a decline in his authority, as he had to moderate his criticisms of the First Front Army and to play down his own claims to rule the party. Ren Bishi, positioned between the authority of the Party Center far away in Shaanxi and the realities of Zhang's power close by, was cautious. Before the reunion, he had already sent out instructions that comments about the split between the First and Fourth

Front Armies would not be allowed and that documents from Zhang Guotao in the name of the "Party Center" were not to be distributed.[28]

Talking to a meeting of party and army activists on June 6, 1936, Zhang Guotao did not use his self-given titles. He acknowledged that the communists in North Shaanxi had made progress and enjoyed success.[29] Zhang claimed that relations with northern Shaanxi had improved recently because of agreement on the Comintern's instructions for promoting the national revolution. Zhang had already agreed to the new policy direction emanating from the Comintern. In fact, Zhang compromised simply to survive. Further, according to Zhang, there had been an agreement between the two groups that both sides would abolish their titles of "Party Center" and let the CCP Mission to the Comintern temporarily exercise the functions of Party Center. The Shaanxi group would become the Northern Bureau and Zhang's group the Northwest Bureau.[30] On military affairs, Zhang made it clear that control lay with Zhu De and himself as Commander-in-Chief and Political Commissar respectively.[31] Finally, in criticizing Mao in Shaanxi, Zhang put himself forward as a faithful follower of the Comintern line, while pointing out that it was only recently that the group in northern Shaanxi had adopted the new Comintern policy on the formation of a united front.

The arrival of the Second and Sixth Army Corps aided the decision to move north to rejoin the Party Center. Ren Bishi had resisted Zhang's attempts to call the meeting to decide the issue a "Party Center conference." It was referred to as a meeting of party and army activists. The Fourth Front Army under Zhang Guotao and the Second Front Army under He Long left Ganzi in early July, marching separately. However, politically leadership was united under the Northwest Bureau (not to be confused with the Northwest Bureau in Shaanbei) as approved by the Central Committee. This must have soothed Zhang's bruised ego somewhat as he was made Secretary, with Ren Bishi as his deputy. The subsequent reunification of the Red Army troops in northern Shaanxi was a victory for the group based there, providing a considerable boost to Mao's position and a major defeat for Zhang.

However, before Zhang's arrival his credibility had been further eroded by Mao in the affair of the Ningxia Battle Plan. On August 12, 1936, the Central Committee put forward a strategic plan to take Ningxia and establish a direct link with the Soviet Union.[32] An integral part of this plan was to reunite the First, Second, and Fourth Front Armies during October and November 1936 in north Gansu. In December, one front army was to be held back to defend the base area while the other two were to cross the frozen Yellow River and seize Ningxia. The plan was revised on August 30. Essentially, Mao's First Front Army was to protect the base area with one part providing support to the Second and Fourth Front Armies. The Second Front Army was to establish a base between the Shaan-Gan-Ning and that of a new base to be established by the Fourth Front Army in south Gansu. It is unclear what Zhang's reaction to this was, but it is unlikely that he would have been pleased, as his troops would bear the brunt of the fighting. Although the plan underwent numerous revisions, the military role of the Fourth Front Army remained the most important, and the most dangerous. Finally, the Army was to hold off Hu Zongnan, who controlled the GMD's most powerful troops in the area. It was difficult for Zhang to object to this, since his troops were the strongest and were the furthest south, nearest the combat zone. By fighting in north Ningxia, the First Front Army had the lightest task and, if the battle was won, would be the first to receive assistance from the Soviet Union.

Zhang was not enamoured with the idea. He moved slowly to avoid engagement, despite promptings from the Central Military Commission in mid-September. Instead Zhang proposed moving his army northwest. Although this was rebuffed by his own Northwest Bureau on September 21,[33] he ordered his Fourth Front Army to move west and cross the Yellow River. This would allow him to avoid direct contact with the powerful GMD forces and would weaken the control of the Central Military Commission (Mao) over Zhang's troops. On September 22, Zhu De informed the Commission of Zhang's view and said that he, Zhu De, wished to follow the views of the Central Committee. Mao succeeded in splitting Zhang's troops and alienating his high-level supporters.

Despite Zhang's protests, the Fourth Front Army did begin to move north on September 29–30, 1936. It was difficult for Zhang to countermand repeated instructions from the Party Center when the leaders of his own Fourth Front Army were not united behind him. Further, Zhang encountered major difficulties in his alternative strategy to cross the Yellow River. This may have been the last straw. On October 9, the forces of the First and Fourth Front Armies combined to fight the Ningxia battle. In a move that would undermine Zhang's strength still further, on October 11, the Central Committee and the Central Military Commission proposed splitting the Fourth Front Army into two. One part was to fight on the north front with the First Front Army, while the other part was to fight on the south front with the Second Front Army and the Shaanbei Independent Army. Confusion abounded over which units should cross the Yellow River. Not surprisingly, Zhang Guotao consistently proposed getting more of his troops over the river to keep them together while, on the whole, the central authorities (Mao) resisted this.

Finally, on October 30, Peng Dehuai decided to organize the Haida battle by uniting the three front armies. The objective was to prevent Hu Zongnan's army from uniting with the local GMD troops in Ningxia. Again Zhang refused to commit all of his troops. As a result, the battle could not be fought according to plan. The two GMD forces were able to link up and cut off the Red Army's main forces (the First and Second Front Armies and part of the Fourth Front Army) from the forces across the Yellow River (the fifth, ninth and thirtieth armies of the Fourth Front Army). Zhang was entrapped; his forces were divided; his key commanders were drifting away; and he had caused a battle to turn out badly for the CCP as a whole. In addition to dilute the influence of the Fourth Front Army and the Red Army Headquarters (Zhang Guotao) in the decision-making arena, the number of members of the Central Military Commission was expanded, thus indirectly increasing Mao's power over Zhang's.

In early 1937, criticism of Zhang increased. On March 31, the Politburo passed a decision on his "mistakes."[34] Zhang's challenge to Mao and the Party Center had failed. As he became increasingly marginalized, and as cooperation between the CCP and the GMD developed, Zhang decided to flee Yan'an. In April 1938 he joined the GMD. On April 18 he was expelled from the CCP, and the following day the party issued an internal party report on the affair.[35]

※

WHY DID ZHANG back off and accept, however reluctantly, the authority of the Central Committee after he had gone so far as to send a telegram urging in effect the overthrow of Mao Zedong ("a thorough inner party struggle") in September 1935 and the setting up of his own Central Committee that he expected to function as the new party center? Mao was able to bring Zhang to heel by first making it clear that the cost of conflict would be that both of them would lose to the real enemy, the GMD. Hence they had to reconcile themselves at least to the point of accepting the rules of the game. But with Mao in effective control of the Central Committee, it was a zero-sum situation. Further, Mao detached two of Zhang's key supporters when Chen Changhao and Xu Xiangqian were reassigned to the Front headquarters with the right route army. This made it difficult for them to act against the official Party Center. Although Zhang momentarily gained Zhu De's support, the former's attempts to set up an alternative Central Committee was interpreted as a breach of the most fundamental of norms governing party discipline. Mao, by seizing power at the Party Center, defined the range of Zhang's feasible options.

Zhang Guotao desperately wanted to maintain the Fourth Front Army power intact and establish his own base. Mao needed to divide the Fourth Front Army, split its leadership, and prevent the "great schism" between himself and Zhang from becoming effective. Zhang proposed a joint strategy and a united force to defeat the GMD and establish a unified base. Mao argued that if a united force attacked and lost, everything would be lost. He proposed an attack by a divided force in which the Fourth Front Army, the strongest, would bear the main brunt of the fighting. From Zhang's point of view, it was an interesting gamble. If he won he could establish an enlarged base in the north with a direct link to the Soviet Union. If he lost, however, the First and Second Front Armies would be intact, but his Fourth Front Army would be weakened. The risk was unacceptable. Zhang then proposed that no battle take place and that his forces move south and then northeast. In turn, this was ruled out by the Party Center. To have acted against its decision would have meant violating the rules, a course that would have been fatal.[36]

Three times Zhang tried to refuse Mao's rules of the game and evade his logic by refusing to move his troops as demanded by the Party Center. But each time the logic of the situation frustrated these efforts. Meanwhile the real game was being played by Mao: that of military power versus political legitimacy. Mao had high political legitimacy and low armed strength. Zhang had high military power and low political legitimacy. Zhang was also vain. he accepted the secretaryship of the Northwest Bureau because it provided him with a position of great prestige. Holding such a posititon, he thought that even if his armies were divided, he might win control over the Party Center, which would give him the legitimacy to challenge Mao. This was the fatal error that led first to Zhang's military and subsequently to his political undoing.

The struggle with Zhang Guotao reveals Mao as a master tactician who played an incredibly intricate game of intrigue. The nuanced manipulation of offices, the moving around of Mao-men and Zhang-men like chessmen, the saving graces provided to Zhang's chief military lieutenants such as Chen Changhao and Zhou Chunquan reveal the ruthless intelligence and cold logic that Mao followed when his interests were involved.

Liu Zhidan and the Issue of Centralized Power

Mao's struggle with Liu Zhidan concerns the relations between centralized and decentralized power. However, key elements of the story remain unclear. The question of local submission to the Party Center is seen in the differing fates of two local leaders, Liu Zhidan and Gao Gang. While Liu was to die a "martyr's death," Gao became one of Mao's most important supporters, guaranteeing Mao the support of the local party apparatus. Liu's death was used to turn him into a hero of the revolution. Edgar Snow portrays him as an exemplary figure: a red partisan, part bandit, part militant communist, who popped up virtually everywhere in Shaanxi, promoting land reform, executing landlords, attracting followers who devotedly followed him.[37]

In the summer of 1935, however, Liu's independent style and policies in the region under his control brought him into conflict with the representatives of the Party Center, Zhu Lizhi and Guo Hongtao.[38] This appeared to mirror Mao's own problems in the Jiangxi Soviet. The early thirties were marked by intense inner-party struggles that took on a sharp ideological tone and resulted in a kind of fratricide. The stress on secrecy, discipline, and reorientation of work by the Party Center for life underground, backed up by the drive for ideological orthodoxy, brought emissaries from the Party Center into conflict with operations in the rural soviets. Ideological correctness became the main weapon with which to attack the local leaders. As in the other base areas, this led to the arrest of local leaders and the increase of factionalism, not only in Shaanxi, but also in Jiangxi, E-Yu-Wan, and Xiang-Exi.[39] In soviets such as in northern Shaanxi, ideological purity was difficult to achieve. The party operated openly as the local government in a complex, insecure environment where it was desperate to hold onto its territorial gains. Compromise was the order of the day. The moderate land policy in the base area included deals made with bandit groups, including the recruitment of bandit soldiers.

When Guo and Zhu arrived, they were given high positions as their standing deserved, but were shut out from real power because they were outsiders.[40] They began to criticize the local leaders for ideological failings. They clashed with the local leaders, Liu Zhidan and Gao Gang, and tried to force them to change their guerrilla tactics and to submit to control by the Party Center.[41] They denounced Liu's setting up of a base in the mountains as the "Shaoshan line" (mountainism).

Liu was a strong character and stood up to Zhu and Gao. He is reported to have said to them, "You come from Beiping [Beijing]. Why then did you not build the base in Beiping? . . . Moreover, Mao built a base in the Jinggang Mountains, why then can't we build a base in the Shaanxi mountains? Shanghai is a nice place. Xi'an is also a friendly place. Why don't you build a base there?"[42] The clash came to a head in the summer and autumn of 1935, when the local comrades were excluded from top leadership positions. While neither Zhu nor Liu possessed their own military power, this situation changed with the arrival of Xu Haidong and his Red Twenty-Fifth Army in north Shaanxi on September 18, 1935, one month before Mao's troops would arrive. Xu and his Political Commissar, Cheng Zihua, teamed up with Zhu and Liu and put the local leaders on the defensive. (Cheng had engaged in a ferocious purge of party members that had taken place earlier in the E-Yu-Wan base area.)[43] The four arrested and killed a number of the local communist leaders, including Zhang Hanmin, who had organized the underground CCP organs while acting as a brigade leader under the GMD general Yang Hucheng. Zhang had deliberately fought badly against Xu's forces and let his men be taken captive. But Xu refused to believe that Zhang had worked underground and had him arrested and boiled alive.

In Shaanbei, a new leading organ was set up to wield party power, its leading positions filled by Zhu Lizhi, Guo Hongtao, Nie Hongjun, and Cheng Zihua.[44] The Military Committee was reshuffled, with Nie placed in charge; and the former Northwest Work Committee was replaced by the Shaan-Gan-Shanxi Provincial Committee. Zhu Lizhi was appointed secretary of the Provincial Committee with Guo Hongtao as his deputy.[45] In the reformed military structure, both Liu and Gao fell under Xu Haidong's command.

Liu had always remained close to his men, who called him "old Liu" although he was only thirty-two years old. He was a superb military commander and strategist. When the Red Fifteenth Army took on the troops of Marshall Zhang Xueliang in the battle of Laoshan, Liu the commander still fought in the front lines and annihilated one division of Zhang's army. At the back of the military formation was Xu Haidong, who had ordered Liu to the front in the hope that he and his army would be wiped out. Instead they took three thousand prisoners and killed the enemy commander. This Red Army victory, which repelled the GMD's third campaign to crush the communist base area, increased Liu's standing. In continuing arguments over strategy and tactics, however, Liu, Gao, and many others were purged and arrested.[46] Liu, although aware of the warrant for his arrest and despite his control of vastly superior military forces loyal to him, allowed himself to be arrested.[47]

During his imprisonment and torture, Liu Zhidan did not break. A "confess one's crimes" campaign began, but he insisted that he could have destroyed his captors and did not because he continued to believe that the base area was more important than who controlled it. This enraged Xu

Haidong. About a hundred of Liu's followers and associates were put in jail, among them Zhang Xiushan, Zhang Ce, Zhang Qingfu, Xi Zhongxun, Gao Gang, and Liu Jingfan (Liu's younger brother, who had served as an assistant to Zhang Guotao). Several attempts were made to break into the prison to free Liu Zhidan. However, Liu is reported to have told his people not to take any action, but to await the arrival of the Central Committee. Many died while waiting.

One survivor estimates that some two hundred were killed in Xia Siwan and one hundred in Guanzhong. At Xia Siwan, the dead were buried in a big hole behind the prison.[48] The place gave off a horrible smell, and local peasants who gathered wood in the area stopped going there. Rumor had it that the ground continued to move because of the live bodies that had been buried there. Some of Liu's followers were indeed buried alive. The secretary of the county, Du Wan, was placed in a hole. Earth was piled up to the level of his chest. His head turned purple and his nose began to bleed. He pleaded with his captors to shoot him, but they did not. Eventually, he suffocated. The seventeen-year-old daughter of the Vice Chairman of the Shaanxi People's Political Consultative Congress, originally a military cadre in the Red Army, was raped and killed. She had just graduated from middle school and had gone directly into revolutionary work. She was buried naked. The wife of the campaign leader took her clothes.

Mao's arrival with the Long March veterans at Wuqizhen in October 1935 changed the balance of power. A member of Liu Zhidan's family reportedly went to Yang Shangkun and Mao, telling them that Liu had been arrested. After an investigation headed by Zhou Enlai, both Gao and Liu as well as the others were released and their positions vindicated. Zhou had known Liu at the Whampoa (Huangpu) Academy and, on hearing the news, sent his men over to have Liu released.

Liu's release created an immediate coalition of interests between Mao's group and the local forces that was to be very helpful for his consolidation of power both within the region and within the party as a whole. However, Mao would not let himself be trapped by local interests. In fact, the arrival of Mao with his Party Center marked the end of partisan independence. The goals of the Northwest were now to be inextricably linked to national perspectives. While Gao Gang thrived in this new alliance, as did some other local partisans, Liu was not to be so easily pacified.

Those responsible for the killings and Liu's imprisonment and torture were not chastised. A number were actually promoted. In December 1938 Gao Gang replaced Guo Hongtao as head of the party apparatus in the

Shaan-Gan-Ning.[49] Gao took over when Guo was transferred to become Secretary of the Shandong Sub-Bureau of the party under the jurisdiction of the Northern Bureau. Guo was moved from this Sub-Bureau in October 1939. Zhu Lizhi remained as President of the Border Region Bank. Cheng Zihua was eventually transferred to work as acting Secretary for the Jin-Cha-Ji Border Region under Peng Zhen.[50] None were disgraced and some held senior positions even after 1949. This was especially the case for Cheng and Xu, but even Guo was a Vice-Chairman of the State Economic Commission on the eve of the Cultural Revolution. By contrast, although he was released, Liu Zhidan remained under suspicion, and his dossier *(dangan)* was marked "serious rightist."

Li Weihan, who ran the Organization Department after the Long Marchers arrived, was responsible for cadre reassignment and thus for dealing with the legacy of the conflict. Much later, when asked about the problem, he replied, "At that time, our thinking was unclear. We were influenced by Guo Hongtao, we elevated Guo Hongtao, listened to him and respected him . . . At that time, we believed Guo Hongtao's words."[51]

One of our interviewees saw this as a case of Mao's trickery. "Mao throws everyone in and lets them fight among themselves. In this way he takes his own control. Mao had his own purposes. The art of political trickery has a long Chinese tradition."

Mao's group regarded Liu as too independent a spirit. There were many who wanted to arrest or kill Liu. Mao sent him on what was called the Eastern Punitive Expedition (1936). At Dongzheng all three high-ranking military leaders of the Twenty-Fifth Red Army, Liu Zhidan and his two Divisional Commanders, Yang Qi and Yang Shen, were killed in battle. Liu's death solved Mao's problem of what to do with him, and even allowed Mao to turn Liu into a hero of the revolution.

Yet confusion surrounds the precise nature of Liu's death. Whether he was sacrificed by the CCP or killed by the GMD remains a mystery. Some informants believe that Liu was too prominent to dismiss, too much the hero to ignore, and too good a military commander to employ merely as an administrative cadre. They believe that Mao had Liu lead the Red Army forces in the battle in which it is said he was killed by a burst of machine gun fire from a watchtower only a couple of hundred meters away. For one informant the story of Liu Zhidan is a parable of the "War of the Three Kingdoms" in one episode of which Zhuge Liang, one of China's greatest military heroes, kills an enemy and then begins weeping and beating on the coffin, ostensibly in grief but actually to make sure that his enemy is not still breathing. Mao is Zhuge Liang.

Liu's Political Commissar, Song Renqiong, places Liu at the battle front, but claims that he was killed by unspecified sniper fire. Some Chinese observers, however, claim that Liu was shot by no other than Xu Haidong or one of Xu's men, on Mao's orders. Xu and his son are said to have complained that the family was not rewarded sufficiently for this act. While there is no hard evidence to support this last account, publication of materials concerning Liu Zhidan, other than that officially produced, has invariably brought controversy.

By contrast, relations between Mao and Gao went from strength to strength. The climax of their cooperation can be seen in Gao Gang's two reports to the Northwest Bureau Senior Cadres Conference (October 1942 to January 1943). Gao's reports and the decisions taken reinforced Mao's view of party history, extolled Mao's supremacy over Wang Ming, and supported Mao's view of economic and administrative affairs.[52] In his reports, Gao sought to vindicate his own previous policies (and those of the now deceased "martyr" Liu Zhidan) and to denigrate those of Zhu and Guo and to link them to the policies and faults of the Party Center at that time. The charges made by Gao were almost identical to those that Mao would level against Wang Ming and his supporters. Gao accused Guo and Zhu of committing the mistake of "left deviation" prior to 1935 and then "right opportunism" after the united front policies went into effect. Gao thus linked the history of the Shaan-Gan-Ning area with Mao's own experiences in Jiangxi, thus validating Mao's stories. The Northwest Bureau provided Mao with a very powerful party organizational base, allowing him to concentrate on rectification of other groups in the party, and so further consolidate his power.

The Struggle for Ideological Control: Mao versus Wang Ming

Wang Ming presented Mao Zedong with his greatest challenge to ideological authority within the CCP.[53] Leadership of a communist movement is aided by a reputation as a Marxist theoretician and philosopher.[54] In this respect, Wang Ming presented a threat to Mao. Wang had received a thorough training in Bolshevik theory while in Moscow and was generally regarded as a theoretician of greater significance than Mao or anyone else in the Chinese movement. Until Mao was able to compile his own party history, Wang Ming's *The Two Lines* was the most substantial review of the party's history.[55] Wang had also been influential in drafting the Comintern's new united front policy and its application to China. He drafted the August First Declaration (1935) that signaled the CCP's clear intent to move from civil war to a renewed form of cooperation with patriotic elements in China.

After initial enthusiasm for the united front, Mao worried about the GMD's capacity to lead the war of resistance. In November 1937, perhaps in preparation for Wang's return to China, Mao tried to stake out his policy for the united front. He stated that the CCP must retain its "independence and initiative." This did not mean that the united front was to be disrupted, but that party members were to remember the differences between the two parties. In Mao's view, the chief danger now was no longer "left closed-doorism" but "right opportunism."[56] Wang Ming, who was about to arrive in Yan'an from Moscow, would receive Mao's scorn as the main "right opportunist" after their clash of opinions about how to proceed with the united front.

Wang Ming had trained with Pavel Mif and under his patronage had ousted Li Lisan from power at the Fourth Plenum in January 1931. While Xiang Zhongfa formally remained General Secretary, Wang had the real power. Even after his return to Moscow, where he headed the Chinese Mission to the Comintern, Wang Ming retained influence over the policy of the Party Center, an influence that was disturbed by the Long March. Up to then, Mao and Wang seemed to have modest respect for one another.

On November 27, 1937, Wang Ming and seven members of the CCP Mission to the Comintern, including Kang Sheng and Chen Yun, arrived in Yan'an. Wang was given a warm welcome. Mao, meeting him for the first time, purportedly said Wang was "a blessing from the sky."[57] But Wang immediately challenged Mao as the dominant ideological force in the party. Mao is supposed to have voted to accept Wang's report on what kind of position ought to be taken vis-à-vis the united front, in part because it appeared to reflect Stalin's views. But Mao had quite other ideas about how the united front ought to be conducted.

Mao had to defeat Wang Ming politically and then present an approach to theory that would not only appropriate the united front as his own, but also undermine Wang Ming's credibility. This latter objective was difficult to achieve because, according to Shum, "Stalin had instructed Wang Ming to overcome the 'leftist deviation' in the Party without directly contesting Mao's authority."[58]

To deal with the situation created by the new arrivals, the Politburo held a conference from December 9 to 14, at which Wang Ming won the support of the majority and established his influence, although his power base remained weak. Wang delivered the keynote speech to the conference while Mao remained silent. Wang's December 27 article called for improving the unification of all work in what became to be known as the policy of "everything through the united front."[59] This contrasted with Mao's calls for "independence and initiative." Wang clearly felt that his was the best way to develop CCP activities outside of the Border Region. While Wang acknowledged that problems still existed with the GMD, he felt that the foundations had been laid for a solid anti-Japanese national united front. This cooperation would be long-term, continuing after the war during a period of national reconstruction. He also called for the united front to be extended beyond the two parties to mobilize effectively other groups for resistance. Although Wang accepted that CCP members could join the GMD government, he maintained that the Eighth Route Army must retain its independence.

The conference resolution congratulating the CCP Mission to the Comintern for its work in formulating the new policies for the anti-Japanese united front appeared to boost Wang's preeminent position.[60] In fact, however, organizational changes strengthened Mao's position. The conference adopted a resolution to convene the Seventh Party Congress as soon as possible. A twenty-five person committee was set up to prepare this congress, to which Mao was appointed Chair and Wang Ming Secretary. This reflected the power relations at the time, and Wang, despite his prestige, must have realized that he could not take over from Mao. Further, on the Comintern's instructions, it was decided to abolish the post of General Secretary in order to encourage collective leadership. Thus, Zhang Wentian lost his position, and a Secretariat was formed consisting of Zhang Wentian, Mao Zedong, Chen Yun, and Kang Sheng.[61] Mao retained his influential position as Chair of the Military Council.

After the conference Wang Ming, accompanied by Zhou Enlai and Bo Gu, left Yan'an for Wuhan to take up his position as Secretary of the party's Yangtze Bureau. This removed him from the Party Center, leaving Mao to run it together with army headquarters. In Wuhan, Wang Ming began to develop an approach to the united front that was seriously at odds with Mao's. Initially dictated by the vastly different conditions in Wuhan, Wang's policy of cooperation and his taking advantage of opportunities to work within the law to expand communist influence paid off.

The conflict between Mao and Wang reached a high point at the Politburo meeting held in Yan'an in early March 1938. The key issues discussed were the role of the CCP in the Sino-Japanese War and the relationship between the CCP and the GMD. As in December, Wang Ming delivered the keynote address while Mao made no formal speech. In spite of this, and although a written version of Wang's report was published and circulated widely, Mao's opposition resulted in no formal resolution being adopted.

Wang's report stated that the united front was to be consolidated in the form of a "national revolutionary alliance"[62] that would resemble the first united front or would be a confederation within which all parties would have political and organizational independence. He stressed the need for a "united army, united assignment, united command, united combat." He also stressed the need for the GMD to formalize the legal activities of other groups. He proposed establishing a national assembly so that other parties could be consulted and encouraged the legalization and development of mass organizations. Finally, Wang stated that the correct military strategy was to use mobile warfare as the main form of combat coordinated with positional warfare. Guerrilla warfare was relegated to a support function.

The downgrading of guerrilla warfare was at odds with Mao's approach, and the question of military strategy took on increased importance in the following months, especially when the fall of Xuzhou to Japanese forces in late May led to Wuhan being threatened. Throughout April, Mao called for the development of guerrilla bases in north China; and in May, Mao stressed that the main task of the Eighth Route Army was to engage in guerrilla warfare and to engage in mobile warfare only where conditions were favorable.[63]

This clash of approaches became crucial as Wang Ming began to participate in the defense of Wuhan. On May 14, the Party Center sent instructions to the New Fourth Army and the Party's Yangtze Bureau telling them to shift their work to the rural areas, where they were to set up guerrilla forces.[64] This was followed on May 22, 1938, by instructions to the Hebei, Hunan, and Wuhan party branches that after the fall of Xuzhou they should focus their work on guerrilla warfare in the countryside and the creation of bases there. The majority of students, workers, and revolutionary elements were to return to their home villages to help with this process. These instructions made party work in Wuhan peripheral.[65]

In stark contrast, Wang Ming, in his public statement of June 15, acknowledged that Wuhan might fall, but mooted Madrid as an example of heroic defense. Wang favored a massive mobilization under the GMD's leadership to engage the Japanese in mobile warfare before they could reach Wuhan. The Eighth Route Army, operating in the enemy's rear, was to be used to destroy supply lines.[66]

Wang's proposals backfired. As always, the GMD was suspicious of CCP calls for mass mobilization and on August 5 placed restrictions on the activities of the local mass organizations. A number of them were closed down, and the activities of the CCP came under close scrutiny by the GMD secret police. Wang Ming's attempt to expand communist influence through legal means ended in failure. His prestige in party circles received another major blow when Wuhan fell to the Japanese on October 25, 1938.

Mao then used the Sixth Plenum of the Sixth Central Committee (September 29 to November 6, 1938) to press home his advantage. His dominance was enhanced by news brought from Moscow by Wang Jiaxiang. Wang relayed information contained in a September Comintern directive and Dimitrov's ideas. The directive approved of the political line of the CCP during the past year in its united front work, while Georgi Dimitrov, the Secretary-General of the Comintern, fully endorsed Mao's leading position in the party. This stripped any claim that Wang Ming could have made to be the "Comintern's man." Indeed, many believe that it was only after receiving this news that Mao decided to convene the Plenum.[67] The loss of Wuhan during the Plenum shifted things further in Mao's favor. By the end of the meeting, Mao had made his differences with Wang clear. The sharpness of Mao's tone in his concluding speeches was aided by the fact that Wang had left the meeting early to attend the National Political Consultative Assembly, apparently believing that he and Mao had reached a compromise. Wang obviously had not made a very good study of Mao as a political strategist.

Mao had no intention of wrecking the united front; he realized it was vital to the CCP's interests. Thus his opening speech praised both the GMD and Chiang Kai-shek personally.[68] Mao even stated that the GMD played the dominant role in the united front. Class struggle was not to detract from the task of national resistance. Mao still proposed that the "new democratic republic" would be based on Sun Yat-sen's Three Principles of the People, rather than on those of socialism. These were all sentiments that Wang could wholeheartedly endorse. He even praised Mao indirectly for the pivotal role Mao played in the CCP.[69]

However, with Wang gone and Wuhan fallen, Mao told a different story. Mao blamed the GMD for not allowing the united front to assume a proper organizational form and harshly criticized Wang Ming's slogan "Everything through the united front."[70] Mao went on to criticize Wang Ming's idea of using legal channels to develop the communist movement and Wang's strategy of moving from the cities to the countryside, a mistake, Mao clearly implied, that derived from the influence of the Soviet revolution on Wang Ming. Mao made it clear that China's revolution would work the other way round: from the countryside to the cities.[71]

The political resolution did not include harsh public condemnation of Wang Ming's approach. It was not necessary to risk upsetting the situation by informing the rank and file. It was enough that Mao had dealt Wang a serious blow at the Plenum by telling the party's inner circle of Wang's short comings. Immediately after the Plenum, the party's regional bureau system was reorganized, resulting in an undermining of Wang Ming's organizational position. On November 9, 1938, Wang's Yangtze Bureau was abolished and its former area of jurisdiction was placed under two new bureaus: the Southern Bureau, headed by Zhou Enlai; and the Central Plains Bureau, headed by Liu Shaoqi.[72] Both Zhou and Liu were loyal to Mao.

Although defeated politically, Wang was still useful to Mao as a straw man to be attacked as Mao moved to justify his becoming the sole voice interpreting the Chinese revolution. Thus, Wang's political defeat was the necessary prelude to his humiliation in the campaign to study party history and the Rectification Campaign. Wang's demise coincided with Mao's desire to place himself as the unchallenged interpreter of China's revolutionary experience.

Mao attacked Wang at the level of theory and discredited Wang's view of CCP history. Mao constructed a party history designed to show that his own correct leadership of the Chinese revolution was intrinsically linked to his correct thought, which had guided the revolutionary process while at the same time being a product of it.[73]

Mao undercut Wang Ming's pretensions to be a theorist by labeling him a dogmatist who derived his Marxist theory from books and not from the practice of the Chinese revolution. After a none-too-successful diversion into lectures on dialectics in the winter of 1936–37, Mao concentrated on promoting himself as a theorist who had fully understood the historical course of the Chinese revolution. Mao's speech to the Sixth Plenum in October 1938 rejected the idea of an abstract Marxism, calling instead for Marxism to be adapted to a local form that people would be able to comprehend easily and thus respond to.[74] In both the process of redefining party history and in defining "sinified" Marxism-Leninism, Wang Ming would come to stand for the antithesis of all that Mao proposed and that revolutionary success in China required.

Wang Shiwei and the End of an Alternative Intellectual Discourse

The humiliation and arrest in Yan'an of Wang Shiwei has come to represent in China the personification of Mao's use and abuse of intellectuals.[75] It also provides a good example of multiple codings of the sort we have been concerned with. On one level it shows how one of the few genuine intellectuals in Yan'an, best known as a translator, became the symbol of resistance to Mao's definition of the intellectual's role: how intellectuals should be subordinated to the revolution as laid down in the "Yan'an Forum on Literature and Art." Wang Shiwei, who stalwartly rejected subordination, became something of a hero. The putative representative of the Lu Xun independent, critical intellectuals (one of the few such intellectuals who went to Yan'an rather than Chongqing or Kunming), Wang's activities coincided with the preliminary phase of ideological purification, from 1939 to 1941, as well as with the first phase of the Rectification Campaign. Wang had joined the CCP in 1926 and worked mainly in Shanghai, where he had come into contact with Trotskyites and translated some of Trotsky's writing.[76] In 1936, he went to Yan'an and became a research officer in the Marxist-Leninist Academy, which subsequently became the Central Research Institute.

Wang became embroiled in a dispute with Mao's supporter, Chen Boda, over the nature and content of revolutionary literature. In view of the importance attached by Mao to literary text, this dispute touched an extremely sensitive nerve. Moreover, it evoked an earlier conflict over the same issue between Mao and China's greatest modern writer, Lu Xun.

Lu Xun, by far the most outstanding of the radical intellectuals of the May Fourth Movement and also a source of inspiration to "real" intellectuals, had never taken kindly to the discipline the party wanted to impose on intellectuals. In Shanghai, were Lu lived, he ran afoul of the local CCP cultural czar, Zhou Yang. An article Lu Xun wrote characterized Zhou as a dandy, a fop, and a vain man who liked fast cars and was ignorant of culture and literature. In return Zhou attacked Lu, who by this time was very ill, removing him from the Left Wing Writers Association, which Lu himself had founded.[77] Shortly afterward, when Lu Xun died, Zhou Yang repaired to Yan'an. When Mao established an academy for artists and writers, he named it after Lu Xun and made Zhou Yang the director. It was a gesture not lost on Wang Shiwei.

In Yan'an, Wang Shiwei was known as one of the "four eccentrics." He was a dissenter associated with Ding Ling and Liu Xuewei, both editors of the art column of *Liberation Daily*. Wang became part of a group who saw the CCP as providing the best vehicle for national salvation but who were not necessarily willing to commit themselves to the party's ideological rigor. They wanted less interference by the party in cultural and intellectual activities, more opportunities for debate, and greater tolerance of differing viewpoints. They also wanted greater freedom to criticize publicly malpractices in Yan'an than the party was willing to grant them.

They interpreted Mao's call for rectification of bad practices in the party in this light. Thus, Liu Xuewei published an article on revolutionary literature in June 1942 in which he criticized revolutionary literature as coarse, dull, and inferior, and urged a higher artistic level. This article was followed up by another on June 7 calling for freedom of thought as the basis of "New Democracy." On September 22, yet another article argued that too much emphasis on politics lowered the development of the arts. On March 9, Ding Ling published "Thoughts on March 8, Women's Day" attacking the party for its treatment of women and pointing out male dominance and sexism in Yan'an society. Mao was upset by the article. A few days later Ding Ling was dismissed as an editor of the art column. A few days after that, Wang Shiwei published "The Wild Lily."

It proved a bombshell. Published in two parts on March 13 and 27 in *Liberation Daily,* the article was, according to Cheek, modeled after Lu Xun's satirical essays "A Rose without Blooms."[78] Attacking Mao's taste for beautiful women, it offered as an alternative to Mao's wife, Jiang Qing, an exemplary model of a woman revolutionary who was executed in 1928. In essence, Wang was criticizing the inequalities perpetuated in Yan'an as leading to the undermining of the enthusiasm of the young. In publishing "The Wild Lily" Wang clearly saw himself as contributing to rectification by exposing the defects in Yan'an.

Given the circumstances, what Wang did was extraordinary. A Marxist militant like the rest of the Yan'anites, holed up in caves during the most difficult days, he began a devastating critical analysis of the situation with a prose poem to the woman he loved. "As I walked alone by the river, seeing in front of me the old fashioned cotton shoes of a female comrade suddenly reminded me of those of Comrade Li Fen, the most beloved first friend of my life. Whenever I think of her my heart pounds and my blood thickens." So begins "The Wild Lily," with a personal lament for a revolutionary martyr. It is a cry from the heart, in the best Lu Xun tradition. It personalizes the world of stylized public experience. It punctures the language of political illusion. It breaks through the conspiracy of personal silences and by so doing deliberately challenges the official position on virtually every aspect of social and political life in Yan'an, especially the role of art and literature and the critical responsibilities of the revolutionary intellectual.

Wang Shiwei deliberately punctured the extravagant claims of egalitarianism made in Yan'an and exposed the differences between those in and out of power. He asserted that in a society in which equality is a chief moral claim, the principle on which the nature of truth itself is to be rerendered, transformed, and redeemed, this principle must not be compromised by hypocrisy. Above all, Wang Shiwei claimed moral and ideological autonomy and the freedom to criticize abuses of power. He believed it was necessary to offer publicly alternative policies to those being proposed. He attributed to the artist romantic purity, which he contrasted (most specifically in his 1942 essay "Statesman-Artist") with the way the party compromised its ideals. In so doing, Wang gained the support of idealistic youth. Ultimately, he was to pay for it with his life.

Wang acknowledged that society in Yan'an was "superior" to that in the "outside world," but he believed this should not be an excuse to turn a blind eye to problems. He attacked the system of rank in Yan'an and the inequalities it produced. Wang felt it was unnecessary and irrational to divide clothing into three and food into five grades;[79] it simply created resentment. Wang suggested that an "iron-like unity" and a more "profound love" would be produced if cadres were willing to share weal and woe with the rank and file.

Wang's exposures drew the wrath of the party elite, which responded by attacking intellectuals for their "petty bourgeois mentality." Almost all of the writers attacked renounced their previous views, the one notable exception being Wang Shiwei.[80] Ding Ling and Ai Qing went so far as to denounce Wang, who was attacked in the communist press and put on quasi trial for his views. However, at first it was not easy to get the Yan'anites to criticize Wang and there were difficulties in arranging meetings to discuss the events. Even Mao admitted in April 1945 that Wang's views had had a powerful impact on Yan'an.[81] Yet Mao waged a strong campaign to eradicate his influence.

Even before Wang's "Wild Lily," party leaders had been disturbed by critical posters that had been put up and proposed that a Rectification Campaign Examination Committee be established to monitor them. Wang Shiwei had vigorously opposed such a committee and, when it became clear that one would be established anyway, he insisted that its members be elected rather than appointed. He also proposed that the directors of all departments and the director of the Central Research Institute be elected as well. He suggested that the writers of wall posters remain anonymous to protect their rights. Wang's proposals found overwhelming support. Elections were carried out; and while those elected were not favored by Wang Shiwei and his group, they were jubilant at this "triumph of democracy." Wang continued to write articles attacking Li Weihan, the director of the Central Research Institute, and he began a wall poster newspaper series called *Arrow and Target (Shi yu di),* the arrow of dissent being fired directly into the target, Marxism-Leninism and the fundamental character of the Chinese revolution. When some of his articles were put on cloth and set up outside the southern gate of Yan'an City, readers "flocked to read them in the way they flock to a fair." Wang Shiwei was becoming a celebrity in Yan'an.[82]

Party leaders were particularly upset by the selections from *Arrow and Target* that were posted at a busy intersection. In late March, General Wang Zhen read them and commented, "Our comrades at the front are shedding their blood and sacrificing their lives for the party and the people of the whole nation while you people are condemning the party after feeding yourselves in the rear areas." After the Forum on Literature and Art, which defined Mao's views on the role of artists and writers in the revolution, Mao asked the poorly educated Wang Zhen to head the artists' rectification study group. Despite Wang's repeated protestations that he was unable to do this, Mao insisted, stating, "It is you who is appointed to do this work. Someone like you without much education should be appointed to deal with the literate."[83] Mao was being pragmatic. While reading *Arrow and Target,* he commented, "Our ideological struggle now has a goal."[84]

It did not take long for the party to react. Wang was attacked both in the press and at his place of work, the Central Research Institute. The nature of the denunciation in the institute and the criticisms in the press set the prototype for the Cultural Revolution (1966–1976). It was not enough just to attack a person's ideas; it was also necessary to show that the person concerned was thoroughly evil and had always been so.

However, Mao at first hoped that private persuasion would prove enough. One of Mao's secretaries, Hu Qiaomu, had two talks with Wang and wrote him two letters. Hu wrote:

The mistake of "The Wild Lily" is, first of all, in its standpoint, which has already been criticized. Second, there are some more concrete criticisms. Last, are its writing techniques. What Chairman Mao wishes you to correct is your wrong standpoint. The article is full of unfriendly feelings towards the leaders and is provocative in winning ordinary people's support to attack them. It is definitely not allowed among party members, no matter whether you are a politician or an artist. The more this kind of criticism draws some comrades together in opposition, the more dangerous it becomes to the party. Thus, it is more necessary to resist [these criticisms].[85]

When the private words failed to have the desired effect, the campaign went public. The Institute launched a "struggle session" against Wang on May 27 that lasted until June 11, 1942. The thrust of the criticism was that Wang's actions had been antiparty and that his viewpoint was that of a Trotskyite. Among the specific charges were that Wang had associated with Trotskyites, that he claimed Stalin was not "lovable," that Karl Radek (wrongly accused of the Kirov assassination) was a good person, that the Comintern must be held accountable for the failure of the Chinese revolution of 1927, that the trial of Zinoviev and the accusation that he was a traitor needed to be taken with a pinch of salt, and that parts of Trotsky's theory were correct. These rather obvious truths were treated as signs of having committed serious crimes. In addition, Wang was accused of slandering party leaders by calling them corrupt, of disrupting party unity, and of using the term "hardbone" (brave) in reference to his friends and "softbone" (coward) for other comrades. Finally, it was said that by describing himself as a modern Lu Xun, he was calling on the youth of Yan'an to embrace him.

The orchestrated campaign began with several people stating that prior to the Rectification Campaign they had manifested an extreme democratic tendency. This required self-criticism. In the self-criticism, it was made clear that while many had become deviationists, Wang was fundamentally different. His mistakes betrayed a pattern. They were not accidental.

Some did not agree. Hence the screws were tightened. Ai Siqi examined Wang's writings in light of Mao's conclusions at the Yan'an Forum on Literature and Art. Ai contended that Wang had abandoned the party's standpoint and sown discord, violating democratic centralism and party discipline. Ideological error was thus compounded by political error. Next came the examination of Wang's thought. By studying the Rectification documents it would become clear how serious his errors of thought and method had become. One had to "cure the sickness to save the patient" by exposing Wang's mistakes. Those who believed that Wang's position was incorrect but his intentions were pure were wrong. His words were "premeditated malevolence." He used the slogan of opposing sectarianism to carry out provocations, and in the name of opposing the "black elements" in the party and promoting democracy, he actually opposed the leading organs. Ai, as recorded in Wen Jize's "Diary of Struggle," personalized the attack:

> This is an exact copy of the old methods used by the Trotskyites in the Soviet Union. Wang Shiwei's thought was that of a petty bourgeois

derived from that of a small ruined aristocrat . . . Like a smuggler, he spreads Trotskyite thought that contains the following major elements: a hypocritical revolutionary zeal that conceals a genuine tragic pessimism; rejection of the united front; the conception of a classless "human nature"; and a factional view of inner-party struggle. His methods are truly ingenious. He knows how to make beautiful disguises . . . He makes use of the reactions of the young to pit them against the old cadres, pit subordinates against superiors and artists against statesmen.[86]

Wen Jize notes that the struggle session ended with lessons to be learned, "a resolute and total opposition to liberalism, strict adherence to discipline, a complete ban on rumor-mongering, heightening of our political vigilance, improvement of our study of the documents and increasing the seriousness of our self-examination."

Wen Jize's account notes that "at the end of Fan Wenlan's speech, the entire hall applauded enthusiastically. Amidst this enthusiastic and victorious applause, the presidium announced the conclusion of the meeting." Even then, and despite the virulence of the attacks, many remained favorably disposed toward Wang Shiwei. To correct the confusion, everyone was instructed to read Lenin's "Party Organization and Literature," Lu Xun's speech at the Founding Congress of the Left-wing Writers Association, Mao's conclusion to the Yan'an Forum on Literature and Art, the first section of the tenth chapter of the *History of the Communist Party of the Soviet Union (Bolshevik),* and selections from the second volume of Stalin's *Selected Works* (about crushing opposition cliques).

Wang attempted to resign from the party, but his request was refused. In his subsequent testimony he withdrew his request, but refused to admit any mistakes. Finally, the members of the Central Research Institute demanded that Wang Shiwei be expelled from the party. The coup de grace was delivered on June 11, when his former colleague and critical intellectual, Ding Ling, denounced Wang and made a self-criticism of her own outspoken views. She said, "We tried everything to pull him out of his latrine, but he wanted to drag us down with him. This is outrageous. Now, we should declare: Wang Shiwei has one last chance to climb out of his counterrevolutionary latrine." Wang was thus turned into an outcast, a warning to others who might challenge the party.

Wang's old enemy, Mao's secretary Chen Boda, led the ridiculing of Wang's ideas in the press. Character assassination abounded.[87] Chen claimed that while Wang liked to use high-sounding phrases about himself, the truth was the opposite. He claimed, "This kind of person has no 'spine' but is like a spineless leech! There is no 'greatness' about him, he is as minute as a mosquito; like the kind that sneak in silently to bite you." Wang was said to have a "very dirty soul" and to exhibit "all the filthy ingredients found in humankind." Referring to "The Wild Lily," Chen claims that Wang's true intent was not to propose genuine equality but to pull others down while promoting himself. As in the struggle sessions, Chen linked Wang to the Trotskyites. For Chen, Wang represented the forces of darkness that sought to lead the youths of the revolution astray.

Wang was arrested on April 1, 1943, together with some two hundred other party and nonparty members. He was portrayed as one of the "internal traitors" who must be detained to prevent them from making contact with the GMD officials who were expected to arrive in Yan'an for discussions. While the others were released a few at a time, Wang Shiwei was not.[88] However, Mao did not want Wang killed and gave explicit orders to this effect. Mao wanted to use Wang Shiwei as a negative model during the Rectification Campaign. When the GMD attacked Yan'an in March 1947, Wang was evacuated by the Central Social Affairs Department, the secret police organization that had been holding him. He was moved to the Jin-Sui Border Region, which was under the control of He Long. In the late spring of that year, he was executed by a prison guard from the detention section of the Jin-Sui Public Security Bureau. Who gave the execution order is unclear, but an unidentified source claims that He Long himself admitted giving the order.[89]

The campaign to silence writers was accompanied by delineation of a "correct theory" on the role of literature and art. Mao provided this in his opening and closing addresses to the Yan'an Forum on Literature and Art (May 2 and 23, 1942).[90] Mao stated that literature and art were not independent of politics. As the party decided correct politics, this meant that literature and art would have to serve the revolutionary tasks prescribed by the party. For Mao, there was no abstract love, freedom, truth, or human nature. Those who believed this had been influenced by the bourgeoisie. There were only forms belonging to specific classes at specific times. Thus, "art for art's sake"—art that could transcend class or party or be independent of politics—did not exist.[91] The role of literature was to reflect class differences, not to obscure them by dwelling on supposed universal qualities. Literature and art were primarily for workers, peasants, and soldiers and only secondarily for the petty bourgeoisie. In the base areas, the writer's task was not to show the darker side of Border Region life but to extol its virtues. The shortcomings in the party's work would be dealt with by the organization itself and not through a public airing in the press. Criticism should be reserved for the Japanese and the areas under GMD control.

Through his idea of the mass line, Mao identified the leaders with the masses and argued that any attack on the party's leaders constituted an attack on the masses. Mao rejected Wang Shiwei's idea that politicians should look after the revolution's material forces while the artist should look after the revolution's soul.[92]

Wen Jize, who recorded Wang's trial for publication in the press, stated many years later, "It is possible that Wang Shiwei spoke the truth, but to speak the truth at that time was not helpful to the Communist Party."[93]

The Depersonalization of Power

The four struggles just described define the immediate context of Mao's politics within Yan'an. The first struggle, with Zhang Guotao, is a rationalistic calculus, a pure game of power inside the framework of a retrieving myth and a projective logic. The second struggle, with Liu Zhidan, was over the direction of power, defining it as top down, not bottom up, despite the illusion of democracy. The third, with Wang Ming, was over whose Marxism would prevail and whose texts would become hegemonic. The Rectification Campaign established a basis for exegetical bonding; it also established the orthodoxy of Mao Zedong Thought, with Mao as the sole and proprietary intellectual. The fourth struggle, with Wang Shiwei, universalized the reach of Mao's word alone.

In two cases the struggle ended in death; in another, exile; and in the fourth, ignominy. Together Mao's four contenders box the compass—that is, they define alternative principles rejected by Mao and so locate a set of boundaries within which Mao emerges as both supreme military figure and cosmocrat. His writings, reedited into a corpus now referred to as Mao Zedong Thought, universalized what began as specific lectures about particular events. The four struggles enabled Mao to situate himself between the rightist and antitheoretical or "pragmatic" line of Zhang Guotao and the more orthodox Stalinist line of Wang Ming; between the decentralizing pull of Liu Zhidan and the tight central control of the Li Lisan line; and intellectually against the elitism and democratism of Wang Shiwei. The discourse explicitly recognized the crucial importance of culture, text, writing, literature, and the arts as weapons of revolutionary theory and practice.

It is in the context of these and other disputes and conflicts that we can see Yan'an forming into a mobilization, or semiotic, space. Like the witches in the demonology of the Puritan revolution, Zhang Guotao, Liu Zhidan, Wang Ming, and Wang Shiwei became the demons of Yan'an. Each represented a lapsarian alternative. With the hardening of Mao Zedong Thought into a discourse, a way of thinking, a mode of dialectical truth, each alternative came to be seen not as different views or alternative truths, but rather as alternatives to the only truth. A space was formed between the lapsarian doctrines and the dialectical truth of Mao Zedong Thought, and into that space the Rectification Campaign was inserted. The result was the formation of symbolic capital as a preorthodoxy and exegetical bonding as a hegemonic hermeneutic; the corpus itself became the norm of discipline.

Moreover, the combination of articulated principle and ruthless struggle is itself part of the story and its interpretation. Coming early in the Yan'an experience each struggle leaves a layer of potential doubt and dissent despite victory. Thus, although success was uneven, particularly in the case of Wang Ming and Wang Shiwei, the Rectification Campaign was an attempt not only to develop a hermeneutic by means of exegetical bonding, but also to make that hermeneutic totally hegemonic as a language separating the enlightened from the unenlightened, and segregating a good communist from the backsliders or dissidents. In this sense, Yan'an was both a moral high ground and a Machiavellian moment.[94]

THREE STORIES

✳

Mao's four power struggles redefined the political cosmology of the party. His next problem was how to enlarge that cosmos to encompass the whole of China. This required a very different strategy from that which enabled Mao to realize supremacy within the party. Lacking the military forces and economic support required to defeat both the Japanese and the GMD, his power would depend on how well he could transform Yan'an into a moral center, a semiotic space in sole possession of an inversionary discourse capable of generating public support. It meant building up and drawing upon symbolic capital so that Yan'an would become a political magnet, attracting and mobilizing young Chinese. This in turn would require constructing within Yan'an an interior system of codes, symbols, and icons capable not only of resolving intraparty factionalism, but also unifying a diverse community. Once this was accomplished, the influence of Yan'an might then push outward.

As a first step toward constructing this system, Mao used his newly realized power to change his role from a predominantly military figure to a storyteller, creating a master narrative of the revolution. He then moved from being a storyteller to a cosmocrat, defining a logic of necessity for revolutionary accomplishment. In this chapter and the next we examine Mao's strategy in each of these roles.

Storytelling

Storytelling is an important, but not well recognized, aspect of political leadership. Walter Benjamin has appropriately described the kind of power it represents: "Death is the sanction of everything that the storyteller can tell. He has borrowed his authority from death. In other words, it is natural history to which his stories refer back."[1] Mao's four victories were not only sanctioned against a backdrop of death but they provided him with both the necessary authority and a history.

Mao's storytelling was accomplished through reenactment, the unification of historical memories and individual experiences. He incorporated his own power struggles within a larger master narrative of the Chinese revolution. Mao was able to transform his own experience into a representation of the general experience. Benjamin puts it very well: "All great storytellers have in common the freedom with which they move up and down the rungs of their experience as on a ladder. A ladder extending downward to the interior of the earth and disappearing into the clouds is the image for a collective experience to which even the deepest shock of every individual experience, death, constitutes not impediment or barrier."[2] One might say that in this case the ladder was a narrative of events that converted time into place by means of the Long March and that so sanctified Yan'an that it became the simulacrum for a projected universal transcendence.

There is nothing mysterious about the storytelling process. People make stories out of events. They do so individually and collectively. Recounting individual stories makes for sociability. Collective stories have political consequences when as myths they purport to be history, as history they are reinterpreted as theories, and as theories they make up stories about events. Theories that become stories create fictive truths. In politics, fictive truth telling and storytelling are all part of the same process by which it becomes possible to interrogate the past in order to transform the future.

Of course, the degree to which this is so varies with time, place, and circumstance. Yan'an, "Mao's republic," is a good example of the way in which fictive truths of the kind we have in mind are generated. Moreover, one can see in Yan'an how stories generate theories and how theories become transformed in the telling, the resultant combination serving as self-fulfilling prophecies (proofs of the correctness of the theory or line).

In this sense, Yan'an represents an inversionary discourse community. Its formation was a consequence of stories told, theories constructed, and the collectivization of both in a mythologic. It includes a sleight of hand, the transformation of individual to collective stories and from narration to text. To make such a transformation requires a strong storyteller, one who can induce individuals to recount their individual experiences and in so doing transform them into a collective experience. In doing this the storyteller generates symbolic capital as an alternative to more conventional modes of power.[3] Symbolic capital can be seen as an endowment of meaning taken from collective experience upon which individuals can draw for their own enhancement. In this sense, collectivization in the form of symbolic capital constitutes a fund of power available to individuals that appears to enlarge their powers. It is less a form of entitlement than enablement: it enables the overcoming of the self through participation in a collective project.

Like virtually all great political ideologists, Mao Zedong was a great storyteller, especially during his Yan'an days. There he and his associates combined storytelling and truth telling. They drew from individuals the materials out of which they formed a collective mythology. In turn, this mythology was made to yield higher truths, a theory textualized as dialectical logic. In this way a discourse was constructed that separated insiders from outsiders. It established a boundary around Mao's followers within the Chinese Communist Party between the CCP and the GMD. Within this boundary individual self-interest was broken down in favor of "collective individualism."

Collective individualism began when an individual went to Yan'an. "Joining the revolution" was made a conscious and deliberate act in which one yielded part of one's persona to the collectivity. This was the first step in a reeducation process in which, through a careful reading of prescribed texts, a form of "exegetical bonding" made each person feel that he or she had transcended individual limitations, had overcome deficiencies, and had therefore gained more from the collectivity than he or she had given up. Mao's stories and theories offered his listeners a supreme sense of insight and interpretative power.

Contextualizing the Stories

Mao was no ordinary storyteller. His stories were carefully contrived, and are repeated in various texts. They do not appear as stories at all, but as historical sequences, each telescoped into the other. There is a long story of the decline and fall of China and the loss of the patrimony; an intermediate one, the struggle with the GMD; and a short one, which covers the bitter internecine conflicts between lines and factions within the CCP. The shorter the story, the more closed down the optic, the bigger the image, and the smaller the field until Mao virtually fills the entire field of vision.

This condensation and intensification of the image of Mao in Yan'an took place over time, as the context became saturated with new meaning. Intensification plus condensation within the space of Yan'an as a simulacrum was essential in the process of generating symbolic capital. In Yan'an three stories were constructed, each representing a different aspect of loss: displacement of the peasant from land and community; the decentering of China and its replacement by outside forces; dismemberment and loss of imperial control. All these losses contributed to an atmosphere of generalized violence, warlordism and banditry, civil and imperialist war, and throughout the country a generalized condition of risk, high uncertainty, randomness, and unpredictability. Simply by connecting loss to remediation, the stories are ordering. That is, they are interpretative devices the ingredients of which point to a future. Yet as stories they are rooted in the experiences of daily life. In such intelligent narration, time is periodized and sensible sequences are formed, each of which is a surrogate for a modified (sinified) Marxist theory of a marginalized peasantry around which is constructed an inversionary discourse. If the underlying theme is an old one (the last becoming first, the slaves becoming the masters), there is, in Marxist terms, a difference. Peasants cannot be the class of the future. In the end, they remain the idiots of rural life. They are a class with radical chains but not a class that can universalize itself, unlike the proletariat as described by classical Marxism. However, if the peasantry is an insurrectionary class, the role of the party is to embody the revolutionary idea. Hence the CCP is the product of these stories. It serves as both the agent of history and the surrogate of truth. A party of truth imposes cognitive controls as an agent of history. By joining such a party one converts his or her own vulnerability into power and control by reducing "the complexity of the encountered environment."[4]

Violence offers ample opportunity for the genesis of storytelling. It generates despair and yearning. People come to believe that only drastic solutions will work, that any authority is better than none, and that the available would-be leaders are wanting—they succumb to corruption; they kill too many people; they demand too much and deliver too little. Such conditions are, on the whole, propitious for totalizing cosmocrats, whether political, religious, or both, who, in a context of high uncertainty, retrieve myths of a golden past and project the logic of a millennial future. When a politics of yearning rapidly goes from despair to redemption it exorcizes cynicism, opening the way for the kind of innocence that favors extremism.

These circumstances prevailed when Mao took command of the CCP. In this context his extremism sounded reasonable. He confronted problems for which others despaired of finding acceptable solutions. His interpretive logic resulted in the reconstitution of power within a symbolic and redemptive moral order. In Yan'an, the moral moment of the Chinese revolution, Mao's storytelling became an act in itself, an assertion of control over violence by means of a first ordering of mind over circumstance.[5] Considered in this way, storytelling and theory construction were part of the same enterprise. Their raw materials were the negative experiences being transcended. What began as a bricolage ended in a system of ideas, a theory. The combination, formed into a discourse, offered the necessary intersubjectivity for collective individualism.[6] With collective individualism at work in Yan'an, each person appeared to become or believed him- or herself to be the real or potential beneficiary of another's experiences.

Mao's version of Marxism, the fictive truths, and the theories he articulated were assertions of cognitive control. His accounts of the decline and fall of Imperial China, the revolution of 1911 against the Qing, and the warlordism and chaos that followed describe a remarkable increase in the complexity of the encountered environment. Sequence, cause and effect, normal expectations, and predictions people made in their daily life were increasingly disrupted. Mao's recounting in narrative form made sense of the disorder. The same is the case with his intermediate and short stories. All three are pulled together in Yan'an in the form of speeches and talks, and reworked into a body of texts. Each of the stories represents a different overcoming project: violence in society, violence over who will control the state, and violence over who would control the party. Mao's rendering of the stories constructs order. This in turn creates a space for theory that results in the formation of symbolic capital, the only form of capital that was available to Mao, and an element that was crucial in his consolidation of political power.

In the process of changing from military figure to storyteller, Mao became a cosmocrat; from being a kind of Odysseus wandering in exile, he became a Chinese Socrates in full possession of logic and word. The point of transition was the period 1942–1944 during what was called the Rectification Campaign. In this period, twenty-two texts were selected for study. The process began at the top of the hierarchy of institutes, schools, universities, and training centers that constituted the core Yan'an. Under a system of exegetical bonding Yan'an became a totalizing and tutelary political system.[7] The process involved a deliberate choreographing of narrative and text in a ballet of fictive and logical truths. This made Yan'an the true model of Maoism (the process was to reappear in monsterous proportions during the Cultural Revolution).

The Preconditions of Storytelling

Rectification was an enforced process of sociation by means of a language to be learned that would allow for demons to be exorcised. The stories were transformed into a logic or a theory, a line, a single unified mode of expression in the face of an otherwise randomized universe. A deliberate and highly contrived ordering process, it located particular targets, surrogates for or expressions of violence and chaos. Order was collective. It contrasted with the condition of "every man for himself"; in fact, that condition was shown to be counterproductive. "Every man for himself" became a definition of anarchy.

Stories or narratives mythologized experiences and provided validity to explanations that then appeared to be empirical. Myths so collectivized produce structures of coherence. As a result of intelligible acts in conjunction with others, and in the context of a collective moral strategy, the universe becomes more predictable. In Yan'an cause and effect were restored as interpretation and understanding. And interpretation and understanding generated cause and effect. The question is, how can this occur?

This question is a general one where conflict is persistent and where central authority seems to have disappeared. The more chaotic the situation, the less likely people are to trust one another and to act in mutual concert. What we witness in Yan'an is a way out of this dilemma. There, in a particular refuge, a "republic of the caves"—indeed, in a condition of what might be called revolutionary Platonism—an inversionary discourse was created that enabled each individual to engage in it by telling her or his personal story in conversation with others, and thus making sensible sequences out of fortuitous events in the temporary sanctuary of what became a mobilization space.

For stories to be shared with others, however, people must want to listen. And the conversation needs to be interesting, or one quickly becomes a bore. Sociation is, in effect, the embellishment of experience through narration. Mao established the conditions for a compelling conversation for that form of dramatic embellishment, which made for a recognizable sociability of the group. But Mao did not draw his account out of thin air. He made sure it corresponded to the stories individuals told each other. Both individual and collective storytelling went hand in hand. It enabled people to learn from each other, recognize certain situations, and anticipate and head off potential pitfalls.

All cosmocratic political leaders share one property. To one degree or another all ask the individual to "give" his or her story to the collective; that is, to the leader. However, since this is also an invitation to lose part of one's mind, as it were, teasing this out of individuals requires that something more be given back to them in return. To accomplish such a conveyance individual stories must reinforce, rather than dilute, the collective one, while the collective one must add more than it detracts from the individual's sense of self.[8] Collective storytelling then has to convince people that giving over their stories *enlarges* their minds and possibilities. They need to be convinced that by so doing they will see more and understand better. Once that occurs so does collective individualism.

Storytelling in this sense requires an agent with a special ability to lift the burden of storytelling from the shoulders of the individual by enabling that person to share it with others—an act of *communitas* as an act of cognition; an "imagined community," as Anderson puts it.[9] This agent must assume a role vis-à-vis the collectivity somewhere between the theocrat, who is realizing the divine will, and the psychoanalyst, who represents agency for the individual.

In this sense storytelling is a catharsis touched with mystery. It is a cathartic narrative that reduces the need for, and the urgency of, the individual story as a drive. By such acts of cognition the property of the story becomes the property of the discourse community.

Narration of even the most shocking events enables them to be interpreted as sensible sequences. In addition, several other qualities come into play. As such stories are shared with others they take on an element of the dramatic, a touch of spectacle, partly because they are all tales of overcoming in the face of tremendous obstacles, and also because the teller needs to make them interesting. The sociability of human groups is not simply functional but a matter of discourse, language, and conversation. Such conversations vary in style, from murmuring, which creates intimacy, to declaiming, which creates hierarchy. The sociability of storytelling also enables the teller to shift, even if slightly, his or her burden. People learn to learn from each other. They are made alert to the typicality of situations; the narratives and stories embody metaphors of understanding. People acquire the sense that they are better able to anticipate events and head off potentially bad situations. And by its very nature storytelling is intersubjective. A person who tells stories only to him- or herself alone is like an artist whose paintings are never seen by anybody else. It is a definition of solitariness.

What were the kinds of individual stories people told each other in Yan'an from which Mao was able to generate collective ones? Here is a characteristic tale recounted in one form or another by many of those interviewed: The second or third son or a daughter of a poor peasant household has been deprived of the family's plot of land because of death, indebtedness, or natural catastrophe and the lack of support from the landlord or the community. The teller describes the decline of the family, the failure of the uncle to help out, and the negative effect of such circumstances on the teller's own personal situation. The starting point then is ground zero: no land; absolute poverty; minimal opportunity; the death of the lineage, which will rupture the worship of ancestors. The story is first about sheer survival: leaving home, being bonded or sold. It personalizes such predicaments: the uncle who steals the widow's little bit of money, how Landlord Han confiscates the last bit of rice while his own family is provided with luxuries and his eldest daughter is sent away to school. The children of Landlord Han do not work; the children of widow Li work for nothing and starve.

In Mao's hands, such individual tales were made prototypical. Like every good storyteller, Mao infused his recounting with both intimacy and familiarity, and outrage. Every one of his listeners knew a version of such a story, and many had similar experiences. Such familiarity adds to the reality. Like music, to know the tune is to enjoy it even more. Widow Li and Landlord Han are generalized surrogates for a great many individual experiences, while the individual experience endows the surrogate with the flesh and blood of direct knowledge. This endowment is facilitated not only by repetition but replication in plays, in opera, in dance. Collectivization in this sense depersonalizes Widow Li and Landlord Han by making them into surrogates of a total history, while the individual versions make the abstracted ones visually and symbolically compelling. Landlord Han may stand for the cruelty of China's decline and Widow Li for the marginalized peasantry, but at the same time everyone knows them both as neighbors.

Collectivization begins when the storytelling agent begins to show that the behavior of Landlord Han is not due to his individual personality, but is a consequence of larger forces: the violation of China by outsiders, imperialists, British, French, American and on, of course, to the Japanese, who want to colonize China as a whole. Personal insecurity, tenancy, and the spread of violence are seen as corollaries of comprador capitalism. Thus, in very concrete ways the story opens up the space for a dialectical logic about the systematic nature of imperialism, semifeudalism, comprador capitalism. The collectivized story is both a symbolic statement and a theoretical *Aufhebung*.

Which brings us back to Yan'an. The Rectification Campaign of 1942–1944 established the authority of Mao as agent. Its object was to induce people to lose part of their minds by conveying their stories (and giving a piece of themselves) to the collectivity. What they gained was a resignification of the events of their own experience, superior insight, and wisdom—a theory of truth open only to those inside, but available to all who come inside. The Yan'anites enjoyed the special privilege of a "people of the book" with the democracy of egalitarian entry. In this setting, text and party document took on the properties of scripture.

If someone continued to have private doubts (and most people retain such doubts no matter how passionately they affirm the opposite), revealing those doubts in public was built into the procedure. Confession was a critical factor. The revelation of private doubt in a public manner, repeated as often as appears necessary, is a method of exorcism. Thus if Mao's rise to power depended on his ability to set the terms of storytelling, his most intense conflicts were with those among the truest believers who claimed the same exorcising rights/rites. Against these enemies he had to establish himself as sole authority. Eliminating rivals, not only as individuals but as surrogates for a party line with its own story and its own logic, was a necessary condition. Only then would party members be able to draw down from the collective more than they contributed to it. Good storytelling of the collective kind therefore must somehow establish truth claims capable of enlarging the individual so that the act of conveyance to the agent is in a sense an act of appreciation, even homage. To the extent that exorcising private doubts depends on faith induced by logic, Yan'an had to represent Mao and Mao had to represent Yan'an. If the ground outside was dangerous, inside there could be no alternative place to stand. And in any case, on leaving that outside world, one left one's former self at the gates. Such storytelling expands one's horizon even as it shrinks it. That is, the storytelling presents a vision of the unlimited possibility of the last instance.

Mao puts it this way. There is an ancient Chinese fable called "The Foolish Old Man Who Removed the Mountains." It tells of an old man who lived in northern China long, long ago and was known as the Foolish Old Man of North Mountain. His house faced south and beyond his doorway stood two great peaks, Taihang and Wangwu, which blocked the way. He called his sons, and hoe in hand they began to dig up these mountains with great determination. Another greybeard, known as the Wise Old Man, saw them and said derisively, "How silly of you to do this! It is quite impossible for you to dig up these two huge mountains."

The Foolish Old Man replied, "When I die, my sons will carry on; when they die, there will be my grandsons, and so on to infinity. High as they are, the mountains cannot grow any higher and with every bit we dig, they will be that much lower. Why can't we clear them away?" Having refuted the Wise Old Man's wrong view, he went on digging every day, unshaken in his conviction. God was moved by this, and he sent down two angels, who carried the mountains away on their backs. Then, with a characteristic twist, Mao says, "Today, two big mountains are like a dead weight on the Chinese people. One is imperialism, the other is feudalism. The Chinese Communist Party has long made up its mind to dig them up. We must persevere and work unceasingly, and we, too, will touch God's heart. Our God is none other than the masses of the Chinese people. If they stand up and dig together with us, why can't these two mountains be cleared away?"[10] What comes through, of course, is the message that enlarged understanding is the basis of resoluteness.

Through such parables and stories people were taught to make comprehensive inferences from circumstances and shrewd judgments about strategy and tactics. And the totality gained flexibility and individual adaptiveness. Both individual and collective narration followed a fairly standardized pattern, from situational beginning to identified obstacles, the defining of a negative pole to be transcended, a testing period, a logic of accomplishment, and a positive pole. Intertwined were themes of struggle, defeat, persistence, and arrival at some defined end point. At each point individuals can insert their individual stories into the collective ones. This comprises a reenactment, which enables the individual to convey and integrate his or her own experience to the more generalized version. Yan'an represents the field of force for mass conversions with Mao as agent.[11] But how did Mao become an agent in the first place?

Mao and the Storytelling Tradition

Storytelling is itself an old story in China. Wolfram Eberhard has shown how the Chinese communists deliberately cultivated the folklore tradition (including overtones of Hunanese banditry from which Mao claimed putative descent). In a foreword to Eberhard's book Richard Dorson introduces this theme as follows:

Conversely, the popular traditions which portrayed peasant revolts and uprisings, from Huang Ch'ao's [Huang Chao] insurgence in the T'ang [Tang] dynasty to the anti-Japanese war, perfectly suited the party's needs, and were encouraged. They were the stuff of reality not fantasy. Cognizant of his rise to power through a people's revolution resembling bandit revolts of the past, Mao gave status to the study of bandit lore. He himself had accepted the support of bandit forces in his uphill struggle with the militarily superior Kuomintang [GMD] armies and pursued bandit practices in marauding the rich landowners and the service corps of the Nationalist forces to feed his own followers. In the epic Long March of 1934 Mao and his Communist troops retreated from Kiangsi [Jiangxi] through the vast stretches of western and northwestern China, and swore blood brotherhoods with the wild Yi and Lolo tribes occupying the area. When Mao came to power he stimulated a review and reinterpretation of peasant insurgence from the late Han to the late Ch'ing [Qing] dynasties.[12]

The model is Confucius, who based his convictions on the retrieved and shared memory of a golden age of tranquillity in the Chinese kingship of the early Zhou dynasty. He blended this memory, as Benjamin Schwartz notes, "with a *conception* of the good socio-politico-cultural order—which he already finds envisioned in the *Book of Documents* and the *Book of Poetry*. When positive memories based on experience are fused with conceptions of an achieved normative order found in the sacred literature, one can readily understand the all-inclusive idealization to which this may lead."[13] Just as Confucius defined the space for the cosmocratic storyteller so Mao defined this space for himself in Yan'an.

Mao's stories were designed to unify a culture otherwise divided between a population largely illiterate and powerless and a thin and powerful sliver of teachers, bureaucrats, and literati. In the past the body of myths, legends, and stories, while they represented a common cultural inheritance, were also part of the great divide between illiteracy—that is, orality and storytelling in the classic sense—and literacy, which of course meant written texts. As performances and activities, and in content, these traditional stories reinforced, as a fault line in society, asymmetries of power and political hierarchy. They represented more or less fixed patterns of deference by ordering a universe of peasants, landlords, merchants, the gentry, the Mandarinate, and the Imperial House in that order. These stories represent the Confucian system of hierarchy, deference, and manner in the home and in society, with honor a function of rank, prestige, and position. In turn rank was associated with literacy, knowledge of the classics, connoisseurship, and artistic mannerism. As in other societies, class, taste, and distinction went along with power.[14]

Mao drew on both oral tradition and literary narratives, but he turned them on their head. From the vast storehouse of China's myths and folktales carried down by voice through the generations or "enscrolled" as literary texts, he selected those with inversionary themes, like *The Romance of the Three Kingdoms* or *The Water Margin*. These stories either cut across hierarchical levels or turned the hierarchy upside down. He also identified previous "truth-tellers," military strategists and wise emperors whom he used to bridge the gap between the illiterate and the literate. Mao was simultaneously the wise man of the oral tradition and the sage of the written one. He embellished the oral stories with the force of a scholarly tradition with well-established criteria of aesthetic refinement. In his hands, traditional culture now combined the popular and the refined while being eliminated as differentiations of class or *Stand*. Like the emperors of preceding dynasties, Mao rewrote history according to his own needs and interests, fully expecting that his versions would become endowed with truth value. For this tradition was crucial insofar as Chinese "history" was always mythmaking, and not merely the professional historians' history, as we understand the term today.

What then could be culled from that tradition? There were, for example, founding myths, which began with the overcoming of chaos, the creation of the world through a series of magical events. There were transformational (last shall be first) myths, in which a peasant warrior could become an emperor. All were common property, defining both the boundaries of the Han community and its interior culture. They gave clan names to the insiders, and in every way marked them off from alien tribes (Yi, Tibetans, and others) and distinguished them from foreigners. The events included dynastic wars, military conquests, peasant rebellions, and Robin Hood–like outlaws performing remarkable deeds.

Mao's stories were never freestanding. They were always worked into a more general argument. They served iconographic purposes—that is, they cultivated an already existing visual imagery, the stories being known by all—and didactic ones. Tailored to meet contemporary needs, the old stories were intermingled with the exploits of the party.

Mao also created a communist story of the descent of Marxism from Marx and Engels, through Lenin, Bukharin, and Stalin to Mao himself as putative descendent. The finger of communist history thus points to Yan'an as an inheritance bringing down to earth the more rarefied reaches of Marxist thought and also the historical struggles of other communist parties, not only in the Soviet Union but also in India, Indonesia, and other countries. Adapting general principles to local knowledge, Mao's storytelling embellished the conditions to which his theoretical positions had to be fitted. He deliberately cultivated the view that he was merely a spokesman and not the founding figure of a myth or a moral architect, while in fact he was acting as both. So much so that Yan'an appears to be a center of light and Mao's stories luminescent.

Yan'an in these terms was the place where an authentically Chinese communist political culture developed through embellishments of Mao's three stories and their reenactment in stories, plays, and theatrical performances. Mao was extremely sensitive to the importance of culture. He knew the propaganda value of *prolekult* during the immediate postrevolutionary period in the Soviet Union. He also knew that to make his stories into more than entertainment would require the help of intellectuals of all kinds— writers, playwrights, musicians, artists, translators, philosophers. His own experience with gifted people had not been terribly successful. Like Stalin he was suspicious of the revolutionary ardor and purity of intellectuals. Weren't intellectuals generally regarded as inconstant and too prone to think for themselves? Too many proved difficult to discipline. At the same time, of course, he recognized that they were important in broadcasting the appropriate cultural formula.[15]

. He also recognized that even a complete break with the past would also require patching. He plundered and reused antique cultural materials as the raw material of doctrinal reconstruction, much in the same way he would later demolish Ming walls and buildings and reuse their stones. He knew as well that a new systemic circle, one that would be permanent, had to be hermeneutically sealed.

The Republic of Clandestinity

Mao began his storytelling in a preliminary way in the late twenties and early thirties, during a period of chaos and while there was a vacancy at the top, both in China as a whole and for the CCP in particular. In this latter instance the cosmocratic pedigree had shifted from Western to Russian Marxism, but had not yet really arrived in China except in a putative way. This left the way open for Mao to use the force of his Odysseus role to invent a Socratic role similar to that of Lenin, but local in style. No previous political communist had tried to do that. All previous party general secretaries, from Chen Duxiu (the Herzen of China) to Wang Ming, were all "pupils" of Marxism insufficiently presumptuous to tinker with the corpus even though they could be fiercely divided over how to apply it to China.

But for Mao to claim to be a Marxist theorist he first had to establish his ascendancy over those better prepared in the canon than he, and he had to innovate in ways that made the spirit of Marxism stronger than the precision of its application. Mao's storytelling begins in his own wanderings. It is his Odysseus role that qualifies him for the Socratic one. His cosmocratic presumptuousness was so breathtaking that initially no one took seriously either himself or the fictive truths he deployed as the analytical truth of Marxism.

Did Mao deliberately set out to tell stories? In general, would-be cosmocrats feel themselves touched somehow by the gods. They recognize in themselves a sense of destiny placed there by the deity. So it was, for example, with Hong Xiuquan, God's Second Son and the leader of the Taipings who had a vision in 1837 about establishing the Heavenly Kingdom on earth complete with miracles, precepts, stories, and an earthly prescriptive cosmology. So it was with Mao. And, like any political figure, he needed examples and events in order to illustrate and, if possible, validate his preferred strategies as a "correct line." Mao became a storyteller precisely because of the practical need to establish his hegemony over others who claimed to be better Marxists than he; and he became an agent because he genuinely believed that he, better than others, saw the principles behind the events.[16]

Mao was able to address his audiences in such a way as to establish mutual confidence. Just as a storyteller makes his audience complicit in the story by weaving a spell, so Mao's audiences became complicit in his way of describing things. He too was able to cast a spell, and of sufficient strength that people would not only listen but also invest their time and energy in thinking about what he said.

Confidence in storytelling is of general importance. But in China it was critical because of the general political conditions prevailing prior to Yan'an. We have already described them as a singularly chaotic. But they were also extraordinarily vicious, both between the GMD and the CCP and within the party. The internal factional fighting was so bad, and secrecy and conflict so pervasive, that we can call the pre-Yan'an period of the CCP an "empire of clandestinity," using the term "empire" to emphasize the spread of clandestinity as a conspiratorial way of life that reached out in every direction, spreading outward from the Soviet Union and penetrating downward from the highest levels of the GMD and the CCP.

A world of conspiracies, intrigues, murders, retributions, and mésalliances with the GMD, the party inherited all the factional splits in the

USSR involving Stalin, Trotsky, Zinoviev, Rykov, Bukharin, and the antiparty rightists and leftists. In addition to the Soviet feuds, which became "sinicized" as swarms of Soviet agents descended on China especially after 1920, the CCP had plenty of its own—Mao against Li Lisan, Mao against Wang Ming, Mao against Zhang Guotao. The Comintern agents made things worse. They helped organize both the CCP and the GMD. They permeated both. Following Soviet models of organization, the structure of both the GMD and the CCP began to look very much alike in formal terms, at least at the top.[17] But at its Second Party Congress, the CCP established the cell system as its organizational principle, thus making clandestinity a principle of party organization. The CCP's and GMD's similarity of structure, combined with the fact that while the CCP joined the GMD, the latter did not join the CCP, became an invitation to internal intrigues and factional conflicts. To make matters worse, the Soviet Union sometimes urged unity and sometimes tried to play both sides against the middle, depending on which Soviet line and agent prevailed at what time. In addition, such conflicts as the Stalin-Trotsky conflict was superimposed on China, as well as other internecine struggles between anti-rightist and anti-leftist blocs in the Soviet Union. All these brought imported notions of terror, betrayal, and murder into the CCP at a very early stage.

At first Mao was not important enough to be involved very much with the stream of Soviet advisors, secret agents, commercial travelers, and so forth. When he did become involved with them, he tried as much as possible to prevent their direct supervision of his activities. Other major party leaders were held on a leash by a Comintern representative, Maring and Borodin for Chen Duxiu, Pavel Mif for Bo Gu and Wang Ming. When such a situation threatened Mao during the Long March, in the person of Otto Braun, the Comintern representative, the latter was effectively repudiated.[18]

Communist intrigue is only part of the story. All the major foreign powers in China, the Japanese in particular, engaged in a veritable orgy of spying, on each other as well as on the different CCP factions and the left and right wings of the GMD. They worked closely with Chinese secret societies (especially the Green Gang), and with the Shanghai underworld, which specialized in extortion, kidnapping, and torture. This involved contacts between Chinese and French, British, American, and Japanese agents at every level. To protect themselves the communists set up elaborate spying networks of their own, which operated within the party as well as outside. The GMD and the CCP each sought to penetrate the other's organizations, the GMD for a time fairly successfully with their so called "AB" (Anti-Bolshevik) Squads. Investigation, accusation, recrimination, revelation, kidnapping, torture, and murder were commonplaces of politics in China.

But in the party there was an additional problem. Because of continuous shifts in the party line and fractional disputes of the most intense kind, exacerbated by mutual accusations of Trotskyism or whatever, between 1928 and 1935 the CCP began killing its own adherents by the thousands. Although documents on this period are still closely guarded by the CCP, information has become increasingly available. Perhaps the most spectacular event of this kind was the Futian Incident, where rival factions of the left, led by Li Lisan (who was eventually put on trial in Moscow), and of the right, led by Li Wenlin, (who was imprisoned in 1931 and executed the following year), clashed with those of Mao. Provincial loyalties exacerbated the conflict; many died.[19] Not until Yan'an were such fratricidal struggles more or less brought under control and the CCP came out of the long night of the underground into relative openness.[20] In Yan'an the killing nearly stopped. In a country so vast that it is difficult to comprehend, the life of a communist was lived on the run, but always with the temporary intimacy of others on whom his or her life depended. Not a few were betrayed and handed over to the GMD for almost certain torture and death.[21] Hence to be in the party, especially in the period from its founding until Yan'an, was to inhabit a world of daily, deadly dangers.

By the same token, the party generated its own interior language. To be a vanguard professional revolutionary meant to belong to an intimate discourse community. The combination gave the party more lives than a cat. It could be weakened, and parts of it could be reduced in number or even destroyed, but no defeat was decisive.

A good deal of Mao's storytelling glosses over this difficult period, except in a fairly stylized relating of key events, which redound to his credit and add to his credibility. Since the party depended on the mobilization of a mass movement the conflict over party lines, especially over the nature of struggle in urban centers versus agrarian ones and positional versus guerilla warfare, determined to a great extent not only the character of the party and its idea of history, but also its military strategy and tactics. Again and again the question was posed of how relevant the Soviet experience was to China. The Comintern tried to keep a heavy hand on the novice party, even imposing its own internal factional disputes within the Soviet Union on China. This meant that admiration for the Soviet model could be a dangerous game. Hence the task of a would-be storyteller was extremely difficult. For if, in order to be credible the role requires a party as both a product of history and a shaper of it, then "overcoming" was a double problem. It meant overcoming all contenders within the party, and overcoming all contenders outside it as well. It was in the course of his personal struggle for power on both counts that Mao effectively transformed the party into his own movement and generalized the movement as a discourse community.

He tells his stories both for those above ground and those underground. He deliberately creates the space for his own texts in the speeches he makes. The early texts, ostensibly of a military nature (on war, guerilla war, positional warfare) and on how to develop supporting peasant clienteles, are actually redefinitions of the nature of communism as laid down both by Lenin and Stalin, and they copy many of the latter's ideas.

Mao as Storyteller

Mao's rise to power is all the more remarkable if one considers that by the time he and his followers arrived in Yan'an they were just a handful of survivors of the Long March, a small band, one of the weaker among the Red Army as a whole. Mao's group was joined by other remnants, among them the local guerilla forces operating under Liu Zhidan (who, as we have seen, had narrowly escaped death at the hands of a factional leader in the Red Army) and Gao Gang (who later committed suicide after being accused of being a traitor). The Long March quickly became a legend in its own right. For not only did Mao outwit Zhang Guotao, his arch rival for power; Mao was not even wounded.[22]

Indeed, for the Yan'anites, the Long March was as much a miracle as the crossing of the Red Sea was for the Jews. Moreover it put Mao on stage, telling stories. Once there, he knew just what to do. He was a master of the second-order discourse. In public he rarely put his own ideas first. He preferred to listen, as one informant put it, "allowing others to make the mistakes." He used his position to summarize orally, integrating the ideas of others in such a way that although the substance was altered, it was done so in a manner agreeable to those who first made the remarks. In this way, he gave the impression that decisions were collective, while the twist he gave them expressed better the general sense of the meaning. He also gave the impression of being modest and deferential to the collective leadership. Summarizing in this fashion also gave him the advantage of a "theoretically" superior venue for his ideas.

Those we interviewed who had known or remembered Mao during the

Yan'an period describe him as "looking the part of the intellectual. He dressed simply and could speak like a peasant, but he was really a teacher. I knew by looking that he was a presence and not a simple teacher."[23] People commented with amazement at his ability to draw ideas seemingly out of the air and then give them a pedigree that made them seem so correct that every sane person would sooner or later have come to the same conclusion.

He also gave the impression of availability and accessibility, an impression actually quite false. He worked at night and slept a good part of the day, appearing in the evening at a performance perhaps, or at one of the innumerable meetings, or giving lectures at the party school.[24] He held his meetings in the evening when almost everyone had gone to bed.

At first, Mao was no great platform orator. Some describe his voice as squeaky and high-pitched. He spoke in such a pronounced Hunanese accent that much of what he said had to be translated into more commonly understood Chinese. His less adoring admirers note the flabbiness of his speeches—a lack of precision, a lack of sureness about the point.

But all this changes when the speeches are written, and rewritten. It is hard to evaluate the relation between Mao's speaking and his writing. People listening to his oral presentations were already familiar with his writings. One might say that since the *writualization* process began very early the very muddiness of Mao's original thoughts and their lack of precision allowed people first to interpret his utterances as they preferred, or as some inner voice struggling to express some higher truth, which caused his listeners to strain in order to hear and understand. Then Mao would rewrite his talks in ways that were clearer, earthy, and more direct. Rewritten as texts, carefully reworked by himself and others, his remarks had force and pungency.[25] Some of those interviewed also characterized him as "like the first Ming Emperor" (a peasant who rose high enough to take power), as "basically a peasant," as "an intellectual," and more frequently than not, as poet, classicist, and calligrapher, one person pointing out that he "could beat both the intellectuals and the gentry at their own games."[26]

Indeed, while those who remember him in these days differ somewhat about his manner of speaking, all agree that he was able to achieve something that no one else could, namely a special kind of listening. When he transcribed events into social texts, contextualizing them in terms of danger, a kind of purity emerged from the squeaky voice. Individual and personal, but disembodied in the thinness of the air, the voice reached to the loess hills on either side of the Agora and echoed back. It was orality itself that became the sign-full event in a barren landscape.

Mao's orality had an essential theatricality as the sound of spoken words took on as much importance as their content. Outside in the wind, or inside in the steamed-up atmosphere of the conference hall, his voice took on a certain ephemeral magic that had to be pinned down in text.[27] The relationship of orality to writing was the act of creating texts as *writuals*, the conversion requiring the listeners to become readers. Doing so put education at the center of the redeeming project. This made it possible to redeploy people from units where old loyalties had been established into new units more under the control of Mao. Men and women were made to puzzle over the meanings of Mao's texts as a matter of life and death. The lesson properly learned was the life saved. In this sense, the kind of symbolic intensification that occurred in Yan'an inscribed and made significant condition, location, space, architecture, terrain. The sheer physical harshness gave a stark sense of reality to the discourse. The difference between Mao as a storyteller and those storytellers who were a featured part of Chinese society for as far back as anyone could remember was that the old storytellers told stories that beguiled and instructed, weaving themes of mystery and charm into the drabness of daily life. Mao's stories stirred one to action, to anger, to make people murmur among themselves. They conduced to thought by forcing the story to a logical instruction, one that had to be dialectically understood. If one began to listen, one began to learn.

Mao's accounts were invariably embroidered with ordinary facts of life. He selected those that were most familiar and then made them yield the unexpected. The words themselves became performatives. First in importance were the action consequences of orality—that is, the actual responses to the sound of the voice in the forum. Second was the locking in of imperatives within a more formalized discourse. Together they produced, to use Furet's terms, a "dramatization" of historical events and a "novelization" of historical processes.[28]

Perhaps Mao's greatest quality was in communicating to listeners a feeling of privileged access to the interpretive wisdom of a mind in motion.[29] We have said that when orality was transformed into textuality, many original meanings changed. The change created what Goffman has called supportive and remedial exchanges, and tie-signs, an insider's language of ritual idiom.[30]

Despite the difficulties of his accent, it is clear that Mao knew how to hold the attention of an audience, establishing a common bond *between listeners* as well as with the speaker. Virtually every major speech of Mao's represents a strategy of intimacy. Each begins with a narrative that defines boundaries of time in terms of the stories themselves, compressing these boundaries into those of space. So strong were the bounds that Mao forged that, unlike conventional storytelling, where when the audience is dispersed the bond breaks, Mao's continued to cast a spell. His storytelling seemed to summarize common knowledge, to establish a tie, a linguistic and experiential basis for a common discourse, punctuated with barnyard humor and classical allusion.

Then there was the Party Center. Within it was Mao, like the point of a tantric circle. At the outer limits were districts and subdistricts. In between was the party and the Red Army. Like a halo radiating outward to other border areas was Yan'an's simulacrum effect. As for the translation of story into text, the written word was published, broadcast, and published from on high by the printing press Mao's followers carried on their backs during the Long March and installed in the Cave of the Thousand Buddhas, the highest point in Yan'an.

Mao's speeches and writings retrieve and rework time. The past is both a golden age and a patrimony lost, a negative pole leading to a time of chaos and an overcoming project. Retrievals established the point of departure for a redeeming narrative, the platform on which to project and construct a millennial end—in short, a logic.

Mao liked to authenticate his stories from below. For example, well before speaking at the Yan'an Forum on Literature and Art, Mao listened to proletarian writers who themselves came from the bottom ranks of society. He knew how to be an audience, an addressee, a listener.

Insight into the way Mao worked is afforded by the case of Cao Meng, a well-known proletarian author. She went to Yan'an in 1941 at the behest of Zhou Enlai, who had met her earlier. She was impressed that of the number of intellectuals who went to Yan'an half were women. For her, it was a place of relative freedom (despite "much bourgeois thinking"). It was also a place where before rectification, a high proportion of Yan'anites were highly individualistic (including "the three mad ones, the four olds, the five eccentrics, the eight blinds, and the nine beauties").

Cao Meng claimed to be a principal source for some of Mao's main ideas at the Yan'an forum. According to her, he came to see her and then invited her to his cave. For three weeks they met every day. Mao directed that her three children be enrolled in a special cadres kindergarten run by one of the Soong sisters. Cao remembers the intensity of the discussion. She was impressed with Mao's eyes (grey), his excellent memory, his lack of interest in clothes (his own were full of cigarette holes), and above all his capacity to listen. She also remarked on his ability to produce a mass of material instantly and derive from it main theoretical principles, which he summed up in the form of memorizable slogans such as "Factionalism is the expansion of individualism."[31] He believed that everyone could transform him- or herself and the environment. He quoted Lu Xun's aphorism "I am like a cow, I eat grass but produce milk." In Yan'an the central problem was the elimination of factionalism. Among his aphorisms dealing with this problem she remembers two: "People first, study second, logic third" and "Preparation, then action."[32] Although his public technique was to speak after consultation and deliberation, and then to let others speak, giving the appearance of modesty, there was always, said Cao, "something of the tyrant about him."

At the center of Mao's storytelling, she said, was his "obsession" with class struggle. Despite his interest in democracy (the "three-thirds system") and the liberation of the people, the dark side of the class struggle made Mao totally preoccupied with conspiracy (making it easy for people like Kang Sheng to use Mao for his own political purposes). Mao himself failed to make the transition from clandestinity to openness.

In this fashion, Mao "learned" what he knew in the first place. He listened for the answer he had placed in the speaker's mouth by the way he posed the question. Well in advance of such conversations he had a clear idea of who would constitute the addressed (the audience) when he became the addressor—workers, peasants, soldiers, or revolutionary cadres. To be effective, listening had to be performative, an engagement of actions through words. "The cadres of all types, fighters in the army, workers in the factories and peasants in the villages all want to read books and newspapers once they become literate," said Mao, "and those who are illiterate want to see plays and operas, look at drawings and paintings, sing songs and hear music; they are the audience for our works of literature and art."

This enabled Mao to prescribe what needed to be done from above. "If you want the masses to understand you, if you want to become one with the masses, you must make a firm decision to undergo a long and possibly painful process of trial and hardship."[33] Knowledge was first to be derived from those on whose behalf it was formed.

Mao used a great many people in the process of telling stories from above, including Chen Boda, Luo Fu, Ai Siqi, and Kang Sheng, and not least of all foreigners who played the role of "witnesses," of whom the most important in this period were Agnes Smedley and Edgar Snow. Smedley was an undisguisedly propagandistic journalist, something of a self-created mythmaker, who deliberately sentimentalized descriptions of life in Yan'an and of her hero, Zhu De.[34] Edgar Snow's *Red Star over China* enabled Mao to tell his story without writing it himself.[35] Mao's exceptionalism becomes unmistakable. Validation by the outside observer no doubt helped Mao to become a surrogate figure for the China to become.[36] Snow as listener made it possible for Mao to personalize himself in a recounted life of periodic wanderings, remarkable overcomings, and above all as an austere seeker after higher truths. The Mao depicted by Snow is undeterred by any obstacle to revolutionary learning. He resists the blandishments of wrong factional politics. He constantly remembers his roots. He periodically returns to the "people."[37] While Snow's account humanizes Mao, it also makes him larger than life.[38]

The Long, the Middle, and the Short of It

As mentioned earlier, the point of departure in all three of Mao's stories is loss. The stories recount China's inability to overcome the negative instance until near the end of the third story, the short one, when the communist movement changes into a Maoist one, which changes everything. The first two stories emphasize China's helplessness and dismemberment. These, of course, show the magnitude of the task, and the remarkable accomplishment of Mao's ascendancy.

Each story gives a defining shape and content to the general cause. The long story is about the fall of the imperial system and imperialist plunder, the intermediate story covers the conflict with the GMD, and the short story is about the internecine party struggles and Mao's coming to power. Each is grist for the next one's mill. In Mao's hands each failure, military setback, or evacuation of a base area is reinterpreted theoretically as an achievement to become an instruction. The Nanchang Uprising was a defeat, but it becomes the benchmark for the founding of the Red Army, that is, Mao's army. The Autumn Harvest Uprising is also a failure, but it is the first act of the agrarian rather than the proletarian revolution. In between these events is the episode of the Jinggang Mountain hideout, where as the result of prior defeat Mao formed his peasant and bandit band and gave it substance as a guerrilla army. Later a major base would be established in Jiangxi, a spartan community where the strictest communism was to be observed, divorce was to be easy, land was to be confiscated and redistributed, and a rigorous equality was to be imposed. The Jiangxi base would serve as the model for Yan'an.

As epic, drama, and passion play, the three stories each deposited its own mystique in a common fund. Each offers a different resonance, adding layers of symbolic density to Yan'an as a simulacrum. Each is retrieved in speeches and used to illustrate texts. Running through them as a common theme, embodied and embellished by all, is political yearning. It is political yearning around which the narratives are composed and the texts constructed.

Through such yearning, people acquire political beliefs so powerful that it becomes urgent to discharge that power in political action, political energy seeking an outlet. Sacrifice and martyrdom add to the pleasure of action. And out of yearning comes the invented real, the fictive truth, the stories in all their palpable tangibility. All revolutions are to a significant degree yearning phenomena.

To make yearning politically significant is at the heart of the storytelling process. The long story, by framing the intermediate one, fits the large historic class struggle into a more immediate rivalry between the CCP and the GMD, pitting Mao against Chiang Kai-shek. In turn this frames the internecine power struggles within the party, and makes conflicts between Mao and his contenders, Li Lisan, Wang Ming, and Zhang Guotao, deadly. Personalization and dramatic impetus builds up as a result. Each story is also self-contained with its own dramatic impact and force. Each provides a symbolic layer to the next, the short story being the most symbolically dense and therefore the most intensely experienced.

Each introduces a set of actors, motivates them, and personalizes them with dramatic presence in the story. Each defines a negative pole to be transcended and a positive pole to be realized, the distance between them defining a normative space. Each event takes on a double meaning, one metaphorical, an event interpreted as another, the other metonymical, the same event interpreted as a surrogate for Marxist theory.

Personalities count for a great deal in all three stories. In the long story is a remarkable Taiping leader, Hong Xiuquan, with his visions of God and Jesus and his texts, which were to be in the hands of everyone, learned by heart, and designed to displace the imperial dispensations.[39] In the intermediate story, two major figures tower over the others, each with a coterie, an inner circle of acolytes, high priests, and lord high executioners. In the short story, Mao emerges at the center, his party stalwarts steeled in many internal as well as external conflicts. As the stories come to an end in the person of Mao, they also come to the end of a great chain of "beings."

Mao's own life is a representation of the representations—an embodiment like that of a Buddha. In his career he became an internal exile twice:

first as a young man, and second in Hunan when he was pushed to the edges of power in the party. This is Mao as Odysseus, for during these periods of wandering he gains in wisdom and shrewdness and also keeps together a small but growing band devoted to reclaiming patrimonies lost and by so doing redeeming society and state. In Mao's account China is in total disarray, the situation is a reenactment of the period of the warring states, and a historical parallel to the post–Qing dynasty warlordism of his own day when the country was similarly divided and engulfed. Living, working, and studying the people, especially in his home province of Hunan, enables Mao to communicate a special thoughtfulness, cunning, and commitment, all based on concrete and empirical study, superior wisdom, and a vision. So Mao becomes the redeeming agent in the very stories he tells.

Everything before the Opium Wars (1839–1842) is prehistory. In Mao's storytelling the Opium Wars are to China what capitalism was to Marx, history with a capital H. Its central theme is China's humiliation at the hands of imperialists. Opium was introduced into the blood of the Chinese body politic as a poison, corrupting and destroying the social and moral fabric of society. It is not an accident that Mao's first published writing is on the relationship between physical and mental health and the need for Spartanism to purify and restore the collective health.

The recounting of the loss of the national patrimony is outlined in a series of episodes that have both time and seriality on their side: the Anglo-French war on China (1856–1860), the Sino-French war (1884–1885), the first Sino-Japanese war (1884–1885), the eight-power allied invasion army at the time of the Boxer Rebellion (1900), the Russo-Japanese war in Manchuria (1904–1905), the Japanese Twenty-One Demands (1915), the Japanese invasion in Manchuria (1931), the Japanese war (1937). The long story represents the fall from grace of the Chinese empire (including the decline and fall of the Qing dynasty and the chaos that came after it) and marks the beginning of the revolution. Its central event is the Taiping Rebellion, a popular and populist protorevolution that involved modernization as defined by a people of the book, and that came to encompass half of China. The long story is an epic by no means exclusive to the CCP. It is also the property of the GMD, one of the several mutual and intricate common bonds these enemies shared.

As for the historical dialectic, the Chinese responses to these events were recorded as follows: the Taiping Rebellion (1851–1864), the reform movement of 1898, the Boxer Rebellion of 1900, and the revolution and downfall of the Qing in 1911. The two sets of events parallel each other.

They take on the relations of cause and effect. The first set are metaphors of violation, expropriation, and pollution. The second are metonymic, with each episode signifying a different aspect of Marxist theory. Together they constitute a mythological accounting of the causes of the decline of China, its displacement as a national entity by imperialists, the transformation of a feudal society into "an alliance between external imperialism and domestic feudalism," a semicolony of which the Chinese revolution was the natural and dialectical result.[40]

The long story represents the *longue durée* of the Chinese revolution. At the beginning there was China the great nation:

> The Chinese nation is known through the world not only for its industriousness and stamina, but also for its ardent love of freedom and its rich revolutionary traditions. The history of the Han People for instance, demonstrates that the Chinese never submit to tyrannical rule but invariably use revolutionary means to overthrow or change it. In the thousands of years of Han history, there have been hundreds of peasant uprisings, great and small, against the dark rule of the landlords and the nobility. And most dynastic changes came about as a result of such peasant uprisings. . .During the thousands of years of recorded history, the Chinese nation has given birth to many national heroes and revolutionary leaders. Thus the Chinese nation has a glorious revolutionary tradition and a splendid historical heritage.[41]

The loss of Han greatness combined with such a "splendid heritage" sets the standard for the redeeming project, which is about the nation and its freedom. In the second, intermediate story, how to redeem China is the main theme and is set in two contexts: imperialism, in the form of the war against the Japanese; and revolution against the GMD.

The intermediate story begins with the May Fourth Movement in 1919 and includes the founding of the party as a direct consequence of that movement. Hence the CCP claims a double pedigree: the sole right to represent the dual revolutionary heritage of the people and their contemporary descendants as the only genuinely revolutionary party; and the May Fourth Movement, the movement for modernization in the name of science and freedom. It is thus a story about how the ideals of the movement (and of Sun Yat-sen, who is the central figure at the beginning of the story) are thwarted by the GMD's ideas about how modern China is to be restructured and ruled. In turn the struggle with the GMD over the inheritance of Sun Yat-sen and his "testament" is over the design for the new China to replace the old.

This story includes the bitter break between the GMD and the CCP on April 12, 1927, when the first united front is shattered by the so-called counterrevolutionary coup staged by Chiang Kai-shek in Shanghai and the martyrdom of leading CCP officials Li Dazhao, Chen Yannian (one of Chen Duxiu's sons), and other "proletarian" revolutionaries. Other events in the narrative stand out like so many stations of the cross, including the Nanchang Uprising, the Autumn Harvest Uprising, the battles in the Jinggang Mountains, the founding of the Jiangxi base, and the extermination campaigns by the Nationalists, the last of which results in the Long March and the Xi'an Incident, in which Chiang Kai-shek is captured by his own general, who is sympathetic to the CCP, and forced to agree to the effective prosecution of the anti-Japanese war as the price of liberation. It is a story of heroics, sacrifices, and betrayals, and the testing of the limits of endurance of the communists, who by surviving become purified and larger than life. China is transformed into a gladiatorial theater in which the two chief wrestlers become Mao and Chiang, surrounded by their retinues and retainers. It is a drama full of the intensity of a wrestling match.

The third, short story is a passion play about the CCP. Its centerpiece is the rise of Mao Zedong to power despite internecine power struggles within the party. It is a duel between Mao and his contenders. It begins in 1921 in Shanghai with the founding of the CCP. It is a dirty story, full of dark secrets, internal intrigue, and secret Comintern interventions. It includes the vicissitudes of Mao himself, his exile to Hunan, his role in the Jinggang Mountains, his chairmanship of the Jiangxi base, and above all his coming to power during the Long March. It ends, as passion plays do, with the leader bringing the survivors into the light—in this case, Mao leading his followers into the light of Yan'an.

The CCP was officially founded in late July and early August 1921. The meeting itself was the stuff of which good stories are made. Interrupted by a police spy, everyone was forced to flee from Shanghai. The last session was held on a hired boat on South Lake (Nan Hu) near Jiaxiang, where Chen Duxiu, Zhang Guotao, and Li Da were elected members of the Central Committee, the first becoming Party Secretary, the second in charge of organization, and the third, propaganda.[42]

Thus the "founding" as an event has a dramatic episode inside it. The party has a "miraculous birth," floating on the waters in a boat, the dry land around it a hostile sea swarming with spies and enemies. Formed under such circumstances, the party requires long evolution, like the legendary egg of stone under the sea that eventually cracked and produced on land the people of China, so qualifying the party to act as the agent of history. Mao was present at the creation. But the story also shows the tasks Mao had to accomplish in order to win the right to become the agent of the party.

This episode, the spy, the water, the dangerous terrain, the trials and tasks are the conditions for Mao's own story of coming to power. It is an overcoming tale in which not only does he defeat his enemies despite serious setbacks, he overcomes his ignorance of Marxism to triumph over those Russian-trained students who represented themselves as the real Marxist intellectuals. His story is also about the evolution of his thought.

Mao's triumph includes his successful negotiation of intrigue and victorious outcome of power struggles among rival contenders within a party whose clandestine character was established from the start. Like everyone else, Mao operated on two levels, above and below ground. On the first level he publicly proclaimed his objectives, while on the second he pursued them on his own terms.

Fictive Truths and Their Mirror Images

Fictive truths can be revealed by their mirror images.[43] The Guomindang portrays the same events but from a completely opposite perspective. The Nationalists share the long story but disagree on its interpretation. The intermediate and short stories they regard as "stories" in the purely fictional sense of the term. According to the GMD, these stories reveal how depraved the communists are.

According to the GMD's version of the second story, troubles begin when, under Sun Yat-sen, the newly founded GMD is permeated by Soviet officials and advisors. Taken in by the persuasiveness of their arguments, Sun is duped into absorbing the CCP into the GMD by the representatives of the Comintern, who have won his confidence. The CCP works within the GMD to try to take control of the nationalist movement. What follows is a record of the GMD trying to extricate itself from the snares of this unholy alliance. The boldness and daring of the CCP endangers the GMD, which splits between left and right, and between Chiang Kai-shek and Wang Jingwei, splits the communists exploit to the hilt. After breaking with the CCP in Shanghai in 1927, the GMD fight against them is extended to all parts of the country. The result is complete success for the Nationalists.

As to the short story, where the CCP struggled within itself to define, out of right and left, the "correct" lines while avoiding "opportunism," the GMD saw evidence of strategic and tactical bungling. Theirs is a story about personal intrigues and power struggles by knaves, rapscallions, and sinister types, and the grand failures their deceits brought about. Where the CCP saw itself playing Robin Hood (in Hobsbawm's sense of the term), with social banditry a heroic and popular endeavor, the GMD saw plain banditry. To the GMD, the CCP base areas were simply repositories for an accumulation of red refugees from other defeats, pinned down temporarily to await extermination. That they continued to be able to make underground forays and engage in troublemaking activities, especially in the cities, was simply a testimonial to how tricky they were. Where the CCP portrayed itself as leading the opposition to the Japanese invader, the GMD saw the invasion as preventing the GMD from finishing the job of cleansing the nation.

The GMD's view of the Long March provides a good example of mirror image. The communists tell the story of a small band of survivors, especially those of the First Front Army, who have made many sacrifices in the course of a year of fighting and survival. They crossed rivers under fire, scaled snowcapped mountain ranges, traveled across treacherous grassland, and passed through lands occupied by the Tibetans, the Yi, and other non-Han (and hostile) peoples. They reached the sky in the snowy alps and were submerged in water. Like the Taipings before them they passed all barriers, claimed heaven and water and land, made all the passages and crossings. So the communist narrative lays claim to China as a whole, its cosmology as well as its terrain.

During the Long March, according to Mao, the correct line is secured. Good and evil are polarized and particularized in the class struggle between the CCP and GMD. At the same time CCP and GMD are bridged by means of a redefined strategy of united front, with all Chinese now united against the common Japanese enemy (this time on Mao's terms, not those of the Comintern and its agents nor Chiang Kai-shek and the Nationalists). As recounted by Mao, "The Long March is the first of its kind in the annals of history . . . Since Pan Gu divided the Heavens from the Earth and since the Three Sovereigns and the Five Emperors reigned, has history ever witnessed a long march such as ours?"[44]

The GMD response is that there are far more compelling examples of such marches, not least of all the case of the Taipings. Furthermore, the communist breakthrough of the Nationalist lines during the Fifth Encirclement and Annihilation Campaign (which began the Long March), actually was a mass Communist evacuation and flight [and] caused the total collapse of the "Central Soviet Area" and six other border or soviet areas. Local guerrilla units in these areas were generally annihilated. Consequently a huge number of Communist Party members and cadres were either captured or surrendered to the Government.

Secondly, a predominantly majority of the once 300,000 man Red Army was routed and liquidated. The Red First Front Army (under Mao) of 70,000 men had no more than 2,000 left when it reached northern Shaanxi . . .

Thirdly, the Red First Army fled to the area of Shaanxi and Gansu simply because it was forced to change its plans again and again under Nationalist military pressures . . .[45]

The victors in this story are the nationalists; the losers are the communists.

In the Nationalist interpretation, Mao's three stories are false in terms of facts as well as in their interpretations; indeed, they are not what happened at all. Mao's stories converted every defeat, retreat, crisis point, into a victory of some sort for the communists. Disasters become magical occasions, and failures superhuman accomplishments. No wonder listeners were amazed. Mao performs as a magician. Communist storytelling is a supreme form of illusion. What intelligent creature would believe such things?[46]

The GMD's version may be closer to the truth. Its protagonists never lost sight of the other Mao, the one rarely revealed publicly, the one that often shocked and dismayed his associates. Behind the Mao of fictive truth was a Mao unmatched in ruthlessness. Mao was a storyteller without appearing to be so and a supreme actor without appearing to be so.

In Mao's stories the Japanese invasion and its connection to fascism, capitalism, and imperialism is a major theme. Yet, in one of his more candid moments, Mao blandly stated that the Japanese war was the key to his success and that without the invasion the communist cause would have been lost. The invasion changed the rules of the game by forcing Chiang Kai-shek into a double front war, which he was less able to fight than the communists.[47] Mao knew how to fight a hit-and-run war against the Japanese and at the same time win pitched battles with the Nationalists, whose soldiers became demoralized. Mao knew he could intensify the struggle against the Nationalists because he knew that in the last analysis it was the Allied powers that would defeat Japan. Yet much of his stories focus on how his forces would save China.

Centering Mao

The GMD's mirror image of Mao's stories may have been the more correct version of events. But the evidence of accomplishment is on the communist side. Whatever the fictive quality of the truths Mao proclaimed, events bore them out. It was not the communists who were overwhelmed by the size of enemy forces, it was the large Nationalist armies that disintegrated. The GMD won victory after victory, but in the end it lost and was forced to flee to Taiwan. The fictive truths of communist storytelling become self fulfilling prophecies, enabling the communists to become virtually miraculous in their own eyes.[48] The GMD rendering was closer to historical truth, except that in winning all the battles they lost the war. For that they do not have a good explanation. And if the GMD did win the battles, all the more reason to believe that the communists' stories, in converting defeats into victories, need to be reckoned with.

To call such storytelling fabrication, in the sense of lying, is to trivialize it. Of course there was manipulation and machination. But to make it work on a collective level, storytelling must do more than tell a story. It must use the art form and the opportunities for dramatic performance that by its very nature it embodies. Among these is the significance of space as an identifiable and symbolically significant place for coming together, for the intersubjective communication of shared experiences, a function of orality first and writing later, of speaking first and modifying afterwards, the oracular pronouncement followed by the logical argument, of event as metaphor and theory as praxis. It is in the immediacy of speech that an initial lexigraphic system of dialectical thinking evolves, one that moves easily between classical references and sinified Marxism, a praxis of developmental socialism that, improvised on the ground, is textualized and writualized.

What Mao does in his storytelling is what Hayden White, in his analysis of narrative, calls the "poetic troping of the facts." In describing the various theoretical facets of narrative, White distinguishes between the *doxa* of history in contrast to fiction and shows how intermingled they can become. Although his analysis begins with functionalism (Hegel's), he goes on to describe different facets of narrative as discourse: as epistemic, as nonscientific representational strategy (Furet); as discursive code (Foucault); as a structure of time, or "time consciousness."[49]

If one applies White's characterizations to the case of Mao's narrative, several aspects are revealed. One is the fictive/factual aspect of the narration, the intertwining of the historical *doxa* with a fictional one. "Today's China is an outgrowth of historic China. We are Marxist historicists; we must not mutilate history. From Confucius to Sun Yat-sen we must sum it up critically, and we must constitute ourselves the heirs to this precious legacy. Conversely, the assimilation of this legacy itself becomes a method that aids considerably in guiding the present great movement."[50]

The representational strategy mentioned by White includes the ordering effect of an account that "fixes" randomness and whimsicality to offer a teleology. The story roots the ideology in "facts": "There is no such thing as abstract Marxism but only concrete Marxism. What we call concrete Marxism is Marxism that has taken on a national form, that is, Marxism applied to the concrete struggle in the concrete conditions prevailing in China, and not Marxism abstractly used. If a Chinese Communist, who is a part of the great Chinese people, bound to his people by his very flesh and blood, talks of Marxism apart from Chinese peculiarities, this Marxism is merely an empty abstraction."[51]

The discursive code mentioned by White depends on making signs out of artifacts. Using metaphors and metonymies Mao creates a code out of elements of a semiology that enables the narrative to endow gestures, acts, dress, dwelling, and above all language and literacy with the power of signifiers while the teleology arranges the signifieds within a revolutionary frame. What is thus formed is a self-sufficient world of language, signs, and symbols into which only the initiated can belong. Such matters are of great concern, for example, in Mao's Yan'an Forum on Literature and Art.

Finally the narrative itself converts time into space by means of a translation process rather along the lines sketched out by David Harvey.[52] In Yan'an time was converted into space to become a moral epicenter different from other border areas, a simulacrum.[53] But Mao's evolution from storyteller to cosmocrat occupying the center of his own tutelary republic is bumpy and dangerous. It does not happen at once. Nor when he begins to turn stories into texts does anyone pay much attention to him as a theorist. Of the various competing party lines, none was his. But what he had always been able to do was gather around him small study and action groups. He had the power to attract people by his ideas and manner even when he was a poverty-stricken and irregular student. A good deal of Mao's life is about centers and peripheries and how to transform the second into the first.

✳

MAO HAD TO confront a number of daunting problems in his own long march to power. What he was able to do, and not in the main centers of party activity like Shanghai or Canton or Nanjing, was to establish bases and guerrilla or peasant forces under his command, forces that were always under pressure and constantly on the move. Mao's earlier career is one of movement, and how to live life on the move was what he wrote about. But he hardly idealized peasant life. As Schram puts it, "For fifteen years, Mao had lived in cities and had, by his own admission, learned to despise the dirty and uncultivated life of the villages. Now in contact with peasants who had risen against the domination of the landlords, he suddenly re-established a link with the world of his youth. Under this stress, his Marxist veneer cracked, revealing the basic personality traits of the young revolutionary, admirer of violence in the service of justice . . ."[54]

An "admirer of violence in the service of justice." Schram's phrase sums up both Mao's attractiveness to others, especially those not too well educated, and his weakness. For Mao, as Schram points out, was not much of a Marxist and not even much of a Leninist when he returns to the people in partial exile from the Party Center, with little influence on the intellectuals at the center and in active opposition to what became the Li Lisan line. As for other founders of the party, like Zhang Guotao, they could not figure out why anyone paid attention to him at all. Indeed, Mao had to gain prominence as a military figure before others would take him seriously.

Hence at the start of his party career, Mao was even in his own eyes, as well as those of others, a negligible figure as a Marxist. Zhang Guotao considered him a romantic. That Mao was present at the party's founding showed that he was the leading spokesperson for communists in Hunan. Yet, while the Comintern representative was impressed by him, Mao was there because the party contained hardly any members outside of a few main urban centers. The party's radicalized May Fourth gentry intellectuals considered Mao, if they thought of him at all, as a provincial representative, a rustic. Indeed he was. Probably if he had not been, he would never have been able to come to power in the fashion that he did.

Not that Mao was odd man out in the party. But he did set himself apart. There was a gulf between him and the May Fourth intellectuals, who represented a kind of Chinese Enlightenment, a movement that advanced such eminently reasonable sounding ideals as science and democracy. Importantly, May Fourth was a ground-clearing enterprise foreshadowing and paving the way for 1949 "just as Voltaire had for 1789."[55] May Fourth represents the entry into China's political life of intellectual activists who, prowestern and iconoclastic, were anxious to break out of the straightjacket of Confucianism and its hierarchical order and assert China's independence as a nation.[56]

A movement of youth against age, and in favor of modernization, it was represented by literary intellectuals who became politicized and attracted to Marxism (and, to a lesser extent, anarchism) because it seemed to combine moral regeneration with the science of modernity.

If most of those who attended the 1921 Shanghai meeting of the CCP were intellectuals, so were the first general secretaries of the party. The first, Chen Duxiu, was Dean of the College of Letters of Beijing University, founder and editor of *New Youth,* and the voice of the May Fourth Movement. The second, Qu Qiubai, was educated in the Soviet Union and taught at Shanghai University. Li Dazhao, co-founder of the party, Mao's own mentor and the person who introduced Mao to Marxism and hired him as an assistant librarian at Beijing University, was the first to write seriously about Marxism. He examined the themes of historical materialism, political economy, and scientific socialism in terms of class struggle, all of which would prove central to Mao's own conception of Marxism. When Li first met him, Mao was barely literate in classical Marxist thought or, for that matter, Leninism. He lacked the language that Marxists used, the inner meanings of dialectical materialism, its connection to a dialectics of nature and a dialectics of class. The term "surplus value," for example, never enters Mao's lexicon, neither does anything but the most superficial reference to modes and relations of production. Mao does better with Leninism and Stalinism because they are more applied. Mao plunged into the realities of violence because he could understand it and because, if Schram is right, it appealed to him.

Mao learned his form of Marxism as he went along, and most of it he improvised out of necessity. It is this improvisation out of necessity that gives his texts their force: the connection of vital events that have storied properties. Hardly an intellectual of the first rank, and showing many of the qualities of the autodidact, Mao could have it both ways. He could appear as one of the people, a man of action impatient with the pretensions of intellectuals, and in his writings show that he could beat the intellectuals at their own game. He did not feel entirely comfortable in their circles. Having been treated with disdain by intellectuals and students at Beijing University, where he was a clerk or Second Librarian, he remained hostile to the intellectuals.[57] He mistrusted their tendency to abstractions, which seemed to him sterile and sectarian, and even more, he mistrusted their lack of experience with everyday life in the raw, something that proved to be Mao's touchstone to power. In one of his earliest writings, Mao says:

> Students hitherto have paid much attention to moral and intellectual education but have neglected physical education. The unfortunate consequence has been that they bend their backs and bow their heads; they have "white and slender hands"; when they climb a hill they are short of breath, and when they walk in the water they get cramps in their feet. That is why Master Yan [Yan Hui] had a short life, and Jia Yi died young. As for Wang Bo and Lu Zhaolin, the one died young, and the other became a paralytic. All these were men of high attainments in morality and knowledge.[58]

Later, of course, he would make use of intellectuals, "leveling them down" to the "masses" in order "to level the masses up," as embodied in the principle of the mass line.[59]

It is ironic that, in the end, none of the intellectuals could match Mao in the sheer quantity of the texts he wrote and the breadth of the issues he wrote about. No other party member writes as much on topics of both immediate relevance and general principle, not Wang Ming, one of Mao's principal antagonists, and not even the philosophers who later in Yan'an would join his entourage, such as Ai Siqi.[60] In this, Mao is in the grand tradition of Marx and Lenin, with most of what he writes considerably better in retrospect than the writings of his more immediate political mentor, Stalin.

Among Mao's earliest writings are those on the body politic. The original themes of loss, pollution, and decline are there from the start. "Our nation is wanting in strength; the military spirit has not been encouraged. The physical condition of the population deteriorates daily . . . These are extremely disturbing phenomena. If our bodies are not strong, we will tremble at the sight of [enemy] soldiers."[61]

Mao becomes the storyteller of his own story. In doing so, he connects the historical frame of the long story of China's fall, the intermediate struggle with the GMD and Chiang Kai-shek, and his interior travails within the party during the republic of clandestinity when he is exiled and peripheralized. He tells the story just after he has taken real power in what will become Yan'an. But he does not tell it directly to a public. He lets it be pulled out of him by an enterprising American, Edgar Snow, the man from Missouri who only tells what he sees and hears for himself. Snow performs the role of expert and reliable witness. Mao describes his early life, his rejection by and of the family, his poverty, his search for an education, his attempts to organize students, his early efforts at writing, and above all his avid search for knowledge without ever having the proper status of a student. His role as a teacher he describes as more or less a cover for political activities. He is restless, an avid reader, a loner. He begins his rise to real power in 1926, when he is appointed director of the Peasant Movement Training Institute under the GMD in Canton. He made a detailed study of conditions in the countryside in Hunan as "inspector of the peasant movement." The investigation in five *xian* (counties) was written up as *Report on an Investigation into the Peasant Movement in Hunan.*[62] It included statistical data, surveys, and a detailed examination of various aspects of peasant life, including taxation, the role of women, and land distribution; it recommended a change in the party line vis-à-vis peasants. Mao's estrangement from the Party Center grew around the same time as the rupture between the GMD and the CCP. Mao in effect becomes more and more a guerrilla commander of an army of peasants.

Intimacy with peasants in Hunan, his work in Changsha, where he was both a student and a teacher, the struggles taking place in Wuhan, and his role in organizing the Nanchang Uprising associate him with the founding of the Red Army, while his role in organizing the Autumn Harvest Uprising (not sanctioned by the Central Committee), and his capture and narrow escape from the GMD all lead ineluctably to his organization of the first peasant army, the "First Division of the First Peasants' and Worker's Army." This coincides with the repudiation of Mao by the party leaders and his dismissal from the Politburo and the Party Front. In the winter of 1927, he and his small band from the First Division flee to the Jinggang Mountains, where together with Zhu De they form their first legendary guerrilla army. "Struggle versus adventurism" is the slogan, which defines Mao's analytical point of attack against the Party Center— that is, the location of the "correct line."[63]

In the conflict with the Party Central in the late 1920s, Li Lisan and his faction, supporting the line of urban revolution and positional warfare, underestimated Mao. Li kept promising that a revolutionary breakthrough would occur as a result of continued attacks against important cities. Li was wrong. Virtually all his battles ended in disaster, in contrast to what was seen (although not by the GMD) as Mao's successes. In various writings, Mao describes in detail the nature of Li Lisan's errors and what must be done, using the events to build up not only a story but also a theoretical basis for his own independent position, a theory of guerrilla warfare and peasant revolution. His dialectical path, deviating considerably from the Moscow line on China, is China's true path.

Snow's book is in good measure Mao's own view of how he became prominent in the party in the late twenties, his difficulties, the resentments, and the factionalism of the republic of clandestinity. It is in this period, while military commander of peasant armies, that Mao makes his famous and very un-Marxist dictum about power growing out of the barrel of a gun. He also prescribes the interactive structure and organization of a guerrilla army as being dependent on a peasant base, using an aphorism about fish and sea, which provides the code and lays down rules of correct conduct for communist soldiers. In this period, too, Mao elucidates the strategy of rural guerrilla warfare in contrast to positional warfare, and lays down the tactics to be followed (for example, "The enemy attacks, we retreat"). The social reconstruction of peasant base areas that support both armies and a communist network in fact constitutes the basis of the border area "governments." At each point Mao is at pains to distinguish strategy from the "putschism" of Li Lisan and the Party Center. In short, Mao's power is first military, and his texts are military instructions, which gradually he converts into a theory of peasant revolution.

But for Mao to become powerful in more than a military way, he needed a place to stand at the center. It was precisely this that was denied him. Pushed to the periphery by the Party Center, his military significance waxed as his political influence waned. Using the Jinggang Mountain hideout as a kind of precedent, and recognizing the significance of some of the border region "soviets" that had been established, Mao found his place to stand in Jiangxi. There he took command not of the party, but of the most important base the party had, while the Central Committee remained in Shanghai. In Jiangxi Mao established a puritanical, tough regime which was the precursor to although a more austere version of Yan'an. In short, Mao created his own base from which he then would establish both a military and a theoretical campaign to capture both the Party Center and the inheritance of Sun Yat-sen from Chiang Kai-shek. He would do this by launching the equivalent of a Taiping Rebellion inspired not by heavenly voices but by his own form of revealed truth. In so doing he would redeem the double patrimony—the national patrimony lost to foreign imperialists, and the peasant patrimony lost to unscrupulous landlords, moneylenders, and the like—and project a future by means of which the body politic is purified and transformed, and the Han regain their glory.

All this is contained in Snow's biography of Mao. It is the story Mao told Snow. Yet, good craftsman that he was, Snow gives it a certain plausibility, and relates it with affection for Mao, especially in his asides and commentary. The Long March becomes a reenactment of Mao's life as a symbolically reconstructed story of China, and embodies the conditions of revolutionary possibility for China. Moreover, just as Mao moves from an Odysseus to a Socratic role, so a transformed China transcends itself through the tutelary agency of the party in connection with the insurrectionary power of the peasantry. The tale of Mao as exile, as wanderer in his earlier years, who gains experience and takes command while resisting false blandishments, sidestepping disaster, and being blessed with miracles, is also the story of the party and the communist movement. Its survival at all, especially given the Long March, is a miracle.[64] Near the end of the March, tired and exhausted, Mao's First Front Army joins up with the superior forces of Zhang Guotao; and Mao, who is forced to flee, nevertheless winds up triumphant in the struggle for power. Mao and his followers straggling into what will become Yan'an itself becomes a miracle of survival. And it is on the Long March, in the military victory over Zhang Guotao in 1935, through ruse, guile, and a masterly game of political Go, that Mao paves the way for his evolution into a Socratic figure, the moral architect of the revolution, displacing all his more intellectual rivals.

Mao's fictive truths then are condensed into two stories: his own life, the personal narrative turned by Snow into a text; and, as part of that narrative, his rise to power during the Long March. Together they "naturalize" his accomplishment. They appear to be part of his own remarkable triumph over past sufferings. Mao becomes simultaneously the higher intelligence of the revolutionary idea and a surrogate for the marginalized peasantry. Just as he embodies both, so will China come to represent their political synthesis. Snow's story contains many notable figures (Liu Zhidan, for example) and descriptions of many worthy and virtuous cadres. There is admiration for Zhu De and Zhou Enlai. But it is Mao who is at the center. It is his life that represents the dedication and supreme act of will that save the party from destruction during Chiang Kai-shek's Fifth Extermination Campaign. In Mao's description, the Long March is the "great passage" over time and space, Han and non-Han areas, the reaching to the heavens in the snowy mountains, the bottom and the wet of the savannah. In claims as classic as any myth, Mao's travels take possession en route of the entire country.

As in Lévi-Strauss's transcription of the story of Asdiwal where, after feast and famine, land and water, sky and underworld are all negotiated by a magical being with special powers, who comes to rest in a mountain halfway between heaven and earth, Yan'an is the halfway point in time and space, a magical accomplishment and a moral triumph. What became the Shaan-Gan-Ning Border Area becomes as well Mao's own surrogate, his creation. In Snow's *Red Star over China,* Mao figures in much the way Christ does in Renan's *Life of Christ.* In both books the remarkable is the rational, and the rational remarkable. At the end of Snow's account Mao is at the center and around him is a small band, some secular priests and retainers such as Chen Boda and Zhou Yang whose job it was to transform Mao's stories and texts into symbolic capital.

4

ONE LINE

✳

We have considered Mao as a storyteller and have shown how each of his three stories telescopes into the other. The more closed down the optic, the sharper the image and the smaller the field, so that by the third story Mao virtually fills the field of vision. This condensation and intensification of the image of Mao in Yan'an took place over time, during which the field became saturated with new meaning. Intensification plus condensation within the space of Yan'an as a simulacrum suggests how symbolic capital results in vast increases in discretionary power.

As indicated earlier, Bourdieu's notion of symbolic capital refers to highly organized and precisely valued nonmonetary exchanges. As with economic capital, value is exchanged for value. The relations of people are defined by exchanges of symbolic capital, with values of that capital realized through exchanges. It is an econocentric model that parallels that of a market. By contrast, in a logocentric model, symbolic capital refers to an endowment, a fund of power on which to draw. It derives from the transformation of people from an aggregate to an internally bonded community as they convey their individuality to the collective. This enables them to make meaningful withdrawals of individual gain from the collective, withdrawals that outweigh their individual contributions. By this means individuals enhance themselves, overcome their deficiencies, and become transformed.

To realize this collective condition, individual conveyances need to be bonded. The bonding material is discourse, language, of a sort that endows acts with special inside meanings. These meanings are built up, or constructed, and become synthesized in the form of a mythologic by means of exegetical bonding.

Symbolic capital in the context of a discourse, or logocentric, model is different from that in an exchange, or econocentric, model. Also, a community generating symbolic capital is different from one generating economic capital. To go from one to the other is difficult. It involves transforming a community in which meaning is organized and sustained by discourse to one in which it is organized and sustained by exchange.

In this chapter, we inquire into the logical side of symbolic capital and how symbolic capital provided Mao with more and more discretionary power as he succeeded in mythmaking and made those myths appear as logical and acceptable as reality.

A good deal of Mao's power can be explained less by the quality of his Marxism than by an ingeniousness born of political restlessness, a desire to reach out to the bottom of society to turn the world upside down. The less theory actually counted, the more it appeared to account for everything. In short, Mao created for himself an independent position in history while at the same time presenting himself merely as its agent. Or, to put it more symbolically, he acted first as a Chinese Odysseus, a wanderer in exile with a redeeming project, a storyteller recounting his trials and gaining wisdom. Wisdom gained, he became a Chinese Socrates, applying dialectical logic to the rationality of the millennium. The events of each narrative contain the lessons of that wisdom, lessons to be taught and learned and treasured within the rules of the dialectical method. It is here that the Socratic factor looms large in Mao the teacher, indeed, in Mao the philosopher-king.

Theory in Mao's mythologic was deadly serious. No doubt Mao could, on occasion, act as a ruthless pragmatist and follow the logic of power to its necessary conclusion. But that would hardly explain the inordinate amount of attention he devoted to serious theoretical matters. While clearly no philosopher, he dwells in his writings on principle and method within a revolutionary context. He says a great deal about man, nature, society. He universalizes particulars and particularizes universals, the latter with great earthiness and as part of his storytelling technique.[1] The central feature in all his theories is class—its relationships, struggles, and alliances. This is basically what his Marxism consists of, but his logic derives from his own experiences and to some extent research.[2] Mao believed that the evolution of mind goes hand in hand with the evolution of society and that verified knowledge is what is realized in social practice. In this sense he moves close to pragmatism.[3] However, to realize anticipated ends human ideas "must be in correspondence with the laws of the objective external world."[4] To discover these laws one must be "scientific." For Mao, "the sciences are differentiated precisely on the basis of the particular contradictions inherent in their respective objects of study. Thus, the contradiction peculiar to a certain field of phenomena constitutes the object for a specific branch of science."[5]

For all the emphasis on laws of history Mao pays most attention to what it is that people have in their heads (and what he can put there). Schram quotes a particularly significant passage: "Men are not the slaves of objective reality. Provided only that men's consciousness be in conformity with the objective laws of the development of things, the subjective activity of the popular masses can manifest itself in full measure, overcome all difficulties, create the necessary conditions, and carry forward the revolution. In this sense, *the subjective creates the objective*."[6] In Mao's practice, the "objective laws" remain on the horizon and the "subjective" becomes the foreground and his primary concern.

In virtually every major essay, Mao deals in some fashion with large themes in the context of specific events. He is good at making connections between abstract thought and empirical knowledge. Like many Marxists, he laid claim to a theory of praxis. While Kolakowski is undoubtedly right that all this hardly adds up to very good Marxism, let alone philosophy, it does suggest that Mao had an extraordinary ability to think on several levels at once, and could grasp the central issues and the large concern.[7] Hence he offered strategies in situations not available to his enemies or even his associates.

While Mao claimed in later life that he preferred the role of sage and teacher over any other, in the early days he used the Chinese classics to illustrate the art of war. Yet even here he moved from the details of everyday experience to principles within which these experiences need to be considered.[8] Mao chides commanders who consider military affairs from a purely professional point of view and eschew politics.[9] He was both a theorist of guerrilla warfare and a political analyst. His redefinition of classes, class struggles, the role of peasants and peasant armies, and the like was heady stuff at a time when the condition of the party was desperate and divided, and seemed barely able to survive.

Despite these preoccupations, in the early days Mao was not taken as seriously as a theoretician as he was a military figure by those in the Party Center. Li Lisan, for example, who accepted the more orthodox (and Soviet) view of the need for urban warfare and proletarian revolutionary consciousness, had little regard for Mao's emphasis on peasant armies and base areas. Later, the "Russian Returned Students" would regard Mao as a rustic when it came to Marxism. Yet the crudeness of Mao's Marxism better fitted the realities of Chinese society. His analyses enabled him to pull a good many rabbits out of the hat and figure out appropriate strategies where others could not. He connected functional tasks to social and military needs within a larger context that made sense not only to intellectuals but also to party cadres and activists.

Hence, while Mao's peculiar and often vulgar interpretations of Marxism were his own concoctions, more in the spirit of Marxism than the real thing, this is perhaps the key to his success. His misreadings made Marxism more appropriate to China than more sophisticated efforts, especially those of the China watchers in the Soviet Union or the more faithful Chinese adherents of applied Soviet doctrines. In any case Mao surely had no monopoly on Marxist misreading.[10]

Frederick Teiwes comments on the way theory and discussion enabled Mao to share power with subordinates.[11] Moreover, as we suggested in Chapter 3, Mao's preoccupation with theoretical questions prompts him to use events as narrative and narrative as fictive truth. His "phenomenology," as he calls it, is the basis for stories and myths around which he weaves his "science" of human affairs.

This view is not at odds with those that interpret Mao as a pragmatist. As all successful political leaders must, he knew how to respond to realities. But if one accepts the political scientists' distinction between pragmatists and ideologues, it is difficult to know on which side Mao belongs. For example, pragmatic political leaders do not create norms but rather operate within them; Mao was out to create his own deontological norms. Pragmatists do not monopolize truth; Mao believed he had special insight into the truth of historical processes in China, with the CCP the historical surrogate of that truth.

Marxism is perhaps the outstanding secular example of how to reinforce ideology with pragmatics. It establishes norms, codes, a discourse, and discourse communities where its norms come to prevail. But its orthodoxies have the virtue of appearing to remain intact while undergoing drastic change.[12] This was also the case with Mao Zedong. At his most ideological, around the time of the Rectification Campaign in Yan'an (1942–1944) when ideology formation was at its height, Mao was also most supple politically. Matters of considered party doctrine (for example, the role of the peasantry vis-à-vis the proletariat, regulations governing gender equality and divorce, the redesignation of class enemies) he would quickly alter depending on prevailing circumstances. Very little was doctrinally sacred. One of the great attractions of Marxism for revolutionary leaders is that as a theory based on dialectics and contradiction it allows one to be both ideological and pragmatic at the same time.

Twists and turns can also provoke ideology rather than inhibit it. Mao's doctrinal formulations, his conceptual jumps, his leaps in the dark toward understanding provided him with new opportunities for strategic decisions, allowing him to interpret circumstances in ways unanticipated and quite beyond the understanding of his enemies both within the party and outside of it. This may suggest that in his heart of hearts Mao Zedong truly believed only in power and would not let even his own ideology stand in the way. But even if true, this would miss the point. The question of belief is independent of both ideology and pragmatism. Is it necessary that the high priest believe his own gods?

Mao thought himself supremely gifted in the matter of theoretical insight and practical wisdom. He invariably kept a jump or two ahead of his enemies. Like Lenin he connected pragmatism to ideology by emphasizing praxis. In that sense pragmatism validated rather than undermined the ideology that went with it. Perhaps the pragmatic in Marxism occupies the middle ground between theory and a praxis of empirical circumstance. The Marxist substitute for epistemology is a way of validating as truth that which works. Such "truths," reincorporated in the theoretical corpus, validate it instead of making it superfluous. Pragmatism works without becoming the more general attitude. It can allow for negotiation and mediation between class surrogates that express fundamental antagonisms and polarization, while ideology sustains the boundaries of a world of many enemies and few friends. The more ideology counts, the more pragmatism is the validating reality, reshaping theory in the light of the reality.

During the twenties and early thirties, during the republic of clandestinity, that underground world the communists inhabited prior to Yan'an, one can speak of ideology over pragmatics. The result was party factionalism, oversimplified sloganeering, unambiguous rights and wrongs, obligations, responsibilities. To be a party member was to take sides. No one could remain aloof. The polarization of conflict between the GMD and the CCP after 1927 in fact fragmented both sides into warring ideological factions instead of generating internal solidarities. In the CCP this was particularly serious. Each line had its own theory, its own interpretation, its own discourse. Each fragment defined a discourse community, each line constituted a world apart, defining insiders and outsiders. To move from one faction to another was betrayal, a crossing of boundaries, a transgression to be undertaken at extreme personal risk.

It was in Yan'an that such conditions underwent a remarkable change. When Mao's ideology and party line prevailed, pragmatism flourished without either diluting or polluting theory. It enabled the most unlikely bargains to be struck. It blurred the distinction between flexibility and radical opportunism. If pragmatist praxis is a doctrine of truths that work, it cannot be used only to justify means but must also be used to reaffirm doctrinal absolutes. Mao neither lost sight of the pragmatics of truth nor doubted the truth of his theories.[13]

As already indicated, Mao adapted Marxist theories to the specific conditions of China by moving back and forth between universals and particulars. Particulars reflected daily life. Universals became scriptural. As the body of texts Mao produced became a corpus he was elevated to a cosmocratic role, surrogate for the CCP as "the party of history," with sole right to decide—literally from moment to moment—whether to fight in the name of principles or bargain over interests.

It is a choice involving more than an appropriate stratagem. It raises the larger question of when or in what situations one might successfully try to transcend reality by means of a logic designed to locate some other order of things, a new code, one that would provide insight by defying the prevailing common sense rather than bowing to circumstances and negotiating them in the best way possible. One reason why Mao was able to move back and forth between these two positions so easily was because the truths he invoked were essentially fictive. One might call him a realist in a world of his own creation—one constituted from his interpretive readings of history and events and transformed into narratives, stories with a hortatory and transcending outcome. To make the fictive true in real life, he applied a teleological logic backed up by force under conditions of war and revelation, circumstances where the line between ideologue and pragmatist breaks down.

Narrating the Text

There was, however, more to Mao's ideology and his efforts at theorizing than simply providing a cover for whatever he intended to do or the line he chose to follow.[14] Evaluating the theoretical debates that went on within the CCP in the thirties, which incorporated the discourse of both Western and Marxist thought (including terms like "dialectic" and "materialism") Werner Meissner concludes that essentially these concepts were not really understood by Mao and were misread by Mao and his immediate colleagues to the extent that they became not truths but "positive myths" possessing "supernatural powers." They were "magic weapons."

Rather, the concepts were foils for Mao, who set in opposition to Marxism their "negative" counterparts, idealism and formal logic, as well as other liberal notions "to be defeated in the eternal struggle between good and evil, light and darkness." These notions were, according to Meissner, part of a demonology derivative in part from that of the Soviet

Union grafted on to the home-grown product in China.[15] Meissner goes on to say that "in reading the texts, therefore, one repeatedly encounters the connection between myth and power—the unity of mythic belief, whose intellectual weapon is the symbol—and rational comprehension of political power relationships. This is the true dialectic of Chinese dialectical materialism."[16]

For Meissner, Mao's philosophical ideas were mainly Aesopian ways of expressing bitter conflicts between CCP factions. He shows how Mao altered his views on matters central to his theories, or how he might appear to alter his theoretical reasons for a course of action without in fact actually doing so, as in the debate over how the CCP should participate in a united front with the GMD against the Japanese. In Meissner's view, for Mao, truth in the last analysis is contingent on power.

But what Meissner ignores is precisely what Mao clearly recognized: that ideology as a form of power requires symbolic capital. Mao was concerned with the embellishment of symbolic capital in terms of conflicts within the party, between the party and the GMD, and between the Chinese and the Japanese. Although these represented separate contingencies, Mao made them all of a piece. The same theoretical structures were set against these conflicts, enabling Mao to play the political power game more shrewdly than his opponents in the party. In addition, this enabled the underlying struggle of the party and of China against Japan to become one and the same. The logic of his theory was to convert weakness into strength. That was for Mao the overcoming and eventually transcending project.

Mao incorporated three elements into his version of Marxism: an interior or local historical pedigree, a universalizable social discourse (with a persuasive logic of truth), and a developmental projective teleology. Wholly without reference to what orthodox Marxism might have had to say about such matters, Mao's version was the ideal vehicle for combining these ingredients.

Hence, even if Mao was never much of a Marxist theoretician, one might say that for pragmatic reasons he took his Marxism seriously enough.[17] Actually, if Mao had been a more rigorous Marxist theoretician, as his Moscow-trained opponents believed themselves to be, the game would have been lost precisely because the discretionary space for a pragmatics of both maneuver and "truth" would have been too narrow.

How did Mao make his pragmatic Marxism mythic? By putting his finger on the problem of the myth in the theory, which is characteristic of all transcending ideological projects. Meissner suggests that for Mao ideology represented an oracular vision. He implies that no matter how personalized his leadership, Mao realized a certain "disembodiment." Indeed one can call him a cosmocratic figure to the degree that he represented agency and "voice"—that is, he served as a mouthpiece for higher forces (sacred) and truths (secular). This combination enables a political fusion between addresser and addressee. It was a fusion that occurred in Yan'an and extended to the other base areas. Yan'an came to represent the ideological climax of the revolution, its disjunctive moral moment when belief burned with a particular intensity. Reading the text collectively, within the framework of study groups and more latterly the Rectification Campaign, produced a certain *jouissance,* what Barthes has referred to as the pleasure in the text.

For each of the three stories, there is a demonology: imperialists and capitalists, compradors and landlords for the first, capitulationists and betrayers for the second, and enemies from within in the third. These last include the representatives of the three "left lines," particularly Li Lisan, and later Zhang Guotao, Wang Ming, and Wang Shiwei even though the struggle with Wang Shiwei was not a line struggle in the strict sense.[18] Each enemy from within represents a dangerous lapsarian alternative to Mao's monopoly of the cosmos. After struggling with them before, during, and after the Long March, Mao winds up close to power. Once his enemies were discredited, Mao Zedong Thought hardened into a theoretical discourse, a total way of thinking, a mode of dialectical truth. Any alternative came to be seen not as a different view, not even an alternative truth, but rather an alternative to the truth itself.

In Yan'an, storytelling was transformed into something quite different when in the space formed between lapsarian doctrines and dialectical truth the Rectification Campaign began. Its consequences went far beyond ideology or pragmatics to the formation of symbolic capital, with exegetical bonding as a form of discipline, a way of defining and internalizing norms.

At that point the narrative speeches and lectures became didactic texts and admonishments. Rectifying the style of work, establishing the proper function of intellectuals (in the Yan'an Forum on Literature and Art) were instructions about roles and role networks. The logic of discourse, symbol, communication, and argumentation became manifest in political structure. Earlier, in his May 1938 lectures at Kangda on "Protracted War," for example, a didactic, schoolteaching, tutelary Mao established the common and distinguishing feature of human beings, their "conscious activity." He laid out a correspondence theory of knowledge between "objective facts" and "correct ideas" leading to an analysis of war and tactics, principles and strategy.

There is, of course, a mass of material with which to enrich these points with greater detail. But our central point is that Mao's storytelling preceded logical construction, that stylized accounts gave way to more detailed descriptions of immediate experiences, and that there was a continuous movement from "facts" to theory and back again.

By incorporating already well known episodes and more recent episodes and events and reinterpreting both for theoretical purposes, Mao made what appeared to be theory construction out of storytelling. Theory is in fact a code that universalizes improvisation in the name of praxis.[19]

To concern ourselves with Mao as a storyteller and mythmaker then means above all to take him more seriously in those roles than that of Marxist theoretician. Meissner shows convincingly how much of what passed for theory in Mao was derivative Stalinism, if not diluted versions of factional theoretical disputes within the USSR and reformulated by certain Chinese communist philosophers such as Ai Siqi.[20] Nevertheless Mao had clear objectives. He knew what it was he wanted to accomplish by these means. One was to gain power over more sophisticated Marxists, especially the "twenty eight and a half Bolsheviks," the CCP communists educated in the USSR. He pooh-poohed their knowledge by drawing from public experience events that could be converted into metonymies for his own "universal" truths. These he elevated to the position of dialectical breaks in historical consciousness. "Leveling down," he then manipulated these into metaphorical narratives. This mass line enabled Mao to recast time from history to situation, situation into the particular space of border areas, and border areas into the simulacrum of Yan'an as a utopic community. Yan'an was made to serve as a moral template, rather than a model, of the China yet to be born.[21] Mao made Yan'an a utopic community mythic in its own time and for most (not all) of its constituents.

Metonymies of the Long Story

To illustrate these general principles let us return to Mao's long story. Again and again the same incidents and events are repeated, in much the same words. The events constitute a metaphorical sequence as well as a narrative. They also constitute a metonymical sequence on which to build up the theoretical statements Mao was fond of. There are many examples

of this in Mao's writing. But it is especially useful to consider the textbook
for students Mao and several collaborators wrote in 1939 in Yan'an, three
years before the Rectification Campaign began, entitled "The Chinese
Revolution and the Chinese Communist Party."

The text is short and consists of two chapters. The first deals with
Chinese society, the second with the Chinese revolution. The first chapter
begins by establishing the jurisdictional boundaries of China, its historical
terrain, its population. It emphasizes that nine tenths of the population is
Han, and goes on to list minority nationalities, among them Mongol, Hui,
Tibetan, Uighur, Miao, and Yi.

These are "locational" or situational facts. The chapter then moves to
prehistory (using the term prehistory as Marx did, that is, as precapitalist).
It portrays China as part of a universal social ontology. Like other societies,
China evolved from classless primitive communes to a slave society, a class
society, and a feudal society; and then, uniquely, China's social evolution
stops. Despite its brilliant cultural achievements—great thinkers, inventors,
scholars, statesmen, artists, and great inventions such as block printing,
movable type, and gunpowder—China is locked into the feudal mode of
production. The reason for this predicament is a critical contradiction in
China's feudal system between peasants and landlords. This contradiction,
according to Mao's text, led to many peasant uprisings, great and small.
The scale of peasant uprisings and peasant wars in Chinese history has no
parallel anywhere else. The class struggles of the peasants, the peasant
uprisings and peasant wars, constitute the real motive force of historical
development in Chinese feudal society, because each of the major peasant
uprisings and wars dealt a blow to the feudal regime of the time and hence
more or less furthered the growth of the social productive forces. However, said Mao, since neither new productive forces, nor new relations of
production, nor new class forces, nor any advanced political party existed
in those days, the peasant uprisings and wars did not have correct leadership
such as the proletariat and the Communist Party provide today. Consequently, every peasant revolution failed, and the peasantry was invariably
used by the landlords and the nobility as a lever to bring about dynastic
change. Therefore, although some social progress was made after each
great peasant revolutionary struggle, the feudal economic relations and
political system remained basically unchanged. It is only in the last hundred
years that a change of a different order has taken place.[22]

Here then is a mythic story, a narrative. The overcoming project is
defined. But it cannot be realized. The transition from feudal to capitalist
society is blocked. It is only when feudalism is exploded by outside forces,

which leads to the primordial condition of chaos and war, that developmental change, the proper subject of theory, is set in motion.

This recounting of China's past establishes three "empirical" conditions from which theoretical generalizations can be derived. Peasant rebellions constitute the motive force of Chinese history. The class basis of the system is such that, despite these rebellions, "Chinese society remained feudal for 3,000 years." During that time, the conditions for a transformational vanguard party were absent. This prehistory suggests that while China is unique in its cultural accomplishment, its inability to move from feudalism to capitalism—that is, to modernity—is the unfulfilled "project."

China's "history" begins with the Opium War of 1839–1842. Mao describes the consequences of foreign capitalism's entering the country in the mid-nineteenth century, and how this changed China into a semicolonial and semifeudal society:

> Foreign capitalism played an important part in the disintegration of China's social economy; on the one hand it undermined the foundations of her self-sufficient natural economy and wrecked the handicraft industries both in the cities and in the peasant's homes, and on the other, it hastened the growth of a commodity economy in town and country.
>
> Apart from its disintegrating effects on the foundations of China's feudal economy, this state of affairs gave rise to certain objective conditions and possibilities for the development of capitalist production in China. For the destruction of the natural economy created a commodity market for capitalism, while the bankruptcy of large numbers of peasants and handicraftsmen provided it with a labor market.[23]

The story accompanying the logic recounts metaphors of loss, violation, and pollution. The moral outcome requires a purification. Loss involves a double patrimony: the nation lost to the imperialists, the land and livelihood lost to the peasants. Violation is both celestial, an implosion within the Mandate of Heaven, and terrestrial, the breaking up of mutual patterns of obligation and restraint. Pollution involves the corruption of Confucian discipline and harmony in the state and the family, and the poisoning of both the body politic and the human body through opium. The story within the story is the Taiping Rebellion, which is about the inversion of the Mandate and the great attempt to establish a peasant order on the ground while seizing the Christian heaven and sinicizing it.

Each metaphor has a counterpart metonym. The Opium War is an extension of China's imperialist/capitalist crisis. The loss of the patrimony involves the loss of imperial hegemony and the break up of the Asiatic mode of production, the class system being replaced with semifeudalism and comprador capitalism. The peasants' loss of their patrimony is a direct consequence of imperialism, which produces a peculiarly unproductive form of primitive accumulation, a consequence of "the collusion of imperialism with the Chinese feudal forces to arrest the development of Chinese capitalism." Foreign intervention then leads to the exploitation and backwardness of China. Mao's is the first theory of underdevelopment applied to a "semicolonial" country. The breakup of the Asiatic mode of production leads to a peculiarly deformed relationship between a newly established and relatively unproductive bourgeoisie and a proletariat that in a sense predates an indigenous bourgeoisie because it is created by the intervention of foreign capitalism. Finally, the events come to stand for the marginalization and the creation of a revolutionary class of lumpens. "Imperialism controls not only China's vital financial and economic arteries but also her political and military power . . . The Chinese people, and particularly the peasants, have become more and more impoverished and have been pauperized in large numbers, living in hunger and cold and without any political rights."[24]

This first chapter combines metaphor with metonym, narrative with text, story with logic to contribute to a Marxist theory of underdevelopment, which is itself a rationale for a long revolution, a revolutionary process grounded in the long story. Time and space are the boundaries. Rupture is intervention from the outside. But it is a theory of absences, lacks, and omissions, which establish the conditions for a new theory of peasant revolution.

Each event in the long story—the Opium War, the Movement of the Taiping Heavenly Kingdom, the Sino-French War, the Sino-Japanese War, the Reform Movement of 1898, the Boxer Movement, the Revolution of 1911—concretizes what are metaphors in the narrative and metonymies in the text. They lead into the intermediate story, which covers events from the May Fourth Movement to the founding of the party. Establishing the party becomes a point of entry for inversionary change. The party is the critical agent in the intermediate story, in contrast to its absence in the long story. The long story, which lasted one hundred years but had "not yet run its course," defines the conditions of revolutionary possibility, while in the intermediate story the revolutionary tasks for the party are enunciated.

The revolutionary task is to combine anti-imperialist war with class struggle, a double-sided struggle requiring protracted guerrilla warfare led by the communist party. As Mao put it, "Clearly then the protracted revolutionary struggle in the revolutionary base areas consists mainly in peasant guerrilla warfare led by the Chinese Communist Party."[25]

What are the structured dynamics? The "motive force" of the revolution in class terms is first of all landlords, "the main social base for imperialist rule in China; it is a class which uses the feudal system to exploit and oppress the peasants, obstructs China's political, economic, and cultural development and plays no progressive role whatsoever"; moreover, a good many landlords are collaborators of the Japanese.[26] Mao goes on to distinguish compradors from the national bourgeoisie: the first is an instrument of imperialism that negates the progressive possibilities of the second. As for the peasantry, who are arbitrarily divided into rich, middle, and poor, all have a potential role to play, the last being the most important. Finally, Mao considers two other classes: the proletariat, about whom surprisingly not much is said; and "vagrants," consisting of "robbers, gangsters, beggars, and prostitutes and the numerous people who live on superstitious practices. This social stratum is unstable; while some are apt to be bought over by the reactionary forces, others may join the revolution. These people lack constructive qualities and are given to destruction rather than construction; after joining the revolution they become a source of roving-rebel and anarchist ideology in the revolutionary ranks. Therefore, we should know how to remould them and guard against their destructiveness."[27]

The chapter concludes with an analysis of the party and its special role. Here the metaphor is of re-creation, the party as a new order, the "inheritance" of Sun Yat-sen; and the purification is the party's Spartanism as it is constructed in the Whampoa (Huangpu) image.[28] The corresponding metonymies include peasant revolution and the disjunctive transformation of a society that is divided between the democratic tendencies of the national bourgeoisie in concert with the proletariat, the comprador capitalism of the major landlords, and the foreign imperialism of the comprador bourgeoisie. It is up to the CCP to act on the "motive forces" by using a dialectical logic, the outcome of which is to link the bourgeois democratic and socialist revolutions.[29]

The style in the essay is didactic. It has little of Mao as a fictive truth teller. He uses narrative structure, chronology, and sequence but as illustrations that require explanation, not to tell a story or capture fictive truth. The text demonstrates Mao's notion of the dialectic as a method of tensed binaries from which a narrative of confrontation and a logic of explanation can be composed. The events described lead inexorably to a disjunctive conclusion. Moreover, the logic is generalized to even broader themes— China and the world, imperialism and impoverishment, modernization and backwardness, Confucianism and Marxism, lumpen peasantry and neofeudal landlordism, capitalism and communism. Each of the binaries is eventful. Each contains a contradiction-transcending instruction. The whole represents the reordering of disordering circumstances.

Indeed order is the number one subtext. Number two is how to "read" historical events according to a golden age, followed by loss, dispossession, patrimony robbed, robbers as enemies of China, subverting Nationalists, invading Japanese. While not included in this essay, Mao's students will also have learned from the intermediate story of the betrayals, the events in Shanghai and Canton, and the defeats by the GMD that almost, but never quite, extinguish the communist movement.

Periodization is crucial, for it fixes time into spatial grids. The beginnings are commonly accepted historical facts located on an "evolutionary" (and basically Stalinist) grid that demarcates societal stages. Movement between stages ascends according to transformational dialectical "laws." "History" moves from primitive communism to slave society to feudal society, the last beginning in China in the Zhou period (1027–256 B.C.).

In the intermediate story the grid follows the general sequence laid down by Sun Yat-sen, the hero of the intermediate story. But the party modifies it to show how it is the CCP that represents the only true follower of the "Three Principles of the People." Differences with the GMD and Chiang Kai-shek are defined in terms of revolution from above versus revolution from below. In this view what the Nationalists wanted was a revolution from above to establish a political framework that would leave existing social structures basically intact. This would take place within a normative order composed of the traditional Confucian qualities of order, hierarchy, and virtue, and combining modernization and capitalism.[30]

Mao's logic required that the GMD position be turned upside down. Make the revolution from below. Use the higher consciousness of the party as the tutelary framework. According to the grid theory, these principles are true because they have evolved according to the evolution of science itself, as manifested in the appropriate party consciousness. Of course as one comes to contemporary events it becomes time to project the Marxist future. Here the grid breaks down. Mao's essay is silent on what happens after the revolution.

For all their ordering, the three stories pose unresolved contradictions. Even using Mao's logic they give rise to genuine theoretical puzzles. Take, for example, the lessons to be learned from the Taiping Rebellion, the centerpiece of the long story. According to the long story, it was the peasants who dared to stand up against the foreign imperialists, who "stole" the national patrimony. The events of the rebellion constitute the narrative of peasant insurrection. This gives Mao the opportunity to reenact what every peasant knows, but on Mao's own terms, since the story contains an infinite number of metaphorical signifiers, not to mention a context of violent confrontation with all the existing reactionary powers—imperialists, landlords, the imperial house, even the convenient target of "Chinese" Gordon.

As an event The Taiping Rebellion is an excellent example of how by instruction a totalized understanding can be achieved. For while everyone knows the story, the public perception is superficial without further instruction, appropriate guidance without which the public perception of the events will not be elevated to a higher stage. The total view is nothing less than an understanding of imperialism itself. "It was only in the second stage that the Chinese people reached the stage of rational knowledge, saw the internal and external contradictions of imperialism, and saw the essential truth that imperialism had allied itself with China's comprador and feudal classes to oppress and exploit the great masses of the Chinese people."[31] Hence the rebellion opens the way for a higher, more general understanding, and not only by a class but by the "Chinese people." The CCP is thus the surrogate not for a class with a higher consciousness, but a society for which new truths are to be revealed, as depicted in Figure 4.1.

Ambiguities, Contradictions, and Lines

For all the prospects for the higher consciousness, it is not always easy in the moment to know what lessons a Marxist should draw from the events. Mao's texts are designed to eliminate ambiguity by laying down the lessons to be learned and the lines to be followed. Moreover, if his line is to generate more power than that represented by any mere aggregate of supporters, it is important that each individual adherent convey his or her own story to the larger one, enriching it by individual experience, and making the whole greater than the sum of its parts.

The problem is that "real" history gets in the way of fictive history. For example, the Taiping Rebellion, while figuring again and again in Mao's stories to the extent that it serves as a marker for his notion of peasant revolution as historical event (as opposed to fictive truth), has troubling implications. It is fine for illustrating social banditry, peasant opposition to landlord usury, the links of corruption to imperialism, the delegitimization of the Qing, and the growing impotence of the Mandarinate to the rebellion itself. It can also be used to establish Marxism as the higher

Figure 4.1 Yan'an as a semiotic space

Narratives/ Texts	Actors	Metaphors	Metonymies	Consequences
The long story	Peasants, imperialists, Qing dynasty	The fall (violation)	Imperialist penetration (pollution)	Loss (displacement)
The intermediate story	Comprador capitalists, imperialists, Japanese, GMD, CCP, Comintern	Chaos (death)	Revolutionary disjunction (inversion)	Overcoming
The short story	CCP factions, Maoists	Redemption (rebirth)	Purification (transcendence)	Logic of necessity
Mao as storyteller	Mao as politician	Mao as Odysseus	Mao as Socrates	Chinese communism
(Fictive truths)	(Choreog- raphy)	(Patrimony regained)	(Texts sacralized)	(Truth revealed)

consciousness of Marxian principle over Christian revelation and logical understanding over revealed truths. But there is also the less convenient matter of how the Taipings themselves proposed to restore the lost patrimony. In fact what they wanted was the status quo ante on the ground, and an ecclesiastical political transformationalism in the superstructure. Not surprisingly, they were profoundly in favor of private property and the restoration of the small freeholders and permanent tenancies that had broken up during the Ming Dynasty. Given these facts, one ought to draw the logical conclusion that a peasant revolution requires a restoration of patrimony not in the form of collective but private ownership. Only then are peasants the universalized and redeeming class.

Similar problems arise in the intermediate story over how to deal with the GMD in the wider context of the Chinese revolution. Must China pass through a bourgeois democratic phase? If so, how long should it last? And why should such a phase be necessary? True enough, Soviet interpretations of the Chinese revolution suggest the CCP could not hope to win a socialist revolution.[32] Hence the insistence on the weaker party joining the stronger one representative of a rising class (the bourgeoisie). While Soviet emphasis on the United Front and Soviet insistence on the CCP joining the GMD as the weaker force piggybacking on to the stronger could be justified on purely pragmatic grounds, the joining of CCP with GMD had the additional advantage of increasing the effective claim of the CCP to the inheritance of Sun Yat-sen, since the CCP could now appear as an authentic nationalist party competing on more or less equal terms with the GMD. But when, how, and under what circumstances should the CCP use its position to undermine and overcome the GMD leadership? How independent in action should the CCP remain? Was party leadership acting from theory or pragmatics when, after the Xi'an Incident in 1936, it officially placed the party in a subordinate position to the GMD and transformed the Red Army into the Eighth Route Army of the nationalist government, with Yan'an itself technically under the control of Chiang Kai-shek? Where is the "revolutionary theory" in a tactical politics of collaboration against the Japanese? These are only a few of the questions that, once raised, touched on profound issues of theory as well as practice.

These issues came to a head in competing lines. The three that Mao had to contend with were those of Li Lisan, Zhang Guotao, and Wang Ming. All were convinced of their own superior insight and knowledge. Zhang represented a "right" line, a pragmatic one in keeping perhaps with his professional training as an engineer. Of the three, Li Lisan's "left" and the Comintern lines were the most serious for Mao to contend with, for both attempted to deal with the questions discussed above. Li Lisan argued that the revolutionary disjunction was about to occur, so that the armed forces of the Red Army had to be concentrated to exterminate the enemy. He argued against protracted war and for a decisive victory now. He supported border regions only as bases to meet larger aims. Li believed that Mao's emphasis on the "lumpen proletariat in the countryside" would lead to "petty-bourgeois socialism." Indeed, Li Lisan attacked Mao on this point directly at the Sixth Party Congress held in Moscow in June and July 1928. He said, "The majority of the delegates to this conference know that this obviously is not socialism, but for many Chinese comrades who are working in the peasant movement in China this is still not clear. I think that such a comrade is Mao Zedong. He possibly even now thinks that we have socialism because we have already raised that slogan. But we must point out that this is not only not socialism, it interferes with the development of actual socialism."[33]

Amidst clashes of the bloodier sort and collisions between lines and factions, theory became practice and practice theory; the larger ambiguities of the long and intermediate stories were resolved by default. Two issues stood out as fundamental: Which is the class with radical chains? How should the answer to that define the role of the party? Behind these questions lay the following problems: Should China head straight for socialism? Or should China opt for a "people's republic" with bourgeois hangovers? On such matters, Mao was inconsistent, swaying with the vicissitudes of the anti-Japanese war and the struggle with the Nationalists (and also in relation to the United States). Certainly over time Mao became less concerned with the Japanese than with the support given both by the USSR and the United States to Chiang Kai-shek.[34]

Why do such issues matter apart from in the heat of the moment? They matter because of the need to sustain revolutionary momentum. These issues, the stories, and their logic as a moral objective needed to continue past the point of the anti-Japanese war. The question was how to square the circle between the democratic line favoring a bourgeois alliance with Chiang Kai-shek and a redemptive vision for China and its revolution.

In this light it is instructive to return to the questions posed by the Taiping Rebellion. Mao's solutions there, although partial, are interesting. They give clues to the way he will deal with other questions. Mao in effect decides that the Taiping basically tried to redeem a lumpen peasantry, radicalize the marginalized, and by saving a pariah caste transform it into a redeeming one. Hence erstwhile small freeholders and tenants should in the first instance be able to reclaim their patrimony, and with that the national patrimony itself would be restored.[35]

Mao's resolution of making the Taiping metonymic figures of the revolution elevates peasant revolution rather than insurrection as the key to the Chinese revolution without making its moral consummation dependent on peasants. A good deal follows from that. It means that the intermediate story can be one of class struggle in which comprador capitalism, imperialism, and landlordism are smashed where they count while allowing harmless remnants to survive. It means destroying the GMD by means of collaboration, a strategy the GMD understood and feared, and one of the reasons it preferred fighting the CCP to fighting the Japanese.

Finally, it meant that all other lines—Li Lisan's, Wang Ming's, and any other predilections by Moscow-trained "superior Marxists"—had to be eliminated and that the party had to evolve into a microcosm of society. The need to move from two lines (Wang Ming's notion, drawn from Soviet analyses of China, and Mao's) to one, Mao's alone, is the lesson of the short story. But in Mao's version, the metonym does not stand for any existing Marxist texts or lines. The theory had to be invented around the metonym; and it goes from class to society, where for Mao it began.

Mao's Inversion

Mao resolves the ambiguities "theoretically" by inventing an inversionary theory within an inversionary model. These terms need to be taken in a context of classical Marxism, which was subject to two main varieties of amendment: *inversionary* and *revisionary*. The revisions gave rise to social democracy, as in the work of Kautsky and Bernstein. The inversions were manifested in the Soviet Union and the People's Republic of China, in the special sense of revolutionary armed communist parties capturing state power.

Classical Marxism is inversionary vis-à-vis liberal democracy and capitalism. It is a negating theory of disjunctive transformation. Despite the enormous significance of it historically and in the politics of virtually every country since its doctrinal inception, it has never succeeded on its own terms. It has never been able to establish a system of self-sustaining norms, structures, and behaviors brought into being as a result of the dialectical conditions of high capitalism. Yet as an inversionary discourse based on class, Marxism has been particularly susceptible to both inversionary and revisionist the other types of amendment. One uses a dialectical logic to establish this or that class as the one with radical change and by so doing designates all sorts of consequences. The notion of "class" lends itself both to historicist interpretations of evolution on the basis of contradictions that define self/other dichotomies, and to a logic of material forces wedded to a logic of projective millennialism.

Lenin's inversion did not change the significance of the role of the proletariat in the classical revolutionary project. For him, the proletariat remained the chief creator of value, but Lenin's shift required that the party act on behalf of a less than fully formed proletariat because of the less than fully realized state of proletarian consciousness. This required the party to use the state to create the material conditions for the universalization of the proletarian class and, by so doing, enable the proletariat to fulfill its designated role as the higher consciousness of human understanding. Lenin accepts the role and place of the proletariat even in a predominantly peasant country.

Thus, Lenin's inversion, while providing for a very different concept of party and state than Marx, is still within the Marxian framework, with economic power as the driving force. In any case, the argument for the revolutionary political project in terms of a totalizing radical disjuncture or break in Russia was to assume a chain reaction. The Russian revolution was to be simply the flashpoint, the spark that would ignite the advanced capitalist revolutions along the lines Marx predicted.

However, the Leninist party must elevate the proletariat to becoming the class with radical chains and a fully formed higher consciousness. In so doing, the party plays a crucial tutelary role not envisaged by Marx. But to do that, it must transform society normatively, structurally, and behaviorally by fundamentally altering both the modes and the relations of production through the application of state power.

The Leninist party therefore serves as the revolutionary wedge, the vanguard agent that triggers the inherent disjunction of extreme and asymmetrical forms of class polarization. In the interim, in the absence of a universalized proletariat the party must universalize itself in society. It speaks in the name of the proletariat to create a dictatorship so absolute that the proletariat can itself be transformed. The state then is the administrative and bureaucratic instrument of the party.

This amounts to an elite theory of revolutionary action. Yet, despite Lenin's success in capturing state power, it failed as a theory. In Russia the proletariat hardly became an enlightened class. Moreover, the rural sectors became more backward even as farms were collectivized and the kulaks liquidated. Stalinism is the result of that theoretical failure. In fact, the Russian revolution was a revolution of force and violence and not one of theory at all. This began to be clear even before Lenin's death in 1924. In effect the party became a class in and for itself with the state its prison colony. Stalin merely carried the logic of Leninism to its full organizational conclusion.

In short, in Russia the party maintained a facade of Marxist legitimacy while reinventing the whole of society as a socialist proletariat with the party at the center. Thus the special role of the Leninist party under developmental socialism is first to generate the disjunctive moment and capture state power. Then, having captured it, its second task is to use the state as its main instrument of power. The state, far from withering away, prosecutes the class struggle for the party. The superstructure thus creates the base. The moral moment of the revolution authorizes power from the top in the name of power from below. Stalin's version of the party–state turned this into a class struggle of state versus society.

If Lenin created the first real inversion within classical Marxism (with Stalin working out the organizational expression), Mao can lay claim to the second. His starting point was a practical one. The Chinese proletariat was too small vis-à-vis the total productive process, far smaller than prevailed in Russia in 1917, when Russia had the fourth largest proletariat in Europe. Moreover, as a class, China's proletariat was even more lacking in revolutionary consciousness than Russia's. It was an insurrectionary, rather than a revolutionary, class. Nor was this likely to change given China's state of economic development, or lack of it. With the proletariat too small and insufficiently developed to carry the revolutionary burden, what China required was a radicalized peasantry.

In both classic Marxism and Leninism, however, peasants are conservative, suspicious, superstitious—the true "idiots" of rural life and, by the very nature of their productive activities, the opposite of an enlightened class. Hence for a China stuck for millennia in the Asiatic mode of production with its static and hierarchical reciprocities, violence caused by injustices could and did explode while providing virtually no base for a genuine Marxist revolution. In Leninism and Stalinism, the transformation of peasant society became a precondition for the transformation of capitalist society to a socialist one through a socialist version of primitive accumulation. But in China, even expropriating the landlords' resources was not likely to accumulate enough for a major industrial transformation. For these reasons, as well as other, practical ones, in China the Soviets preferred to follow Marx, at least to the extent of favoring a bourgeois democratic revolutionary phase. In concrete terms, this meant favoring close links between the CCP and the GMD.

Mao then had the special task of turning sporadic peasant and proletarian uprisings and a predisposition to insurrection into a revolutionary movement. Despite official descriptions of vast organized peasant movements evolving under his guidance, nothing like that ever took place. Indeed, one of the reasons why in the republic of clandestinity the conflicts were so deep-seated was that it was never clear that Mao would have any greater success in mobilizing peasants and making them the class with revolutionary chains than more conventional Marxists such as Chen Duxiu, Li Dazhao, Qu Qiubai, Li Lisan, or Wang Ming, with their preoccupations with the proletariat. Nor did Mao ever challenge directly the conventional Marxist view in principle. Rather, he set about establishing the conditions under which the classical Marxist and the Leninist views of the central role of the proletariat might not be true enough, while also arguing that the peasant predisposition to revolt could be transformed into a theory of peasant revolution.

Hence, the peasantry, the class Mao chose as the one with radical chains, was the opposite of the most "advanced." Rather, it was the most functionally superfluous, the least economically significant, and the most marginalized. It resembled most those lumpens for whom Marx reserved his greatest contempt. Dispossessed, it had nothing to take over. Worse, what it had been dispossessed from was property. Claims to restore the patrimony, however, raised the spectre of private capitalism as the logical outcome of a peasant-based revolution.

Initially Mao did not claim that the peasantry was an enlightened class or the class of a higher political consciousness. He saw it simply as a class from which sufficient numbers could be recruited to support guerrilla armies. He saw it as a class whose grievances had in the past produced, and would continue for some time to produce, explosive potential. Mao therefore did what neither Marx nor Lenin nor, in principle at least, Stalin did. He made revolutionary consciousness a function of violence.

Here is where story and text intersect. The long story is a descent into violence and the breakdown of order. Violence was thus the generalized condition of China. It was the occasion for a projective logic, a taking of possession, a repossession *by means of violence* using a myth and a logic for its framework. Order took the form of revolutionary consciousness.[36] The victims of violence would use violence to establish order. Mao's inversion makes Marxism into a theory of revolutionary violence closer to Bakunin's anarchism rather than a communist solution.[37]

What Mao did was not to make the peasant class the agent of a revolutionary future, but to extend its insurrectionary role into the present. In this respect, the real class with revolutionary chains is not the peasantry in general, but only its most marginalized fringe, the most functionally superfluous. This turns the functional dynamic of Marxist classes on its head: the least enlightened class in theory becomes the most enlightened class in fact. In terms rather similar to Hegel's master and slave, Mao argues that those at the bottom have a special insight into the top, while to the top the bottom is invisible.

Mao's Marxism, if that is the word for it, is first of all about events that people experience. It is situational and contextual. It is about China and the events of China. It requires a transformation from story to theory. In making the transition or, better, combining the one with the other, it becomes essential to depend on the CCP for more things than Lenin had ever envisaged. Mao has to make the party into a miniaturized version of society, the party-state in miniature. This is what he attempted in the Jiangxi base and later in Yan'an. His is a theory of revolutionary simulacra. Moreover, simulacra of the party-state produce missionaries, who spread out to other areas, behind enemy lines and within the GMD. The Jiangxi soviet and Yan'an border areas are really centers for a radical inversionary colonialism. Mao's inversion is thus a colonialism of the disjunctive transformation.

Clearly, Mao is the opposite of a classical Marxist and even very different from a Leninist. Yet, by offering a theoretical basis at every step he avoids the charge he made against Li Lisan and Wang Ming, that they were "adventurists" and "putschists." One might think that revolutionary violence in the context of more general violence as a theory would represent little more than terrorism. Yet Mao succeeded in making this into his own theory of the revolution in the revolution. Precisely because it is so difficult to create a revolutionary consciousness among a group that considers itself so victimized that its margin for risk is small, providing them with a pedigree by means of a retrieving narrative is the best way to give them a place to stand in history. From this place, the sharply marginalized peasants can see a place of their own in a historical process not of their own making. In this respect, their consciousness becomes different from that of the Taiping. Instead of a blind lashing out at the powers that be, Mao's peasants learn by constructing an articulated principle of revolutionary peasant action. Thus, the "slaves" are provided with a logic of struggle and historical references to previous and future struggles.

In fact, a peasant revolution does not require the mobilization of vast numbers of peasants. It has only to mobilize a few, establish a wider sympathetic clientele among them, and use them to lend authenticity to intellectuals who, by going to the countryside, gain not only folk wisdom but also the legitimacy to act in the nation's name and on its behalf.

Nor does Mao's inversion actually require the peasantry to become the class with radical chains. Mao's inversion is more ingenious than that. Lenin shifted the focus from advanced capitalism and a universalizing proletariat to high imperialism and an incompletely developed proletariat. But the difficulties of that theoretical twist pale compared with the conditions of the Chinese revolution. For Mao had to find a role for the peasants that made them the salt of the earth, a role more significant in their consciousness than mere insurrectionary violence might offer; they needed a deep sense of grievance, a yearning for justice while still lacking the larger vision that remains open to any proletariat. However, unlike the proletariat, there is no way in any Marxist theory that the peasantry can become the class of the future. Quite the contrary. By the very nature of the productive process, it is a class that would be marginalized even more if modernization and industrial development were finally to get under way on a large scale in China. It is a class of the past, not the class of potentiality.

Mao recognized this. In Yan'an the possibility of rendering the "peasant other" into a redeeming national class became the object, while the Yan'anites and their associates in the party and other border regions were in fact the nucleus for a wholly new society waiting to be born. It was a society in which the actual peasantry did not figure at all—though in Ya'nan it was not necessary to provide even an outline of what that future society might be. Nor did Mao have to design a structure for developmental socialism. It was enough to create an exemplary utopic community, a freestanding moral community, which, because it possessed all the right answers, could beg all the right questions.

Tutelary Party/Utopic Community

In Mao's inversion the task of the communist party is even more significant than Lenin's. For the CCP is not only a tutelary party, it is also a substitute for a class with radical chains. It is the party that must make the revolution by capitalizing on what insurrectionary tendencies exist in whatever sector of society, peasant, proletarian, gentry. Hence Mao's tortured and inconsistent efforts to identify different classes within the classes and point out which need to be eradicated and which can be cooperated with (at least for the time being) are inconsistent and unconvincing. He needs something more than the party; he needs a community that is not a class but that contains different class elements whose original functions have disappeared. This is the real significance of the border regions. They became substitutes for revolutionary classes. Mao's revolution by means of simulacra centers on Yan'an as the most important.

Yan'an was a place where time was converted into space, the conversion achieved partly through Mao's recounting of himself and partly through the fact of the Long March. Yan'an becomes the surrogate for the larger historical vision, the fictive truth of the long story. Indeed, Mao's vision, already in place in his earliest works, needs this space to concretize the fictive truth of the long story by bringing it literally down to earth.

Yan'an can be seen as a semiotic theater of revolution as well as a substitute for a genuine revolutionary class. It has all the elements of drama. Within Yan'an, the audience goes through a double conversion, first into students and then into actors. This transition is fundamental. An audience, after all, is passive: it looks and listens as the play casts a spell. Students are active; indeed, they become part of the performance. With the theater as classroom the spell remains after the performance is over; something is learned permanently and, more important, is incorporated into one's persona.

Yan'an had both drama and schooling. It was the center where people came to see and listen as audience, either outdoors or in meeting halls. The space outside or inside, was broken up into classrooms, that were structurally organized around "universities," diverse educational and research institutions. Other functions were performed as well: work and production campaigns; the pursuing of redemptive tasks by means of transformational projects and instructional strategies; the organization of syllabi, lectures, research, and so forth; and the creation of military strategy, the methods of fighting both the Nationalists and the Japanese.

A community in learning acquires the proper language and codes, as well as dress, attitudes, and conduct. In Yan'an, students in the "tutelary position" knew that they would not only learn but also become cadres. Preceptorship was followed by administration. One learned how to be a good communist so well that, as one interviewee put it, "anyone could tell a communist from a noncommunist."[38] In Yan'an all the improvised rules and practices, the shaky mixtures of ideas about relationships with peasants of Jinggang Mountain experience and the somewhat more stringent and austere codes of Jiangxi, were reorganized in elaborate legal codes and a "constitutional system" known as the New Democracy, or "three-thirds" system and based on a series of concentric circles. The external boundary of Yan'an was marked by Nationalist and Japanese areas, broken up by other border regions and liberated areas. Just inside Yan'an proper were the rural districts and communities operating under the "three-thirds" system. Within that area is greater Yan'an City and its civil administration, and inside Yan'an City is the charmed circle of intimates we call the Yan'an simulacrum. In this small circle the issues of the party reign supreme, and from this circle the body of texts and logical principles emanates.

Each narrative included elements of the magical or the fabulous, a structure of suspense, a climax, and a denouement. These became the focal points of logical explication.

In White's terms this revolutionary storytelling tradition is redolent of the Paris Commune more than the October Revolution and has affinities to the Levelers and the Diggers in England, and the Jacobins of the French revolution. However, it also embodies the codes of the Leninist inversion. All share one characteristic: each is "a society of all-round non-specialists helping each other to arrive at truth through the community."[39] That idea would prompt the Yan'anites to reject not only Confucianism and familism, feudalism and capitalism, but also individualism, on grounds that it would lead to anarchy. Instead, Yan'an favored a dialectical reason applied to Chinese conditions that would allow a communitarian circumstance, a mutualism of necessity.

Holding the whole thing together was a system of reportage that covered all activities in remarkable detail. Each person was evaluated according to recognized rules governing courtship and marriage, education, military life, the printing and use of money, economic and productive enterprises, land use, the creation of weapons, the training of guerrillas, the spinning of fabric, the building of roads, physical training (including basketball), military training, and above all textual exegesis. So complete was this system of reportage that measuring a Yan'anite's communist consciousness was more frequent than taking his or her temperature.

Reportage and administration imply hierarchy; and if egalitarianism is the norm, hierarchy must be justified. The old hierarchy of the Mandarinate, with its stylized and scriptural learning and its rigid forms, justified itself. The bureaucrats were the people of the book in a country of the illiterate, the one-eyed kings in the country of the blind. It was precisely this self-legitimizing body of norms that Yan'an meant to explode. The book, not to mention literacy itself, now was to become common property. The tutelary party in China would become the voice of the marginalized peasant.

This brings us to the central weakness in Mao's theory. Mao's was a theory of peasant revolution based on symbolic capital. But after the revolution succeeds, and after the peasantry provides the economic capital for the party-state, the peasantry must wither away, because it has no potential of universalizing itself in a highly developed, modern nation.

Mao wanted to universalize the normative, structural, and behavioral balance established in Yan'an. His major problem was finding a suitable structural alternative, one that would reinforce the norms and behavior of Yan'an while serving as the functional mechanism of development. But he could never find the right combination after Yan'an. He found contradictions galore; but no matter how hard he tried to systematize these factors, to segregate the benign from the malignant, and to render class struggle into a principle that would realize the norms acquired in Yan'an and the behavior of a model communist, he failed. Yet despite Mao's failure, it remains the idée fixe for most of the surviving Yan'anites, especially those at the top.

The fundamental character of Mao's normative principles, as they were worked out in Yan'an, where the social structure created willy-nilly fit so perfectly with desired behavior, could never be comparable to Soviet-style bureaucratic state structures. Hence almost immediately after the People's Republic was established, all the elements that Mao had fought against— opportunism, bureaucratism, "mountain-topism," neofeudalism—returned, this time inside the party. While Mao's inversion could solve the contradictions of the stories he told, it could not resolve the contradiction of a normative system emptied of content, and behavior drastically altered given the nature of the structure of society being imposed. Yan'an was where the Chinese communist ideal got stuck, because it was there that its stories and its logic reached an apotheosis.

Missionary Intellectuals

The problem in Yan'an was to find a genuine revolutionary nucleus, the class with radical chains in full possession of a higher consciousness. For Mao this had to be the intellectuals.[40] Yet because of the previous role of the intellectuals in China's history, their position, their character as a *Stand,* they had to identify completely with the most marginalized. The intellectuals had to be the class for the lumpen peasantry and not a class for themselves.

Because of this, Mao's revolutionary intellectuals could not be too intellectual. Mainly bright children of gentry, bureaucrats, and professionals, some were artists and writers. Most were students from middle and high schools; some were schoolteachers; some were university or technical institute graduates. Very few could be called "real" intellectuals, even in China.

Mao's task was to elevate these "intellectuals" to an understanding of his notions of the dialectic direction in which to go, while keeping control over them so that they did not join the wrong faction. He had to seal them off from influences other than his own. The simulacrum formed at Yan'an was perfect for this. It became a charmed circle. It was difficult to get there but even more difficult to leave. While it would be wrong to say that he made them a captive audience, it is fair to say that, once inside, to leave for doctrinal reasons required one to escape.

It was in Yan'an that education became rectification, a process involving exegetical bonding. When the proper missionary spirit was instilled intellectuals became cadres, fanning outward to the other base areas, proselytizing among peasants, engaging in underground work, organizing in the trade union movement, or, using the "three-thirds" system as the framework, becoming involved in administration in the border regions. It was in Yan'an that the peasantry as a class with insurrectionary chains was connected to the party of radical brains, the latter learning from the former and the former being transformed by the latter into a revolutionary class. Hence those most given to thought without action became activists, and those given to act without thought become thinkers. This was Mao's vision of how to realize the higher revolutionary consciousness. It contained his definition of equality. He wanted nothing less than to draw more of his intellectuals from the peasantry; and, if not converting intellectuals into peasants, he sought to put intellectuals on intimate terms with peasant life.

In Yan'an, most people, with the exception of a few "real" intellectuals, found this very satisfying. It appealed to intellectuals because it gave them power while making them modest, and work to do without giving them airs. And in a country where to be an intellectual was to belong to a *Stand,* this position was even more appealing to sympathetic foreigners. Mao's CCP obligated itself to both peasants and intellectuals, but only so that the second could be used on behalf of the first.

The methods of instruction were systematic. The long, intermediate, and short stories were part of the instruction. In the study groups, the turning over of the meaning of words and phrases and the learning of certain stock ways of saying things converted the larger discourse of Marxism and the dialectic to a specific Chinese language of the text.

This produced an interior language that was originally shared by those in Yan'an and would become the meta-language for the instruction of others. The stories and the texts had to be translated for peasants and outsiders; they had to be made into a common sense. But for those in possession of the meta-language, it was like belonging to a secret society, an inscripted band. With exegetical bonding, an intimacy of language was followed by an intimacy of association.

This posed an interesting problem. How could the preceptual quality of the community be sustained without the new literati hardening into a radical replication of the old, and so become increasingly divorced from the people it was now dedicated to serve? To make matters more complicated, it was the radical literati who called for the greatest egalitarianism. That is, the most qualified intellectuals were the most concerned with egalitarianism. And ironically, because of their gifts as intellectuals, they were more subject to Mao's hostility.

Despite all the emphasis on equality, plenty of inequality and hierarchy remained, most of it justified on grounds of function. Rank was differentiated by the material used for uniforms; the higher cadres enjoyed better food and access to horses. Perhaps the most fundamental differences had to do with the circulation of women. Especially early on in Yan'an, there were far fewer women than men. The senior cadres had mostly left their wives behind, and many wives had been killed. And while it would be wrong to say that these senior cadres had their pick, the women having their own ideas about such matters, the higher a man was in the hierarchy, the greater his degree of sexual choice, Mao himself being the supreme example.

In Yan'an in 1986 questions on such matters were discussed with a Red Army soldier from an illiterate peasant family and a veteran of the Long March. Stuffed into a uniform now several sizes too small for him and wearing his decorations proudly, he seated himself stiffly on the edge of a couch and gave precise, but not very informative, answers to questions. However, when asked about equality, he exploded: "What equality? Those intellectual women would never sleep with us!"

The power of the discourse, important as it was for the students and the intellectuals, was in some respects even more important for peasant soldiers, a good many of whom had little esteem when they joined the revolution. Easier to enlist than to discipline, especially those captured from the GMD armies, the peasants were quick to run away unless they felt somehow an integral part of the overcoming project. In the beginning, at least, the large objectives, pursuing the war against the Japanese and the revolution against the Nationalists, were circumstances they had to deal with rather than principles to fight for. For this reason, they also had to become "students" and, in a step-by-step process, moved from instruction in basic literacy to technical instruction (in, say, radios or electricity) to eventually, at least for some, more theoretical work.[41]

The issue of subjectivism was central to the tutelary process. It posed the question of how one became an individual rather than a category without becoming individualistic and subjectivist, a self rather than an "other" without becoming egocentric or liberalistic. For a good many people that issue was not easily resolved. A celebrated writer such as Ding Ling solved the problem by defining "selfness" as becoming a "radical woman."

Which brings us back to Mao's logic as an inversionary discourse. One of Mao's objectives was to secure his own particular version of Marxism as a deontology, a freestanding body of normative principles. The logic on which the principles were based had to be made explicit. It is in this respect that Mao's republic is closest to Plato's. And as with Plato's republic, the point was to make the transition to a self-sustaining moral system irreversible and timeless under the guidance of philosopher-kings. Mao's inversion imposed on the intellectuals a tutelary role that at the same time had to inspire and be inspired by those at the margin. It was this unity of opposites that gave Yan'an its special quality as a simulacrum. Unlike Plato's republic, however, Yan'an began as the conversion of time into space. It could not, by the same token, convert space into time.

The Cosmocratic Frame

These were the contexts in which Mao demonstrated agency and so connected a past of lost patrimonies to a millennial vision via revolutionary transformation. Among his abilities was an ability to give voice to ideas better than all others and to use the events of his life as a metaphor for China's search for the right road.

He had a capacity to connect story and theory, narrative and text, myth and logic by using the same events twice, the first time as sequence and the second as principle. Fictive truths served as evidence for logical principles, the structure behind the event. Logical principles project a millennial solution. The fictive truths are composed of metaphorical markers and metonymical meanings for the logical structure. A symbolic social text also becomes an analytical written text. Praxis in this sense is in the use of the first for the second to create an internal dialogue, a discourse. The addresser inducts the addressee into a new language in a reconstruction of social reality so total that to share in it is to be part of a discourse community.

To invent this totality and establish a discourse community such that it can generate symbolic capital is the fundamental objective. For Mao, fighting the Nationalists and the Japanese constituted the raw materials for the process; but, while these were ostensible reasons for revolutionary war, they were means to the larger end, the disjunctive and redeeming transformation of China as a whole. They gave to the communists that necessary urgency required to sustain a revolution of the *longue durée*.

Within this frame, Mao shifts back and forth between narrator and logician, storyteller and teacher, contextualizer and textualizer. He is the addresser and his audience is the addressee. But he needs something more active than an audience. The addressees must listen and internalize the principles learned. The audience becomes a student body. It learns a language. It forms a discourse community. In the ballet of Odysseus and Socrates the two come together in a more elevated cosmocratic role for Mao himself.

This follows from the implications of our phenomenological model, that human beings have two propensities, one to storytelling and the other, equal and opposite, to logical explanation. Mao's political leadership includes an exceptional ability to take command of both storytelling and logical explanation and make each contingent on the other in a context of shared and experienced events. He establishes a link between himself as addresser and his followers as addressees in such a fashion that a conveyance of the individual story to the collective occurs. The conveyance makes possible a new form of community based on symbolic capital.

The object is nothing less than a complete reconceptualization of the universe of experience and the language people use to explain it, the interior goal being a new *doxa* and *habitus*—in short, a new normative, structural, and behavioral synthesis. Revealed to individuals is that insight into the larger scheme of things such that they become different from their former selves, and distant from others outside the community. Veterans of Yan'an use terms like "soaring" to describe their experiences there—an odd choice of term, since conditions of life on the ground kept pulling them back down to earth. Reality in Yan'an might be described as drudgery touched with excitement.

Mao uses his three stories to create the space for his version of Marxism. But it is also clear that he used theoretical criteria in order to construct the stories in the first place. Just as Mao received "instructions" from "below" by talking to people and suggesting the answers he wanted to hear, so he embedded in his stories the kind of logical lessons he wanted to derive. Mao was at one and the same time the voice speaking to a listening audience and a teacher lecturing a student body. At first the stories do not appear to have a logical purpose; the agent as voice hides the logic in the story so that it is not visible to the audience. But as they become more symbolically dense and metaphorically enriched, the stories soon offer a logical explanation that is used to interpret the surface tale. The ability to combine these ingredients is Mao's special quality.

His combination of myth and theory contains innovative leaps of considerable daring that better trained but more orthodox Chinese Marxists would never have attempted. Mao used his own version of the dialectic against both classical and Leninist Marxism while claiming their pedigree. He charged the orthodox with stereotyped thinking and divided them between "left" and "right" deviationists, opportunists and adventurists.

The fact was that with or without theory, Mao proved to be more correct than his opponents within the party, and eventually he came to prevail in the Party Center. So much so that the Party Center in due course would rewrite history just as the emperors did, and place Mao at the center of events in which in fact, if he was not at the periphery, he played only a secondary role.

Mao realized a vision of totality. He turned China upside down by institutionalizing his vision in structural terms, while universalizing it to fit the new circumstances. What he failed to reckon with sufficiently early was that older modes of thought thrown out the back door have a way of coming in by the front. Not even the Cultural Revolution could prevent the erosion of the vision, the corrupting of behavior in the form of *guanxi* socialism, and the revival of bureaucratic neofeudalism. Nor could it in the long run exorcise capitalism, which the post-1978 reforms have invited.

But not even today can the reformers among the old Yan'anites countenance the desire for individualism and liberalism, democracy and science, the original objects of the May Fourth Movement now so attractive to a younger generation. There is still the desire to sustain a monopoly of truth. Hence their effort to modernize economically but not politically while opening the door a little to diverse opinions shows that they accept the logic of liberalization but not the practice of democracy. How far one can go politically was sharply defined in a new simulacrum, this time for democracy, the student protest in Tiananmen Square.

II

YAN'AN AS A
MOBILIZATION SPACE

✳

Revolution must not only be considered in its overtly
known and conscious ins and outs, but in its brute appearance, whether it is the work of Puritans, Ency-
clopedists, Marxists, or Anarchists. Revolution, in its
significant historical existence, which still dominates the
present civilization, manifests itself to the eyes of a world
mute with fear as the sudden explosion of limitless riots.

Georges Bataille, "Propositions"

5

THE SURVIVING YAN'ANITES

✳

Many of those we interviewed looked back less in anger or repentance than nostalgia or, better, fondness for the worthier possibilities Yan'an offered. This attitude is common among the survivors of the Yan'an period. The more one interviews old Yan'anites the more one becomes aware that all remain marked by the experience. Most were young when they went there. Most received their most formative education in the context of a revolutionary simulacrum. They persist in professing a kind of sweetness about past sufferings no matter what their private emotions were at the time. They share a preoccupation with virtue that would bring joy to the heart of the most divine Puritan. These feelings are all the more intense because each of them went from being considered a revolutionary hero in the 1950s and early 1960s, with a secure place in society, to a traitor during the Cultural Revolution.

After several interviews with the same individual, we became aware of other characteristics as well. These former Yan'anites tend to disapprove of the path China took under the later Mao, not to mention the later Mao himself. But they also disapprove of the present course, the *guanxi* socialism that replaced the earlier tradition. They still inhabit a world of fictive truths and logical explanations. They learned their lessons using particular texts out of which a language was constructed—a language only they can fully speak and understand.[1] Hence, they are set apart not only by shared experiences but also by the instruction they received. Whatever else they may have been—soldier, artist, factory worker, cadre—they are above all Yan'anites, teachers at heart, the didactic impulse never very far from the surface.

Their nostalgia is less for the revolutionary band itself than the juxtaposition of purity and danger. More than loyalty, this tension produced bonds that were different from friendship or kinship and that personalized shared obligations to principle while it depersonalized commitment to individuals.

This was the special quality of the Yan'anites as a revolutionary band. This gave the group its privilege, distinguished it from conventional political groups, and provided it with the right in its own eyes to pass judgment on the laws and powers of the state from which it claimed to be exempt.

Today, no matter what their subsequent experiences, the historical Yan'anites represent a revolutionary alumni. They remain a discrete discourse community. They are acutely aware not only of the power of the word, but the codes that give it power, and these they still defend. They are sensitive to the canon of expressive formula and alert to even slight variations, to be sniffed, felt, and read as a peasant reads the wind.

All of them were taken by surprise by subsequent events, which normalized the revolution without institutionalizing its consequences. Almost all experienced this process from positions of power. They understood the strenuous efforts in China to sustain revolutionary momentum. But, in a sense, Yan'an was not a good preparation for what followed. It involved too much foreshortening of time and intensification of meaning. People were unprepared for the long term and its new hierarchies, as well as the practical difficulties and limitations imposed by intractable realities. Yan'an was a place where fictive truths created power. But, of course, such power creates its own realities.

For Yan'an was also a place of struggle, with the GMD, with the Japanese, and with its own inhabitants. Each of Mao's four struggles for power had to be won to elevate Mao from a local Odysseus to a Chinese Socrates. While each constituted an important dimension of power essential for his monopoly of truth, they also served as "trials" or obstacles necessary to be overcome as part of the transition of Mao from an agent of history to agency itself.

But who were the objects of these endeavors? For whom did Mao come to represent agency?

Those in Yan'an joined a band whose defining characteristic was the substantive redefinition of the situation with acts and intentions following from that. A context such as this is quite rare and depends, as we have shown, on both fictive and logical elements. Once formed into a discourse shared by all those within a mobilization space the new interpretive scheme becomes objectified in the terrain itself.

Those who shared the discourse made up the core of Yan'an. One would expect them to be a band of ideological fanatics. What is so surprising is that, with few exceptions, there is virtually no evidence of fanaticism. (In the case of Kang Sheng, at the time—as distinct from in retrospect—his motives seemed to be above suspicion.)[2] Mao himself was frequently described as exuding a certain common sense, the kind of practical wisdom that seemed to characterize Yan'an more generally. As Shum Kui-Kwong put it, "In this light what is generally called Yan'an Communism (in itself a misnomer) is characterized by moderation, reformism, and pragmatism rather than radicalism or revolutionary romanticism."[3] What one needs to add however, is that what emerges from these interviews is the seriousness with which learning was regarded. There was a sustained enthusiasm for virtually incessant political discussions that must have been exhausting. Participation in meetings and debates on resolutions was required. Nothing could be taken for granted.

One can say that Yan'an generated its own internal information, with politics less a system than a kind of energy—and that there was a surplus of such energy, which was expended in a variety of virtually superhuman activities, and which was communicated to other base areas and behind enemy lines.[4]

Paradoxically, excepting those at the top, very few Yan'anites ever knew or seemed to want to know what was going on at the Party Center. There seemed to be a good reason for everything that happened.[5] They had almost no concern with higher CCP politics. Most preferred to leave things to those responsible, letting the leadership concern itself with the important issues. They trusted the leadership to make the best decisions on their behalf; they had little direct involvement in the decisions themselves. They did become involved in determining how best to carry out such decisions. Thus, despite the appearance of unity in Yan'an there was a world of difference between those at the top and those at the bottom. At the bottom, one shared and learned through discussion, and then carried out one's assignments.

In this way, political beliefs were deliberately embedded in the Yan'anites' daily tasks. All the intentionalities—the purposeful and meaningful wider objects of meaning—were routinized and collectivized, from the time they had to go to bed at night to when they were to get to work in the morning, to when and where they bathed, to appropriate attitudes to have toward the wounded or the sick. Yet no one mentioned the word "regimentation." So much did belief became a *doxa*, a communist ordinary, that the rhythm and routine penetrated all thinking and action, movement and stasis, separation and association, and, not incidentally, improvement and promotion.

What sharply cuts through Yan'anites' consciousness, especially in retrospect, are the Rectification and "Rescue" Campaigns. The impact of these campaigns is clearly demonstrated by the differences between our interviews and those conducted earlier in Yan'an.[6] Prerectification Yan'an had a much more experimental atmosphere. There was greater freedom to try out new approaches. In theater, for example, one might try new themes; writers and artists might try to break with literary or artistic conventions. The revolution was the new, liberating China from the old. But increasingly after 1942, and beginning with literature and the arts, new political orthodoxies began to take over.[7]

To Each One's Own Yan'an

One of the first things one notes in the interviews is that almost everyone has, to one degree or another, his or her own Yan'an. Much depends on when they went there and in what capacity, as soldier, student, intellectual, or cadre. There are certain categories of people: the "four eccentrics" (Wang Shiwei, Xiao Jun, Sai Ke, and Xian Xinghai), the "five olds" (Dong Biwu, Xie Juezi, Wu Yujiang, Xu Teli, and Lin Boqu). Also depending on time and role, participants periodize Yan'an differently. Some divide it into four parts (military, student, rectification, stable political community), some three. For most, however, it is divided into two periods: prerectification, the period from 1936 to 1942, when Yan'an was a remarkably open community; and after 1942, when rectification engaged everyone in a highly systematic program of exegetical bonding, including textual analysis, and through this bonding created a discourse with its own interior language. It is in this latter period that we can begin to see how personal conveyance to the collectivity occurred "voluntarily, but not spontaneously," as one participant put it, and how symbolic capital was created.[8]

The common point of departure in all the personal stories is "joining the revolution" and "going home," as going to Yan'an was called. It represented both a psychic crossing and a physical one. To get to Yan'an was never easy. For many it represented a profound rupture, a separation, even a transgression of conventional life. One crossed all boundaries, in the mind and on the ground: ideological, jurisdictional, affiliational, territorial. So to "go home" was to "go over" (exactly how total this crossing was most did not realize until too late). Going to Yan'an was an act of rejection before it became an act of commitment. And because it usually meant a break with family, work, school, local authorities, or the GMD it took time and preparation to work up the courage to do it, a gestation period in which most became extremely vulnerable to the GMD authorities. They might have the "wrong" friends; they might read the wrong books. All this could be reported to the GMD. One entered into an atmosphere of clandestinity. Moreover, to make the break required organization. The penalties for getting caught were detention, often torture, sometimes even death. This was so much the case that as they recount their transition, the interviewees have two subjects: themselves, and themselves as China. Indeed, one might say that no matter how personal their account, their real subject is China. Each participant came to see her- or himself as a surrogate of the revolution. How each regards the consequences, however, varies a great deal.

But no matter how they feel about what the revolution produced, participating in it, as one of many, was a crucial experience. All were very young. All felt they made events happen. In this sense our interviewees became agents of historical truth. It set them permanently apart from ordinary people.[9] Moreover, they were in one fashion or another all elevated to the status of true heroes of the revolution before being cast down, beaten, and demeaned. What these informants remember about Yan'an is not only its benign and utopic side, but the first indication of what would happen in the Cultural Revolution. In retrospect they all remember the flaw in utopia.

These are some of the things one needs to know in order to contextualize the interviews. In addition, it is important to note that most of these stories have been retold and relived many times, to the point where distortions are perceived as realities. With each telling, the negative pole becomes redefined and simplified, the break marked by a particular event. Memory changes actual circumstances and situations.[10] What is said must be taken with more than the usual pinch of salt. Yet much mutual corroboration also comes through, enough to provide something of the feel of how life was lived, especially when the interviews are interpreted in the light of more contemporary accounts.[11]

Four distinct categories of Yan'anites can be identified. The original group consists of remnants of the First, Second, and Fourth Front Armies that made the Long March to the border area. The second group, the main core, consisted of young students, a significant proportion of intellectuals who had left school and begun to work, cadres reassigned to Yan'an, and peasant-soldiers who showed promise and were seconded to Yan'an to become students, as well as locals who entered the educational system at the base and were sent on for increasingly higher levels of education and training. The third group consisted of the larger base area population organized in county and district jurisdictions in what came to be called the "three-thirds" system of democracy. The fourth was outside Yan'an itself but linked to it in terms of both organization and effective participation in the discourse community.

These categories overlap. Students at any moment numbered about 50,000 and could include members of the other three groups. Of those who came to Yan'an from the outside, some did so because they feared remaining in Japanese-occupied China. This occupied area included Beijing, where students were forced to learn Japanese. Most of the students were motivated primarily by a combination of hatred for the Japanese invader and contempt and dislike of the GMD. Almost all held progressive, radical views. Most had interrupted their schooling in middle or high schools, technical institutions, colleges, and universities in order to fight the Japanese.[12] Many were party and army cadres undergoing higher training. Some students were officers of the Red Army, including generals in need of political education or simply more advanced training in logistics or strategy.

Taken together, these different roles and networks constituted the structural frame of Yan'an. Extending the roles and networks to other base areas and behind enemy lines or in "white areas" (areas controlled by the GMD) became the primary consequence of participants' education and training.

Very few Yan'anites were "real" intellectuals, if we take a Lu Xun as the exemplary figure. Other "real intellectuals" like Lao She, a liberal and progressive writer, went to Chongqing or Kunming. They regarded Yan'an as somewhat remote from their own sense of Chinese political life, and found the place both barren and primitive in every sense of the term.[13] While only a few "real" intellectuals, such as Ding Ling or Wang Shiwei, did go to Yan'an, many intellectuals were formed there. Among them were individuals who became important in the subsequent political life of China, such as Li Rui, who was for a while Mao's secretary, or Wen Jize, who was extremely important in creating a radio broadcasting network. In Yan'an, Wen had been the record keeper at the "trial" of Wang Shiwei. Others would later become some of China's most distinguished filmmakers, photographers, leaders of dance troupes, and writers.

Among the most important intellectuals were those engaged in writing or literary work; translators of Marxist texts, for example, played a critical role. The newspapers were crucial. A printing press, disassembled and carried on the backs of the Red Army soldiers during the Long March, was reassembled at the highest point in Yan'an, the Cave of the 10,000 Buddhas. Anchored to the stone floor, surrounded by these figures of the Buddha, Yan'anites published first the *Red China News* and the *New China*

Daily, both of which were combined in 1941 to become *Liberation Daily.* Articles, directives, speeches of Mao, and more dangerous *zawen* (polemical essays) were not only the main intellectual fare, the base upon which everything was discussed, but the guiding voice of political life. These pieces set, explained, and put down the agenda. They communicated items of common concern. They literally orchestrated one campaign after another. Yan'an was a place where the written word was indeed crucial for the discourse, the language formed. Yet, for the most part, the journalists and newspaper workers, one hundred or so in all, had little if any previous experience.[14] The editorial groups, all of whom used the one printing press, were intense and hardworking. All were closely connected to institutions such as the Academy of Marxism-Leninism or the Central Party School.

Yan'an formed a kind of theater, or agora, where large numbers could sit and listen to their officers or leaders face to face, and within the sound of the human voice. Through the many meetings, one spoke into a sea of faces. Within this theater were traveling troupes of actors and actresses who put on melodramas and acted out stories for their audiences, who usually sat in the open air. Performances were frequent and highly professional, and great efforts were made over the costumes.[15]

To younger people, the atmosphere resembled a scouting, YMCA, or Outward Bound camp. Since it was very expensive to get to Yan'an, the children there tended to be from either well-to-do or extremely impoverished backgrounds. The former were struck by how harsh life was in Yan'an, while the latter found it something of a promised land. The well-to-do found the basic necessaries of life either absent or in extremely short supply. For those from the south, eating millet instead of rice became the symbol of hardship. There was, however, a sense of the heroic about doing without and a pride in collectivized poverty. Life in Yan'an was regarded as a kind of Spartanism in which the body was purified and hardened, the precondition of a virtuous communism.

Students and Intellectuals

For the very young, who arrived with their parents and "grew up drinking the water of the Yellow River," their idea of Yan'an was formed both by the vicissitudes of getting there and by the network of institutions into which they were inducted. Yan'an for them "nestled" in the mountains and they "nestled" in Yan'an, in kindergarten and primary school. One woman, a very important economist now in her early sixties at the Chinese Academy of Social Sciences (itself a distant successor to the Yan'an Academy of Marxism–Leninism), went to Yan'an as a child. Her description captures this sense of nurture particularly well.

She described "her" Yan'an as a "spirited, colorful world" and her own experiences as "rich." She was nine years old when she arrived, and fourteen when she was sent to the army to do radio code work. The life she describes in Yan'an is based almost entirely on educational experiences. In her case, Yan'an became home after two years of wandering under conditions of extreme danger to herself and her mother.

She came from a rich but declining landlord family. Her mother, orphaned at an early age, was brought up by an uncle, a rich merchant. A very strong woman, her mother refused the marriage the uncle had arranged for her and went to Beijing University, where she fell in love with a Mongol student. The uncle refused to allow an "interracial" marriage. As a result, the mother left home and went to Shanghai where she married her Mongol, who became a professor in Beijing. Because of his leftist, progressive views, he fled to Chongqing when the Japanese took over Beijing, leaving his wife and four children behind. His wife, who did not want her children educated either in Japanese or under the Japanese and who did not know the whereabouts of her husband, decided to go to Yan'an.

Leaving her youngest child behind, and taking with her a young, rich cousin, whom she wanted to save from a future she knew would work against him, she made her way to Shanghai. She arrived penniless, having sold all her belongings. From Shanghai the family made its way to Yan'an in stages. At each stop the mother would find a teaching job and stay just long enough to accumulate enough money for the next stage of the journey. Since it was extremely difficult to get to Yan'an, her route was circuitous, from Shanghai to Hong Kong, then to Burma, Kunming, Chongqing, Xi'an, and finally Yan'an. All told it took two years, infinity to a child. Miraculously, in Yan'an they were reunited with the father, who had become a high-ranking cadre in the Central Party School. Her mother was made a teacher at the North Shaanxi Public School. The daughter went to kindergarten; the rich cousin, to a science institute.

The kindergarten became the girl's cocoon, and her permanent memory of Yan'an, even more so than the primary and middle schools she also attended in Yan'an. The kindergarten was a boarding school some eighty miles from Yan'an City. There were no classrooms. Teaching took place in the open air; when the weather became too bad the children were sent back to their families elsewhere in Yan'an. Our informant recalled that, prior to 1940 and the production campaigns, they had no stockings, and in winter they had to share overcoats. They received one-half kilogram of rice per day.

Despite such hard conditions, this kindergarten was a special place. Consisting of some five hundred children (mostly of cadre families with a few locals), volunteer teachers, and outside support (some even coming from one of the Soong sisters), the kindergarten was very much an elite establishment. The reason was simple. Senior cadres did not have time to be parents, not only because of their practical responsibilities but also because they were often students themselves. Studying as well as working, they also had to forage for and cut wood for cooking and making charcoal (for heating the caves they occupied), grow their own vegetables, extract cooking oil, and make cloth and clothes. Hence they could not be expected to cope with small children.

The woman we interviewed noted that the vast majority of children in the kindergarten, primary, and middle schools came from much the same backgrounds. Asked about children from peasant families, she said there were some from the immediate vicinity, adding that a number of the most important of today's political leaders who came from peasant stock had attended that kindergarten. Most peasant children, however, were not allowed by their parents to go on to primary school, since the children were needed for work, the area being one of the most desperately poor in China. Thus, one could say that the kindergarten was a good example of what might be called functional inequalities—that is, inequalities that enabled individuals to perform better in their main jobs.[16]

What she remembered best was the nurturing attitude of the teachers, whom she described as "more than teachers, not like teachers today." She described their extraordinary kindness and concern, how they would wash the feet of children who were in danger of getting blisters and so not being able to walk properly, and the compassion with which they treated bed wetters. Above all it was the teachers' absence of anger, even in the face of the rigors and extremely harsh conditions of life, that impressed her most.

Once in primary school, the children began learning to read and write Chinese, and to study Chinese culture, mathematics, and world affairs. They wrote on the ground. They used wooden tablets, which they hung around their necks, for math. Each student was given one piece of paper per day.

Among the things that struck our informant was that there was less discrimination between men and women teachers than now. Of her schooling in general she said most of the learning was "just storytelling.

We received education almost unconsciously." She described how one accepted whatever job one was given. There was no such thing as a good or bad job. Just as all work was necessary and therefore equal, so, despite disparities of class backgrounds in Yan'an, all people were equal. When asked to define equality, she replied that it was "mutual responsibility." All work was necessary; therefore, people were equal.

Here then is Yan'an seen through the eyes of a child. It is protective, warm, and affectionate. After two years of danger and wandering she was placed under the protection of family and school, and was united with her father, a high party cadre. Yan'an had this nurturing effect on many. It formed their sense of how the world ought to be, despite, or perhaps because of, its harsh physical conditions.

✳

ANOTHER PERSON we interviewed went to Yan'an as a young married man and became a journalist for the Xinhua News Agency. He made a sharp distinction between the Yan'an he admired most and the Yan'an that evolved after the Rectification Campaign. Arriving with his wife in Yan'an via Xi'an in 1939, the man says the first thing they noticed was a sign saying "Fight Liberalism." He was also struck by Yan'an's emphasis on enlightenment and harmony.

The young man came from a well-to-do family. He had a strict Confucian upbringing and retained strong filial principles of obligation, but now they were given to the party. When he and his wife decided to go to Yan'an, they left all their possessions behind. Passionately anti-Japanese, they regarded themselves as progressive. They considered Marxism a non-hierarchical way of fulfilling Confucian ideals of virtue.

Early life in Yan'an was open. What impressed him was that superiors did not impose their ideas. They used reason instead. You were allowed to keep your viewpoint and talk about it. There was no limit except that one could not openly attack communism. Yan'an was thus, before 1942, democratic. It was governed by the rule of law.[17]

The main job was study. Students lived eight to a cave. A bugle awakened them at 6:00 A.M. in summer and 7:00 A.M. in winter. In the mornings there were lectures, in the afternoon and evenings self-study and production work. People went to bed around 9:00 P.M. because there was no electricity and no kerosene lamps. What light they had in the evenings was from homemade lamps: containers with a bit of cooking oil and a cotton wick. They had Sunday off; that day they would bathe in the river. Because there were no radios (only very high-ranking cadres had them) they relied on newspapers, the most important after 1941 being *Liberation Daily*. Movies were run on a manual projector. Films were mostly Chinese with an occasional Russian one. Life was hard, but happy.

Our informant regarded himself a "real" intellectual. He was a close friend of Wang Shiwei, who, as we have seen, became one of the prime targets in the early days of rectification. Like Wang, he found a great many things wrong with Yan'an he felt could easily be set right. The kindergarten, he said, was only one example of the many distinctions being made among Yan'anites, despite the verbal emphasis on equality. He noted sharp discrepancies in material conditions, and was taken aback by what he saw as privileges of rank. It bothered him that some people had to walk, while the senior cadres rode on horseback. He did not believe that the small inequalities in Yan'an were small at all; rather, they were more offensive and visible than in society outside Yan'an where there were no pretensions to equality.

He also believed in democracy, which for him meant decentralization and local autonomy. For the party, however, democracy meant centralization. He advocated decentralization against centralization. For these and similar reasons, he and some of his friends became partially "estranged."

However, the party showed him the error of his ways. He was given to understand that such criticism represented petty bourgeois characteristics and that these were personal defects. To become a whole person, one had to rid oneself of such defects. One had to engage in "ideological remolding," a purification rite whereby one eradicated "evil" ideas. This process caused him to view absolute equality as a liberalistic-anarchist notion that did not take into account the differences in need and work that a society requires. He came to see that the notion of total equality was infantile.

He discovered that he was, without knowing it, a "liberal" and that liberalism was egoism. It attached more importance to the individual than the collectivity. It was liberalism that led people to speak behind each other's back instead of airing views frankly and face to face in public. He was made to understand that the self needs to diminish in favor of the collectivity so that the collectivity could enhance the self.

As for democracy, the party taught him that decentralization would dissolve the necessary solidarity of the collectivity and that democratic centralism is the true essence of democracy. Particularly after 1942, he was made to realize that these petty bourgeois "deficiencies" were defects in understanding. He was "invited" to improve his understanding of communism. In doing so he received certain benefits. For example, before remolding he was subject to great fluctuations of mood. If there was a victory against the Japanese, he felt exultation; a defeat filled him with despair. Indeed, during the dark days after 1940, when the GMD imposed its blockade, he became fearful and became disillusioned with the whole enterprise. He thought it would fail. Ideological remolding taught him to emancipate himself from this way of seeing things. He realized how necessary it was to understand the larger forces behind an event and to translate defeats and victories into tactical terms. A defeat now could be the basis for a victory later. One did not become Olympian, but one had to sense the larger principles at work underneath the shifting sands of events.

Specifically he learned the following:

1. Although one could see communism as a system in which people do not have to worry about where such necessities of life as soap, fat, meat, and shelter come from, this conception is superficial. Communism is a system, an idea, an outlook, a way of looking at the world according to dialectical principles.
2. Social and political life will always evolve through the following stages: primitive society, slave society, feudalism, capitalism, socialism, and communism. Capitalism brought about the demise of feudalism. Hence China was engaged in a double revolution, first capitalist and then socialist, the two together realizing themselves eventually as communism.
3. The fundamental principle of the CCP was to serve the people; hence, a good party member had to be the first to worry about the world but the last to enjoy its benefits.
4. A good party member embraces three working principles: combine theory with practice; remain close to the masses; and engage in continuous criticism and self-criticism.
5. Party education must always govern one's personal life.

Taken together, these five concepts "constitute norms governing our behavior." Once he realized this, our informant says, "I was no longer afraid of harsh conditions."

Despite his best efforts as a communist, he confesses to still having residual petty bourgeois characteristics. These were revealed to him during the Cultural Revolution. He still lacks the necessary revolutionary passion and determination. He thinks this is true of many if not most intellectuals. He believes that the best way to understand Mao Zedong Thought is to know "who Mao's targets were at every moment."[18]

This second view of Yan'an is that of a total and wrenching upheaval, a negation of self brought about by rectification. This was a common experience of progressive intellectuals who, thoughtful and sincere, came to Yan'an because they were anxious to do their duty in the anti-Japanese war, convinced that Chiang Kai-shek and the Nationalists were corrupt and incapable of redeeming the Chinese people. While our first case is a story of growing up in Yan'an, our second is a story of giving up the self for to live a life of the self is to live the wrong story, a life of error despite good intentions.

❊

THOSE FROM the "highest" families sometimes found communism literally forced on them by the GMD. Rebellious rather than radical, and threatened with punishment for relatively mild forms of protest, they became radicalized, sought out others, and then, under fear of arrest and maltreatment, located party units. They became communists as much from a reaction to the GMD as from any positive attraction to Marxism.

One woman, also an economist, describes this pattern. Her great-grand-father was a county head and an official of the Fourth Grade in the Mandarinate. Her grandfather was a famous Confucian scholar. The family came from Guilin, which she saw as the most feudal area of China. As she put it, she got into trouble "because I liked reading." There were only a few schools for girls, and she found her life in a girls' middle school very restrictive. She became involved in a protest and was expelled. She moved on to a more liberal school, where the superintendent was the uncle of a revolutionary leader (later killed in the 1946 plane crash in which a number of high-ranking CCP cadres were killed). The school was unusual for its time because it took in both boys and girls. There she learned to write much better.

She then went on to higher middle school and became friendly with a girl whom the local authorities did not like. The provincial government asked that this girl be removed from the school. Our informant and her friends protested to the Bureau of Education, and once again she was expelled.

It was now 1936 and she was sixteen. She went to Chongqing to enroll in a higher middle school sponsored by Christian missionaries. She refused religious instruction and could not be convinced of the existence of God. Within six months she was expelled for the third time.

Although not a Christian, she was fed up with the GMD educational system and decided at the urging of a classmate to join a Self-Reliance Reading Society at the YMCA. There, she and some friends organized a

Marxist reading group, which read the work of writers such as Mao Dun, Lu Xun, Ai Siqi, and Maxim Gorky. Her home became a meeting place for what her parents thought were Christian youth. Indeed, she became chair of the Self-Reliance Reading Society. Of course she did not tell her family her views.

She developed contacts with underground party groups, one of which tipped off a radical uncle of hers that the GMD was about to take her into custody. In those days, a high proportion of women and young girls so taken were raped, tortured, and killed. Through a friend of the uncle, she fled to an Eighth Route Army branch headquarters where she stayed for several days under the wing of the secretary of the Southern Bureau, and then proceeded to the Eighth Route Army office in Xi'an. There, with a nineteen-year-old girl, she disguised herself as a soldier, got into a truck, and proceeded past a GMD roadblock designed to catch students en route to Yan'an.[19]

In Yan'an her first assignment was to edit a history of the youth movement. She then asked to be able to continue her studies and was assigned to an institute that worked mainly with self-study rather than through course instruction. It did not undertake much research. You could, however, with others, set up courses as the need arose. In contrast, the Academy of Marxism-Leninism had lectures and courses. But, as she puts it, her real education began with rectification in 1942. She was assigned to the third department of the Central Party School, where intensive rectification was undertaken. Before this she was procommunist but not theoretical. Now she studied Marxist theory. What she absorbed was not only specific knowledge but the right point of view about life. If one lives for one's self, becoming selfish, one will not be respected. Life should be devoted to the emancipation of the masses. But to do this properly one had to understand Marxism. Hence the Rectification Campaign was for her the beginning of her real education. Unfortunately, early on, Kang Sheng, one of those in charge of instruction and an "extreme leftist," undertook a so-called Rescue Campaign. In this he made several "mistakes," one of which was to believe that people from the wrong backgrounds and the "white" areas were likely to be spies. Not only had she come from the wrong background and come from a white area but in Yan'an she had the misfortune to be working under someone Kang Sheng believed was a spy. Kang Sheng also held the view that especially women from the wrong background were spies—woman spies being something of an obsession with him. As a result, our informant was treated very badly until Mao called the Rescue Campaign off and chastised Kang Sheng.[20]

Rectification formally began on February 1, 1942, with Mao's speech "Reform in Learning, the Party, and Literature."[21] Our informant and her co-workers were provided with a book that was compiled for study but never published for outside consumption, entitled "Documents of the Rectification Campaign." It included such essays as Mao's "Combat Liberalism" and Liu Shaoqi's "How to Be a Good Communist" as well as others by Chinese and non-Chinese writers. "We studied the documents by ourselves. Two or three times a week we had a group discussion. It was our job to study and not to send comments back to the Central Committee, but some comments did find their way back. We accepted what the Central Committee said."

Her knowledge of Marxism now became deepened in four ways. First of all, she learned how to better achieve her goals. Her original concern was based on two goals: how to make China prosperous, and how to make it powerful. But she and her friends in the party had no idea how these goals could be realized. They did not know how to proceed towards them. Mao's theory taught them to learn the message from the people. "Now we realized that our knowledge was too abstract. We discovered that our world of study, which we thought was broadening us, actually represented a cramped view of life. Coming closer to the people gave us a wider view."

Second, she learned to base her understanding of Marxism on principles, not characteristics. "We now understood that socialism had two stages: a lower one, socialism; and a higher one, communism." The first represented distribution according to work and the second according to need. The first represented a strategy for achieving the second, which was the final goal.

Third, she came to understand that in order to achieve this goal a methodology was required. Its object was to combine theory and practice correctly. Most of the ideas for the methodology were found in a book by a Soviet philosopher entitled "Basic Readings for the Cadres."

Finally, she clearly understood that the party was the pioneer of the working class, that Mao's thoughts were the thoughts of the party and the working class, and that he was only expressing the correct interpretations of large historical tendencies.

What comes through in this interview is, first, the tension between this woman's class background and the appropriate way to connect to the Chinese people as potentiality. Rectification became a means for her to make that connection. Once she had made it, she was able to understand how Marxism-Leninism, as a body of universal truths and methods, would show how, with the peasantry, Chinese potential could be realized. For her, study was itself a form of fulfilment. The idea of communism being the final stage of evolution represented a symbol she could fill up because it was intrinsically empty. She could convert all her yearning into a powerful unity of self and community, China and the world, according to dialectical rules of total transformation. Yan'an enabled her to arrive at what might be called a "symbolic infinitude."

✳

A LEADING journalist who had been with *Liberation Daily* all his working life called Yan'an the "sacred place of the revolution." When he went to Yan'an at the end of 1937, he was a university student from Sichuan Province, the son of a rich peasant who took part in anti-Japanese activities. He became a member of a group called the Revolutionary Liberation Vanguard, which was sympathetic to the CCP and took the position that there were only two choices for Chinese students, slavery or fighting back. He went to Yan'an via Xi'an on foot. Before arriving in Yan'an itself, he was sent to a Youth Training Class at a training college run by a famous Fourth Front Army General.

There people studied party policy on the united front, guerrilla warfare, the principles of the "New Democracy" movement, and its relation to Sun Yat-sen's alliance with Russia on the one hand and the CCP's alliance with workers and peasants on the other. The program usually took two to three months, but our informant proceeded more quickly. Most of the participants had no background in Marxism-Leninism, and had a letter of introduction from some Red Army officer or CCP official. Our informant had already studied communist ideas, and he had letters from the Youth Wing of the Revolutionary Liberation Vanguard. He walked for eight days. The journey to Yan'an was very dangerous, since the GMD had set up road blocks to intercept the students. Anyone caught was arrested.[22] With two others, he made his way to Yan'an without any armed Red Army squad accompanying them.

He entered Kangda in February 1938 for the fourth course. The aim of this university was to train three kinds of people: military cadres, political workers, and "organizers of people." Although originally Kangda was established to train Red Army members, by the third course, it began accepting students as well as soldiers. At the time, Lin Biao was president.

The students at Kangda were divided along military lines into brigades, squadrons, and teams. There were eighty to ninety students in a team. The training course took six months; our informant's ended in September 1938. The curriculum consisted of political economy, philosophy, guerrilla warfare, and party history, plus occasional lectures on current affairs and the politics of the united front. Everyone also underwent military training. In the war games, students were divided into two teams, the enemy and the CCP. They were observed by instructors, who would comment on their performance. Everyone also participated in student activities, including those of the National Salvation Clubs, where students would put articles and written comments on the walls for others to read and discuss.

Our student was then assigned to the Academy of Marxism-Leninism under president Luo Fu (Zhang Wentian), then Secretary General of the CCP. Here the courses were more regular than at Kangda and covered political economy, philosophy (taught by Ai Siqi), and world history. Each lecturer compiled his own materials. There were many other lectures as well, such as Liu's "How to Be a Good Communist." Mao also lectured to large crowds. His lectures were highly philosophical. "He was good at explaining very complicated philosophical ideas in very simple metaphors, especially using some practical Chinese expressions," according to our interviewee. Perhaps Mao's most influential lecture was "On Protracted War." Most of Mao's writings in this and the earlier period were originally lectures. Students never criticized the lectures because they all agreed with them. After each one, they organized discussion sessions to deepen their understanding of the main points.

"On Protracted War" made a deep impression on our informant. This lecture shows how Mao's mind works. In it, Mao pointed out the two dominant views in China about the anti-Japanese war. One was that China was too weak to fight the Japanese and would be subjugated if it tried to fight back. The other was that the Japanese would soon be defeated. Mao showed that both these views are wrong. He contended that China would win by means of a protracted war. "This seemed exactly right to me," said our informant. The other lecture by Mao that made a deep impression on him at the time was given at the Yan'an Forum on Literature and Art.

"The curriculum of the Academy of Marxism-Leninism had three parts," said our informant: "philosophy, social science, and political economy. The books that most influenced me were Marx's *Communist Manifesto*, Engels' *Socialism, Utopian and Scientific*, *The History of the Communist Party of the Soviet Union (Bolshevik)*, Lenin's *Left-Wing Communism, an Infantile Disorder*, and Stalin's *Introduction to Leninism*." He also found Stalin's essay on dialectical and historical materialism particularly valuable.

"We came to regard Yan'an as the big school of the revolution," he said. "There we had two kinds of education: the kind you learn from books, and the kind you learn from experience. We were inspired by the Red Army during the Long March. We were told of their crossing the snowy mountains and the grasslands. We were taught military discipline by Red Army instructors from the Long March."

Soldiers and Commanders

Just as experience, the second kind of education at Yan'an, was different from the kind of education gained from books, the soldiers at Yan'an were different from the intellectuals. Some of these differences are immediately apparent in interviews with former Red Army and Eighth Route Army veterans. One former commander from Sichuan Province came from a very poor peasant family. His family had to pay the landlord a rent consisting of sixty percent of their farm's annual yield, retaining just forty percent for itself. Their own grain would last for about six months, after which they had to borrow from the landlord. As a result, they were constantly in debt. Some "spies" infiltrated the landlord's establishment, learned the layout, and stole weapons from him. There were six warlords in the area, but the Red Army "got rid of them and [the] captured weapons."

Near his village, the Red Army had set up a district soviet, and a smaller primary unit soviet nearby. It consisted of a guerrilla team, a Young Pioneer League (young people from sixteen to eighteen years of age), and a Children's League (children from twelve to fifteen). The slogans were antilandlord and antitaxation. The message was that the peasants must not fear abolishing taxes, overthrowing the landlords, and redistributing the land. The appeals were almost all local and agrarian.

The person we interviewed was the youngest in a family of three children. The eldest was taken away by the GMD, the second joined the Young Pioneers, and he joined the Children's League. At that time, there were no uniforms, just arm bands and hats with a red star. There were only a few weapons other than bamboo spears so every ten days or so they would go near the GMD areas and shoot rifles simply to show the GMD that they were armed. They had to hide in the mountains to escape detection from the air, and they would engage in small skirmishes with the enemy at night. They obtained food mainly by helping themselves to granary reserves kept by the landlords, but often they only ate one meal every other day. Despite these difficult conditions the unit he belonged to expanded, mainly because the message their propaganda teams brought to the villages was that if you join the Red Army you need never fear the landlord. Our informant became literate "on the march." In a column, each soldier carried a paper with two characters written on it, which the person behind would study. By the end of each march, those characters would be learned.

When he was old enough he joined the Red Army. He became a member of Zhang Guotao's Fourth Front Army and as such made the Long March. He described the conflict between Zhang's Fourth Front and Mao's First Front Army from the point of view of a soldier. He knew little of the rivalry between the two men but was bewildered by sudden changes in marching orders when, in 1935, Zhang Guotao's tactical and strategic preferences were directly opposed to Mao's. When he was assigned to a commander of logistics he became more aware of the intensity of the conflict, which ended tragically for the Fourth Front Army when it was divided, cut off, and partially destroyed. He was one of a group of six or seven hundred soldiers who managed to escape to Yan'an. However, it was not until 1937, when Zhang was "exposed" in Yan'an, that he realized what had been going on. He believes that the Soviet Union supported Zhang Guotao's desire to march to the Soviet border area. While he came to understand that Zhang Guotao opposed Mao, he did not answer when asked if he thought Zhang was right to do so.

In 1937, Yan'an was primarily a military base and had just recently become a legal area as a result of the reestablishment of the united front with the GMD. Although there were many young students around it was only in February 1938 that the party began to recruit large numbers of them. Then, from February to December 1938 alone, some eight thousand students came to Yan'an from Xi'an.

For him there were three stages in the evolution of Yan'an. The first stage, prior to 1938, was military; then Yan'an became a cadre training and educational center; and then, after 1942, it became a community. In his view, the Rectification Campaign was necessary because the intellectuals knew too much theory from books but did not have any practical experience. He does not mention Wang Ming.

Before the Japanese bombing of Yan'an in 1938 people lived mostly in abandoned residences, although some preferred caves. After the bombing, they dug caves. However, it was clear to him that Yan'an was a place that would eventually have to be abandoned. The only time he met Mao

Zedong was when they were preparing the line of retreat from Yan'an and Mao made a short speech saying, "We shall meet again at the Yellow River."

✳

ANOTHER ARMY view of Yan'an is afforded by a former guerrilla commander, for whom Yan'an was a "peaceful paradise." A thin, wiry chain-smoker, very compact and looking much younger than his years, this man was the son of a small or middle peasant from a tiny village in the Northwest. At age sixteen he was forced to marry a girl two years older than himself, whom he later divorced. After that he says he had no time to be married until 1949.

When he was a schoolchild there was a constant battle between the old-style teachers, who followed the tradition of the "Eight-Legged Essay," and those who followed the tradition of the May Fourth Movement. The contradiction between them was intense and drove some of the teachers away. One teacher could not reply when asked by the students what the purpose of education was. His replacement, a communist, told them the purpose was to become communists. Through this teacher's influence he decided to learn about communism. At age seventeen he joined the party. There were two communists in his entire village, himself and his uncle. He got involved in underground work, transmitting documents written in secret ink or hidden in his shoes.

People knew of Mao Zedong because of the Hunan investigations and the essay "A Single Spark Can Start a Prairie Fire."[23] They knew of the Jinggang Mountains and Zhu De. They had heard of the left line favored by Xu Haidong, and they admired Liu Zhidan. They knew that Mao corrected "leftist" and "rightist" mistakes.

After 1927 he had to leave the village; he went to work underground. In 1929 his home was one hotel room after another. He was constantly on the move. He would occasionally return home for one night and two days. Sometimes he only got home once a year. His parents were very worried, his father in particular. When he returned, they were very happy to see him, but they feared that they too would get into trouble. In 1934 all his family members were driven out of their homes, and their land was taken. (Their property was returned in 1937.)

After spending time in underground work, he joined a guerrilla detachment that saw constant engagements. They had their own revolutionary base area, which was linked to others. They belonged to a division made up of seven independent battalions and several dozen guerrilla detachments. There were about a thousand men in his detachment, although sometimes they would have double that number. He remembers the first time he killed one of the enemy and how happy he felt. He could only think that if he did not kill the enemy he would be killed himself. The only time he was a little nervous was in his first battle because he knew that "either you eat the enemy or he eats you." His detachment had very little communication with other areas. They had no communication with Yan'an in the early days and did not know, for example, of the Xi'an Incident. His detachment was highly autonomous.

When not fighting they engaged in education. Peasants needed to be taught to aim their rifles. Without training they would just point and shoot, not bothering to aim at all. They also had to learn to read and write. They studied their own battles to learn from them. They had a party commissar as political instructor who taught them basic literacy and provided an introduction to world affairs. They also learned the "three points of discipline" and the "eight points of attention." Military instruction was the most critical and urgent part of the curriculum. They learned a lot about small arms. The detachment was supplied first by the Japanese and later by the Americans. The best pistols were German Mausers. The best all-around weapon was the carbine. But, he said, the machine gun was best of all.

Sometimes a new recruit would be in the detachment for only two hours before being killed in battle. Many of his detachment were killed when they were only sixteen or seventeen years of age. Sometimes they would take a column of recruits to the base area and en route be attacked and many wiped out before the newcomers had even held a gun in their hands. They lost soldiers in every battle.

Their area was completely surrounded by warlord armies and the GMD. At first named a Red Army Detachment Commander, he rose to become political commissar for the division. The first leaders from his division began going to Yan'an for training in 1937; he went in 1938. It was a peaceful place. In his base area there was no food and one constantly had to forage for it. But food and drink were plentiful in Yan'an. He was assigned to the party school for study, but after one week he was sent to reclaim waste land for a year. In December 1939, he graduated from the school and was sent to study at the Academy of Marxism-Leninism. Again after two weeks they sent him out as a cadre in the production campaigns. After that he graduated from the Academy and was sent first to the Northwest Bureau and then to Yan'an City. Eventually, he became chairman of the Yan'an City Committee and remained there for thirty years—

except for the three years he spent in a cow-shed and the seven years in forced labor during the Cultural Revolution.

His earliest days in Yan'an were the best. It was peaceful. He had confidence in the party leaders. Zhu De was very even-tempered. There was no tension between leaders and no gossip. "If the heavens fell down, the leaders would pick it up." The committee of which he was chairman was elected by the party congress of the city. Yan'an City was composed mainly of cadres, students, and intellectuals, the latter including students from middle school or above. The city itself was organized in four districts, each with its own administrator. Each district was divided into smaller *danwei* (units). He and the committee were, in effect, the Yan'an City government and were also responsible for "guaranteeing" the party's Central Committee, the Northwest Bureau, the Border Region Government, and the Headquarters of the Eighth Route Army. In 1943, Mao asked him what he thought about his post and how he felt about his work. He replied, "Very comfortable." Mao replied, "It is said that it is the officials in the capital that have the most difficult job." He was apparently a very efficient administrator and helped organize subsequent production campaigns. The worst period for him was during the Rescue Campaign of Kang Sheng. But everyone knew that Kang Sheng had made a mistake.

Top party leaders went to the countryside quite often. Somewhat surprisingly, he said that apart from Mao, it was Bo Gu who knew most about peasant affairs. He himself and his committee members also went frequently to the countryside, especially in summer. On one occasion, he remembers, it was very hot, and they took off their clothes and went for a swim in the river. Then they saw Mao walking by. They were extremely embarrassed, but Mao only smiled and said, "It's hot."

✳

WE ALSO interviewed four men who joined the revolution as ordinary soldiers. All came from poor peasant backgrounds. They joined the CCP under fairly similar circumstances. One said the Red Army came through his village after leaving the Jinggang Mountains, and he tagged along as the Army continued on its way. A second had tried to join the army at age fifteen. After first being told to go back home as he was too young, they allowed him first to become a "Little Devil" or "Red Devil." He became a guard of the Front Line Committee and eventually became Mao's personal servant on the Long March. The third joined the party in 1930. After living a harsh life as a cowherd for the landlord, he became an apprentice, but was working under such miserable conditions that the

Red Army was for him a means of escape. An underground party committee in his village arranged matters for him. The fourth was simply
hungry all the time. He wanted food and had heard that the Red Army
fed its soldiers and did not abuse them too much like the warlord armies
or the GMD generals did.

All four took physical hardship for granted as a way of life. Its absence,
rather than its presence, was something to be remarked on. Hardship was
life itself. Most had bitter stories to tell of uncertainties. All regarded the
Long March as a remarkable experience, but not for reasons of physical
hardship. That they withstood easily (all four being very young at the
time). All of them were given education. The young soldier preoccupied
with food learned to be preoccupied with theory by eventually going to
Kangda.[74] Others were sent to party schools and Red Army training
centers. All talked about learning correct theory, which to them was what
Yan'an was all about.

One of the soldiers who had been sent to the North Shaanxi Public
School and was then reassigned to another institution describes rectification
in the following terms:

In 1934 the Fifth Extermination Campaign was defeated when we
escaped encirclement and began the Long March. Comrade Mao
Zedong won military power at Zunyi in 1935. We learned that the
Wang Ming line resulted in terrible mistakes. Positional warfare was
responsible for the loss of 90 percent of our base areas. All our work was
lost. The masses complained. We needed to know right from wrong.
Comrade Mao Zedong told us that the military question had been
resolved but not the ideological question. Rectification was designed to
tell us right from wrong and make the reasons clear. The Rectification
Campaign was the result of demands from the Red Army and the cadres.
In 1943 Comrade Mao Zedong told us that we had to rectify three bad
tendencies: dogmatism, sectarianism, and stereotypical writing. In my
party school there were three classes. I was in the second class which had
over two hundred students. It was made up of local and county-level
cadres. We had twenty-two documents to study plus two books, which
were collections of materials from before and after the Sixth Party
Congress.[25] Rectification continued for seven months. For the first four,
we studied the twenty-two texts and analyzed them. During the last
three months, we summarized the articles in the two books, to contrast
the wrong line of the documents by Wang Ming with those of the

correct line. By struggling against the Wang Ming line we discovered the right way.

The interviews with these four participants tended to ramble, and the soldiers at times became involved in reminiscences. However, three main themes emerged.

First, they took personal hardship for granted. Unlike the students, these soldiers rarely discussed food or physical difficulties. Events were struggles, and in the Red Army each was simply a challenge to be overcome. The demarcation points in their individual stories were battles, to be sure, but they were described mainly as postings. The four described them geographically, where they were sent, according to the type of unit; and according to responsibility, with responsibility accorded on the basis of training and education. One had been literate before Yan'an; the other three had to learn to read and write. All four were sent to Red Army schools, where they received additional training to become specialists in some field; and all were sent to party schools to learn Marxism. They described an extraordinarily well-organized yet highly diverse structure, with continuous meetings, discussions, and instruction on virtually every subject. Party directives were discussed. As the four tell their stories, they describe themselves emerging and becoming more differentiated or "individualized" with each new post.

One was sent to a party school and became a telegrapher, then a communications specialist in charge of highly sensitive coded materials. He was never allowed to go outside by himself. The members of his unit traveled in groups of three, to avoid either betraying or being betrayed. Another became Mao Zedong's batman. He described how he had to take care of Mao's horse, make sure the dispatches were properly mounted, make Mao's bed, and generally provide for Mao's necessities.[26] Another became a propaganda worker and then was sent by the army to organize union workers, eventually winding up in Yan'an as the manager of a machine shop employing one hundred workers.

In short, once they left the poverty-stricken life of the village and joined the Red Army, these men entered a world not only of military action, which they expected, but also of a wide range of activities that continuously challenged them and where they felt themselves enlarged and expanded. Eventually, if they did not become intellectuals, at least they became knowledgeable about Mao Zedong Thought. They could recite Mao's principles, but not in a mechanical way. Each did so with an air of personal discovery and amazement at how rich such ideas were and how related to his own experiences. Geographical, organizational, and educational factors all played a part in this sense of personal growth. They became aware of China as a whole country rather than just as their home province, and they developed a sense of the interconnecting networks between the Red Army and the party.

They liked Mao for several reasons. One was that "he had gone on foot to do research in five counties and had studied and knew Chinese society. He was the first to deny reform and emphasize revolution, define the role of the party, and emphasize armed struggle." Mao made them understand the need for cadres and organizational work if the armed struggle was to succeed. "Comrade Mao Zedong himself made the transition from idealist to materialist, who took from Confucius 'respect others, respect old people, love children,' but rejected its 'respect the emperor, respect the father.'"

Recalling his earliest days of service, one of the soldiers described Mao and Zhu De as being very close to ordinary soldiers. "Zhu De was in general command with Mao as political commissar. The two were inseparable." After Mao became chairman of the Jiangxi Soviet government, the soldier was reassigned to the guard of the Central Committee, which was then enlarged to form a model regiment.

> The regiment was sent to Fujian province. One day the regiment received a telegram from the Central Committee saying that they would have an important task—to receive Li De [Otto Braun], the Comintern representative. We were worried because we were operating in GMD-controlled territory and it was dangerous. A detachment was sent to get Li De. Although we did not realize it at the time, strategy changed after Li De's arrival and the Red Army began to lose battles. Later we heard that Mao had lost his power and that Li De and Wang Ming were in control.

But Mao and Zhu De never lost influence with the ordinary soldiers. In the winter of 1932, Mao went away for a long rest. Luo Fu (Zhang Wentian) never came to visit him, but others did. Later on, during the Long March, he noticed that Luo Fu was not respectful to Mao. It was only then that he and his fellow soldiers learned that Mao had been "excluded."

In describing their daily activities none of the four dwelt very much on the fighting that, especially in the early days, was more or less continuous. Even before they got to Yan'an, army life was about education and training. They never mentioned the monotony or boredom common to most soldiers. In Yan'an, their education became both more specialized and more political.

A second theme that runs through these interviews is the discrepancy between how the students and intellectuals regarded the soldiers and how the soldiers viewed the intellectuals. Asked about the first intellectuals they met and their reaction to them in Yan'an, the soldiers' response was that they had been nervous. They were nervous of the intellectuals in part because they thought they would appear ridiculous, uncouth, or stupid. Class and status in China were so bound up with being an "intellectual" that their reaction was not surprising. More surprising was that it did not seem to occur to the intellectuals to be nervous about peasants and soldiers. There might be difficulties in communication. They might have to study how to "learn from the people." But no intellectual interviewed ever used the term "nervous" when speaking of their relationships to peasants, workers, or soldiers.

When asked what made them nervous, the soldiers replied that the intellectuals wore funny hats and that there were other external things that they found curious about them, but what bothered them most was the way men and women associated so freely with one another.[27] The soldiers were shocked by this and considered it very wrong. The senior cadres who had left their wives behind, or divorced them, or lost track of them married the young women students, who on the whole did not consort with any but their own kind. Perhaps the sexual relationships between the soldiers, highly avoidant and with a mixture of barnyard humor and extreme shyness, was the most difficult for them to talk about. When asked about Mao's behavior with women, they laughed and refused to discuss it.

The third theme was the Rescue Campaign and its significance in changing their attitudes towards the intellectuals. This campaign, the intense part of which probably lasted only a few weeks in early 1943, made the soldiers very sympathetic towards the intellectuals. One of the ex-soldiers said, "They were terribly frightened. The Rescue Campaign terrified them." The campaign was based on the assumption that most of the intellectuals from the white areas were GMD spies or members of the Red Banner (a supposed pro–Zhang Guotao formation). Since a very high proportion of the intellectuals in Yan'an had come from either the white or the Japanese-controlled areas, almost all were rounded up. "So many were arrested that the caves could not hold them all," one interviewee told us. Nor was it only intellectuals who were involved. The soldier who had become the manager of a shop said that out of a hundred employees, sixty were picked up for questioning and many were arrested. At another shop nearby with thirty employees, four or five were arrested. In one place, the person arrested was in charge of food, so the members of the unit *(danwei)* went hungry.[28] Many local organizations protected their members by protesting. Our informant was asked to go to many meetings at which people confessed, but eventually he stopped going because he could not bear it. Everyone knew the confessions were false. The Rescue Campaign made the cadres and the army particularly sympathetic to the intellectuals. At the same time their own sense of inferiority completely disappeared.

Musicians and Artists

The Rescue Campaign affected virtually everyone, including some of the singers and musicians. One, originally from Xi'an, came to Yan'an from Mongolia at age sixteen. He was one of the "boy soldiers" or "Little Red Devils" described by Edgar Snow. In fact, he is one of the three in the front row of a photograph taken by Snow and published in *Red Star over China*.[29] He learned to play the flute and other instruments. "The Shaan-Gan-Ning Border Region was divided into five areas," he says. "We formed a small musical troupe which went around helping to form local groups so that they could perform in these areas. We were little more than children. I also wanted to write and wrote a play in two days. But it was not performed."

The songs he wrote were more successful, and some became famous Yan'an songs that are still sung. He and others in his group considered themselves more composers than players. The nature of the songs they composed changed radically after the Seventh Plenum (1945). Before that, they were told to write songs about the anti-Japanese war. After the plenum the focus was on fighting the revolution against the GMD. For example, the famous song "Once We Defeat the Japanese Soldiers We Can Go Home" was changed to "Once the Revolution Succeeds We Can Go Home." Another example of this change is in the opera "The White Haired Girl." During the anti-Japanese war the wicked landlord is not killed in the course of the opera. After the struggle shifts to the revolution, the landlord is killed at the end.

The composer was part of a small group of singers and players who regularly performed for Mao, Zhu De, and Zhou Enlai. They called themselves the Shaanxi Players. He played the drums and the flute for their dances. After playing Mao would invite them to have noodles. There were regular Saturday night dances for the top leadership, and the Shaanxi

Players came to know many visitors, including Agnes Smedley, Edgar and Helen Snow, and Anna Louise Strong. Agnes Smedley liked to dance, but she was clumsy. Anna Louise Strong was too big and too fat. Helen Snow was the most beautiful. Everyone loved her. She did tap dancing and tried to teach Mao to do the Charleston.

They were very upset when Mao switched wives and married Jiang Qing. When she was at the Lu Xun Academy she was very boastful. The way she caught Mao was this: Mao loved Beijing Opera. She would have his favorite opera performed frequently, she taking the role of the innocent young woman in the opera. But in real life she was not an innocent young woman. The interviewee came to know her very well but did not like her at all. When there was a dance and she came past them they would spit behind her.

Even though very young at the time of the Rescue Campaign, he was accused of being a spy. He was denounced by his *danwei* and even by some of his friends. However, someone had told them that he was a spy, so they thought they were doing their duty. He was put under local arrest in the *danwei* and not allowed out. So many people were accused at that time that he was not brought before Kang Sheng or any of the higher authorities. Eventually he was freed and rehabilitated. Mao told the members of his music troupe, "If someone calls you a spy, come to me and I will tell them you are not a spy." Our composer believes, however, that there were many spies during that period who were sent in by the GMD.[30] Asked about the Wang Shiwei affair, he said that it affected only a small group in the cultural field and was not well known at the time. Everyone believed in Mao. They liked the way he spoke. He had a warm, gentle, intimate style.

✳

AMONG THE more interesting people of those we interviewed was a film director who had been at the Lu Xun Academy in Yan'an and had known Jiang Qing since 1936. The film director lived in a double apartment when we met him and kept birds, which were allowed to perch freely throughout the living room and a glassed-in balcony. Very much a free spirit, much less disciplined in his way of thinking and speaking, and much more outspoken than the others, he remembers the early days of the anti-Japanese war before rectification as an extraordinary moment. For seven years he fought in the mountains, sometimes with nothing to eat except grass, which was boiled in water with a little flour. He wrote poems on stones, and also painted pictures on stones in the mountains so that someone would find them one day and wonder about them. His group opened many theaters in the countryside and wrote plays that required no costuming or backdrops. Eventually, he joined Ding Ling in the North West Frontier Stage Group, which was extremely free. He could write whatever he pleased. There was virtually no interference from above. He made pictures. He took part in performances. They played in courtyards and places where they thrashed wheat. It was realist theater. For a while they used a captured Japanese soldier to play the part of a Japanese character in some of the plays. They even played behind Japanese lines in occupied areas, sometimes not far from Japanese rest houses or destroyed pagodas.

Peasants would invite them in, and people from the village would gather. They provided food cooked earlier in containers so that it was not necessary to light fires at night, which might betray them to the Japanese. He and his group also formed a Military Working Group, which put on skits in which he acted. They carried guns so that if the Japanese came on them unexpectedly they could try to protect themselves. Their main strategy, however, was to withdraw.

Although the director had been very much a city person from Shanghai, during these years, while he was constantly on the move and living with peasants, he forgot about city life. In 1943, during the Rescue Campaign, he was sent to Yan'an to teach at the Lu Xun Academy. Since he had worked in the white areas, his friends were afraid to recognize him. People were afraid. The fear remained pervasive even after the campaign was over.

Our informant had no direct experience of Wang Shiwei and was not in Yan'an during that affair. He knew that "Wild Lily" was regarded as an anticommunist *zawen*. It seemed to him that the fate of Wang Shiwei was intended to teach the intellectuals a lesson. He could never understand why Mao relied so heavily on Kang Sheng. The purpose of the Rescue Campaign was to protect the party, but Kang Sheng went overboard and for a while Mao seemed afraid to rein him in.

Many people in the lower echelons of the art circles were really stupid, according to the director. They did Kang Sheng's dirty work and turned in their friends. "In our hearts we remember what they did. We say hello to everyone, but we remember, we remember. We often name dogs after these people. We talk about everything as a joke." But rectification itself was necessary. "If you did not rectify revolutionaries you would never have been able to make the revolution." He himself thought he had nothing to fear because of his experiences at the front. He did not think he needed rectification but that, in general, it was a good idea to try to summarize the party experience, especially in the countryside.

His first contact with Jiang Qing was in 1936. He knew her, and all her past lovers, extremely well. Although in the theater section at Lu Xun, she was a poor actress. He could not understand why Mao took to her. "She had her method of getting Mao to listen to her," he surmised. She and Mao came together while her main lover was elsewhere in China. Today this former lover lives in Paris. Our informant helped established the Yan'an Film Studio, which Jiang Qing was also involved in, and where he made his first film, *Model Laborer*.

The director thought Mao an interesting man who had a zest for life. He saw quite a bit of Mao and took many pictures of him. Occasionally Mao would ask him for all the names he knew for a plant or a flower. Once he went with Mao to a river. Mao asked him if he knew the name of the river. He did not. Mao provided the name and told him it was named after a goddess.

He and Mao shared something of the spirit of the restless wanderer. Mao was endlessly curious. For example, he asked about cameras, so the director "talked to him about aperture, light, and film." Mao liked being photographed and encouraged it. Both of them believed that "life is the basis of art." Our director believed in particular that "without life we can not create." But the Yan'an forum was terrible. "Mao made art utilitarian, a matter of conscious policy. This was very wrong. People need to enjoy the beautiful." Many people believe that art should be used in politics. While Mao opposed art in "slogans," he "had many contradictions. For him, words were soldiers."

The director had many friends among the foreigners in Yan'an, including Norman Bethune, George Hatem, and Agnes Smedley. He felt that they really understood that China was feudal and backward. "Sometimes I thought they were more concerned about this country than I was." Smedley was wonderful. She had a hard time. She lived in a cave. But she loved the revolution, was very sympathetic, braved every hardship, and took the Yan'an message to the world.

He remained a free spirit until the Cultural Revolution. Then he and his family were singled out for special punishment by Jiang Qing. His sister, a famous actress, was beaten to death by the Red Guards. His own wife was killed. Everything, including the Song and Tang pots he collected and hundreds of photographs of Mao, were all destroyed. "Today in our society people have no life, no experience. Without life one can not understand."

✳

AMONG THE intellectuals in particular there is retrospective sadness. Among the artists there is much more cynicism. The artists lived for their art and played the game of survival. But even among them there is a sense of having participated in something extraordinary at Yan'an.

Yan'an Recollected

If one had to describe Yan'an in terms of these interviews one could perhaps call it utopic, rather than utopian, and situate it between nurture and rupture. Nurture there was, as embodied in the nostalgic, even elegiac, first interview, Yan'an seen through the eyes of a child. Around and outside there was the danger of war and revolution, but it was distant and far away. But for others, given subsequent events, particularly the Great Leap Forward and the Cultural Revolution, Yan'an was, even within its nurturing, a kind of rupture. For almost everyone the Rescue Campaign cut through Yan'an like a hot knife as the Great Error of Yan'an. While clearly more frightening to the intellectuals than to the others, the Rescue Campaign prompted these "others" to feel sorry for the intellectuals. One might say that the campaign was, in its day, a hairline crack that in retrospect became a fault-line break. No matter how one felt about Yan'an, Kang Sheng became the "evil wind" in the moral paradise, always there underneath the surface, the sorcerer's apprentice. But this introduced a difficult question. Who then was the sorcerer? No one could afford to give the answer.

However people felt about it, the Rescue Campaign produced some unanticipated consequences. It became the turning point in the relations between the old Red Army soldiers, particularly Long March veterans from poor peasant backgrounds, and the intellectuals—especially when some of the intermediate-level military cadres were caught up in the campaign simply by the very nature of the work they were doing. For example, the soldier who had become a telegrapher was accused of being a spy simply because of the secret nature of his work with sensitive documents. That the musician was accused bemuses him to this day. He thinks it was because someone high up in the party had told subordinates that people like him, who had worked in white areas or behind enemy lines, were spies and, being gullible and wanting to do the right thing, the subordinates turned him in. At the time, most believed that if one had nothing to hide, he or she would have nothing to fear. But in hindsight, all the interviewees saw the Rescue Campaign as the dress rehearsal for the Cultural Revolution.

In telling their stories, the narrative events selected by the soldiers were quite different from those of the students and intellectuals. The soldiers' recollections have much to do with regimental groups, unit assignments, and particular jobs more than battles, skirmishes, and actual fighting. The context is the major shifts of power within the party as reflected in defeats and victories, and factors such as whether one survived Nanchang and went to the Jinggang Mountains, or whose regiment or army one was with on the Long March, or whether one was in underground or open work. Hence the soldiers' terrain was defined in terms of the movement of armies, which forces went north or east, and of course the major battles in which they participated. Significant dates included those of important Central Committee meetings, enlarged plenums, and significant directives from the Central Committee. Few seem to have grumbled at undesirable postings, mainly because, as one person put it, "complaining was against the spirit of Yan'an."

For students, events were demarcated in terms of graduations and schools attended, courses taken, and major texts that had to be studied. Both soldiers and students contextualized their Yan'an lives in terms of the long story turning into the Long March, China *as* history becoming China *in* history. In turn, they lived the intermediate and short stories, the latter in terms of Mao's conflicts with Zhang Guotao and Wang Ming (and, for the intellectuals, Wang Shiwei).[31]

For most, the short story involved sharing in the life of Mao in Yan'an, and their sharing their lives with him. Virtually everyone had seen him, talked to him, or heard him talk, and in general regarded him and those in his circle with admiration and respect. Except for those who perhaps had cause to know better, struggles such as those with Zhang Guotao and Wang Ming were widely considered victories not only for Mao but also for the party in general. Moreover, Mao was regarded as remarkably free of vindictiveness. After all, it was not he who threw Zhang Guotao out of Yan'an; the latter chose to flee. Members of Zhang's own bodyguard who had accompanied him to Chongqing pleaded with him not to go over to the GMD but return to Yan'an with them. They themselves turned back, going to a Red Army outpost in Chongqing, which arranged their trip back to Yan'an.

As for Wang Ming, Mao did not have him shot, as may have happened in the days of the empire of clandestinity, but instead made him president of the Woman's University. At the time, people thought it was a very clever way to be insulting and generous at the same time.

Among the most remarkable aspects of these stories is the interviewees' recounting of daily life—how far they had to go to use a toilet when living in caves, what happened if they were chronically ill, and above all what their attitude was to members of the opposite sex. A high degree of avoidance of the opposite sex was invariably described, coupled with laughter at lapses from grace. One woman said that she and the other women in her cave would go as a group to bathe in the river. They would be accompanied by men from a nearby cave. When the women undressed and went into the water the men turned their backs, and the women did the same when the men went in. Asked if they peeked at the men, one woman giggled and said, "Of course." But in general sexual conduct was highly regulated, particularly because of the ratio of men to women.[32] Despite the imbalance, senior cadres who had left their wives behind seemed to have had their pick of young women. It was not uncommon for wives to be twenty or thirty years younger than their husbands.

The interviews offer a picture of Yan'an as a critical part of what became whole lives—a special period as a result of which people's whole lives were altered drastically. Take, for example, the story of an old woman who, many years before, became an underground worker, a role particularly dangerous for women who, if captured, could expect to be raped and tortured before being killed by the GMD. A wisp of an old lady at the age of eighty-two, her straight grey hair pulled back in a bun, dressed in a high-necked Mao jacket, white blouse, trousers, and black canvas and rope shoes, she described these hazards from the perspective of the alternative, a life of drudgery. Risk and danger were preferable for someone like herself, who came from a poor peasant family and at the age of seven began to work, tending bullocks. At age twenty-two, in 1927, she joined the Communist Youth League.

She had never attended school, but in 1928 the Red Army set up night schools. Here she learned to read and write so well "that Mao began sending the League secretary to talk to me." Because she was smart, small, and ordinary looking she seemed ideal for secret work. At that time, the CCP was waging a particularly strong campaign against the landlord class. She was recruited as a scout to locate those who had become GMD informants and spies. For a year she engaged in such activities in the white areas. In addition, she painted communist slogans on walls and distributed newspapers through clandestine networks. In 1928 she became part of a nine-person team, one of five in her district. Although the youngest, she was quickly put in charge of all five teams. She assigned three to the front. One team did medical work, carrying stretchers and caring for the wounded even though no medicines were available. A second team consisted of organized troupes of singers and dancers, who put on performances for soldiers and in nearby villages. A third team was engaged in propaganda against the enemy. Another acted as a service team, doing the laundry, washing, and cleaning. The fifth was a production team.

The propaganda team was concerned with the enemy. For one's own troops, the emphasis was on education. For the enemy, it was propaganda. They painted slogans on rocks. They would call to enemy soldiers by megaphone and urge them not to fight the communists but to join the revolution. Many enemy soldiers surrendered with their guns. The entertainment teams put on dances for them, the production team brought food, ducks and eggs. Drums were beaten. The enemy troops were warmly welcomed. Those who wanted to return home were given "road fees," a small sum with which to travel. Others enlisted in the Red Army.

The production team helped families whose men were in the army. They assisted the family with planting and harvesting. They reallocated land so that each peasant had two "measures" of land. If a family had several sons who could not join the Red Army because they were needed on the farm, the team would ensure that they had "labor power," freeing the sons to go to the front. They did any kind of work, caring for the sick and the elderly, for example. She and others would often go to the mountains to collect herbal medicines.

Though a good deal of the heavy work was done by women, the production team also formed squads of "needleworkers" who would sew for the soldiers. The soldiers treated the women very respectfully. They never did anything improper. If the men made advances, the women immediately stopped their work. Discipline was very strict, both in the Red Army and among the teams. For example, one of the rules of the army was to avoid bathing near women.

The main problem for our informant was that she had no time to be married and have a family. People like her who were married could not keep their marriages working. They moved around too much as individuals, or in groups where loyalty was to the group, not the spouse or parents. With underground work one could not be committed to a husband and to the party at the same time. Many of the team members were captured by the enemy. One of the women members of the propaganda team was shot and killed while using her megaphone. Our informant herself was captured when she was acting as liaison for the Party Center. When caught, she had in her possession an important secret document, which she managed to swallow without being observed.

She escaped and joined the Red Army in 1930, working in the same region. After the army left, she turned to underground work. In 1934 the situation got very bad, and she and her comrades had to hide in the mountains. The GMD got their relatives to persuade some of them to come down, promising they would not be killed. Of those who did come down, all the educated women were killed; the uneducated and illiterates were beaten and fined, but not killed. Our informant also came down and was bound and beaten, her arm broken in a number of places so that it still gives her pain. A relative paid twenty silver coins in ransom, and she was freed. She suffered a lot in those days and prefers not to talk about it. She returned the ransom money after Liberation.

After the Red Army left the area, the enemy was able to control it without too many troops. Only then (in 1936) was she able to marry a veteran party member who had joined the army in 1927 and was team leader at the township level. She bore him two sons. Only once was she able to meet Chairman Mao, but he made a big impression: "He had very long hair, his clothes did not fit, and he displayed a good temper to people."

There are many other stories to tell and people who want to tell them before they die. One of the most senior cadres who subsequently had a distinguished career in the Chinese Academy of Social Sciences (in between long periods in prison), Wen Jize, is collecting the stories of a thousand "martyrs" for his book on the heroes of the revolution. There is now no dearth of memoirs. And there are many anecdotes about Mao by those who knew him well or were associated with him during this period, several with unusual perspectives. For example, we interviewed Mao's "official" photographer, Wu Yinxian, several times in 1986, 1988, and 1989, always in his small, comfortable apartment filled with books and photographs of Yan'an days. He came from poor peasant stock, taught himself photography, and was much influenced by the early Russian films of Pudovkin and Eisenstein. Now in his nineties, and retired from his post as Chairman of the All China Photographers Association, he was already established as a photographer and moviemaker by the early thirties. Going to Yan'an in 1938, he remained there until 1945, making movies and taking photographs, particularly of the production campaign and, of course, Mao himself.[33] In his view, Zhou Enlai was the easiest of the party's leaders to photograph because he was so photogenic. Wu Yinxian describes how Mao, despite his apparent modest demeanor and lack of concern for appearances, liked having his photograph taken and took care to present himself as a friendly intellectual, never in a real uniform, using his "Mao tunic" as a compromise between a kind of Nehru jacket and a uniform. Wu was particularly fascinated by the way Mao's hands fluttered when he spoke to form patterns of their own, like birds in flight. Indeed, he took hundreds of photographs of Mao's fluttering white hands, not at all the hands of a worker but those of a scholar, one with a certain delicacy that wields the brush. Today, Wu Yinxian feels well rewarded for his work, which has been recognized by a citation from the International Institute of Photography in New York. More recently he was honored as photographer of the year in Arles, France.

At the opposite extreme, we interviewed a retired general who had been literally chief torturer and executioner under He Long.[34] Now retired and living in the main army base outside of Beijing, the general was happy to receive us. His wife served orange drinks and beer in their large, airy, and comfortable ground-floor flat as we talked. The general described the various kinds of torture he used. After each description he would give a little giggle and say, "Well, everybody knows that." Sometimes they buried people alive, or left them to a slow death. The simplest method of getting rid of people was to tie them together and make them walk into a lake or river, where they would drown.

This general described Mao as a "quick killer" who eliminated the AB squads with despatch and finished the job. The Second and Fourth Front Armies in Hubei were "slow" killers because it took them a year to finish off the so-called Reformist Faction of the GMD. Those who followed the leftist line were the worst killers, according to this general, and of these, Xu Haidong was the most notorious. They went after communists, not the enemy, calling themselves the "Counter-Revolutionaries' Campaign." According to the general, people were often boiled alive or buried alive. A common procedure after a victory over CCP soldiers unfortunate enough to have followed the wrong line was to line them up in two columns, the winning commander going down the center between them to pick out this one or that one with the comment, "All right, it's time for you to be killed now."

We also interviewed a soldier who rose to become a general in Mao's bodyguard. He described how Mao became so accustomed to sleeping on a hard bed that he continued to do so even when he lived in relative luxury after coming to power. He began to describe some of Mao's activities on the hard bed, but was stopped by his daughter, who had come along with him. He remembered the first time his unit captured Japanese prisoners. They were intensely curious about the Japanese enemy because "even when badly wounded the Japanese never let themselves be taken prisoner and would kill themselves." The effect was to make them believe that the Japanese were not quite human beings. When they captured three Japanese soldiers, it was a major event, in part because of the victory and in part because of this intense curiosity. Asked if they hated the Japanese, he said one didn't really hate someone who was so strangely different. But even on closer inspection the Japanese continued to astonish him and his associates. A great event was capturing a Japanese colonel who then was converted to the communist cause. When he identified himself and broadcast appeals to his fellow countrymen urging for them to desert, they did so, and in substantial numbers, much to everyone's surprise.

A good many of those interviewed were second- and third-echelon cadres, such as the teacher in Nanchang who had learned to be a teacher in Yan'an and continued in that occupation all his working life, or the woman from a very poor background who became literate in Yan'an and, assigned to underground work, performed remarkably daring feats, winding up as a kind of keeper in the *danwei* of a factory. Or the "proletarian writer," a woman from a cripplingly poor family who barely survived being sold into bondage to become an important writer. She continues to see Yan'an in the bright colors of socialist realism, treating more intellectual writers like Ding Ling with a certain contempt. On the whole, however, such personal reactions were remarkably lacking. While people differed in their views of Yan'an, it was about how they experienced it rather than as an experience. Indeed, in all the interviews we conducted with people who had been in Yan'an in whatever capacity, we sensed that Yan'an had given them a certain ease with themselves that was very different from the undercurrent of restlessness and bitterness that prevails almost everywhere in China today.

We also sensed an intimacy without complete equality, despite Yan'an's emphasis on principles of egalitarianism. People determined one's position in the hierarchy by the material of one's clothes and, above all, the food one had to eat. One soldier defined his rank as "middle food"—he was a fairly high-ranking cadre but not at the highest level. One could be irritated by such "ranks," but people (except for a few of the intellectuals) not only accepted it but also thought it necessary: all were opposed to "infantile leftism," or excessive egalitarianism.

The disparities of social background were more troublesome in the early days, but the Rescue Campaign did a good deal to diminish the ordinary

soldiers' resentment of the intellectuals. Yet in retrospect it is quite remarkable how little overt friction there appeared to be, compared to accounts
of what happened after the Hundred Flowers campaign and the careening
left–right course Mao and his cohorts traveled after coming to power. It is
especially surprising because in Yan'an everyone was thrown into such
proximity and intimacy that all differences, however small, were magnified.
Such a situation could have easily led to intensified resentment and petty
jealousy. Instead, people ignored their differences. People seemed to reach
out to others almost like religious communicants. Above all, what Yan'an
did was, in Israel Epstein's words, to expose "the GMD and all its
imperfections. Yan'an was like a different country, a different world."[35]

Indeed, it *was* a different country and world, one with its own language
and way of thinking. It was held together not only by enemies at the gates
but also by a powerful interior moral force, the fund of symbolic capital
Yan'anites shared, that "enabled each to understood more or less what the
other was thinking and doing." Our interviewees all describe their own
individual experiences in terms of the prescribed and textual form of Mao's
logic. In effect they grounded his discourse in themselves. Each individual
contributed his or her own experience to the totality of what Yan'an
meant, while drawing down net gains: a deepening of the sense of persona,
the sense indeed of overcoming, of becoming educated. It is this sense of
drawing down and being uplifted one finds in the actual interviews—what
we have been calling collective individualism, so very different from the
methodological individualism characteristic of normal politics.

What else do these interviews tell us? They illustrate the power of what
we have called conveyance. To go to Yan'an constituted a rupture, a break
with friends and family. To arrive there was immediately to be placed in
an instructional group, an organized setting in which the central activity
was to learn. Individuals were assigned to a unit. In the process of receiving
instruction they were encouraged to convey their life story to the collectivity. In return, they received a theoretical method of instruction that
enabled them to take better charge of their own lives. They grew; they
overcame themselves and their inadequacies. The political result of everyone's acting out a similar conveyance is what might be called the "double
covenant"—for example, between Mao and the individual and between
the individual and the party. That indeed was what it meant to become a
Yan'anite. Individuals conveyed their stories, and in return, they learned
and shared in a theoretical discourse that enabled each to understand better
the events of the story in the context of a wider historical process. Locking
the two covenants in an overcoming project that defined a negative pole
enabled individuals to transcend themselves and society to transform itself.

Each individual described a patrimonial rupture followed by a suturing process similar to being born again. At the societal level, Yan'an imposed a peace over the prevailing general violence. Mao's stories and texts contributed to the collective suturing in well recognized form—nationalism and socialism, both of which took on sacral qualities in Yan'an. Socialism took the specific form of Mao's Marxism. Hence for both the individual and the collectivity, ends become redeeming and salvational and obstacles merely tests of the individual's moral character and collective will.

Yan'an left a definite imprint on its veterans. A few look back on Yan'an days sceptically, recounting their personal associations with Mao himself with a certain irony. But such cases were the exceptions and only emerged in a third or fourth interview spread over several years.

Most of those who had been literally "brought up" in Yan'an continue to see themselves as beneficiaries of its collective individualism. They remain in their own minds "recipients." Indeed, most of them had arrived in Yan'an looking for belief and so were prime candidates for Maoism. If at any point they had doubts, these doubts had been so publicly exorcised on so many occasions that even today the interviewees all used the same terms of reference in describing their individual circumstances. As for their general attitude toward Yan'an, one might describe them as serious but with an appealing good humor. These were qualities that prevailed in Yan'an at the time, despite the grimness of actual conditions.

None of those interviewed decided to join the communists after having had a good look around, sizing up the relative strengths and weaknesses of contending forces, and deciding to cast their lot with Mao on the basis of shrewd calculation. In their reactions to conditions in China they ignored such options as exit, voice, or loyalty in favor of a fourth, conversion.[36]

In this sense, the Yan'anites always considered themselves an elite, albeit of that special radical sort (not unknown elsewhere) that enabled them to regard themselves as an anti-elite. Compared to most religious movements, the Yan'anites may have been more deeply sincere, if not devout. In a religious movement, one does not have to be a true believer so much as to take the observances seriously and speak the language of the church. In Yan'an, one had to prove one's mettle as a true believer through the discourse. Hence in interviewing survivors we cannot help feeling that we are examining the long-term effects of a conversion.

What becomes clear in the interviews is that to this day to speak of "Yan'anites" is to emphasize not only an ecclesiastical aspect of politics, but also the specific discourse in which it is grounded and the language that becomes part of the interior bonding out of which the community is

constructed. This ecclesiastical quality structured the meaning of action in
a fashion that made the actions come alive with meaning. One could say
the initial push came from the original moral endowment provided by the
Long March. Yan'an, the direct product of that exceptional event, represented a triumph over both hostile nature and hostile forces. Survival itself
was made possible only by the sacrifices of a small band purified by
struggle, a crystalline residue left after everything else was burned off.[37] It
was these qualities that created new conditions of possibility not seen
before in China. The story became a record of exceptional acts of service
and sacrifice, sanctifying the community in advance for those who came
to it subsequently, its discourse defining the party as the chosen agent of
historical evolution. By the same token, it set narrow limits on acceptable
heterogeneity. Conduct or principles outside stringent limits constituted
not some mere transgression but was a violation, with punishment more
likely to be "repressive" than "restitutive," to use Durkheim's distinction.
The more people recruited from outside, the more intense the process of
exegetical bonding. Moreover, as people came in from the outside,
whether they were army personnel, students, intellectuals, or cadres, the
more necessary it became to mobilize effectively all resources and to
harness energies.

    The two things that emerge from the interviews as the major events in
Yan'an are, first, the external pressure, which began with a blockade by
Chiang Kai-shek as early as 1940 and which reached a peak in 1943; and
the Rectification Campaign, preparation for which began long before
1942, the year it was officially launched. Connecting the two events are
Mao's writings of the period, most particularly those in which he deals
with economic crisis in direct terms. The text he writes, *Economic and
Financial Problems,* is down to earth and very concrete. Here Mao assesses
what has already been accomplished and what needs to be done in the way
of improved "management" and how private and public property ought
to be coordinated within a civil society that is part socialist and part
capitalist.[38] He makes his views known in his usual way, using storytelling
to reveal the more general logic. His stories are examples that refer to
Individual X and Individual Y as real people whom everyone knows or
knows of. Mao names names. He locates people in their places. He
describes their locale, setting, and family circumstances in considerable
detail. In the course of his descriptions, he discusses grain growing, charcoal burning, sheep pens and horse stables, tools and agricultural practices,
the value of the water content in mud for fertility, the difference between
communist cotton production and others, and the purpose of hoeing

weeds (not only to get rid of the weeds but to help the seedlings). The stories and their contexts particularize in the form of on–the–spot description of practical nurture and cultivation. In turn, these descriptions and vignettes are linked to generalizations about the revolutionary enterprise. "If you talk of revolution, then in the final analysis apart from economic work and educational work (including theoretical education, political education, military education, and national education) what other work is worthy of the names [sic] central or primary work? Is there any other work that is more revolutionary?"[39] In a certain sense this intersection of life, work, and principle is what all those interviewed had in common.

Almost entirely absent from our interviews is any working sense of history. Family was the beginning point, and the break with family was the necessary precondition of revolutionary activism. It is difficult to know what people made of Mao's own excursions into historical parallel. He made a good deal of the way in which his peasant revolution reenacted not only past peasant uprisings but also the texts and writings of the Taipings. These texts and writings defined the nature of truth and righteousness with China as a "holy continent," while others laid down the concrete prescriptions for an agrarian utopia.[40] If Mao's points made an impression on our interviewees at the time, they did not seem to be remembered.

Rather, almost everyone saw Yan'an in terms of immediacy. They agreed with Mao when he said that, in the end, actions speak louder than words. Performance counts. "Talking of education or study separately from economic work is merely using superfluous and empty words."[41] And in case someone might miss the point, Mao elaborated further on who he had in mind and what he meant:

Because we have many comrades with leadership responsibilities who still take the attitude of neglecting or not paying much attention to economic work, many other comrades copy them, being willing to do Party, government, army and educational work, or to work in literature and art but unwilling to do economic work. Some female comrades are unwilling to marry economic workers, implying that they consider them dishonourable. They consider that marrying the head of a mule-and-horse team would be an insult and they would rather marry a political-worker. In fact all these viewpoints are very wrong and do not match the situation in this time and place. We must make a new division of labour. We need some revolutionary specialists who are separate from production affairs. We also require some doctors, literature and art workers, and so forth. But we do not want many people like this. If there are too many then danger arises. If those who eat are many and those who produce are few, if those who are employed suffer and those who benefit are comfortable, we shall collapse.[42]

Here Mao comes close to his own version of the Platonic state.

Performance counts for political workers as well as for the economist or artist or literary worker. Performance demonstrates how well an individual has become assimilated into the discourse community and how well that person has absorbed and internalized the writuals. Everyone must be socialized in the way under the Taipings everyone had to be saved.[43] No one was to be exempt, not even those at the very top. Socialization was to occur not only by study but also by the emulation of exemplary behavior. If one's service was lacking, it was cause for public comment and self-study, a matter of concern not simply of the individual but of the entire unit. It is in this sense that "Mao's republic" as a simulacrum in the end took over and became reified as the real thing, to remain embedded in Mao's own thinking about how a virtuous society must work. Yan'an represents the Mao most at home in the revolutionary world he created— so much so that one must also ask why Mao and no one else was able to succeed to this degree, although there were other border regions with powerful leaders. None other was quite able to gain the conveyance of individual stories to the collective, but more, to encourage an interpersonal transference both to Mao and through him to the collectivity as a whole. There are no doubt practical reasons for this. Mao's stories and theory were articulated against the actions of his competitors, such as Li Lisan, who favored a line that failed when implemented and led to disaster. In a sense the others left Mao in possession of the field, for Mao's actions were by contrast more right, or successful, and so validated his mythologics.

But there was more than that. As these interviews show, Mao was everywhere, but he was elusive. His presence was always felt. He was there, and with authority. But he was rarely seen acting out that authority. He slept during part of the day and worked at night, which added to the creation of the mystery of his communion with himself and a world of his unique understanding. He was friendly and accessible, but rarely gave orders. He could become angry, but rarely did ordinary people see such displays. Quite the contrary, he generally appeared conciliatory and even-tempered. He did not abuse the transference. Most people regarded him as there to help.

There was, then, an intimacy that was in part real and in part false. This desire for intimacy has been described extremely well by Lowell Dittmer: "Mao's conception of the proper relationship between leader and led is unmediated contact, and he deplores 'bureaucratism' *(guanliao zhuyi)*."[44] But it is intimacy at a distance. This may well have contributed significantly to his later failure to grasp the rather elemental fact that coming to power is vastly different from being in power. It is not possible to maintain norms and behavior of the kind realized in Yan'an when the urgent need is for economic capital, the formation of which requires the restructuring of the entire economic and productive structure. One might say that Mao sought a quick and massive return on symbolic capital by means of the economic capital it could produce, the labor theory of value providing the cover for a massive job of primitive accumulation. It led to many unanticipated "contradictions."[45] At a minimum, such a project was virtually guaranteed to erode symbolic capital much faster than it could possibly generate economic capital.

But there are other factors to emphasize in accounting for Mao's success in Yan'an, and these have to do with more than intellectuals, students, and party cadres. If there is an inner core to Yan'an, one grounded in its educational structures, so there is a wider Yan'an closer to the rest of society, which we have so far virtually ignored. But there is a sense in which that, too, is the "real" Yan'an, though it differs substantially from the Yan'an of the intellectuals. What unites the two is a shared discourse, the language both have been taught to speak. What they speak about is another matter. We turn next to this wider Yan'an, the Shaan-Gan-Ning Border Region, which, though well beyond the simulacrum, gave life and (despite its bitter poverty) nourishment to the center.

6

THE TERRAIN ON THE GROUND

✳

If in Mao's inversionary theory the peasantry represents an insurrectionary class, one that is both a surrogate for displacement, dispossession, and dispersion, as well as a national symbol of loss and depatrimonialization, Yan'an constitutes the margin of the margin. Far from major centers, Yan'an (or the Shaan-Gan-Ning Border Region more generally) was the perfect symbol of decline. Poverty-stricken and forgotten though it was when Mao arrived there at the end of the Long March, it had a glorious history as the "cradle of Chinese civilization where the state of Ch'in [Qin] once rose to create the first unified empire," as Mark Selden put it.[1]

For this reason, Yan'an is not such an unlikely place for the revolutionary movement to resurface as it might appear at first glance. There were other reasons as well. It provided a good redoubt for the exhausted troops of the Red Army. It could be defended relatively easily and was far enough from enemy lines, Japanese and Nationalist, to require an attacker to provision his armies over long distances and difficult terrain. But it is doubtful that Yan'an could have survived, or maintained its authority as the seat of the Party Center, if it were not also akin to those redemptive religious movements whose power is of the word and the interpretive discourse so created. Without that generative power, Yan'an would have withered on the vine, its networks and links to the rest of China shriveled and broken. The power that radiated from Yan'an was secular, of course, but it was a utopic community in which theory and story were so combined that they drenched with larger meanings the actions and thoughts of those who composed it.

We have already suggested how this interpretive discourse was totally engaged with events that were familiar and experienced by all and how, transformed into stories and a logic, time became converted into space—not just any space, but a space with Mao at the center. Once established, Yan'an also began transforming space into time by projecting solutions, the "New Democracy," the structure of society, the characterization of a historical process as a future strategy of the next stage. Thus, while Yan'an began as a redoubt of last resort in a revolutionary war its inhabitants were losing, it became the simulacrum for a successful revolutionary movement.

That said, we need to distinguish more sharply the Yan'an that forms the simulacrum from the entire Border Region. One can speak of the core, the discourse community and its composition, and the wider Border Region as a whole. Thus to speak of Yan'an as the mobilization space of China's communist revolution is to include the entire region, its resources, the food grown, the crops sold, the factories constructed, the recruits raised from the peasantry and villagers as well as the military, the educational and party organizations at the center. But the closer one gets to the educational core, the more one can speak of the "real" Yan'an in the sense of the discourse community. For it was there that we find its moral center.

We do not want to draw the distinction between core and periphery too sharply, for that would be misleading. Perhaps it is best to regard Yan'an as a series of overlapping jurisdictions—educational, military, party—with a civil administration for the region as a whole: the Shaan-Gan-Ning Border Region. We can consider this larger terrain in two very different ways: one is as a break with traditional patterns of power in China, especially what has been called the Confucian ethical system; and the other in terms of factional conflict within the party. In terms of the latter, Yan'an transformed the party from a clandestine underground empire to a "victory over the sun" (to use the words of the radical Russian opera). In terms of the former, Thomas Kuo describes the Confucian system as follows:

> The Confucian ethical system was the real framework of Chinese society. That system divided the people into two classes, the "governing class," or the "mind laborers" and the "governed class" or the "body laborers." The former class was supposed to work with its brains. Its members might hold government offices by passing the civil service examination. When they retired they had distinguished gentry status and could become local leaders in their communities. In reality, they were the natural bridge between the government authorities and the local communities. Besides political privileges, the gentry class also shared most of the nation's wealth and expected to be served by the other class.[2]

We will discuss the "victory over the sun" phenomenon in the next chapter when we analyze the core Yan'an. For the moment, we are concerned with the larger terrain. For although it would be scarcely correct to say that the Confucian two-class system actually existed in the Border Region, this area was so impoverished that it raises the question of whether Mao was able to generate for the wider region the same kind of hard commitment to, and understanding of, the revolution as at the core.

In turn, this also raises the question of practical policy, of how to administer a large and poverty stricken territory. To what extent was it transformed? To what extent did Mao leave things as they were? More particularly, how important was his "three-thirds" system of government in winning local support?

The analysis is made more difficult because there is no consensus among scholars about what it was that ensured Mao's success. A good many hypotheses have been advanced about the support won by the CCP, some even doubting that the peasants played a critical role. Mao himself recognized in the Jinggang Mountains that peasants tended to be lukewarm to appeals to nationalism, although they were responsive to the ideas of class struggle against landlords. Some of the different explanations for Mao's success put forward by Chalmers Johnson, Donald Gillin, and Mark Selden have been admirably summarized by Shum Kui-Kwong in his book *The Chinese Communists' Road to Power*.[3] Shum doubts that the support of the peasantry alone, "whether obtained primarily through nationalism or social revolution or both," was the answer to the communists' success in China. He places more weight on the united front as the critical factor, combining as it does the weight of both the rural and the urban elites.[4] Indeed, contrary to conventional wisdom, in the period after 1937, the rural elite was more readily attracted to the CCP program of resistance than was the local peasantry.[5] The threat posed by the Japanese bonded the CCP and the local elite together in an uneasy marriage of convenience.

This turns one's attention to the political elite and leaves the larger question of popular and mass support still open. It also raises the question of how much popular support is ever effectively mobilized in modern revolutions other than in the form of mass meetings and military recruitment. In fact what peasant support meant in Yan'an is difficult to say. It hardly meant economic support, for the region was on the whole too poor to give anything. One can say the peasants gave more than passive support—that is, they did not betray the Eighth Route Army. The CCP won over enough peasants and indeed gentry to act as the eyes and ears of the government in the local community, and if it did not alter class relationships in conventional Marxist terms, it provided venues for mobility for those seeking them.

Such support was particularly important because it suggests how in practical terms the civil administration of communism was to work, at least as it became idealized in the New Democracy. This concern shifts the focus from the interiority of the communist movement at its Yan'an core to how it looked from a different class or territorial perspective. One might ask to what extent the movement attracted those in rural areas and in the peasantry.

Up to this point, the Yan'an of which we have spoken is the core Yan'an, where intellectuals, students, and higher-level cadres came to represent a kind of radical gentry. They were concerned with egalitarianism as a principle. They needed to find the right balance between pursuing such principles—for example, in eliminating the landlords—and temporizing in the face of realities. In fact, most Yan'an administrative policies relevant to the rural areas were dictated by larger needs and outside circumstances. In these terms, there are two Yan'an's. One is the Yan'an of the radical intelligentsia, the miniaturized space defined in terms of its hothouse theoretical debates, filtered outwards through its networks of educational, military, and party centers. This center set up fields of force radiating outward to other, very different parts of the Border Region itself, and behind Japanese lines and white areas, not to speak of other border regions and military camps and outposts.

❋

PERHAPS THE best way to begin a study of the wider Yan'an is with a brief description of how Yan'an looks today. It remains remote, despite the coal dust from the factories that have been built there. An ancient, small, propeller-driven Ilyushin makes the trip from Xi'an twice a week; but, with no radar, bad weather often disrupts the schedule, sometimes for days. There is a battered bus, but it takes forever and in any case goes through areas officially closed to foreigners; a taxi is too expensive for most. Those arriving by air will see, near the new landing strip, the original one, now used mainly as a road by cyclists, who move out of the way when a plane comes in. Fronting the landing strip is the old Catholic Church, still standing somewhat forlornly nearby. In some ways visiting Yan'an today makes it more rather than less difficult to envisage what it was like as a utopic community, let alone in its second reincarnation during the Cultural Revolution, when thousands made their pilgrimage to it like Muslims on the hadj. For those who search for curios, many Red Guard lapel buttons are for sale, left over from the period, which feature on a red enamel ground the Yan'an pagoda, which still stands overlooking the city. The fabled caves are of course are still there; those once occupied by major figures are now museums. In front of the well maintained and freshly whitewashed caves are small identifying plaques.

One quickly discovers that Mao had an eye for a view: except for his original courtyard abodes, the caves he occupied enabled him to look out over the surrounding territory. Swept clean, the *kangs* (clay heaters) look strangely unused. With spare bits of furniture, tables, chairs, the folding "transams" (lounge chairs) emphasizing the peripatetic character of armies on the march, the caves feel comfortable, light, and pleasant. Objects similar to those used at the time are on display—enameled teacups, spectacles, writing brushes, dispatch cases. These are the only remaining signs of the intense activity that took place here.

The caves for senior ranks were fairly large, with two rooms, one serving as an office and the other a connecting bedroom. In the back of the cave, tunneled far into the loess, was the air raid shelter. The overall effect is similar to period rooms in a museum. Despite the generous use of photographs, it remains difficult to imagine the sounds and scenes as they must have been, the clink of weapons and gear, the snort of horses. Missing is the sense of constant movement, couriers, dispatch riders, delegations, clusters of militia, or the smell of cooking pots, manure. Today the hills are peaceful. It is difficult to conjure up the real life of years ago, which recedes more and more into the neat descriptions on the walls and black-and-white photos of the inhabitants. Yan'an has become so distant that it is like looking through the wrong end of the telescope. People have become specks, lacking substance—all the more so when generalized theories of class, or peasant, proletarian, or military populism are used as explanations of what went on here.

Certain things do remain, however, such as a sense of the intimacy of the leadership. Here at the foot of Phoenix Mountain is the cave of Liu Shaoqi, next to Mao's. Just over there is the cave of Zhu De, and a step or two behind that of Zhou Enlai, all clustered around the courtyard of the army general staff. Mao's cave, the office and bedroom where he wrote "On Protracted War," "On Contradiction," and other lectures, features photographs of the top leaders sitting together on the now empty benches, or standing stiffly for the photographer. In one photograph one can make out the notice "Don't tie horses here."

The Date Orchard, the last place Mao lived in Yan'an, had the best view. Set back on the hillside overlooking Mao's cave was Jiang Qing's.[6] Mao's had the usual *kang,* a muslin-canopied simple bed, and some transams. Through the rice paper window screen one has a view of a small field where Mao is said to have cultivated crops during the production campaign. The scene is not only peaceful but graceful—a false impression when compared to the reality.

Today's Yan'an in no way resembles the attractive city described by contemporary observers before it was destroyed by Japanese bombing in 1942. Nym Wales considered it a classically beautiful small Chinese town, in sharp contrast to the harshness of the surrounding areas. Lying about 2,500 feet above sea level, Yan'an, said Wales, was "the quaintest and most picturesque little fortress city imaginable . . . set like a jewel in a crown of hills, each crowned by crenellated walls and towers of defense."[7] The surrounding hills and the muddy river that wound around the city provided a natural defense, while the ancient pagoda perched on the hill above provided a traditional talisman to ward off bad luck and ill fate.

Today, the caves look over a town dominated by the squat, vaguely sinicized, Stalinist cement hotel, with its dark interiors, vast empty corridors with cuspidors at every turning, and cavernous entry and reception halls. Its rooms are shabby, and the food is poor. But there is plenty of vitality only a few blocks away in what looks like the old part of town where cooks, with the flair of magicians hand-pull noodles before one's eyes. Small wooden shops painted red or green abound, as do tiny restaurants, food sellers on the streets, and provision stores with brightly painted signs. All are testament to a relatively cheery commercial life, which spills over into the streets like a Muslim bazaar. But none of the buildings are as old as they look, and none are from the "old days."

Indeed, it takes a sharp eye to find some of the buildings from Mao's Yan'an days: the brick meeting hall downtown, the Assembly Hall built near the caves, a large building constructed between 1940 and 1942 where today twenty-four banners still hang from the walls, marking each year of the struggle from 1921 to 1945. Here the Seventh CCP National Congress was held in 1945, with 544 representatives and 208 observers, where Mao delivered the opening address on China's destiny and closed with his rendering of the "foolish old man who moved the mountain." Not too far away is the long, low complex of wooden buildings that comprise the General Headquarters of the Central Committee, where in 1942 the Propaganda Department of the Central Committee held the Yan'an Forum. Eighty-eight people attended, including He Jingzhi, the author of *The White Haired Girl,* China's first "real opera."[8] Perhaps the best reminders of the old days are the pagoda, which still stands atop the high hill above the town, across the Yellow River; and, at a similar altitude but on another hill overlooking the city, the Cave of the 10,000 Buddhas, where the communists reassembled their printing press after the Long March. Not far away is Xi'an, where the great Qin emperors were buried with their armies of life-size men and horses, only recently excavated and now on display.

What made Yan'an all the more appealing to the foreigners who, like Snow, spent some time there, was the idea of it as a "republic of the caves."[9] They were reminded of Plato's republic. Where previous knowledge had been perceived as shadow play and reflections, now it came out into the sunlight, the schools, outdoor classrooms, and light of Mao's teaching revealing the hidden structures behind more ordinary recognition.[10] So for Edgar Snow, "the man from Missouri" who knew a truth or two when he saw it, or Agnes Smedley, the Montana miner's daughter whose life left little to the imagination, and Anna Louise Strong, the Congregationalist minister's daughter with a settlement-house passion for reform, as well as others, Yan'an came to be the center of an intensely concentrated experience in alternative living and learning. They were the "witnesses" to the reality of a Yan'an that can also be called a *political imaginary*.

Not so imaginary was how the area around the city, once rich and famous, had become miserably poor—so poor, it was said, that many peasant women were unable to go outside their homes because they did not have enough clothes to cover their nakedness. Pretty as it might have been, Yan'an City was situated in a border area that had become one of the most devastated regions in all of China.

Yan'an at the Margin

What was life like outside the charmed circle? For most of the permanent inhabitants of greater Yan'an, in the Shaan-Gan-Ning Border Region, life was little more than one disaster after another. When Mao Zedong led his fatigued troops to Wayaobao he found one of the poorest and most unpromising environments imaginable. It must have been quite a shock to the Long March veterans to wind up in such a desperately poor place. Perhaps it was a good thing that at the beginning no one had a precise idea of where they might wind up because if they had known it would be Yan'an, many would not have begun the march.

Conditions in the region were appalling. Aridity is the word that best describes the general conditions, and yellow is the color—yellow dust from the loess-covered hills, yellow dust billowing behind people or animals as they moved. Baron von Richthofen noted in the late nineteenth century,

"As far as the eye can see . . . all this is loess. We are here at the very center of the loess region. Everything is yellow. The hills, the roads, the fields, the water of the rivers and brooks are yellow, the houses are made of yellow earth, the vegetation is covered with yellow dust . . . even the atmosphere is seldom free from a yellow haze."[11]

It is this ubiquitous yellow that gives the Yellow River its name, and also the name of the first "yellow" emperor of China who established power in this area. In the fertile Wei River valley, the Emperor Qin Shihuang and his ancestors developed the culture and traditions that many feel still condition the political culture of northern China. It was also here that the emperor began the consolidation of the frontier walls that led to the creation of the Great Wall of China, designed to keep out barbarians. A tiny section can still be seen behind Yan'an City. Originally a symbol of China's power, the Wall came to represent China's insularity and backwardness, its isolation from the rest of the world.

We have mentioned the small communist base in the area and Gao Gang and Liu Zhidan, the two remarkable guerrilla leaders who headed it. They were in place when Mao arrived in 1935 with the tattered remnants of the Red Army and a vague plan to set up something approximating the Jiangxi base that had been lost to the Nationalists. Mao had yet to consolidate fully his power. Intractable political problems remained to be dealt with, as did the difficulties of turning a poverty-stricken area into a military base camp capable of becoming economically self-sufficient.

Yan'an did have one advantage: it was relatively safe. Yan'an City, where Mao eventually made his headquarters, was situated in the heart of this loess land in the subregion of Yanshu. It lay across the historic invasion route from Mongolia to the Wei River valley. To use the much-quoted words of British consul Erich Teichman from his tour of 1916, "We had heard much of the terrible bitterness of this road, and certainly what with the ravages of the brigands and the natural infertility of the soil, the few inhabitants were poor to the verge of starvation. Yenan seems to be the center of the most desolate area, by far the poorest region I have traversed in China outside the actual deserts."[12]

By the time Mao arrived, the area along the Wei River valley, once the cradle of Chinese civilization, was effectively cut off from the developing mainstream of Chinese society. Its isolation was heightened by the poor transportation and communications not only within the area but also between the area and the rest of China.[13] Not only was the northwest one of the worst places to settle in China because of frequent drought and famine, but it also was inhabited by bandits and warlord troops who preyed on each other and the local people. Indeed, the area was so desolate and devastated that it seemed forever condemned to be poor.

The climate did not provide enough rain in predictable amounts to ensure sustainable agricultural activity. Its average twenty inches of rainfall per year was concentrated in the spring and summer months. Although loess soils can be made fertile, they are not capable of holding sufficient water for long enough periods. Soil erosion had long been a major problem. Winters were long and cold, with some five months a year being liable to winter frosts. A restricted growing season forced idleness on many peasants who could not find alternative work during these slack seasons.[14]

History had not been kind to the area. During the mid-nineteenth century the local Muslims had rebelled to gain independence from the Qing. That conflict and the lengthy suppression that followed coupled with a drought that affected the Wei River valley, drastically reduced the local population. Shaanxi's population shrank from 12 million in 1875 to 8.09 million in 1884.[15] The conflict also left its mark on the population of the Yanshu subregion. The population in Yan'an county declined from 61,200 in 1823 to 18,198 in 1909; Bao'an's declined from 51,500 in 1823 to only 170 in 1868 before recovering somewhat to 5,241 in 1896.

Within this generally bleak description one must note certain variations. There was considerable diversity within what became the Shaan-Gan-Ning Border Region as a whole. Situated in the bend of the Yellow River in the high loess plateau and ranging some 450 kilometers from north to south and 400 east to west, the south of the region was bordered by fertile plains that ran along the Wei River. This area formed the historic core of Shaanxi Province.[16] Along these plains one could find both extensive farming with holdings covering some four hectares (in Pucheng county) and more traditional intensive farming, such as in Zhouzhi, where farms only averaged one hectare. For both types of farm, wheat and millet were the main crops. Their cultivation might be supported by a little cotton or poppy production.

To the north, the landscape gradually changed into the loess mountains familiar to those who picture Yan'an as a republic of the caves. These loess-covered hills were shaped by the weather of centuries into a criss-cross pattern of ridges and gullies. To the northeast of Shaanxi, the land, while arid, can be made quite fertile; but to the northwest, especially the further reaches in Gansu and Ningxia, the land becomes semidesert, its population sparse and scattered. Families trying to carve out a living in these steep hills were rarely successful over the long term. Lack of alternatives to farming left them idle for large portions of the year. Poor communications made finding other sources of work problematic. Travel was difficult: violent storms frequently washed away the few roads in the area, or made them rutted and difficult to use.

The entire Border Region was afflicted by drought and famine. From 1928 to 1931, before Mao's arrival, the region had suffered the Great Northwest Famine.[17] Relief was virtually nonexistent. Cut off from the rest of the world, the region suffered alone, in silence. Eventually, the scale of the tragedy drew the attention of the GMD and foreign relief agencies. Indeed, it was these relief measures that connected the region to the world outside and helped at least the more accessible part of the population to revive.[18]

Yan'an and the counties in the surrounding subregion of Yanshu had a number of distinctive topographic features. Subtle variations of soil and climate within this mass of loess land created distinct ecological environments within which the Communist Party cadres learned to operate.[19] The area around Yan'an incorporated in the Yanshu subregion totaled some 23,000 square kilometers and was very sparsely populated.[20] Population density was extremely low and remained low even after the communists began large-scale population transfers from Suide in the early and mid-forties. Thus, in Yanshu there was an abundance of land with scattered hamlets within which social differentiation was not very marked.[21] This contrasted with Suide, where there were growing social divisions and a large pool of underemployed peasants who could provide landlords with cheap labor. While hamlets in Yanshu ranged from 1.2 per 10 square kilometers (Zhidan) to 3.8 in the most populated county (Ansai), the averages ranged from 3.52 to in Suide to 8.5 in Mizhi. Generally, in northern Shaanxi the power of the local elites was weak because of the large distance between settlements and the difficulties of travel between them. In Yanshu, this was even more marked.

The climate of the area made land suitable for cotton growing. Land holdings were relatively large, many landlords having acquired large tracts of land in the mid-nineteenth century as a result of the Muslim rebellion. Land was leased in sections to poor immigrants. Huge estates incorporating vast areas of uncultivated hill country were a distinctive feature. With labor a scarce commodity, male workers would often be hired in, frequently in the form of labor gangs that would move from holding to holding to carry out essential tasks.[22]

This abundance of land is at variance with the usual perception of China as an overpopulated area with busy peasants engaged in labor-intensive rice cultivation. It made Yanshu distinct from neighboring Suide, where land was scarce. A speculator's market for land did not exist. Peasants could shop around for the best deal for rent. Rents in Yanshu could be as low as 5 or 6 percent of the tenants' crop (in Zhidan) or as high as 20 percent (in Yanchuan and Yanchang). Average rents in neighboring Suide ranged from 35 to 50 percent.

Those who were enterprising could reclaim wasteland for agricultural development. While there was plenty of land for those who wished to cultivate it, lack of access to such things as capital and seed grain made it difficult for itinerant laborers to settle into their own holdings. Land rentals played a less oppressive role in the life of the peasant than did the punitive loans and the unpredictable taxes that would be levied by the local authorities. Unfortunately, the vast majority of these random taxes did not go into infrastructural development but into maintaining war chests for the constant fighting that plagued the area.[23] Thus, when the CCP sought issues on which to mobilize the peasantry in the Yanshu region, it found that taxation and, to a slightly lesser extent, usury were the key issues. The peasants' anger fell on the "local tyrants," people who might or might not have been landlords, but who certainly had the connections and power, including armed militia, needed to get their way in the villages.[24]

Peasants in Yanshu, like those in the larger region, had to be able to diversify, for they could not make ends meet from agriculture alone. The weather and the many natural calamities led to frequent harvest failure, which increased the farmers indebtedness and caused frequent ruin.

Apart from the natural disasters, disease,[25] and the constraints of the economic environment, the area into which Mao moved was also beset by warlordism and roving bandits.

After the collapse of the Qing dynasty in 1911, like so much of China, the region fell prey to warlordism. Political power and authority extended only as far as the gun could command. Qing power was replaced by the local forces of the Gelaohui (Elder Brother Society), a secret society that quickly penetrated the cities to fill the power vacuum. Subsequently, power was fought over between various local forces, the Anhui armies (whose representative was appointed governor in 1935), and the Zhili armies.[26] Eventually, with the ascendence to power of Feng Yuxiang in 1926, the area achieved a period of relative calm that lasted until the onset of war with Japan in 1937. The communists were able to infiltrate the spaces left by the warring groups in northern Shaanxi. Banditry was rife. Rural Shaanxi was not a safe place to venture out into after dark. Perhaps it was, as Nym Wales noted, a "wistful hope in the magic of a name" that led to many settlements in the area containing the name "peace" (an).[27]

Establishing the Shan-Gan-Ning Border Region

If the Border Region was one of the worst places to make a living, one might expect it to become most hospitable to the revolution. To some extent this was so. It does not take a genius to convert people living under such vicissitudes to a cause that promises reform, stability, and release from arbitrary taxes and levies. If, on the surface, at any rate, it was hardly the terrain on which to construct a utopic community in an age of capitalist reproduction, in terms of actual living conditions, most people had a lot to gain. However, for new recruits passing through en route to party headquarters, it must have appeared to be the opposite end of the civilized world. Just getting there was no mean achievement; to prosper under such conditions was an extraordinary accomplishment. For the outpost to succeed on its own terms and far beyond anyone's expectations required that the new recruits be imbued with missionary zeal, and the economic and social conditions of the permanent inhabitants drastically transformed. How to do both at the same time became Mao's strategic problem. He had to build up the interiority of the core as a discourse community in order to generate symbolic capital, and then deploy that capital to generate economic capital in the countryside. Doing this required all Mao's imagination and skill as a political leader.[28]

His accomplishments were so great that they aroused wonder and envy among many GMD officials (who tried unsuccessfully to emulate some of Mao's policies). And as the area evolved as a Border Region, it began to exert more and more of a pull on the rest of China. It was not simply a matter of spinning theories or even winning victories in battle, although both were important. More than anything, Mao succeeded because he managed to create self-reliance and autonomy in the region and so inspired others to think that, if he could transform this area, he could do the same for China as a whole. As time went on and what was happening in Yan'an became better known, the GMD stepped up its pressure on the region. But the more Yan'an was pressed by hostile forces, the more its attractiveness radiated outwards.[29] Here in Yan'an, a border area in the classic tradition, were the marginals who would redeem the rest of China.[30]

This quality of redemption was enhanced by certain external factors. While Mao had been acquiring power on the Long March, a fundamental shift in Comintern policy with implications for China had taken place. The idea of a united front of all elements, classes, and nations in the fight against fascism had been proposed and accepted by the Comintern in July and August of 1935. This new policy was applied to China by Wang Ming, the head of the CCP mission to the Comintern in Moscow. Its implementation after 1937 became, as we have seen, a major focus in the struggle between Mao and Wang Ming. Wang Ming's own ideas had been evolving from the notion of a united front from below to a united front from above.[31] Indeed, the Japanese occupation of northeast China in January 1933 had caused the Central Committee to suggest a shift in policy in the Manchuria region.[32] The Central Committee thought that it would be possible to cooperate with the national bourgeoisie if a solid united front from below had been assured. This, according to the Central Committee, would ensure the proletarian leadership in the united front.

The clear signal that the CCP was to make the strategic shift from civil war to a new united front came in the August First Declaration of 1935 issued in Moscow in the name of the CCP and the Chinese Soviet government.[33] This declaration, drafted by Wang Ming, called on all to resist Japan and criticized "scum" and "traitors" such as Chiang Kai-shek, Yan Xishan, and Zhang Xueliang, who had not adopted a policy of resistance to Japan. According to Wang, the CCP was willing to set aside differences and cooperate with all those prepared to join a government of national defense that would pursue a ten-point program to expel the Japanese. The suggestion was now clearly for a united front from above.

This shift in strategy set Mao and the party leaders a new problem to ponder. Having just escaped destruction by GMD forces, it was beginning to appear as if they would once again have to contemplate cooperation. Their formal response came in December 1935 at the Wayaobao Politburo meeting.[34] On the military front, they decided to build up troop strength in 1936 for a direct fight with Japan, and would adopt widespread guerrilla warfare in a shift from regular warfare.[35] Politically, they decided that the Japanese invasion of the northeast and the threat of further advance necessitated adopting the broadest political front possible to oppose Japanese imperialism and Chiang Kai-shek.[36] This front that the party intended to lead would include workers, peasants, the petty bourgeoisie, the national bourgeoisie, rich peasants, and small landlords. The greatest manifestation of this new united front was to be the government of national defense and the united anti-Japanese army. This conciliatory approach was reflected in both the moderation in policy and a change of name, from the Worker and Peasant Soviet Republic to the People's Soviet Republic. Rich peasants were to enjoy the same rights as the rest of the population and would not have their property confiscated, while industrial and commercial entrepreneurs would be welcomed to invest in the area.[37] Criteria for party membership were relaxed, and "left closed doorism" was seen as a greater danger than "right opportunism." Party members were called on to respond flexibly to the changing circumstances and not to use ideology as a dogma.

Mao's main objective in 1936 was to consolidate the new settlement in north Shaanxi. To achieve this end, it was important to forge an alliance with the local GMD troops of Zhang Xueliang's Northeast Army and Yang Hucheng's Northwest Army. A truce with these local troops would not only eliminate an immediate threat to the Red Army but also would drive a wedge between the base area and the GMD central army. It is difficult to say whether Mao had any broader scheme in mind at the time, but the logic of the alliance would propel events forward and result in a second united front with Chiang Kai-shek. After patient and careful probing, the CCP succeeded in establishing preliminary contacts with both Zhang Xueliang and Yang Hucheng in the early months of 1936. In April, the CCP negotiator, Zhou Enlai, and Zhang met in secret and agreed to end the fighting and to open trade. The opening of trade was an economic boost to the beleaguered base area.

To consolidate their relationship with the Northeast Army, the Party Center issued an internal directive on June 20, 1936, outlining a number of principles on how to deal with the united front.[38] The policy outlined in the directive provides a striking contrast with the CCP reaction to the Fujian rebellion in 1934. Instead of resorting to slogans about unending class struggle, the directive stressed the Northeast Army's patriotism in resisting the Japanese invaders. This patriotism was to be encouraged. At the same time, the directive outlined a number of tactics for future work, such as negotiating with the Northeast Army's senior officials while agitating among the rank-and-file soldiers and establishing secret CCP organizations within the army.

Although the communists had been forced to abandon Wayaobao to Chiang Kai-shek's troops in late May 1936, their agreement with Zhang afforded them some respite so that they were able to establish themselves more firmly in North Shaanxi during the latter half of 1936. With cooperation secured, the CCP began to tone down its criticism of Chiang Kai-shek. On May 5, the CCP sent an appeal to the Nanjing government asking for a cease-fire and unity in the struggle against Japan, and sent a similar secret message to the GMD on June 20.[39] On August 25, Zhang Wentian drafted an open letter on behalf of the CCP commending Chiang Kai-shek for his opposition to infringement of China's territorial integrity and referred to him as Generalissimo.[40]

Finally, on September 17, 1936, the Politburo passed a resolution on the new situation that suggested an agreement be reached with Chiang

Kai-shek.[41] This shift in policy to "dine with the devil" needed to be handled delicately to prevent confusion or opposition within CCP ranks. Thus, while the resolution called for GMD participation in the united front, it informed party members that this did not mean an end to criticism of the GMD, nor did it mean that the ultimate goal of socialism was being rejected. The resolution pointed out that the largest political party in China, the GMD, had not yet joined the anti-Japanese united front but that the GMD itself was now internally divided on the question of how to oppose Japan. Popular pressure would cause the GMD to waver and eventually decide to participate. The CCP proposed the formation of a democratic republic, a form of government that it felt would have a more universal form of democracy than that practiced in the soviets and would be more progressive than that under the GMD. According to the Politburo, this form of government would provide the political basis not only for mobilizing the people against Japan but also for assuring the victory of socialism in the future.

For Zhang Xueliang, these overtures must have contrasted markedly with Chiang Kai-shek's continued belligerence. When, in early December 1936, Chiang flew to Xi'an to supervise the campaign to eradicate the communists, Zhang and Yang kidnapped him. This "Xi'an Incident," although not a part of CCP policy, was to be of great benefit to the CCP in the consolidation of Yan'an. After consultations with the Comintern in Moscow, the CCP decided to resolve the situation peacefully. The CCP's objective in the negotiations had been to extract as much as possible from the situation by realizing a peaceful agreement with the Nanjing government. In this, it was entirely successful.

Among the consequences of the Xi'an Incident was the arrest of Zhang Xueliang when he accompanied Chiang Kai-shek back to Nanjing and the disbanding of the Northeast Army. The Red Army immediately took advantage of the Northeast Army's withdrawal and moved quickly to occupy Yan'an, which then became the capital of the Shaan-Gan-Ning Border Region for the next ten years. The area under CCP control now extended close to Xi'an, and secret party branches were established in a score of counties. Militarily, the threat to CCP existence in North China had been removed.

The incident provided the link between the phases of civil war and the national war of resistance, and the CCP adopted a moderate tone in its communications with the GMD as it pushed for further collaboration. Protracted negotiations followed, and the CCP offered a number of concessions in return for immediate preparation for war with Japan and democratic reforms. The CCP effectively promised to give up Marxism-Leninism and accept Sun Yat-sen's Three Principles of the People as the guiding ideology of the whole nation, stop the land revolution, abolish the soviet system, and change the name of the Red Army to the National Army.

These protracted negotiations were speeded up by the Japanese advances that began in July 1937. Chiang Kai-shek accepted communist troops as part of the Nationalist Army, and on August 21 the GMD Military Commission issued an order naming the Red Army the Eighth Route Army of the National Revolutionary Army. On September 22, the cooperation between the two parties was formally recognized, with each party issuing its own statement. Finally, in November the remaining guerrilla forces in central China were renamed the New Fourth Army.

The agreement with the GMD led not only to a moderation of the land policy but also to a new form of government. Until the united front was established, the Northwest Office of the Soviet Government incorporated the administrative structure of the former Central Government from the Jiangxi soviet to run the base area.[42] The organization thus paralleled that of the former soviet structures with an executive committee of the Soviet government headed by Mao Zedong and a Council of People's Commissars of the Soviet government headed by Ma Mingfang. The Northwest Office was chaired by Bo Gu from November 1935 until his replacement by Lin Boqu. On its arrival in north Shaanxi, the Politburo comprised Zhang Wentian, Mao Zedong, Zhou Enlai, Wang Jiaxiang, Bo Gu, Chen Yun, Liu Shaoqi, Deng Fa, He Kequan, Peng Dehuai, and Lin Yuying, with Zhang Wentian as General Secretary.[43] In March 1937, the soviet area changed its name to Special Area and, with the agreement with the GMD, the name was changed again to the Shaan-Gan-Ning Border Region.[44]

With all the main traditional centers of China—Canton, Shanghai, Nanjing, and Beijing—now under Japanese occupation and Chongqing, Yunnan, and other areas under the GMD mired in corruption and arbitrary rule, Yan'an became an object lesson in basic living. For many students and intellectuals it came to hold great appeal for its simplicity and rusticity. Moreover, under the stabilizing conditions of the united front the communists were able to construct a model political structure—the three-thirds system of local administration, a framework enabling them to consolidate power in the countryside.

While Yan'an's "democracy" never became a blueprint for the next stage of the revolution, Mao always leaving the way open for improvisation, it provided the kind of mandate that no Chinese government had been able to achieve since the fall of the Qing. And, whatever its internal organization, the leadership never lost sight of the original revolutionary project.

The Social Structure of the Greater Shaan-Gan-Ning Border Region

One can imagine the reactions of the local peasantry to the arrival of Mao and his lieutenants in the area. Most were probably indifferent; many were hostile. Organized opposition could be expected from local landlords, bandits, and GMD representatives. The problem from the start was how to fashion a policy internal to the region that would reflect well on the larger character of socialism. Simple military control and rule through repression would have made the CCP indistinguishable from the warlords whom they now intended to replace.[45] As a result, Mao and his supporters found themselves faced with having to devise policies to suit the locality without compromising the party's general principles, while at the same time avoid forcing the potentially hostile groups into outright opposition. What was later elevated to the idea of the "New Democracy" began as an improvised attempt by the CCP to neutralize or co-opt local elites and gain the support of the local peasantry by means of social reform. The CCP defined economic and political relationships in the villages in terms of class rather than traditional forms of patronage and familial relationships. The introduction of class as the defining characteristic in village life was new, certainly in Yanshu, where economic differences were small and difficult to perceive.

The party had to first win the acceptance of the local peasantry and, second, mobilize them for practical support, and having mobilized them, keep them under control. The politics of mobilization in the post-1937 period was complicated not only by the problems arising from the use of class labels but, more particularly, by the need not to alienate the local elite, a need partly created and defined by the Japanese invasion.

In the first phase of territorial expansion and consolidation, from 1934 until the "land revolution" was brought to a halt in late 1936 and 1937, the party operated a policy of thorough land redistribution. This was easier to carry out in the scattered hamlets further away from major urban centers than those close by, where landlords and the local elite might be more willing to fight to protect their interests. Thus, while thorough land redistribution was carried out in virtually all of Yanshu with the exception of Fuxian in the southwest, land reform in Guanzhong and Suide was patchy at best, and large areas did not undergo any redistribution or were only partially affected.

Selden's culling of the relevant data shows that, on the whole, land reform removed the most glaring inequalities in the countryside and improved conditions for the vast majority of poor residents. As Selden wrote, the "entire class balance shifted to the center with the elimination of extremes of wealth and poverty as well as gross forms of exploitation,"[46] a conclusion shared by the CCP, with its own surveys on land redistribution. Not surprisingly, those surveys that were published confirmed that the CCP succeeded in its intention to increase the number of middle peasant households at the expense of the rich and the landlords, and increase the living standard of the poor peasant households.

Selden quotes figures for 321 families in the Third Township in the Yanquan district, which lies on the road to Yan'an. These figures show that all the landlords who had been operating in the area before land redistribution had been removed by December 1939. Correspondingly, the number of middle peasant households increased from 50 to 123, while the number of poor peasant households declined from 204 to 136.

A similar picture of the thickening of the middle at the expense of the extremes is also available for other areas that underwent land distribution in this period. A 1941 survey conducted by Chai Shufan, Yu Guangyuan, and Peng Ping in Suide and Mizhi found a similar decline in landlord households with a consequent rise in the number of middle peasant households (Tables 6.1 and 6.2).

However, minimizing the extremes did not mean that rural life became easy. Particularly in the Suide area, the more glaring inequalities in the village had been removed, but poverty remained. The land-scarce but labor-abundant economy meant that redistribution of land still resulted in holdings relatively small by comparison to those in Yanshu. This may account for the fact that in the case of Yanshu the number of rich peasants increased, while in Suide the number of rich peasants decreased markedly as the peasants' land had also to be redistributed in order to make a difference. After redistribution, the poor peasants still only had 7.3 *shang* of land on average to farm in Yanjiachuan and 8 *shang* in Yihe township. Middle peasants were not much better off, with 12.2 and 12.1 *shang* respectively.[47]

Lack of land to redistribute was not a problem in Yanshu. Here, the tendency towards concentration of land had been reversed. As Keating has noted, "In a depopulated countryside, the flight of a just a few big

Table 6.1 Class composition of families in Third Village in Yihe District (Suide)

Class	1935		1941	
	No. of households	%	No. of households	%
Farmhand	25	11	0	0
Poor peasant	139	61	114	42
Middle peasant	32	14	154	57
Rich peasant	22	10	2	1
Landlord	2	1	0	0
Other	7	3	0	0
Total	227	100	270	100

Source: Chai Shufan, Yu Guangyuan, and Peng Ping, *Suide Mizhi tudi wenti chubu yanjiu* (Preliminary Research into the Land Question in Suide and Mizhi) (Beijing: Renmin chubanshe, 1979, originally published 1942), p. 105.

Table 6.2 Class composition of families in the Third Bao of Yanjiachuan District (Suide)

Class	1935		1941	
	No. of households	%	No. of households	%
Farmhand	44	13.5	1	0.3
Poor peasant	178	55.5	125	33.7
Middle peasant	85	26.5	236	63.9
Rich peasant	8	2.5	4	1.1
Landlord	3	1.0	1	0.2
Other	3	1.0	3	0.8
Total	321	100.0	370	100.0

Source: Chai Shufan, Yu Guangyuan, and Peng Ping, *Suide Mizhi tudi wenti chubu yanjiu* (Preliminary Research into the Land Question in Suide and Mizhi) (Beijing: Renmin chubanshe, 1979, originally published 1942), p. 105.

estate-owners and the division of their properties among relatively small populations resulted in substantial land grants to the poor: families often received more than they could farm without hired help."[48] As a result, not only was it unnecessary for the party to attack the rich peasants to free up land but also former landlords could be given enough land from which to make a decent living. This avoided the kind of resentment that occurred in other areas.

Territorial Administration and Local Politics

Political difficulties with the GMD, compounded by the harsh realities of life endemic in the area before the arrival of the communists, called for an integrated strategy. Earlier, we have described the two roles Mao played so successfully, both of which were necessary for his ascendence to that of cosmocrat. With his arrival in the region, he assumed a double obligation, to redeem the peasant patrimony for the peasant and the national patrimony for the people. The second required a nationalist goal; the first a revolutionary one. It was within this double framework that Mao came to the region. But he was also armed.

Mao had made it very explicit that for him, as for any good commander, military power was required to establish control. Impoverished and weak as the Red Army was, it had sufficient power in the Shaan-Gan-Ning to allow the party the time and space it needed to devise policies that would both stabilize and mobilize the region. A continuous and ubiquitous CCP presence backed by armed force induced the local elite either to cooperate or acquiesce in CCP rule. The lack of alternatives for the local elites was vital. Just as the CCP survived in those areas where it had earlier gained local military superiority over the GMD (as in base areas around Wuhan from 1928 to 1934), so it succeeded where the invading Japanese forces had driven out the GMD (as in north and northeast China from 1937 onwards).

Communist partisans had been active in Northern Shaanxi since the summer of 1927, when the first united front with the GMD collapsed. In broad outline the development of the movement there was much the same as in the rest of China. Secondary school and college students radicalized by the May Fourth Movement formed the core. In the region such activity was concentrated in the Yulan middle school in northern Shaanxi. It was here that the two main leaders of the Shaanxi movement, Liu Zhidan and Gao Gang, received their education and were introduced to the rudimentary ideas of Marxism.[49] As in other parts of China, the first united front with the GMD gave the communists a chance to expand their numbers and influence—a situation that was overturned when in the summer of 1927 the GMD turned on its communist allies. Just before the crackdown, the party in the Shaanxi-Gansu area numbered just over 2,000 members (Table 6.3). The organization was dominated by "intellectuals" (52.1 percent) with not quite 4 percent drawn from the working class (Table 6.4). After a number of failed uprisings and false starts, Liu and Gao put together a coalition of supporters favoring the strategy of rural uprisings, the strategy proposed and developed by Mao.

In 1931, Liu led the rump of his men to conduct guerrilla operations from the Huanglong mountains in north Shaanxi. Gradually, as their activities spread, the group was able to establish a presence on the Shaanxi-Gansu Border and to push activities further into the Guanzhong area. As in other areas of China, and in contradiction to the policy of the Party Center in Shanghai, compromise was the order of the day. Radical demands inspired by ideology would not have made much headway. Many of the early recruits to Liu's forces were bandits, not displaced proletarian fighters. The prevailing party policy of pushing radical land distribution was not followed, since the main problems in the area were usury and taxes; in any case, the area was agriculturally flat on its back after the 1928–1931 famine. Moreover, as Selden has noted, it would have been irresponsible to carry out land redistribution when the partisans could not

Table 6.3 Party membership in Shaanxi, 1924–1927

Date	Area	District comm.	Municipal comm.	County comm.	Special party branch	Branch	Member-ship
Oct. 1924– Nov. 1926	Northern area Henan-Shaanxi area	2 1			3 3	2	
Nov. 1926– Feb. 1927	Joint Conference of Party and League	4			9	11	388
Feb.–July 1927	Shaanxi-Gansu area	7			41		2,177
July–Sept. 1927	Shaanxi Province		1	7	32	153	1,681

Source: Yan'an Revolutionary Museum, Ziliao xuanbian (Selected Materials) (Yan'an: May 1981), vol. 1, p. 20.

be sure of holding on to the area. It would have left the local population to the mercy of vengeful returning elites.[50]

Eventually, the partisans were able to establish two soviets in the region, the Shaanxi-Gansu Soviet and the Shaanbei (North Shaanxi) Soviet. The Shaanxi-Gansu Soviet was formally established in 1932, the North Shaanxi Soviet, in 1934. Almost immediately, in July 1933 the movement in Shaanxi suffered a major setback when its main armed forces were defeated by GMD regiments and some one hundred sixty party and youth corps members either were arrested or defected. This led to the disintegration of communist influence in the Weibei area. In February 1934, the Shaanxi-Gansu Border Region Revolutionary Committee (centered on the counties of Bao'an, Heshi, and Qingyan) was established as a provisional Soviet government. Then, in late 1934, the North Shaanxi Revolutionary Area was founded centering on Anding (Zichang). As with the central China bases, these became targets of GMD forces when the encirclement and annihilation campaigns were launched. The first and second campaigns ended in victory for the communists. This led them in late 1934 to convoke the First North Shaanxi Soviet Congress, which was held in Anding in January 1935. A Shaanxi-Gansu Provisional Soviet government was set up, as well as a Northwest Work Committee and a Revolutionary Military Committee to coordinate the guerrilla activities. It was during this period that the major conflict described in Chapter 2 broke out between Liu Zhidan and Gao Gang on the one hand and Zhu Lizhi and Guo Hongtao, the two Party Center delegates, on the other.

Table 6.4 Class origins of the party members of the Shaanxi-Gansu Area Committee, March 1927

Class	Number	%
Peasants	654	30.3
Workers	82	3.8
Intellectuals	1,125	52.1
Soldiers/police	112	5.2
Other	185	8.6
Total	2,158	100.0

Source: Yan'an Revolutionary Museum, *Ziliao xuanbian* (Selected Materials) (Yan'an: May 1981), vol. 1, p. 22.

The augmentation of guerrilla forces with Red Army troops provided Mao with the necessary military power to control the region. Once established in the base along the Shaanxi-Gansu border, CCP troops began to reach out into the counties in Yanshu. Frequent skirmishing ensued, in which the Red Army was not always victorious. In July 1936, the Central Committee was forced out of its first headquarters in Wayaobao, and moved to Bao'an (later renamed Zhidan). In spite of the new united front, it was only after a year-long siege that Yan'an City at last fell to the communists. The two main soviets, the Shaan-Gan (Shaanxi-Gansu) Border Soviet and the North Shaanbei (Shaanxi) were merged. CCP accounts claim that by the end of 1936 all or part of 37 counties in the region were under CCP control and that this amounted to some 130,000 square kilometers.[51] While the GMD managed to draw back some of the areas, the second united front, which began in 1937, allowed the communists to consolidate what was then termed the Shaan-Gan-Ning Border Region.

After the second united front was consolidated, a government structure was instituted based on provinces that fell under the jurisdiction of the Nationalist Central Government. The arrangements for the organization of the new Border Region were outlined in principle in a document of May 12, 1937.[52] This allowed for elections (including stipulations on universal suffrage for all over sixteen years of age) and gave all political parties and mass organizations the right to nominate candidates. However, as Selden has pointed out, the elections were predicated on sustained communist rule. (The election process was later modified significantly in the 1941 elections when the CCP decided to implement the three-thirds system of government.) Under the 1937 policies, the electors voted in councils at the township, district, county, and regional levels. These legislative organs were in turn to elect their own executive organs. The organizational outline stipulated that township heads should be elected every six months and that the councils (originally called representative congresses) should come together once a month. At the district level, the head was to be elected every nine months, with the council meeting every two months. At the county level, the time periods were respectively one year and six months, while at the Border Region level, it was every two years and every year.[53] In practice, however, the councils, as with all CCP legislative organs, did not play a prominent role: they met infrequently and thus offered little guidance over the various permanent organs.

The most important government organ was the Shaan-Gan-Ning Border Region government, which was set up in September 1937 and operated until 1945 under the chairmanship of Lin Boqu. From 1939 Lin presided over many departments: the Secretariat; the Civil Affairs, Finance, Education, and Construction Departments; Public Security Headquarters (Army); the Public Security Office (Police and Intelligence); the Audit Commission; and the Supreme Court.[54] Further, a number of auxiliary agencies came under the administration of the Border Region government. These, eventually numbering some thirty-five, dealt with areas such as taxation and health, and included the Border Region Bank.[55] This government was elected by the Border Region council, the first of which had been elected in the winter of 1937. In addition, the Border Region council had to approve all departmental appointments of the Border Region government. However, elections in general had been interrupted by the thrust of the Japanese troops in the summer of 1937. In fact, the regional-level council did not even meet until January 1939, when it was convened under the chairmanship of Gao Gang. The 197 elected and 12 appointed members represented the city of Yan'an and all the counties that came under the jurisdiction of the Border Region. Mao Zedong was elected to represent Xinning county and serve as General Secretary; Zhang Wentian and Gao Gang were elected for Dingbian.[56]

According to Selden, by 1941 there were 7,900 full-time government officials of whom about 1,000 worked in central government, while 4,021 worked between the regional and the township levels and 2,879 at the township level.[57] This was considered too many to retain once the Border Region had to tighten its belt after the crisis of 1941.

The jurisdiction of the Border Region fluctuated with the ebb and flow of the conflicts with the Japanese and the Nationalists. By February 1941, the Border Region government presided over an administrative structure of twenty-nine counties with 179 districts, 1,063 townships and 6,703 natural villages containing a population of almost 1.5 million. Directly under the Border Region government were five subregions:

1. Yanshu: Yan'an City and the directly administered counties— Yan'an, Fu, Ganquan, Gulin, Yanchang, Yanchuan, Anding (Zichang), Ansai, Zhidan (Bao'an), Jingbian, and Shenfu.
2. Suide: Suide, Qingjian, Wubao, Mizhi, and Jia.
3. Guanzhong: Xinzheng, Xinning, Chishui, and Chunyao.
4. Sanbian: Dingbian and Yanchi.
5. Longdong: Qingyan, Heshui, Zhenyuan, Huanxian, Quzi, and Huachi.[58]

Paralleling this governmental structure was the party, the most powerful organization in the Border Region. Indeed, the party apparatus gained in importance once the crisis of 1941 caused the Border Region to adopt a mass campaign approach to resolving problems. This culminated in the Northwest Party organization's having a key role under Gao Gang in the Rectification Campaign. However, Gao Gang gained control of the local party apparatus only after Guo Hongtao was transferred out of the Border Region in spring 1938. Indeed, according to his own account, Gao and the other local cadres were excluded from the First Congress of the Border Region Party Congress, held in May 1937. This was set to right by the time the Second Congress was convened under Gao Gang's direction in November–December 1939. From then until 1946, Gao headed the local party apparatus in its various forms. On May 13, 1941, the Northwest Bureau of the Central Committee was formed under Gao's leadership through the amalgamation of the CCP Central Committee Bureau for the Shaan-Gan-Ning Border Region and the CCP Central Committee Northwest Work Committee.

Unlike the administrative and functional departments that fell under the governmental apparatus, the party committees were intended to ensure that party policy was implemented through the mobilization of key elements among the Border Region population. At the Bureau level was the secretariat, headed by Gao Gang, and committees for party affairs, youth, the military, propaganda, organization, workers, peasants, women, and the united front. Under this level came the committees for the three provinces under the jurisdiction of the Border Region, the four subregions, and the committee for those counties directly administered from Yan'an. At this level was a secretariat and committees for youth, women, propaganda, organization, and military affairs (in Suide headed by Wang Zhen). At the Yan'an level there was also a united front department and a peasant and workers' department. In essence, the organizational structure was the same at the county level. Below this level were the party branches with a secretary and an alternate and committees for propaganda and organization. The basic level of the party structure was organized around cells.

Mao's New Democracy

The principles of this new-style Border Region were governed by Mao's notion of "New Democracy." Mao realized that it would be necessary to adopt policies for power sharing and to moderate economic policy in areas under communist control in order to win over other groups in the united front. Having defeated Wang Ming politically and rejected his notion of the united front, Mao was faced with having to provide a viable policy alternative, one that would neither drive away current supporters nor alienate potential new supporters. The need to rethink economic policy was heightened by the economic crisis that faced the Shaan-Gan-Ning in the early forties. In addition to countering the perceived failures of Wang Ming's approach to the united front, Mao also had to provide an alternative vision to GMD rule. By 1939, serious frictions had brought the united front to a possible breakup; at this point the CCP had to offer its own alternative. Articles began to appear and discussions took place about the nature of the Chinese revolution and the similarities and differences between the CCP and the GMD.[59]

Mao outlined his views on government and the strategy for attaining power in two important articles in October 1939 ("Introduction to the Communist") and January 1940 ("New Democratic Politics and New Democratic Culture"). While the former was intended for party members and not for public consumption, the latter was intended for the public at large to persuade them that the CCP had something to offer them.[60] As a result, the statements in "Introduction to the Communist" are harsher than in the latter piece. Thus, as Stuart Schram has pointed out, while "Introduction to the Communist" does not raise the question of who should exercise hegemony in the united front (it simply assumes that it is the CCP), "New Democratic Politics" skirts around the issue of communist leadership.[61]

In "Introduction to the Communist," Mao proposed the "three magic weapons" that would bring the party victory: the united front, armed struggle, and party building. For the united front, Mao proposed "unity and struggle." This meant that the alliance with the national bourgeoisie had to be maintained. Failure to do so would, according to Mao, result in "left opportunism." The bourgeoisie was to be struggled against by "peaceful" and "bloodless" means. However, opening up the system meant that the party would have to strengthen itself. Otherwise, it would commit the error of "right opportunism" and fall prey to those vacillating elements, especially among the big bourgeoisie, who sought to suppress the CCP. Party building would require the definition of ideological doctrine and the unification and rectification of the party on that basis. Mao argued that discipline and organization would have to be tightened and a resolute struggle conducted against erroneous tendencies. This would become the major focus of party work during the Rectification Campaign of 1942–1944. This would ensure that this time, when the split in the revolutionary forces occurred, the "proletariat" would be ready for the fight.

Mao's effort was to try to unite the party by appealing to all elements.

He argued for staying within the united front while holding out the prospect of future revolutionary struggle against the bourgeoisie. Although "New Democratic Politics" had a much more conciliatory tone, it showed that Mao's views had shifted substantially from his position at the Sixth Plenum (October 1938) and also reemphasized that the CCP had its own ultimate objectives. Although, as Schram writes, proletarian leadership of the united front was "covered with a rhetorical figleaf,"[62] for the first time since the outbreak of war, the CCP publicly put forward its claim to lead the revolution. According to Mao, the bourgeoisie had both revolutionary characteristics and a tendency towards compromise. As a result of this tendency towards compromise, the proletariat would have to assume leadership in China's struggle against imperialism and feudalism by default. During this first stage, there would be a "revolutionary democratic dictatorship" of several classes. In the second stage, the nonproletarian classes would be transformed gradually and the new democratic revolution would progress into its socialist stage. Although Mao said that the first phase would take a long time to complete, he was vague about when the change of stages would come about and criticized as "leftist" those who thought that socialism could be implemented before the new democratic revolution was completed. However, the article did return attainment of socialism to the CCP's political agenda.

In line with the view that it would be a long time before socialist construction was on the agenda, Mao outlined a moderate economic policy that would appeal to non-CCP elements. Private capitalist production would be allowed as long as it did not dominate the "livelihood of the people on a national scale." In the countryside, a rich peasant economy was proposed with only "big landlords" having their land confiscated and redistributed. This economic program was depicted as being in line with Sun Yat-sen's ideas.

As a political program, "New Democratic Politics" was well designed in its appeal to the party faithful by reasserting socialism as the party's final goal. At the same time, it sought to isolate the GMD by offering the "intermediate elements" a future stake in the revolutionary struggle.

The Three-Thirds System of Government

In the potentially hostile environment he found himself in, it was crucial for Mao to keep the local elites in the Border Region on his side, something that was perhaps even more important in the other communist base areas. Like the Shaan-Gan-Ning, they tended to be situated in poor, remote areas, often on provincial boundaries.[63] By early 1940 the most important of these other bases were Jin-Cha-Ji (Shanxi-Chahar-Hebei),[64] Jin-Ji-Lu-Yu (Shanxi-Hebei-Shandong-Henan), Jin-Sui (Shanxi-Suiyuan), and Shandong.

The situation was quite different in these base areas than in the Shaan-Gan-Ning Border Region. Shaan-Gan-Ning, apart from being the home of the Party Center, was beyond the reach of Japanese attacks and, having been formed earlier, it was almost entirely consolidated. By contrast, the other base areas led a precarious existence, always prey to Japanese attack and with significant populations of landlords and other elements who might become hostile to the communist presence. This meant that policies had to be more flexible and accommodating to a wider range of class interests. The Jin-Cha-Ji, in particular, served as a model for other base areas and also for Yan'an when the Party Center began to formulate its administrative and economic policies.[65] In 1939, Mao gave his seal of approval to the base area by writing the calligraphy for, and promoting, an account of the Jin-Cha-Ji Border Region as part of the development of a policy platform to counter Wang Ming's.[66]

Mao's thinking not only led to economic moderation but also had a major effect on the structure of Border Region administration. The experience of government in other regions led Mao to put forward officially in March 1940 the "three-thirds system" of political power.[67] In all political organs, communists were to be restricted to one-third of the positions with a further one-third for nonparty left-wing progressives and another one-third for "intermediate elements" who were neither left nor right. Mao pointed out that the middle bourgeoisie and enlightened gentry had up to then been excluded from power and that nonparty people who worked in government organs had been made to feel uncomfortable by having to "live, talk, and act like communists."

Mao's proposals were discussed, and on August 13, 1940, the CCP's Northern Bureau published the "Current Administrative Program for the Jin-Cha-Ji Border Region," more commonly known as the "Double Ten Policy."[68] It was a program that seemed to offer something to everyone, and gave significant concessions to the traditional elites in order to gain their support. Only the land and property of the worst "traitors" were to be confiscated; others could keep their property and continue to receive rent. Under the three-thirds system, they would be assured of positions in the local assembly as long as they did not transgress the anti-Japanese policy. Commitment to social reform was maintained, and workers were pledged an eight-hour workday. Peasants were guaranteed low rents and a progressive tax system, while the fears of landowners were eased by outlawing rent strikes and promising that payment would be enforced. This program provided the basis for the May 1941 Shaan-Gan-Ning policy that in turn became the model for the other bases.

In his work on the "Yan'an Way," Selden saw the second united front as containing potentially conflicting goals. He saw the communists, on the one hand, seeking the political participation of the traditional elite and the achievement of moderate socioeconomic and political reforms while, on the other hand, attempting to strengthen the grip of the party over the entire region and to build a firm base among its allies. In fact, these goals did not conflict. Mao and his supporters, such as Peng Zhen from the Jin-Cha-Ji, saw the three-thirds system of government not only as being compatible with CCP rule but also as providing the precise mechanism to strengthen the party's grip over the areas under its control. In this respect, it is important to bear in mind that the system was first implemented in the Jin-Cha-Ji, where party hegemony was far from complete, and in the Suide and Longdong regions of the Shaan-Gan-Ning Border Region, where party control was recent and insecure.[69]

This is the process that Hartford has termed "power management." The policy program and the administrative regulations were designed to neutralize the threat from the local elite by coopting them into the power structure and appearing to give them a place in the new political structure.[70]

In May and June 1940, the Border Region government carried out direct elections in the three counties of Suide, Wubao, and Qingjian for each county's heads of the Baojia and Lianbao systems and the county head. Before the subregion council was formally elected, between July 28 and August 4, 1940, the Suide garrison convened a temporary council to form an interim popular organ. Elections were carried out in accordance with the three-thirds principles, with the local gentry, the anti-Japanese political parties, and the organizations to save the country and the local governmental organs in the military selecting 75 councillors for participation. Of those elected, 17 were CCP members, 9 were from the GMD, and the rest had no party affiliation.[71] In the Longdong subregion, a temporary council was also selected by the political parties, local military, and mass organizations. Of the 75 selected, there were 5 CCP members and 5 GMD members, the remainder being drawn from the wide range of organizations in the region, such as other anti-Japanese parties, the women's federation, the chamber of commerce, and the trade unions. Clearly, at this level at least, the three-thirds proportions were somewhat lopsided, with the CCP drastically underrepresented. However, the election of the temporary county government councils in Suide and Longdong showed the advantage of the three-thirds system. In this indirect election, the CCP could exert its influence. For example, in Zhen county, the county government invited 35 people to form the government executive committee. Of these, 14 were from the CCP, 10 were GMD members, and the remaining 11 had no party affiliation.[72]

In his 1941 report on the Jin-Cha-Ji, Peng Zhen made the intention of the three-thirds system perfectly clear.[73] He showed how, by means of policies such as rent, interest reduction, and popular elections, the party penetrated into local society and increased its influence. Peng's main concern was how to build political power in the base area in such a way that party committees would be able to retain control of the policy process in the decentralized and fragmented situation. His intention was to break up the old power structure but to do so without alienating the powerful traditional elite. It was necessary to give them a stake in the running of the base area while, at the same time, making sure that the party could guide the political process. For Peng the three-thirds system was important and appreciated by the old elite. This made them, according to Peng,

> visibly happy and they realize that, under these circumstances, supporting and joining the anti-Japanese democratic governments is much more beneficial to them than blind opposition. Thus, they turn to supporting democracy. Some happily and loudly sing "even the best of dynasties is inferior to us"—this is the concrete attitude of the landlord class on the question of democracy. If one asks the landlord class why its attitude toward democratic politics is "opposition first and acceptance second," then its answer will certainly be, "Now I have lost my previous dictatorship and the new government treats me decently."

The old system was replaced with a system of village councils, which in turn elected the local administrative officials. This indirect system of election was designed to prevent the traditional village leaders from automatically ensuring their election to official positions. This forced them to ally with others within the councils where the CCP would have an automatic one-third representation.[74] However, for Peng, this system of popular elections to village councils required a widespread expansion of party organization in the villages combined with well-organized, politically motivated masses. Rather than weakening the party's role in the villages, Peng argued for a strengthening of the party apparatus at the village level to ensure that the local elite would not be able to dominate the political

process. Application of the three-thirds system of government in the villages would mean that each village would have a party branch with a "considerable number" of party members.

Further, by abolishing the requirement that candidates for position as district or county head would have at least two years' administrative experience, Peng opened up candidacy to a wider group than the old administrative elite. However, Peng was quite aware that the three-thirds system of government could not be rigidly applied. Rather, it was to form a general guideline for controlling political power. Indeed, Peng even suggested that a number of CCP members should resign if they won over one-third of the seats.

The policy governed the new elections for the various councils that were elected from 1941 onwards. Lin Boqu, reporting to the Shaan-Gan-Ning senior cadres conference in March 1944, provided statistics on the results of the elections in fourteen counties in the Border Region.[75] Of the 10,926 representatives elected to the township councils in these counties, 2,801 (25.6 percent) were CCP members, 352 (3 percent) belonged to the GMD, and the remaining 7,773 (71.4 percent) had no party affiliation. In eight of the counties, CCP representation was under one-third, while it exceeded one-third in the remaining six. For eight other counties, for which Lin gives more abbreviated information, the percentage of CCP representatives ranged from a low of 13.8 percent (Suide) to 29.3 percent (Heshui). Nearer to the center of the revolution, CCP representation rose. In Yan'an of the 1,291 township councillors elected, some 42 percent were CCP members.[76] In the election for the 323 members of the executive committees in Yan'an, the percentage rose to over 50 percent.

At the county level, there was a tendency also for CCP representation to increase. For example, in Yanchuan of the 99 councillors elected, 45 were CCP members.[77] The figures provided by Peng Zhen for the earlier elections in Jin-Cha-Ji showed much higher CCP representation at the county level. The average CCP representation was almost 50 percent for the twelve counties in the Beiyao and Wutai districts. Representation ranged from a low of 34 percent (Wuan) to a high of 74.5 percent in Hangtang (Table 6.5). Peng also provides evidence that CCP representation increased the higher one moved up the administrative ladder.

The social composition of those elected in the Shaan-Gan-Ning showed a predominance of poor and middle peasant representatives, with the former accounting for around 60 percent and the latter around 20 percent of the total in the fourteen-county survey. Landlords accounted for only about 1 percent (134 of 10,765) and rich peasants 6.2 percent (686 of

10,765). This did not mark a significant change over the situation in the 1937 elections at the township level for the four counties of Yanchang, Anding, Gulin, and Quzi for which we have figures. Here 71.4 percent of the representatives had been poor peasants, 17 percent middle peasants, 2 percent rich peasants, and 1 percent landlords.[78] All four counties, however, had undergone thorough land redistribution.

Peng Zhen's figures for elections to the seven counties in the Jin-Cha-Ji paint a similar picture. Workers, poor peasants, and middle peasants comprised 87.1 percent of village councils, 91.6 percent at the district level, and 82.1 percent at the county level. By contrast, landlords, rich peasants, and merchants made up 12.9 percent of village councils, 8.4 percent of

Table 6.5 Background of county councillors in thirteen counties in the elections of 1940

County	Number of county congressmen	CCP members		Progressive elements		Neutrals	
		No.	%	No.	%	No.	%
Wutai	60	27	45.00	24	40.00	9	15.00
Tang	63	25	39.68	22	34.92	16	25.40
Manchen	45	26	57.80	8	17.80	11	24.40
Dai	45	27	60.00	9	20.00	9	20.00
Zhun	35	20	57.10	7	20.00	8	22.90
Dingxiang	33	12	36.30	12	36.30	9	27.28
Quyang	56	28	50.00	12	21.43	16	28.57
Wuan	44	15	34.09	15	34.09	14	31.82
Pingshan	67	27	40.29	33	49.25	7	10.45
Jianping	72	25	34.72	25	34.72	22	30.56
Fuping	36	22	60.00	7	20.00	7	20.00
Laiyuan	49	34	69.38	8	16.32	7	14.28
Hangtang	51	38	74.50	4	7.84	9	17.65
Total	656	326	49.70	186	28.35	144	21.95

Source: Peng Zhen, *Guanyu Jin-Cha-Ji bianqu dangde gongzuo he juti zhengce baogao* (Report on Party Work and Specific Policies in the Jin-Cha-Ji Border Region) (Beijing: Zhonggong zhongyang dangxiao chubanshe, 1981), p. 46.

district councils and 17.9 percent of county councils. However, as Peng pointed out, this latter group was overrepresented in terms of its relationship to the population as a whole (7.9 percent). The problem of electing peasants and workers at the higher levels of government was compounded, in Peng's view, by the fact that their low educational level made it difficult for them to work competently. In addition, Peng suggests that the higher levels of government adminstration were not so important for them. They only viewed the village council elections as important.

At the level of the Border Region Council, the communists held a clear majority of the seats. Between November 6 and 21, 1941, the first Border Region Council met. Including alternate members there were 217 councillors of whom 123 were communists (56.7 percent) and 24 were GMD members (11 percent). The salvation society had 1 representative, the various minorities of the Border Region had 9, while the other 61 representatives were soldiers or came from various mass organizations. Of the councillors, 183 were elected directly, with one councillor being chosen by every 8,000 citizens. The government invited 36 people.[79] Where the CCP could exert greater influence, as in the indirect election for the Border Region executive organs, it took care to ensure that the balance approximated more correctly the three-thirds principle. Communists exceeded one-third of the positions in the original list of 51 candidates for the Standing Committee members (changzhu yiyuan). Consequently 6 CCP members withdrew their nominations. The three-thirds principle was fully honored with the election of 3 communists among the 9 finally elected. The same process occurred with the election of the Border Region Government Council. There were too many communists among the 39 original names, and as a result, 12 candidates withdrew. With one communist too many still remaining, Yu Teli also volunteered to withdraw. This resulted in 6 communists being elected to the 18 places on the Border Region Government Council.[80]

As in other fields, the party proved adept at learning from its experiences in Yan'an. As a result, the Border Region government used the experience to tighten up the procedure for the township elections in 1942. On March 6, 1942, it sent a letter of instruction on the three-thirds system to all counties about to undergo reelections between August and December.[81] The letter brought successful results, but the policy was still not implemented in all counties throughout the region. In the 1941 elections in Qingliu township of Qingjian county, 16 of the 36 councillors who were elected were CCP members. CCP members accounted for just over half of the head and deputy heads and six committee heads. Communists headed three of the sixteen natural and administrative villages. After the 1942 election, the picture had changed. Three of the five township officials were noncommunists, and only five of the village heads were communists.[82]

At the county level, in May and June 1942, various counties, including Yan'an, Yanchi, Ansai, Shenfu, Ganquan, Chishui, Quzi, and Yanchang, held their second council meeting. This time, to ensure that the balance was correct, some 100 CCP members voluntarily withdrew to allow non-CCP members to be elected. In this way, it was estimated that by the end of the year twenty-two counties had completely realized the three-thirds system.[83]

CCP–GMD Relations and the 1941 Crisis

By 1940 the united front began to dissolve. The blockade imposed by the GMD and the subsequent economic crisis that hit the Border Region in 1941 had a major effect on policy and led to the adoption of the campaigning style that Selden has termed the "Yan'an Way." Most important, as the campaigns spread out beginning in 1942, the party apparatus became increasingly dominant in people's lives, organizing campaigns and rallying mass organizations to meet the party's goals and objectives.

The Border Region was also affected by the increase in Japanese military activity that followed the "100 Regiments' Campaign" launched by the CCP in north China.[84] While the campaign may have boosted the morale of the resistance in China, it resulted in a major Japanese backlash during the years 1941 to 1944 in north China. The Shaan-Gan-Ning itself did not come under attack, but the pressures on the base area increased, especially financially. A large number of soldiers and cadres were withdrawn to the Shaan-Gan-Ning from other base areas, such as the Jin-Cha-Ji, increasing the strain on the Border Region's finances.

The problems caused the main emphasis of work to be shifted to practical and immediate ways of coping. The ecclesiastical quality of the community ensured that no trial would be considered too great to overcome. It also meant that every individual was constantly being tested by the elements as well as the enemy. There was a Jobian aspect to the whole enterprise: how well one withstood such trials was a testimonial to one's revolutionary will and character.

An ethos that might be called "controlled voluntarism" prevailed. Backsliders were treated with severity and firmness, a mixture of generosity and ruthlessness depending on person, place, time, mood, and circumstance.

Those who resisted or did not conform were considered morally lacking or, in the language of the day, "softboned." Above all, education increasingly emphasized that every act was a surrogate for something larger than itself, the entire Border Region a surrogate for a China yet to be built. Among the general effects of the GMD blockade was a heightened sense of urgency and beleaguerement.[85] People believed that spies had infiltrated. It was in this environment that the Rectification Campaign was organized and launched in 1942. The crisis made mobilization essential. The Rectification Campaign was qualitatively distinct from the campaigns to increase production and to simplify the Border Region government. It belonged to a different political agenda.

By 1939, relations between the CCP and the GMD had begun to sour. CCP expansion brought it into conflict with local GMD troops, culminating in what the communists termed the "first and second anti-communist upsurges" (December 1939–March 1940 and January 1941). If it had not been obvious before, the Southern Anhui Incident of January 1941 made it clear that the alliance between the two parties was dead, in practice if not in theory. While this incident marked the worse of the clashes between CCP and GMD forces, the GMD did not release its economic stranglehold on the Shaan-Gan-Ning.

The GMD blockaded the Border Region in 1939 and, to make matters worse, cut off its subsidies. The economic blockade severely affected the trade potential of the Border Region. Inflation became a serious problem; money received from the GMD declined to one-seventh of its original value by 1940.[86] In 1941 the GMD cut off the subsidy altogether. After the second united front was agreed upon, the Nationalist Government had agreed to provide 1.2 million *yuan (fabi)* per year for support of government expenses and 6 million *yuan* for military expenses. The importance of this aid is shown by the fact that in 1939, Nationalist subsidies accounted for 89.66 percent of the total Border Region budget; in 1940, a year when the communists complained of the GMD withholding funds, the subsidies still accounted for 73.5 percent of the budget.[87] In 1941, the first year without GMD support, the budget showed a deficit of 5.8 million *yuan (bianbi)* (around 15 million *yuan* in *fabi*).

Selden's stress on the effect of the economic blockade and the increase in Japanese military activity does, of course, explain why the communists faced such difficulties in 1941. However, this explanation overlooks the inherent weakness of the Border Region economy that the subsidies had papered over. Chen Yung-fa's study has demonstrated that the CCP, despite the land revolution, had failed to establish a sound financial base and depended financially first on confiscation of the property of enemy classes and later on outside help to maintain its solvency until 1941. The GMD subsidy helped the CCP meet its political objectives by operating a low tax policy that was exacted only on the rich peasantry. In December 1935, for example, some 52 percent of CCP monthly revenue came from confiscations and attacks on local gentry; this rose to 56 percent by the end of 1936. One of the first results of the economic blockade was to force the CCP to increase taxation on the local population, but even this was not enough to compensate for the lost revenue.[88] By 1943 the Border Region Government was suffering from a deficit of 30.4 percent on its annual budgetary needs.[89] As Chen Yung-fa notes, "It was this heavy dependency and lack of an independent revenue base that accounted for the severity of the economic problems faced by the party during the three difficult years."[90]

To deal with the huge problems facing the Border Region, the party resorted to mobilization techniques in the hope that people's enthusiasm would overcome the obstacles. In the following years, the party sponsored campaigns for rent and interest reduction, large-scale production campaigns, and the mutual-aid movement. Their apparent success in turning around the Border Region economy has been praised by foreign writers and CCP historians alike. For CCP historians, this success lies at the core of the "Yan'an Spirit" that has been subsequently invoked when the party has found itself confronted by major challenges or seemingly insurmountable problems. The appeals to dedication and selfless sacrifice were most important for convincing the faithful that they were engaged in an honorable exercise. This helped them implement a production and self-sufficiency campaign that was later turned into legend: a Border Region that pulled itself up by the bootstraps when confronted by overwhelming odds. The reality was somewhat different.

The economic blockade led to a campaign known as "Crack Troops and Simple Administration." The objectives were to try to reduce the size of the bureaucracy and the regular military organizations while improving the overall quality. (With the base area's revenues shrinking, it was not possible to maintain such a large administration.) The policy itself was adopted by the Border Region Assembly of Representatives in November 1941 and promoted throughout the administration from December onwards.[91]

On December 4, 1941, the Border Region government sent out a directive to all counties highlighting two main problems in the administrative structure.[92] First, there were too many people and organizations at the top while, at the lower levels, the quantity and quality of cadres was deficient. This meant that in some places good policies were not being implemented. This top-heavy structure was to be corrected by transferring down senior personnel and decentralizing some decision-making powers. However, the directive pointed out that only a limited number should be transferred from the county level to the village level. In the military, the surplus officials could be transferred to production work as a part of the drive for self-sufficiency. Second, the directive stated that government work at all levels had to be systematized in order to improve it. The lack of a clear system was creating problems. To guide the movement, a rectification committee *(bianzheng weiyuanhui)* was set up to be in charge of the investigating and rectification of government organs, the merging or abolition of superfluous organs, and cadre reallocation.

However, it proved difficult to reduce the size of the bureaucracy and the number of officials. As a result, the official media published frequent reminders on the importance of the campaign.[93] In January 1944, Li Dingming summed up the progress of the campaign thus far to the Border Region Council of Representatives.[94] According to Li, one-quarter of the units of various departments, sections, and administrative councils had been either reduced or combined. Li also claimed success in terms of personnel reduction and even admitted that a few organs were now short of staff. At the central government level mergers between various departments and the general office meant that personnel had been reduced by 40 percent.[95]

Two methods were used to remove surplus personnel. The first was to send them to school, a measure that would not have lightened the load on production. The second was to send them off to engage in productive work. At the level of the Border Region government, the majority were "sent to school." According to Li, some one hundred fifty senior and middle cadres were sent to school to "improve them and for them to become more cultivated." However, at the lower levels of administration, the majority were sent to engage in production.

Despite such reports of impressive achievements, other accounts suggest that the campaign was less successful than was hoped for. Early in 1943, as a third wave of the campaign was to be launched, the Chairman of the Border Region government, Lin Boqu, stated that currently there were 8,200 cadres serving in government at all levels; this was more than the total of 7,900 that was noted at the beginning of the movement in December 1941. In addition, 3,300 students were supported by the government at the middle-school level (excluding the military schools), and a total of 22,500 were "eating the government's grain."[96] Li Dingming pointed out that due to the fact that those in school consumed government grain and that dependents had often not been reassigned, some 1,000 to 1,500 people above the quota were still consuming government grain in 1944.

The major campaign launched to deal with the economic problems was the production campaign. While the Rectification Campaign in the party was to lead to a harsher atmosphere for members, the party's economic policy showed continued commitment to building alliances with nonparty elements. Radicalization within the party was not allowed to spill over to economic policy. On January 28, 1942, the Politburo approved a Central Committee decision on land policy in the base areas.[97] The decision was designed to appeal to all classes in the rural areas. Although the peasants were described as constituting the "basic strength" of the resistance effort, most landlords were described as being anti-Japanese and even some of the gentry were said to be sufficiently enlightened to support democratic reform. After rent and interest reduction had been completed, landlords were to be assured of receiving their outstanding money. The decision pointed out that in areas where this policy had been carried out more extensively, participation by the local population in the war of resistance had been higher. Further, the decision recognized that the capitalist mode of production was "the more progressive method" in China and that the bourgeoisie, particularly the petty and national bourgeoisie, was a relatively progressive force. In short, the decision was an appeal for evenhanded treatment by local officials of the different classes in the base areas under CCP control.

In December 1942, Mao Zedong delivered a major report to the Northwest Bureau's senior cadres conference that outlined the economic principles of his Republic.[98] In general terms, the report was a response to the economic crisis that was facing the Shaan-Gan-Ning Border Region. In line with the united front approach, Mao sought to bring together all groups to play a role in strengthening the local economy. Mao acknowledged that improving the standard of living of the local population was the key to engaging its help in the war of resistance.

According to Mao, the only way in which living standards could be raised was through the development of the private sector, essentially the agricultural, handicraft, and commercial sectors. Thus, the positive role that rich peasants could play was acknowledged, and previous "leftist" deviations that had frightened the peasants into not producing for fear of being labeled as enemies were criticized. Party officials and the army were to cease being a burden on the local economy by trying to achieve self-sufficiency in production through running their own agricultural, industrial, and commercial undertakings. The new policy was to promote a mixed economy that would even acknowledge a certain level of exploitation. (This was justified by the overwhelming stress on the need to develop production.) To raise productivity, Mao sanctioned the use of mutual-aid teams for the exchange and contracting of labor. These teams were to build on the traditional methods of cooperation, such as the pooling of labor or animals or the hiring of labor teams. They were to evolve voluntarily and were not to be forced on the peasantry. However, the party sought to draw out this form of cooperation from short-term, seasonal cooperation to broader-based, long-term cooperation.

For the most part, the party simply tried to ensure that the market operated smoothly, but it also tried to stimulate the development of consumer and producers' cooperatives. As his model, Mao put forward the Southern District Cooperative. The ideal form was for the cooperative to be owned and controlled by peasant shareholders. Mao saw this form of economic organization as linking government activity to that of the people, as the management of the cooperative was expected to look after the interests of the shareholders and find ways to implement government policy. As Mao pointed out, the cooperative, in the midst of a small-scale peasant economy, was to play a pivotal role in implementing the government's economic policies and in organizing and encouraging people to develop the economy.

Finally, it was in this context that Mao stressed the need for party, army, and government to strive for self-sufficiency. Mao noted that the army was the best in self-sufficient production because of its labor power and organization. As a model, Mao put forward Wang Zhen's 359 Brigade and its Nanniwan farm to the south of Yan'an. According to Mao, the brigade had "grasped the primary importance of agriculture," thus ensuring that the economic base had a secure foundation. This base had been used to develop industry, handicrafts, transport, and a commercial outlet.

The results of this reorientation of production and the self-sufficiency drive were good, but were not so spectacular as to resolve the Border Region's financial crisis by themselves. In 1943, the production drive intensified, stressing self-sufficiency. The objective was to make both the Border Region and the military organizations and other units self-sufficient. While many units did attain self-sufficiency, such units generally becoming models for others to emulate, the production campaigns still fell short of resolving the problem: the budget deficit was relieved only by some 20 percent.

What really contributed to the "Yan'an Spirit" was, as Chen Yung-fa has demonstrated, opium production and its export. This was what ultimately enabled the Border Region to overcome its financial crisis. The party was careful to ensure that opium use did not spread through the region under its control, but it desperately needed the money from the export of opium to other areas of China in order to keep the economy afloat. One of the main investors in the Local Product Company that was set up in Yan'an to promote the sale of opium was none other than Wang Zhen's model 359th Brigade.[99] In 1943, without the inclusion of opium revenues, the trade deficit for the Border Region was either almost 4,000 million or 4,800 million *yuan bianbi,* depending on which source one uses. If the opium factor is included, the deficit is effectively halved. By 1944, the figures are even more telling. The first source shows opium exports turning a deficit on trade of some 6,750 million *yuan bianbi* to a profit of 15,631 *yuan bianbi;* in 1945, a deficit of almost 1,000 million is changed to a profit of 3,000 million.[100] Indeed, even as early as 1942, profits from opium production were said to account for 40.9 percent of revenues.

Once the financial crisis eased, the party halted opium production. It had been a temporary expedient to save the revolution, a necessary evil to keep the revolution alive. However, it destroyed the myth that the Border Region could have survived without external trade. If one consequence of Mao's policies was the generation of symbolic capital, one must also add that the economic base of Yan'an depended on the poppy. As Chen Yung-fa wrote, this reveals the realistic rather than the romantic Mao. The Rectification Campaign that was launched in 1942 would reveal yet another Mao.

7

YAN'AN AS A
REVOLUTIONARY SIMULACRUM

✳

As suggested at the beginning of the last chapter, in studying Yan'an one needs to distinguish the core from the larger Border Region, just as one needs to separate the three-thirds system of government and the overlapping jurisdictions of party, civil, and military administrations from the essential Yan'an organized around educational institutions. These educational institutions were the chief instruments through which Mao's discourse was transmitted, communicated, and taught. Within the core, the discourse represented a unique vocabulary. It had its own signals, codes, and triggering phrases, each consistent with the other. It used its own standardized tropes. The core became the simulacrum, a miniaturized space for the discourse community, so much so that one could call it not only utopic, but also *utropic*—that is, a kind of utopia constructed of tropes toward which outsiders were attracted.

Inside this utopia there was a high degree of mutual obligation and predictability. Outside it, both these features were virtually absent. Internally, the discourse ordered social life through storytelling and logical interpretation. Externally, in an effective network of organizations it was what bound people together. Together, in the context of a logocentric model, was a complete system of metaphors and metonymies. Manifested within the corpus of Mao Zedong Thought, this abstract ordering had to be realized in the form of concrete experience. For Mao, Marxism meant the interpenetration of work and knowledge. In the core community, these ingredients were combined so effectively that the discourse became a *doxa* with Yan'an the *habitus*.[1]

The core Yan'an also represented a public space, an arena, a stage, and a dramatic setting. The discourse was naturalized by people poring over the text, interpreting their experiences, and expressing themselves in public utterances that bound addresser and addressee. The audience so unified consisted of more than listeners, and as leaders became connected to the led, myths became logical; logic, experience; and experience, truth. In this way, a master narrative was formed, a self-constituted synthesis: symbolic capital.

Within both the public space and the primary units the same vocabulary prevailed. The primary unit reinforced the public space, and the public was drawn down to the primary. Conduct included a complex signaling system in which enthusiasm, brightness, and willingness replaced assertiveness, moodiness, and fear. Yan'an was the bright way as well as the right way, and any individual doubt became a condition of self-criticism. Indeed, one came to believe in the richness of the interpretative scheme, while the scheme itself was reduced to code phrases, which in the mouthing seemed to add to individual profundity (without which the brightness would appear too superficial). Outside observers were convinced that this process produced a remarkable sincerity of both individual and institution, and commented on it.[2] They were less inclined to notice how formulaic the interpretative scheme had become and that any variation could be considered grounds for reeducation and rectification.

Performance mattered a great deal. The agoras, the public arenas of Yan'an, became the sites for changes in the formula, where displays of the power of orality marked the occasion for changes in textuality. The formation of a new text became a critical event. These were the moments when new truths were discovered to add to the extant corpus. They were expressions of Mao's unfolding vision of dialectical truth through the public display of his praxis of contradiction. Such occasions excited the Yan'anites. They produced hubbub and discussion. In this sense, in the miniaturized space of the core Yan'an, narrative and orality and textuality and theater became performance.

On an everyday basis an institutional network, simple in form but elaborate in structure, was established. It was composed of nuclei that we shall call *primary units*. The structure of the core community was based on these primary units. But primary units, affiliated with educational bodies, schools, colleges, institutes, and training centers, were linked to party, army, and civil administration. It was inside these primary units that people lived and worked; they constituted the cellular structure Shue described so well.[3]

Such units assumed particular importance for students. Almost all of them had left their families behind and indeed virtually all previous associations and affiliations. In the absence of family, primary units became substitutes, but with one critical exception. There was no father. As a result, and as revealed in some of the interviews, one's self-esteem became bound up with how one was perceived by, and how well one interacted, with one's primary group. Emotions were disciplined, since within the unit there was no privacy. In fact, there was a virtual absence of private space. Not surprisingly, the new discourse, the vocabulary, the formula were not only learned in schools but also absorbed through daily participation in one's unit of affiliation *(danwei)*. Education in Yan'an was associated with the elimination of any sphere of private space. One needs to visualize this core as constructed out of primary units of affiliation, each a representation in miniature of the Yan'an public sphere as a discourse community. The public sphere, in turn, is an enlarged version of the primary unit. Filiation was complex, but the unit structure remained very simple. Wherever one was posted subsequent to a particular educational experience, the same structures were replicated and the same discourse prevailed. All organizations and work units were built up out of similar primary units, and all work units contained their own living units in a pattern extending throughout. All administrative systems *(xitong)* followed the same formula.

By the same token, each primary unit provided a concrete context for the system of signals and codes—the same system of denotations and connotations in which the ends of winning the war against Japan and revolution hid the fact that the ultimate design was, prescriptively, utterly vague. This is one reason for describing Yan'an more as a utropic than a utopic community. Of course, there was a set of working political rules and procedures following the principles of the three-thirds system of government. These established the formal conditions for participation in the Border Region as a whole, and elsewhere as well. Within the core, the linking institutions and organizations in the party and the military replicated stable contexts for meanings. Far more important than either constitutional, procedural, or legal rules was the structure of the discourse itself as a stable contextual meaning structure within which the crucial revolutionary metaphors communicated specific referents.[4]

What made Yan'an possible as a discourse community is both its meaning structure and its reliance on an educational structure for the building blocks of the utropic community. Of course, given the larger mythological context, this educational structure does not simply convey conventional knowledge but starts with disjunctive breaks and ruptures of the conventional discourse. It provides the contextual frame for its own language and sets of metaphors, and grounds these in experience and work. It creates new meaning, provides a new structure of logic, and expresses that structure in texts. The texts furnish revolutionary metonymies. The entire process constitute not only a discourse of its own but also units for the production, proliferation, and dissemination of the discourse. One joins the revolution as a discourse community. The primary units of affiliation are educational, so we will begin our examination of Yan'an as simulacrum with an examination of the educational system, then move on to cultural diffusion, rectification, and exegetical bonding. All these are welded together in what Mao called the Yan'an "smelter."[5]

Raymond Wylie points out "prior to 1935, selected cadres from national Communist parties were sent to Moscow for advanced training in Marxism-Leninism . . . After the Comintern's Seventh Congress in 1935, there was an increasing emphasis on the development of higher party schools in individual countries." Accordingly, after arriving in Yan'an the party set about establishing a range of schools, covering subjects from ideology to the arts (see appendix). Wylie goes on to note, "This proliferating educational system, developed side by side with Mao's growing power in the party, gave Mao the means to exercise a degree of ideological control over the party that had never been possible before. It was this educational system that was to serve as the incubator for Mao's Rectification Movement of 1942–43."[6] According to Li Rui, who for a while served as Mao's personal secretary, in the forties at any one time there were approximately 50,000 cadres of which a large proportion of the younger ones had come through the Yan'an educational network.[7]

If education characterizes the structure of the core, radical students gave it a distinctive flavor. Most were young and from the white areas; a good many had a middle-school education. They responded well to the highly structured but often informal methods of instruction. Organized into study and work brigades along semi-military lines, their affiliational units were mainly residential and tied to a particular school, college, university, technical institute, or training college. With a high proportion living eight to a cave, the result was "deep imprinting," especially on the military and civil cadres who, in increasing numbers, were products of the Yan'an network of educational institutions.

In this living and work setting, informal though it was, nothing was left to chance. One was not allowed to talk about trivial things. Gossip was a guilty pleasure. Each person demonstrated his or her fair share of concern with such questions as ideas and representation, materialism and idealism, reflection and reality, universals and particulars. So insistent were these as topics of study, debate, and reflection that everyone was able to look back with astonishment at what their discourse had wrought. They felt their minds materializing as power. Of course all this heady philosophical talk was not for everyone. But everyone did have to learn about theory and practice, universals in particulars, and the concrete and the abstract as a kind of catechism.

This is why discourse as hierarchy, language as power, and class and the derivation of wisdom were among the most serious concerns in a Yan'an ostensibly devoted to war and fighting. Even war and fighting were made to center around education, giving a military form to the group life. This extended to the curricula and the interpenetration of the higher knowledge with its truths, to the revolutionary culture and its diffusion. Indeed one can see manifested in the core of Yan'an virtually all the Platonic concerns. As in Plato's *Republic*, there are plenty of bolstering myths where reason leaves off.

In this loose sense, the term "revolutionary Platonism" applies very well to Yan'an. The point is that we are not dealing simply with propaganda, although propaganda would become the job of many Yan'anites, but rather a totalized and in its own way hermetic system by which one observes "reality," finding in it facts that reinforce truths.[8] Most of the recipients of this educational system had a great deal to absorb in quick doses. As students their tenure tended to be very short. Hence the need to drench them as much as possible in the totality of the revolutionary experience. It should also be said that student life, while hard, was exceptionally lively, so imbued were people with an original sense of mission and a cultivated desire to learn.

Indeed, Jane Price has called Yan'an the "student city."[9] The training institutions constituted a miniaturized universe of their own within the larger frame of the military and the administrative organization of both the party as a whole and Yan'an as a Border Region. While certainly not insulated from the rest of Yan'an, these educational institutions did share a certain interiority, and this fact had several consequences. People formed cohort friendships and sustaining commitments while subscribing to communist norms of impersonality of association. Furthermore, inwardness diluted the harshness of the terrain and made people less fearful of externally generated crises, like the GMD blockade.

The Evolution in the Revolution

Mao liked to call himself a teacher. From the beginning, he managed to combine the two roles of teacher and revolutionary. The student study society he had helped set up in Changsha in 1918 became one of the best known among the many founded around that time, including the Marxist Research Society, the Awakening Society, the Socialist Youth League, and the Mass Education Speech Corps.[10] It was significant that Mao's group was called the New Citizen Study Society *(Xinmin xuehui)*.

The history of the Communist Party and the evolution of its tutelary role in China cannot really be separated from these study groups and the party schools, which evolved into a ramified system of institutes and other bodies including, for example, the Shanghai University.[11] Military instruction was also intertwined with politics. For example, Zhou Enlai was the political commissar of the Whampoa (Huangpu) Military Academy, the political work of which was dominated by communists and the left GMD. As soon as the Jiangxi base was established various military and other training institutes were founded, most importantly the Academy of Marxian Communism, founded in March 1933 "to commemorate the fiftieth anniversary of Marx's death," and the Red Army Academy, in both of which a good deal of experimentation went on with methods of instruction and the teaching of senior cadres.[12]

The educational system in Yan'an was influenced in part by the early Soviet experience. Large numbers of young Chinese attended such institutions as Sun Yat-sen University in Moscow, as well as the University of the Toilers of the East and other Soviet educational bodies, where there was extensive and explicit use of cultural materials for propaganda.[13] Their experience helped define the role of Chinese communist educational and cultural activities.

Mao's own ideas about education both reflected his ambivalence about intellectuals and resembled the Leninist ideal of instilling revolutionary perspectives. His methods, however, were more experimental. Mao put his views on such matters very succinctly in a comment on the May Fourth movement:

> In the Chinese democratic revolutionary movement, it was the intellectuals who were the first to awaken. This was clearly demonstrated both in the Revolution of 1911 and the May Fourth Movement, and in the days of the May Fourth Movement the intellectuals were more numerous and more politically conscious than in the days of the Revolution of 1911. But the intellectuals will accomplish nothing if they fail to integrate themselves with the workers and peasants. In the final analysis, the dividing line between revolutionary intellectuals and non-revolutionary or counter-revolutionary intellectuals is whether or not they are willing to integrate themselves with the workers and peasants and actu-

ally do so. Ultimately it is this alone, and not professions of faith in the Three Principles of the People or in Marxism, that distinguishes one from the other. A true revolutionary must be one who is willing to integrate himself with the workers and peasants and actually does so.[14]

Before the communists were able to establish a solid presence in the area, there had been virtually no provision for education in the Border Region as a whole. Even basic education was extremely poor. Across the region illiteracy rates ran at about 90 percent; in some counties, such as Huachi and Quzi, the literacy rate was no more than 0.5 percent.[15]

In the twenties, the only districts in north Shaanxi with a middle school were Suide and Yulin. As in other areas of China, these two schools provided the initial cadre for the communist group in the Shaanxi area. Li Zizhou, one of the founders of the local movement, taught at the Suide Normal School; Li and Wei Yezhou, who worked at the Yulin Middle School, had both been influenced by party founder Li Dazhao. The list of graduates of the Yulin school reads like a who's who of the early Shaanxi party apparatus. Graduates who became active in the movement included Liu Zhidan, Gao Gang, Xie Zichang, and Wang Ziyi.[16] By July 1927, when the CCP fully recognized the important role of the peasantry, it also noted the respect schoolteachers enjoyed in the local communities. As a result the party called for the election of primary schoolteachers to the area executive committees of peasant associations.[17] This was in marked contrast to the disdain with which such groups were viewed by the party when it tried to organize urban China during the early twenties.

Once the communists consolidated their base they sponsored a major expansion of primary and secondary education. This expansion grew even more rapidly after the Border Region government was set up. In the winter of 1935, the soviet set up 5 new primary schools in Yan'an county with about 70 pupils, and in 1936 another 25 were added with 500 pupils. The conditions of guerrilla warfare meant that when the Border Region was set up only 120 primary schools, with some 2,000 pupils, came under its jurisdiction.[18] However, between 1937 and 1945 the number of primary schools increased from 545 to 1,395, with the number of pupils rising from 10,396 to 79,500.[19] The number of schools dropped temporarily in 1942 when the Border Region government launched the "Put the Stress on Quality, Don't Emphasize Quantity" *(zhongzhi bu zhongshu)* movement. This enforced retrenchment caused the number of schools to drop to 847.[20]

The primary schools were not excluded from Yan'an's drive for self-sufficiency. The regulations for primary schools promulgated in February 1942 called for educational methods to be linked with "production, society, the home, and struggle against the enemy." To deal with the financial problems facing the Border Region in general, the system of part study and part production was adopted. Productive work was also seen as good experience that would help pupils prepare for future life. No moment was left unused. On Sundays and in their spare time pupils engaged in sponsored social activities and were urged to "carry out anti-Japanese war propaganda, ferret out traitors, join in spring planting and autumn harvesting and mobilize new soldiers." In just six months, primary school students in Yan'an county planted over forty *shang* of land, found two hundred opium burners, and hunted down forty-five fugitive soldiers.[21] In addition, primary school pupils were expected to encourage others to act as models for others to follow. For example, the "young gentleman's system" *(xiao xiansheng zhi)* comprised attempts to persuade relatives to follow their example and become literate. In Suide city, within one month, 700 women and children were encouraged to enter literacy groups through this method. In September 1937, the Border Region government launched a major literacy campaign, and by 1938 there were 5,834 such literacy groups with nearly 40,000 people participating. These were small teaching groups, often consisting of no more than the members of one family. As the movement wound down, so did the number of groups: in 1941 there were only 1,973 such groups with 12,259 students (see Table 7.1).

During the same period, the number of middle schools increased from one in 1937 to seven in 1945 with the number of students rising from 250 to 2,443.[22] On September 8, 1938, the Yan'an middle school was set up. However, because of the Japanese air raids, in November it was shifted to Ansai county. On September 6, 1939, it was merged with the Lu Xun Normal School to form the Border Region Normal School. Students attended the Yan'an middle school for a period of between three and six months. In September 1940, the Longdong middle school was set up, effectively taking over the Mizhi middle school (set up in 1926). This was followed by the establishment of the Sanbian Public School.

In line with the 1942 regulations for the administration of middle schools, the length of junior middle school was set at three years, with senior middle comprising a further two years.[23] As in the primary schools, middle schools stressed participation in production; even more than in the

Table 7.1 Part-time education in the Shaan-Gan-Ning

Type of group	1937	1938	1939	1940	1941
Literacy groups:					
No. of groups		5,834	3,852	3,580	1,973
No. of students		39,983	24,107	23,725	12,259
Night schools:					
No. of schools		599	535	545	505
No. of students		8,245	8,086	8,706	7,905
Half-day schools:					
No. of schools		236	202	379	393
No. of students		3,994	3,323	5,833	5,990
Winter schools:					
No. of schools	382	728	643	965	659
No. of students	10,337	12,824	17,750	21,689	20,619

Source: Yan'an Revolutionary Museum, *Ziliao xuanbian* (Selected Materials) (Yan'an: May 1981), vol. 1, p 35.

primary schools, middle schools stressed participation in the revolution. Participation in production was seen as a way to help cover school costs and reduce dependence on the government. According to the regulations, middle school pupils had to participate in production for between twenty days and one month every year. Thus, in 1941, the students of the Longdong middle school reclaimed eighty-five *mu* (almost 15 acres) of wasteland and produced various goods valued at 124 million *yuan bianbi*. Middle schools also served as training grounds for the revolution. The students supplemented Border Region work by taking notes for the government, writing reports, filling out forms, helping township and village cadres propagandize policies, laws, and directives, carrying out "social education," conducting hygiene movements, and organizing mass production. The vast majority of graduates were immediately sent into action. Of the fifty-two graduates from the Longdong middle school in 1942, forty-eight went into revolutionary work, one died, and three returned home.[24]

    A main focus of attention for the party was the development of supplementary schools and all forms of part-time and on-the-job training. It was important to ensure that as many adults as possible carry on with their regular work as they continued their education. Ever since it was founded, the party saw the expansion of this kind of education as an important part of communist policy. Acquiring basic skills in literacy was combined with the teaching of basic communist policies and objectives. In Beijing in the early twenties, for example, communists made some headway against a reluctant population through the use of workers' supplementary schools, where education was used consciously as a form of agitprop. Through literacy campaigns, ideas such as the eight-hour workday were introduced. However, party activists were wary of declaring themselves to be communist.[25]

In Yan'an, wide use was made of night schools, half-day schools, and winter schools to rapidly expand access to basic education. All these forms of education were geared to ensuring that production not be disrupted at the expense of learning. In 1938, there were 599 night schools in the Border Region with 8,245 students; by 1941, the numbers had declined to 505 and 7,905 respectively. During the same period the number of half-day schools increased from 236 to 393, with the number of students increasing from 3,994 to 5,990. Winter schools increased from 728 with 12,824 students to a peak of 965 with 21,689 students in 1940 before the number of schools dropped to 659 the following year, although the number of students remained relatively steady at 20,619 (see Table 7.1).

One other form of training was the midday school, which took advantage of the midday rest period for educational purposes. This type of school focused mainly on women. Finally, there were "touring education" groups that would move from village to village. In addition, there were ten performing troupes and 3,371 reading newspaper groups in 1941, one for every 450 people.[26] All the different forms of part-time education shared the idea of linking basic literacy with an understanding of the objectives of the Communist Party. Teaching materials, while simple, would contain easily understandable messages explaining how the peasants' misery derived from the repression of the landlords, the warlords, and more recently from the Japanese invaders.

A distinctive feature of Yan'an in the education field was the high number of institutions that were specially geared to training to party, military, and government cadres (see appendix). These schools had the task of ensuring that cadres would be faithful to party policy and would know how to function within the intricacies of the united front; the schools also were to instruct the new recruits and those who had made their way to Yan'an in the norms of Mao's revolution.

At most only some 25,000 party members had made it from the south to the north during the Long March, and the movement was severely short of cadres to staff its apparatus. This shortage became more acute as the Border Region expanded in territory and in population. Education levels among Border Region cadres were low. For example, literacy rates in

Ansai county were 57.1 percent for district heads, 85.7 percent for self-defense corps heads *(ziweijun guanzhang)*, 100 percent for women federation heads, 67.1 percent for union heads, and 28.6 percent for security assistants and Salvation Society heads.[27] This, of course, did not bode well for the cadres' understanding of the intricacies of Marxist-Leninist theory (perhaps a factor that was conducive to their accepting a bastardized version of it). Many of the better educated patriots who had come to the Border Region also did not have a solid understanding of Marxism-Leninism.

This situation led to a major effort first to expand cadre education and then to ensure that cadre education conformed to the needs of the Rectification Campaign. In spring 1939, cadre education was placed under a special education department under the leadership of the CCP Central Committee. Zhang Wentian was appointed head with Li Weihan as his deputy. In June 1940, that department was merged with the Propaganda Department to become the Propaganda and Education Department, which was revamped again in October and renamed the Propaganda Department, though it retained control over the education of all cadres. Propaganda and education were seen as indivisible. In November and December 1939, the Second Congress of the Shaan-Gan-Ning Party passed the "Resolution on the Question of the Education of Party Cadres," which set down some basic guidelines for the objectives of the training. It called for illiteracy among party cadres to be eradicated during 1940 and set a target for all cadres to recognize at least 1,000 characters. To meet this objective, the Border Region Committee of the party published a basic book for cadres containing 1,000 characters. To facilitate the training, they were split into three levels: senior, middle, and beginners. The senior classes included the following subjects of study: Chinese, math, history, geography, and *Jiefang ribao* (Liberation Daily); the middle level covered Chinese, history and geography, knowledge of the natural and social sciences, math, and *Qunzhong bao* (The Masses). The beginners' level had to study volumes one and two of the Cultural Exercise Book (including materials for the study of Chinese), general knowledge about the natural and social sciences, and *Qunzhong bao*. In 1940, to help with understanding of theory, three books were issued for study by cadres at the county and subregion level. These materials were volume two of *Communism and the Communist Party (Gongchan zhuyi yu gongchandang)*, and volume one of the *History of the Chinese Current Revolutionary Movement (Zhongguo xiandai geming yundongshi)* and the *Short History of the Communist Party of the Soviet Union (Bolshevik)*. In

December 1940, Lin Boqu wrote to county heads and *Zhuanyuan,* (commissioners) informing them that they would also be required to "study conscientiously" *On Leninism, On Protracted Warfare, On the New Period, New Democracy,* and key articles published in the Party Committee of the Border Region, "Discussion of the Township Soviet Movement" *(Lun xiang su gongzuo),* the weekly *Jiefang,* and *Xin Zhonghua bao.*

Having provided its members with basic literacy, the party was moving to ensure that they also appreciated ideological correctness. Of course, the party had operated training schools before arriving in north Shaanxi, but it was in Yan'an that the schools were to be shaped more directly by Mao and his supporters. It was through these training institutions that Mao would direct his reeducation campaigns.

The most important training institute for the military and its cadres was The Chinese People's Anti-Japanese Military and Political University *(Zhongguo renmin kangRi junzheng daxue, Kangda).* Kangda was formally set up on January 21, 1937, in Yan'an under the directorship of Lin Biao with Liu Bocheng as his deputy. Luo Ruiqing served as dean of the faculty and Fu Zhong as head of the Political Department.[28] Kangda had been reorganized from the Shaan-Gan-Ning Red Army Military Affairs College *(Shaan-Gan-Ning hongjun junshi xuexiao),* which had been set up in Wayaobao in October 1935; it owed its ultimate origins to the Red Army Academy in Ruijin.

With each student intake Kangda became increasingly diverse, reflecting the changing circumstances of the base area and the party's changing policy. At first the students came mainly from the military and military-political arenas. Later, as the united front developed, classes became more "intellectual," with most of the students drawn from the white areas.

The first students were virtually all from the Central Red Army and the Red Twenty-Fifth Army and had participated in Long March. The students were split into three groups. The first contained only 35 of the most senior cadres, headed by Chen Guang; the venerable students included Lin Biao, Luo Ronghuan, Luo Ruiqing, Tan Zheng, Yang Chengwu, Zhang Aiping, Wang Ping, and Su Zhenhua. The second group had 225 students consisting mainly of battalion and company cadres. The third group comprised some 800 students, mainly drafted from squad and platoon leaders and a number of veteran soldiers.[29] The first and second groups focused on military affairs, politics, philosophy, political economy, Marxism-Leninism, the history of the Communist Party of the Soviet Union, and military strategy. In particular, they studied works by Mao on the Japanese invaders and on China's revolutionary war. The emphasis of training for the third group was simply on raising literacy levels.[30] For this group, military affairs were given secondary importance; only the basic principles of policy were to be taught.[31] The three groups graduated in December 1936.

The second intake, which began study on January 20, 1937, also was dominated by military figures, but the school had already adopted the role of training the educated youths who were beginning to arrive in north Shaanxi.[32] Some 80 percent of these recruits were drawn from the Second and Fourth Front Armies of He Long and Zhang Guotao respectively.[33] In effect, those loyal to the two most independent military commanders were reassigned by means of a progressive educational process that presumably would lead to better postings and thereby diminish any residual personal loyalties they might feel for their former commanders. The total of 1,362 students was divided into fourteen groups; upon graduation in July 1937, the entire class left for the front. By then Kangda was under the control of an Education Committee especially set up by Central Military Commission. The Committee was chaired by Mao Zedong.[34]

The third group of students enrolled (August 1937 to May 1938) contained 477 educated youths, 37 percent of the total of 1,272 students.[35] The intensifying conflict with Japan meant that the fourth intake (April 16, 1938, to December 1938) included a large number of recruits that came from the white areas (83 percent of the total enrollment). Enrollment rose to 5,562, of whom Eighth Route Army, New Fourth Army, and underground cadres filled seven groups of 907 students, while another thirty-one groups were filled by 4,001 students who had recently arrived from outside the Border Region. Another five groups were made up of 654 women students.

By the time of the fifth enrollment, which began on January 28, 1939, Mao suggested that branches be set up behind Japanese lines to help further the training programs. Initially, two such branches were set up; this grew over the years to a total of twelve, the last being the Taihang Branch, set up in spring 1945.

The establishment of branch agencies behind Japanese lines led to an emphasis on the recruitment of military cadres. On January 27, 1939, Mao Zedong, Wang Jiaxiang, Tan Zheng, Luo Ruiqing, and others sent a telegram to the General Front Committee and the Military Regions stressing that the primary objective of Kangda was to train political and military cadres for the Eighth Route Army and the guerrilla units. This meant that future emphasis was to be on recruiting from among Eighth

Route Army soldiers and cadres, with graduates being assigned to the Eighth Route Army.

Thus, the fifth intake was the last that was dominated by educated youths from the white areas. The central campus and the two branches had a total of 13,390 students, among whom were 2,987 Eighth Route Army cadres (22 percent) and 10,403 educated cadres from the white areas (78 percent). Of this fifth class, 64 percent had a middle school education, 26 percent had attended only primary school, and 10 percent had been university trained.

During this fifth class, the GMD tightened its blockade on the Border Region. This forced Kangda to move out of Yan'an, first to Wuxiang in Shanxi and then eventually on to Zixian in the Shanxi-Hebei-Shandong-Henan base area. This caused a change in recruitment patterns: the number of educated students from outside the base areas plummeted, while the number of worker and peasant students increased. Some 86 percent of the recruits in the sixth training class (April 15, 1940, to December 1940) came from poor and middle peasant or worker households. Not surprisingly, this had a major effect on the quality of the recruits. Now only 2 percent had received a university education, while the illiterate or partly illiterate accounted for 43 percent.[36]

It was not until January 1943 that Kangda was brought back to the Shaan-Gan-Ning. As a result, rectification came late to Kangda, beginning in August 1943 and continuing until November 1944. Study had begun while still behind enemy lines; it stepped up with the formation on July 15, of a Rectification Cadre Training Class *(Zhengfeng ganbu xunlianban)*. To strengthen leadership over the class, a General Study Committee was set up with Xu Xiangqian at its head. Initially, study focused on Mao Zedong's works "The Reconstruction of Our Studies," "Reform in Learning, the Party, and Literature," and "In Opposition to Party Formalism" together with Liu Shaoqi's "How to Be a Good Communist Party Member."

A number of Mao's key works from the late thirties originated as talks at Kangda, including "On Contradictions," "Strategic Problems of China's Revolutionary War," and "On Practice." It was here also that the long story became a part of the curriculum as a description of China's decline, and the intermediate story as the struggle with the GMD. In fact, the list of lecturers reads like a Who's Who of the communist leadership. For those from the base areas, Mao lectured on strategy and tactics of the Red Army and dialectical materialism. Other courses were taught by other prominent leaders. Zhu De and Lin Biao taught a course on the history of the founding of the Red Army. Other party luminaries lectured on the history of the Chinese revolution, tactics and strategy of the Chinese revolution, Leninism, materialism, political economy, guerrilla warfare, and military affairs. For the white areas, Mao, Ai Siqi, and Zhang Wentian lectured on dialectics, and Lin Biao on guerrilla warfare. Other courses were a history of the Chinese revolution, the study of political economy, Leninism, and military affairs.[37]

It was also at Kangda that the *qifa* method of teaching was adopted. Jane Price describes it as follows: "At Kangda the *qifa* method was contrasted to the traditional lecture format, rote memorization, and simple questions and answers. It was defined as 'a method of investigation moving from induction to deduction.' A practitioner of *qifa* proceeded 'from near to far, from concrete to abstract, from part to whole,' thereby grasping from one incident or example the law of development of a complex phenomenon."[38]

As in other institutions, study was combined with the students discussing written essays about their attitude towards the party. Readings would then be discussed. In our interviews it was made clear that the instructional materials were by no means casual. Pedagogy counted for a very great deal, with educational method a matter of great concern and subject to continuous revision. In turn, each school had to teach literacy and help semiliterates to learn. Informal discussion took place in Lenin rooms or "salvation rooms," where newspapers and other materials were available for discussion. The process of learning was thus one of living and helping. A missionary factor was built into the student role.

Kangda served as a major recruiting ground for the party. In particular, it served as a major source of educated cadres. Some 70 percent of the educated youths who enrolled in the second class, and 67 percent of those who enrolled in the third group, joined the party. Among the fourth class, only 11 percent had been party members at the time of enrollment, but by graduation party membership had risen to 71 percent.[39]

In addition, a number of other institutions were engaged in training personnel for united front work—the North Shaanxi Public School *(Shaanbei gongxue)* and the Chinese Women's University *(Zhongguo nuzi daxue),* to mention just two. The Public School was set up in August and September 1937 in Yan'an under the directorship of Cheng Fangwu and was situated in the Qingling foothills to the east of Yan'an. It functioned until its reorganization in August 1941. The School's primary purpose was to offer a short-term training program of two to three months for "patriotic intellectuals" who came from outside the Border Region. In total, it graduated 13,000 students.[40] A small number of students from this school moved on to Kangda or other party schools for further training; a similarly small number went on to work in the GMD-controlled areas. The vast majority went to the front or worked behind enemy lines and in other base areas.[41] Most of the students in the school were well educated and committed to the anti-Japanese cause. The training program was directed toward introducing them to the political program of the CCP. To ensure that this objective was met, most of the CCP's senior leaders, including Mao Zedong, Zhang Wentian, Kang Sheng, Li Fuchun, Ai Siqi, and Li Weihan, spoke to the students on military and political affairs.

The Women's University was formally set up on July 20, 1939, in Yan'an under the directorship of Wang Ming, although Li Fuchun took over later as the leading official. It was situated outside of Yan'an's north gate in the caves, across the river from the Central Party School.[42] Through twelve training classes it graduated around 1,000 students.[43] The training programs were specifically designed for women who would join the work to mobilize female cadres. The intention was to train women cadres imbued with a sufficient level of political consciousness. On opening, the school enrolled 500 students spread over eight classes: six general classes, a senior class, and a special class. In addition to these eight, there was the Shaanxi cadres' class. Students in the general classes were recruited from among patriotic youths who came from the white areas. Classes one and two trained cadres for the women's movement; classes three and four were from the women's brigade at Kangda who had received some military training; classes five and six had no distinguishing features. Leading women cadres from the ranks of the Red Army and well-educated intellectuals from enemy-occupied areas, including students from Yanjing University, made up the senior class. The class for Shaanxi cadres specifically trained women officials for the Border Region. The special group comprised those who had been through the Long March and who had battle experience but whose cultural level was rather low. This group was counted as worker-peasant cadres.[44]

The Women's University offered both compulsory and elective courses. Among the compulsory subjects for the ordinary class were political economy, Chinese revolutionary history, the history of the CCP, the history of societal development, the Three Principles of the People, the women's movement, and health education. The senior class also took Marxism-Leninism and Party Construction. The special class also took classes in basic literacy. Among the electives were military education, foreign languages (Russian, English, and Japanese), journalism, stenography, accounting, and medicine.[45] Normally, the school adopted a system of half-day study and half-day work to allow the students to engage in other activities such as agricultural production or road repairs.

Party organization within the university did not operate openly, but every week convened a secret organizational activities meeting. These covert meetings were referred to as the group cadre meetings *(ban ganbu hui)*.[46] Interestingly, the university came under the leadership of Wang Ming and a number of the Russian Returned Students. In September 1941, in preparation for rectification, the Women's University was merged with the Youth Cadre School[47] and the Shaanbei Public School to form Yan'an University, under the leadership of Wu Yuchang.[48]

The most important institution for the training of party cadres was the Central Party School.[49] According to the December 1941 resolution on cadre schools in Yan'an, it was described as a "higher and middle school for the training of all those Party cadres concerned with practical work, and of the military and political working cadres which stand above the area committee and regimental levels and have a capacity for proper independent work."[50] This was the successor to the Academy of Marxian Communism that had been set up in Ruijin. The Central Party School was set up in Wayaobao in December 1935 when the long marchers arrived and was initially headed by Dong Biwu. The school followed the party leadership via Bao'an to Yan'an, where in late 1937, Li Weihan succeeded Dong Biwu as director. Li remained director until 1940, when he was replaced by Deng Fa. Deng remained in charge until the shake-up of the Rectification Campaign. At this time, Mao took over temporary leadership supported by Lin Biao and Peng Zhen. As rectification wound down, Peng Zhen took over from Mao.

The school was situated in a Catholic church in a valley a few miles to the east of Yan'an. Some 300 students were enrolled, and cadres from the white areas were invariably required to follow a course at the school.[51] Generally, a limit of 300 to 400 students was maintained.[52] In its early years, the program of study ran for three months and covered political economy, the history of the Communist Party of the Soviet Union, Leninism, Chinese problems, world politics, philosophy, dialectical materialism, communist party work among the masses, and military training.[53] This program came under attack with reorganization for being too abstract, and study was redirected towards more practical issues. At the same time, the period of study was increased to two years. Following reorganization, 25 percent of the students' time was spent on current affairs, 17 percent on China's situation and revolutionary strategy, 30 percent on party construction, 23 percent on Marxism-Leninism, with the remaining 5 percent being reserved for group research projects.[54]

Initially, there was only one branch in the school, which was made up of students at and above the level of the prefecture party committee and brigade level. In addition, there were a few students from below the prefectural level who had been selected as representatives to the Seventh Party Congress. Originally, the branch was headed by Huang Huoqing, but when he was made secretary, his job was taken over by Gu Dacun. A second branch was formed from the original students who were cadres from the county and regimental levels. Delegates to the Seventh Party Congress were excepted. This branch was headed by Zhang Dingcheng, with Sun Zhiyuan and An Ziwen as his deputies.

On May 4, 1943, the Central Committee decided to merge the Central Research Institute into the Central Party School to form the third branch. This group comprised more educated students, many of whom were well-known literary figures. The branch was headed by Guo Shushen, with Zhang Ruxin and Yan Dakai as his deputies. The problem of the low literacy levels of some of the original cadres from worker and peasant origins among the original Military Academy and Party School students caused a fourth branch to be set up. The specific purpose of this branch was to enable the students to become literate while they participated in rectification. The branch was headed by Zhang Qilong (later Zhang Bangying), with Cheng Shicai and Yang Shangkun as his deputies.

Finally, in early 1944, the fifth and sixth branches were formed. These were created through the merger of the Northwest Party School with the Central Party School. This had been proposed by the Northwest Bureau and was accepted by the Central Committee. Most students in the fifth branch were drawn from county or regional cadres within the Shaan-Gan-Ning Border Region with a small number of regiment and battalion level cadres who were veterans of the Long March. The branch was headed by Bai Dongcai, with Qiong Xiaochu and Chao Zhipu as his deputies. The sixth branch comprised county and regional level cadres and "educated" elements from behind enemy lines or GMD-controlled areas. It was headed by Ma Guorui. This brought the complement of the Central Party School to 3,000 students, with another 3,000 serving as functionaries.[55]

The premier institution for the party in the theoretical sphere was the Central Research Institute. It was set up in May 1938 as the Academy of Marxism-Leninism in Yan'an under the leadership of Zhang Wentian, with Wang Xuewen as his deputy.[56] At its most expansive, there were a total of six groups with 300 to 400 students. Ordinary students were admitted through examination and had usually passed through another training institute such as Kangda, the Party School, or the North Shaanxi Public School.[57] During the reorganization of 1941, it was renamed the

Central Research Institute and, while Zhang Wentian remained director, Fan Wenlan was appointed his deputy. According to the December 17, 1941, regulations on cadre education in Yan'an, the Central Research Institute was to be a "higher research organ for the training of the Party's theoretical cadres" and came directly under the Central Propaganda Bureau.[58] Later it came under the leadership of Li Weihan. The main party and administrative work was carried out by Xu Jiansheng (general secretary), Li Yan (secretary of the party committee), and Li Qing (secretary of the office for guiding research).

The institute had a total of nine research departments: Chinese politics (headed by Zhang Ruxin), Chinese economics (Wang Sihua), Chinese history (Fan Wenlan),[59] Chinese cultural thought (Ai Siqi),[60] Chinese arts (Ou Yangshan), International Affairs (Ke Bonian), Russian (Shi Zhi), Chinese Education, and Chinese Journalism (Li Weihan).[61] The objective of the education department was to provide a theoretical basis and practice for the theory of New Democracy. In order to carry out its work, it was subdivided into three groups: the education group for the anti-Japanese base areas, a group for education in the GMD-controlled areas, and an educational research group for behind enemy lines. Study in the department was to be based on the methodology and theories of Marxism-Leninism, but Chinese social conditions were also studied.[62]

Among the general courses offered were philosophy, political economy, Marxism-Leninism, Chinese revolutionary history, western revolutionary history, Soviet party history, and party construction. Among the key teachers were Wang Xuewen, Chen Changhao, Ai Siqi, Wu Liangping, and Yang Song; guest lecturers included Zhang Wentian, Mao Zedong, Zhou Enlai, Liu Shaoqi, and Chen Yun. Mao delivered an important report calling on party members to "seek truth from facts," while Liu delivered "Training of the Communist Party Member" and Chen Yun spoke on the theme of party construction. The well-trained graduates turned out by the Central Research Institute were often sent to staff the various party schools and often came from, and returned to, senior party positions elsewhere.

Education as a Culture of Socialism

Our description barely scratches the surface of the kinds of materials taught and the varieties of programs and instructional materials offered. The diversity, seriousness, and centrality of the entire enterprise composed the essential Yan'an, providing it with such special characteristics that it can be described both as a mobilization space and a simulacrum. But it was not only by means of formal instruction that Yan'an achieved such stature. As noted earlier, Yan'an defined and prescribed a total way of life. To transmit revolutionary ideas and principles into daily life, and daily life into revolutionary ideas and principles, was the communist ambition. Culture, or cultural transmission, was considered essential. Indeed, this was virtually designed as a formal educational program, and there was almost as much debate over how and what to write and for whom, and the nature of revolutionary art, music, and theater, as over the right or the wrong line.

In the next chapter, we will deal directly with the way in which discourse became bonding and how as a result symbolic capital was generated. For the moment we want to concentrate on cultural capital, the product of Yan'an's educational system of universities, colleges, schools, and research institutes, as well as its organized cultural activities.

If one were to try to describe sinified Marxism as a cultural system as it prevailed in the thirties and early forties, it might be said to be composed of several overlays on an original Chinese base, part Confucian, part Buddhist (in terms of enlightenment and "the way"—the "correct" code and pattern of responsibility). Among these overlays, one might include an eighteenth-century European idea of secular rationality and a considerable interest in science; Rousseauean emphasis on the general will as an appropriate principle of democracy (democratic centralism); a nineteenth-century evolutionary principle cast in mode of political economy but with overlays of Darwinism; and some notions that mutualism (an anarchist principle) is an improvement over alternative forms of collective association. The first represents an inner knowledge that binds together those who possess it; the second and third take the form of developmental modernization; and the last suggests a utopic socialist condition to be realized.

Mao put the matter as follows:

To nourish its one culture China needs to assimilate a good deal of progressive foreign culture, not enough of which has been done in the past. This includes not only today's socialist culture and new democratic culture, but ancient foreign culture; for example, the culture of the Age of Enlightenment in capitalist countries. Anything that we can use today should be assimilated. However, we should not swallow this foreign material uncritically, but must treat it as we do our own food—first putting it in the mouth and chewing it, then submitting it to the working of the stomach and intestines with their juices and secretions, and separating it into the nutrient to be absorbed and waste matter to be discarded. We must not absorb it uncritically and completely. The so-called proposition of "wholesale westernization" is a mistaken view. China has suffered a great deal in the past from the mechanical absorption of material from the West. Chinese communists should have the same attitude to the application of Marxism in China. They must fully and properly integrate the universal truth of Marxism with the concrete practice of the Chinese revolution, that is to say it will be useful only in a national form. It must not be applied subjectively and as a mere formula. Those subjective Marxists who use it as a formula are simply playing the fool with Marxism and the Chinese revolution, and there is no room for them in China's revolutionary ranks.[63]

For these different themes to blend in a plausible and systematic way requires a master narrative, an integrated vision, and a set of educational practices to go with them. The master narrative was created by Mao and his associates to represent something both universal within Marxism and yet specific to Yan'an. However, his pronouncements did not appear as from on high. Rather they seemed to be derived as a common sense from the people, uttered through Mao who in turn became the voice of the people themselves. It is in this context that the importance of orality as an art form, as a pattern of performance in the specific guise of lectures and speeches, brings the cosmocratic Mao into the close proximity of his hearers. And once the key utterances became the key texts, writualized in a process of exegetical bonding, it is possible to speak about the formation of symbolic capital.

So considered, Yan'an in the light of its evolution moves towards truth as both a living abstraction and an intensely concrete experience. The structure and the form of both are embodied in the educational system. The dissemination of its principles is through the cultural system, with its articulated structure of theater and drama, writing and literature, arts and performance. Mao used both the abstract and the concrete to define the discourse and the discourse community.

In terms of our general model, internalization goes together with socialization in the way theory and practice do. It is only when one has the appropriate knowledge and conviction that performance can reinforce conviction, the functional being incorporated in the motivational, and the latter endowed with the power of revolutionary purpose and discipline.

In Yan'an—that is, the core Yan'an—the emphasis was on the recreation of the individual so that he or she added to the collectivity and also became its surrogate. So closed, this political hermeneutic circle literally draws in to the collectivity the private intellectual property of the individual in story and narrative, the basis for our conveyance theory of collectivized power. In other words, the educational/rectification process realizes the individual in the collectivity and by doing so realizes the community itself.

We have put the primary emphasis on Yan'an as an instructional and learning republic. We have revealed the revolutionary Platonism hidden within an educational structure that provides everyone with access to higher truths, with learning, the process of self overcoming. Pupils at every level of educational skill in Yan'an became the objects of learning, but they were also targets in the campaigns that the party launched. The extensive network of cadre training schools, moreover, defines the main purpose: to create a unified discourse for those who matter most. In short, higher education was cadre education. The objective was not to make the students think critically with respect to Marxist Maoism but only in relation to liberalism and conventional thought. Education was to ensure that they understood party policy and had the necessary technical expertise to implement that policy in their own particular field. Having set up the "academy," however, Mao and the party could not entirely exorcise opinions and reflexes of residual intellectual independence.

Cultural Transmission

Associated with this ramified institutional network of schools and universities was an elaborate program of theater, arts, music, and literary productions, both for internal consumption within what might be called the charmed circle (the inner core and its immediate clientele) and for the extended Yan'an (both military forces and party workers, but even more importantly, peasants and locals). Both Mao and Chiang Kai-shek understood very well the power of discourse and the role of intellectuals. Chiang persecuted radical intellectuals with particular vehemence. Mao recognized that his instructional republic depended on education and culture, the two being connected both by artists, writers, and intellectuals organized in such bodies as the Lu Xun Academy as well as by troupes of performers and writers associated with educational institutions. Mao knew perfectly well that his was a discourse community, and if the discourse somehow eluded his control, the leakage and erosion of power would be great. Hence, there were complicated issues for him to resolve related to theory and the nature of discourse, as well as strategies of effective presentation, pedagogy, and performance. For the educational side, the instructional community of schools, colleges, universities, and institutes, it was particularly important to find the correct line and avoid left or right deviationism. The main ideas of Mao's own version of Marxism were laid down in his Kangda lectures on dialectical materialism in 1936–1937 and in two key essays, "On Practice" and "On Contradiction." As for cultural diffusion, the key document is Mao's Yan'an Forum on Literature and Art.

Mao was quite explicit in his stress on cultural transmission and its importance and the significance of cultural capital over economic capital; as he said:

> There are a number of different fronts in our struggle for the national liberation of China, civil and military, or, we might say, there is a cultural as well as an armed front. Victory over the enemy depends primarily on armies with guns in their hands, but this kind of army alone is not enough. We still need a cultural army, since this kind of army is indispensable in achieving unity among ourselves and winning victory over the enemy. Since May Fourth, when this cultural army took shape in China, it has aided the Chinese revolution by gradually limiting the sphere of China's feudal culture and the slavish culture that serves imperialist aggression, and weakening their strength, so that now reactionaries are reduced to resisting new culture by "meeting quality with quantity": reactionaries aren't short of money, and with some effort they can turn out a lot even if they can't come up with anything worthwhile. . . . Our meeting today is to ensure that literature and art become a component part of the whole revolutionary machine, so they can act as a powerful weapon in uniting and educating the people while attacking and annihilating the enemy, and help the people achieve solidarity in their struggle against the enemy.[64]

However, the role arts and literature were to play in Yan'an was more complex than this quotation suggests. At one level, they were simply used as a form of pleasurable propaganda as well as powerful weaponry, rousing people to the realization of just how villainous the Japanese or the landlords were. Certainly a good deal of ingenuity and creative craftsmanship went into the plays, dramas, stories, and graphics that were produced by those who felt themselves playing an important role in both the revolutionary engagement and the war against the Japanese. In this vein, theater and dance troupes entertained not only in Yan'an and its villages, but also in other border regions, in the white areas, and behind Japanese lines. Several of the artists, photographers, dancers, and writers we interviewed commented that life, in this early period, was relatively free. There was considerable improvisation and artistic adaptation. Those familiar with communist graphics of the early twenties in *The Masses* and with German literary productions like *Die Weltbuhne* will recall the black-and-white woodblock print or etching as almost standard proletarian art. These were produced in great number on the old printing press in the Cave of the 10,000 Buddhas. However, eventually the Chinese found them dull rather than powerful and introduced multicolor woodblock prints, with happy themes rather than the more somber portrayals favored by the western radical left.

For others, of course, other issues were at stake—the question of freedom, creativity, intellectualism, and the arts. For them, the issues were no different than for artists and writers in the early days of the Bolshevik revolution when, in an explosion of artistic and literary experimentalism, literary and artistic freedom became the essence of the revolution itself. Indeed, to produce a revolutionary art was to break not only with the past, but also with conventional artistic and literary forms. This was precisely the view of many of the avant garde revolutionary artists and writers in the early days of the Russian revolution. Among them were some of the most powerful creative artists and writers of the twentieth century, artists like Popova, Kandinsky, Lissitsky, Malevich, Goncharova, and Tatlin, poets like Mandelstahm or Mayakovsky.[65] They developed institutes, workshops, *prolekult* centers, committees. Their idea was to convert the base, to reach out to a public who might at first be shocked by their work but would sooner or later succumb and by doing so find their capacity for life itself vastly enhanced. "Going to the people" meant that groups like the Suprematists under Malevich or the Constructivists under Tatlin designed not only posters for propaganda but also clothes for workers, and teapots and plates, "interpenetrating" art with a life of design.

There was a big difference between Mao's thoughts on education and his views on culture. Much of what he had to say about education derived from his own experience, while his views on culture were much more derivative of Soviet thought, most particularly Lenin's and Stalin's. Lack of experience in the cultural field made it difficult for Mao to use culture to elevate himself to the center of the pantheon. He did not become the personification of wisdom and the purveyor of truth overnight. Furthermore, his efforts were not well received by many intellectuals. They were increasingly concerned with the hypocrisy of his efforts than with the rationale behind them. This was certainly the case for those few "real" intellectuals who had inherited the independence of spirit and the desire to experiment with form as represented by the Lu Xun tradition.

Many Chinese intellectuals were aware of these same trends and tendencies in the USSR. Debate was expressed in the form of discussion over cultural nationalism versus internationalism. This debate, an old one among Chinese intellectuals, divided Chinese students in the Soviet Union at the various universities into nationalists and internationalists on the issue of how sinified an authentic Chinese Marxism ought to be. This concern could be traced back to earlier debates among May Fourth Movement intellectuals about such matters as westernization and modernization, the Romanization of the Chinese alphabet, and how to deal with local dialectical differences. Indeed, the concerns went back to the nineteenth century.[66]

From the standpoint of revolutionary Platonism, perhaps most important of all was the larger question of whether an avant garde, or even worse, intellectuals as a class, could be tolerated when they had an unfortunate propensity to reproduce themselves as a class. In Russia, they created a revolutionary art that broke with artistic traditions and modified the canon, thus becoming separated from the masses, either by intent or default. In China, they were often critical theorists, with the potential to serve as an independent force precisely at the moment when it was necessary to create a discourse community with a common language and a shared view of truth.

In Yan'an, the debate on such matters was joined by Zhou Yang and Chen Boda (who often acted as Mao's intellectual alter ego until he fell from grace in 1970). However, these larger issues and the matter of the relationship between culture and power were already very much on Mao's mind. In fact, Mao began his major discussion of democracy not with an analysis of democracy but with cultural transmission. He does so in an oddly hesitating manner:

> I am an outsider as far as culture is concerned and have only just begun to study it. Fortunately, there are many comrades in Yan'an who have written at length on the subject. My rough and ready words may thus serve the same purpose as the gongs and drums announcing a theatrical performance. Our words may contain a grain of truth for the nation's advanced cultural workers and we hope they will participate in discussion and help us to reach correct conclusions that will meet our national needs.[67]

No matter how tentatively put, there is little doubt that Mao's thoughts on culture were reinforced by Stalin, for Mao goes on to quote him approvingly in the same text. The issue is not only the role of cultural workers but also the question of how national and internal, and how universal and international, the cultural references should be. Like the narrative of the long story, the question of culture connects to history and the authenticity of the communist movement within each country.

Complicating the matter of cultural diffusion, in Mao's eyes, was the neo-feudal overlay and especially the combination of the Confucian ethic and the historical role of the Mandarinate in China and the part played by intellectuals and scholars within it (something that intrigued Max Weber). These circumstances were compounded, however, by the dramatic and startling difference between intellectual and avant-garde circles in the Soviet Union and China. In China such circles were virtually absent. There was a real dearth of both, not just in Yan'an but in modern China as a whole. There were plenty of literary societies like the Society for Literary Research or the Creation Society, which stood more or less for art for art's sake. There was as well an extraordinary list of people engaged in both kinds of enterprise. But an authentic avant-garde can hardly be said to have flourished.[68] Nevertheless, especially in Shanghai there was a remarkable, if small, group of artists, writers, and intellectuals. But their ranks were decimated by the GMD, particularly between 1927 and 1936. In 1936 Mao Dun prepared a list of fifty prominent writers killed or imprisoned, representing a virtual writers' who's who.[69]

For Mao, this loss made it all the more important to recruit as many intellectuals as possible to enable the party to carry out its tutelary rule by means of education and culture. As described earlier, Mao's inversionary discourse elevated the peasantry not as a class for the future but as a rebellious and insurrection prone resource to be mobilized. Hence it was up to the party to perform a mobilization function while taking on the role of a protoclass for the future, one that would generalize itself first in the name of a peasantry and eventually in the name of the proletariat. The party would provide direction, and it would use the intellectuals for this purpose while preventing them from taking control. In turn, this allowed Mao to transform his public persona from that of a predominantly military theorist and strategist possessing a rustic view of Marxism to that of a Marxist wrestling with the larger issues of how to apply principles to conditions, and from there to political teacher.

Many of these issues came to a head in Yan'an well before rectification, in the form of a conflict between Zhou Yang and Xiao Jun. Their conflict prefigured the great debate over art and literature that would later become part of the Rectification Campaign. What is interesting throughout this time is that the intellectuals appeared to loom so large and their cultural production appeared so important, when in fact the intellectuals were few and far between, and virtually no avant garde existed at all. This suggests the great importance Mao attached to the discourse of the discourse community and reinforces our interpretation of how important symbolic capital actually was in Yan'an. Indeed, there was a certain tenuousness in Mao's monopoly of symbolic capital, a potential leakage in his possession of the fund of truth, he feared that his entire mythologic might be exploded by those few intellectuals who chose to resist him, especially through satire and humor. In a universe where symbolic capital counts for a great deal, those who generate the discourse—the intellectuals—hold the key. Hence the paradox. The tutelary role of the party, combined with the centrality of education and the significance of its mythologic, underscores Mao's republic as a kind of revolutionary Platonism. But it was the need to avoid becoming dependent on the intellectuals that triggered the Rectification Campaign. The struggle against Wang Ming and his line was not the fundamental reason for launching the Rectification Campaign. If Mao had placed less emphasis on the significance of the discourse, he would not have seen the intellectuals as so much of a threat. For despite their historic prestige and status in China, intellectuals were not highly regarded in radical workers' circles.

Kyna Rubin describes the conflict over the role of the intellectuals in her discussion of the tense relationship between Zhou Yang and Xiao Jun.[70] Zhou Yang defined the cultural project in the following terms: "expose the dark versus praise the bright." The participants in the debate were the Lu Xun Academy of Arts, where Zhou was dean, and the Yan'an branch of the All-China Writers' Resistance Association, led by Ding Ling and Xiao Jun. Rubin refers to Zhou as a literary "czar" and "faithful enforcer" of Mao's political codes in the literary realm. Indeed, Zhou has been held personally accountable for the persecution of many of China's leading "counterrevolutionaries" and "rightists" during the purges of the last four decades. For these activities, he apologized publicly at the Fourth National Writers' Congress in 1979.[71]

Zhou Yang permitted himself, says Rubin, "a certain degree of professional empathy for writers struggling with conflicting inner responses to the disenchantment tearing at the seams of Yan'an's bright exterior, at the same time he pleads with writers to conform to Party needs by focusing on the sanguine Yan'an."[72] However, Zhou argued that while writers are the "flesh and blood of the revolution," they are unable to keep up with the consciousness of workers, peasants, and Red Army soldiers. In short, the people's consciousness is not only more advanced than that of the intellectuals but in addition the intellectuals, instead of leading, are falling behind. He advocates "frontlinism" as a way of deepening the intellectuals understanding of war:

> The relationship between art and life is similar. You must be able to "enter" as well as "leave." This is a delicate dialectical relationship. One must have the ability to penetrate life, yet transcend it at the same time. Transcending life can only come after penetrating it. To drown in a sea of facts, unable to view human life in its entirety or see its essence from a defined ideological level, is what we call "not seeing the forest for the trees." In philosophy this takes the form of narrow empiricism, in literature, naturalism. We adopt neither.[73]

Echoing a theme we heard in some of the interviews, Zhou connects theory to a kind of transcendental tranquility:

> Detachment in the mind of a writer is the pure state of universal understanding. Does this state exist above and beyond all material objects, without any ties to them? Does it imply a Kantian "disinterested mind" and a lack of enthusiasm for life? Detachment means none of these. Rather, it comes from tasting life deeply while controlling the emotions. Great thinkers and writers have all been able to maintain tranquillity of the heart. They have fought tooth and nail with life. They have identified its every fibre, found its heart, grasped all its laws. Therefore they are calm and unperturbed before any change.[74]

The reply, a rather mocking one, came from several writers, of whom Xiao Jun was perhaps the most significant. He too believed that it is necessary to "experience life." However, prefiguring the Wang Shiwei affair, Xiao argues that it is time to point out the "black spots" in Yan'an and, by criticizing them, eliminate them. For Xiao, covering them over will also make them worse.[75] Hence, the intellectual and writer as critic becomes the essential role (and not as a producer of symbolic capital).

Mao tried to put a stop to the debate with his Yan'an Forum on Literature and Art. By then, his earlier diffidence has entirely disappeared. He makes his arguments forcefully and insistently.

> Since the audience for our literature and art consists of workers, peasants, and soldiers and their cadres, the question then arises of how to get to

understand and know these people properly. To do this, we must carry out a great deal of work in Party and government organs, in villages and factories, in the Eighth Route Army and the New Fourth Army, getting to understand all sorts of situations and all sorts of people and making ourselves thoroughly familiar with them. Our workers in literature and art must carry out their own work in literature and art, but the task of understanding people and getting to know them properly has the highest priority. How have our workers in literature and art performed in this respect until now? I would say that until now they have been heroes without a battlefield, remote and uncomprehending. What do I mean by remote? Remote from the people. Workers in literature and art are unfamiliar with the people they write about and with the people who read their work, or else have actually become estranged from them. Our workers in literature and art are not familiar with the workers, peasants, soldiers or even their cadres. What do I mean by uncomprehending? Not comprehending their language. Yours is the language of intellectuals, theirs is the language of the popular masses. I have mentioned before that many comrades like to talk about "popularization," but what does popularization mean? It means that the thoughts and emotions of our workers in literature and art should become one with the thoughts and emotions of the great masses of workers, peasants, and soldiers. And to get this unity, we should start by studying the language of the masses. If we don't even understand the masses' language, how can we talk about creating literature and art?[76]

The passage is as remarkable as much for its tone as its message. Mao repeats "uncomprehending" again and again throughout the talk. If one were to read the passage aloud, in the orality in which it was presented, it would sound like drumming. It would also sound threatening. It makes no effort at finer distinctions. The "many" writers and artists who stand aloof because they are unfamiliar with the language of the people are self-evidently empty, their works necessarily insipid. Hammered home is the myth of peasant wisdom, a romantic punitivism. Workers and peasants constitute a reservoir of deep knowledge without direct access to which artists and writers are the losers. The people, the ultimate source of both deep knowledge and inspiration, are the sole source of authenticity for creative work.

But of course since the peasants and workers (who in another context Mao treats as a blank page) are not themselves able to articulate their wisdom, the artists and writers become translators and mediators between the people's spokesman (Mao himself) and the people. This position elevates Mao, stifles independent creativity in the name of inspiring it, and is part of a more general plan to convert the intellectuals into the service of discourse—transmitting and enriching the language of Mao Zedong Thought as a form of discipline as well as a method of understanding.

It is in this context that the conflict between Wang Shiwei and Mao must be understood. Wang Shiwei was one of the very few intellectuals who refused to go along with the Yan'an Forum. He is contemptuous of the idea of "engineers of the soul" taken over by Mao from Stalin. He writes in his essay "Politicians—Artists":

> The politician and the artist each have defects. For the sake of successfully attacking the enemy, uniting with friendly armies and strengthening himself, the politician must be worldly wise, have an excellent command of cunning methods and be good at dealing with both enemies and friends. His defects come from just these merits. When these skills are used in revolutionary tasks, they become the most beautiful and glorious "arts of revolution." But apart from a truly great politician, none can avoid some desire to use these skills for their own reputation, position and profit and thus to harm the revolution.[77]

It was clear from Wang Shiwei's other writings that Mao was not a "truly great politician."

On the question of souls, Wang says the engineers of the soul must first

> reform their own souls to become pure and bright. To purge one's soul of the filth and darkness within it is a difficult and bitter process, but it takes us along a great road that must be taken . . . Old China is a pus-covered bloody society full of filth and darkness. Those Chinese who have long lived in that society have naturally become corrupted in it. Even ourselves—the revolutionary warriors creating a new China—cannot be an exception. This is a cruel fact. Only if we bravely face up to it will we be able to understand that in the process of reforming the social system we must at the same time seriously and deeply reform our souls in order to speed up the accomplishment of the first [task] and to guarantee its success.[78]

Finally, to make sure that, in particular, Zhou Yang understands his import, Wang says, "Lu Xun fought all his life. But even those who have the slightest insight into him certainly can comprehend that in the midst of his fighting he was very lonely."[79]

Some Implications of Revolutionary Platonism

There is no place for loneliness in Mao's republic. For loneliness implies a separation from the rest. It makes for dissent, for a refusal of the discourse. It makes loneliness and creativity part of the same phenomenon—an independence of mind that refused the new *doxa* as well as the old. It is, in short, the highest threat to a politics of the seamless web in which each person has a part to play in a highly orchestrated political process.

The paradox is that with revolutionary education the task can never be mere transmission of knowledge. In Mao's terms, education is a consequence of the class struggle itself. Through it everyone gains the opportunity to "level up"—to improve their knowledge and overcome their deficiencies. The job of the intellectuals, artists, and writers is to make leveling up possible in a process leading to self enlightenment. But to do that they must subordinate their independent judgment and level down. Mao's own writings identify the process. Most of them combine earthy anecdote with classical or folkloric reference, moving from concrete description to abstraction and thus to a policy defined in principles—formulaic instructions. In this way, knowledge and culture become accessible to the masses while a more ramified logical explanation is given to the intellectuals and the better educated. "Leveling down" and "leveling up" become embodied in the same texts and performance. In this way knowledge also becomes situated within the larger code, located in terms of a concrete problematic. Mao problematizes first and analyzes second. And he wants the intellectuals, writers, and artists to do exactly the same thing, but as cultural translators and transmitters.

There is in this, as Wang Shiwei points out, a revolutionary cunning. Mao's basic argument is that leveling down is in reality a form of leveling up, since peasants and workers have the only true fund of wisdom. Without that wisdom at their disposal, the intellectuals can not be fully formed human beings. Hence Mao's notion of education remains almost as hierarchical as in the old Mandarinate, but top and bottom have been inverted.

And so has the theory of truth. For Mao, the dialectic is a way of penetrating false consciousness to see a higher truth behind the world as conventionally perceived. His method of locating that truth is dialectical (whether it is more Chinese or more Marxist is pretty much irrelevant). But if the higher truth is in the people, they become the final authority. In effect, Mao's is a form of revolutionary Platonism, an inverted Platonism, but a Platonism nevertheless. What the peasants and workers represent in Mao's republic are a substitute myth for the myth of Er in Plato's. Instead of a mythic heaven, there is the myth of the base over the superstructure that justifies precisely the opposite, the use of the superstructure to transform the base.

One can see the reasons for this inversion. While knowledge and cultural diffusion are fundamental characteristics of education and education is for everyone, it requires a continuous process of deepening and enrichment. If it were only designed to enable people to level up, to improve themselves and their capacities, it would generate new class boundaries. In Mao's theories, the myth of the wisdom of the multitudes creates the conditions for the rationality of ideas. As with Plato, the system of representations of logical "truths" has its logical limits. It is at this point that myth takes over.

Education means a hierarchy of knowledge. Mao separates insight and knowledge for some purposes and reunites them for others. Education also dilutes hierarchies by making knowledge accessible. But that means the teachers are placed at a strategic juncture in the society. In their claims to independence they can also claim certain exemptions as a class. To avoid becoming a class of philosopher-kings, intellectuals must level themselves down as they make culture and knowledge accessible, and level themselves up by becoming enriched with the popular knowledge they need to synthesize and comprehend. This is the basis of the mass line. It draws on basic folk wisdom and the shrewdness of people living in a world of work and risk.

Mao made such matters quite explicit. He pretty much sweeps those with intellectual pretentions into the dustbin, including all those who might look down their noses at him. He decries the lack of good Marxist theorists of Chinese political economy, or politics, or war while leaving open the space for new opportunities. China as a semicolonial and semifeudal country "treasures" intellectuals. "However," says Mao, "we know that there are many intellectuals who consider themselves very learned and who make a great display of their knowledge, not realizing that this attitude is harmful and obstructs their progress. One truth that they should realize is that a great many so-called intellectuals are actually exceedingly unlearned, and that the knowledge of the workers and peasants is sometimes somewhat greater than theirs."[80] It is a theme to which Mao returns in the Yan'an Forum on Literature and Art.

Despite his attitude towards intellectuals, one might say that Mao's republic was more egalitarian in principle than Plato's but no less unequal in terms of acceptable differentiation. Both offer a rudimentary hierarchy functionally necessary to a relatively primitive level of organization and differentiation, a division of labor self-evidently applicable and explicable. Both favor open competition and educational competition without discrimination.

Of course, no Platonic invention has been called upon to deal with practicalities of work and power, and if by chance such a thing might happen, it would no doubt fail. Mao succeeded remarkably well as a cosmocrat both in terms of numbers of people who became part of his discourse community and the efficacy of their knowledge. And Mao always connected efficacy to both theory and praxis. Moreover, to be enhanced by praxis was not enough. Theory required a method so that people could be shown how to make it work.

Situation was crucial. In Yan'an, abstract theory was not acceptable by itself. Theory and practice had to be made to come together, not only in exhortation but in the practical overlap between the production and rectification campaigns. In these we see at work not only a moral architect but also that rather more rare circumstance, a political economy, with Mao giving detailed descriptions of economic practices in a context of organization, efficiency, and production.[81]

It is in terms of the educational system that the tutelary role of the party becomes explicit. The structure is itself a form of political organization. Each institution is, moreover, organized around a core curriculum designed to break with all previous political models and surviving networks and alliances and to rupture prevailing patterns of mutual obligations.

Each reassignment to a unit was in itself significant. It was in Yan'an that the *danwei* became virtually all important as a primary affiliation and a nuclear unit of one's social existence. The *danwei* system became more important than family. All decisions about the self, about education and work, took place in consultation with the members of the unit. In the unit, all functional activities converged within such a degree of intimacy and interiority that the unit came to have a virtual monopoly of control over one's daily life. It was also the venue for scrutiny, struggle sessions, and often reassignment. The educational structure then was based on what were at one and the same time graded and specialized schools, units of work and living, and units of primary affiliation.

Theory and practice in terms of the unit meant unifying education and production, the one functional, the other "revolutionary" (moral). How well these two fused became particularly visible to others in one's unit. It was in the unit that the evidence of how and what each individual learned became manifest. The unit in effect destroyed one's political individuality while, at the same time, dissected a person's individuality. Because of this everyone had to not only continuously offer evidence that they thought about themselves as revolutionaries, but also reveal all their doubts and hesitations. By discovering their limitations, others helped their comrades to overcome them. Hence if education defines the tutelary quality of Yan'an, it also specifies the appropriately tutored response: to identify and eliminate bad thoughts, shaky commitments, self-doubt, and liberalistic political commitments by the mechanism that connected private reflection to public self-criticism.[82]

Perhaps the most interesting aspect of all this is less the conformity this system produced than the curious way in which it destroyed individualism by focusing on individuality. Self-criticism as a public phenomenon, preceded by the exhortation to pitiless reaching into the self to identify basic weakness, must have been, for those who took it seriously, as drastic a reconstruction of the self as one can think of. This is where Yan'an departs most from a radical version of a Platonic republic based on reason to something more akin to a religious community in which Mao's own version of truth becomes a religious phenomenon. In the guise of a war and a revolution, the true purpose of such a system is to make evil inaccessible. It is in this context that we need to examine what we can call the moral moment of the revolution—that is, the rectification process, which we consider in the next chapter. Rectification comes close to making Maoism a secular religion with sacral characteristics.

For this, the communists in effect expropriated the strong educational traditions of the Mandarinate with its respect for knowledge as power and made it accessible to all—a revolution in its own right. By this means, the sheer practice of living in a utopic and salvational community turned the usual world upside down. Moreover, just to ensure no one got the wrong idea, Mao enunciated the doctrine of the mass line as a way of underscoring as principle what could never be true as fact: that the most educated had more to learn from the people than the people had to learn from them. Invoking this principle of inverted hierarchy was good for the exercise (in name rather than practice) of a carefully cultivated egalitarianism (not equality), which, constituted at the tutelary center of Yan'an, disguised how the system really worked. This inversion, portraying peasants and workers as the true fund of wisdom, was of course a very anti-Platonic assertion.

Leveling up and down is embodied in the slogan "from the masses, to the masses." As Mao explained it:

> This means: take the ideas of the masses (scattered and unsystematic ideas) and concentrate them (through study turn them into concentrated and systematic ideas), then go to the masses and propagate and explain these ideas until the masses embrace them as their own, hold fast to them and translate them into action, and test the correctness of these ideas in such action. Then once again concentrate ideas from the masses and once again go to the masses so that the ideas are persevered in and carried through. And so on, over and over again in an endless spiral, with the ideas becoming more correct, more vital and richer each time. Such is the Marxist theory of knowledge.[83]

And such is the power of voice and utterance. For if one purifies knowledge in this continuous process, the person articulating the theory does not speak with his or her own voice, but is simply giving voice—the people are speaking through that person. Utterance means the people replacing the voice of god in a more religiously inclined and revelatory movement. In effect, the relationship between a Marxist theory of knowledge and the organization of education must be embodied in institutions that not only teach substance but also enable utterance, and insofar as the process Mao describes becomes permanent, he who has the voice is the power.

This is not so different from the Platonic ideal of the philosopher-king, who also represents utterance and voice, but not utterance from the people but from rationalistic knowledge and the voice of teacher and sage. This focuses attention on the educational system as the meaningful boundary of Mao's republic and the nucleus of the revolution. These, unlike those of Plato, which sprang full blown from the mind of Socrates, have a history. There is an evolutionary pattern to the actual institutions themselves, especially those that in the critical years of 1939 to 1944 confronted the double bind of the GMD blockade and the ensuing production campaign and the Rectification Campaign, which sought to elevate these educational principles into a system. Where the production campaign was a matter of self-sufficiency as a key to economic survival, the Rectification Campaign represented a crystallization of knowledge leading to an increasingly integrated collectivity despite functional differentiation. The more diverse the skills and the more complex the community became, the more necessary it was to be united by a single political discourse. By this means, moreover, productive economic purposes would also serve higher political ends by bringing revolutionary principles literally down to earth and elevating productive practice into universalized principles of a utopic community. Knowledge and self-consciousness of the process became an essential requirement of the small but rapidly growing body of highly trained party members. This in turn enabled their commitment to become missionary, their conduct exemplary, their practices efficient. It is only by such means that a new and displacing normative, structural, behavioral balance could be achieved. Indeed, only then, by means of the internalization of normative prescriptions and the socialization of new roles, would its utopic projections be universalized. "Mass line" to the contrary, Yan'an as an instructional republic was from the start the representation of a few who made the discourse community into a chosen people. As Mao put it in 1940, "Beyond all doubt, now is the time to expand propaganda about communism and strengthen the study of Marxism-Leninism. Without this, we shall not only be unable to lead the Chinese revolution forward to the future stage of socialism, but also we shall be unable to guide the present democratic revolution to victory."[84]

Here then is the materialized Chinese version of Mao's revolutionary and Platonic republic. A party elite replaces the Mandarinate, if not as philosopher-kings at least as a theoretically enriched class. There is also a class of warriors and guardians in the Red Army, as well as peasants and workers, who provide the material necessities. There is also a sense that other classes do not count except as enemies or partial enemies to be dealt with sooner or later. These other classes, rich peasants and certain categories of landlord, for example, might be temporarily tolerated in light of the larger anti-Japanese coalition. However, none of them, and no other classes, are essential to the enterprise.[85] In Mao's own version of a Platonic republic, then, one finds a functional theory of class, the enlightenment of the party to replace the philosopher-kings, and superior qualities to adhere to the guardians, the communist military. Competitive recruitment exists within a meritocratic educational structure at the very center of "egalitarian" Yan'an. Finally, the dialectical search for a higher truth that underlies the realities one perceives constitutes an ongoing project, one that enables Mao to continue to play the Socratic role and to write the texts that become the writuals of learning and rectification. Nor does the resemblance end there. Like Socrates, Mao cares little for dress or appearance (not to mention wives and family). He prefers the role (guise) of teacher. He is obsessed with the particularities and forms of discourse, both of which are fundamental to the structuring of the community. When he opposes empty formalism and the "eight-legged essay," it is in the first instance to engage intellectuals and Marxists with the complexities of actual life and in the second to cast out the ritualized respect for the superiority of the Mandarinate and its Marxist equivalent.

Like Plato, Mao is deeply concerned with the uses, and corresponding dangers and diversions, of entertainment, the arts more than music. Indeed, he is preoccupied with the importance of culture and how and what should be transmitted. Furthermore, one could expect each class to strive to perfect its performance and individuals to live up to the ideal roles they defined, whether as theorist, political commissar, guardian, or producer.

III

THE POWER OF
SYMBOLIC CAPITAL

✳

Even when things happen in the best way, there is still
no tendency for distribution and virtue to coincide.

John Rawls, *A Theory of Justice*

8

EXEGETICAL BONDING AND THE
PHENOMENOLOGY OF CONFESSION

✳

Themes, mythic stories, logical constructions, metaphors and metonymies, the mandated cosmos and the role of Mao as the purveyor of an inversionary discourse of his own all come together in Yan'an in the form of symbolic capital. But producing the right combination for the generation of symbolic capital depends on the molding of belief. Such molding is by no means simple. In Yan'an, it took the form of a textual exegesis that sought the total restructuring of mind and outlook in accordance with principles and precepts laid down by Mao and his associates. Something like this is intrinsic to every communist party, but in no other had there been such a high degree of orchestration and mobilization—and success— as in Yan'an. In this chapter we examine exegetical bonding in its most extreme moment, during the Rectification Campaign (1942–1944), which in retrospect became one of the distinguishing marks of the Yan'an period, and which would reach monstrous proportions during the Cultural Revolution.

The object of the Rectification Campaign was systemic change, irreversible and decisive. It was to set the stage for the next round of struggle. The organization of the campaign was systematic.[1] Key writings of Mao were sifted, recoded, and presented to the entire core Yan'an. The practical task was the total reeducation of the community. For this purpose, the entire instructional apparatus was mobilized. This required first that the educators themselves be reeducated; the place to begin was near the top of the political hierarchy. Bewilderment on the part of the participants had to precede reeducation, and reeducation in turn resulted in exegetical bonding. So effective was the process that one might say that the last reserves of individualism were wiped out, completing the conveyance of self to collectivity. As this conveyance occurred, so symbolic capital was generated. People felt themselves transformed from within, by their own efforts as well as the efforts of those around them. Yan'an changed drastically from an essentially voluntaristic community into something much more rigoristic, a discourse community in which structures were more highly institutionalized, norms internalized, and behavior socialized.[2]

Exegetical bonding enabled the party to extend its tutelary role. The entire organizational structure of the core Yan'an was mobilized for this purpose. What was sought was nothing less than both a totalized and integrated view of the revolutionary process and a shared understanding of specified ends. The space for differences in views was drastically narrowed, if not entirely erased. Yet this was done in ways individuals felt enhanced their more common knowledge. They were also made to feel that they had gained a deeper insight and understanding and were more comfortable and fluent in the political language they were being taught. Individuals in groups had to study and learn from required texts; the main themes of those texts established filiational lines between self and community, and reforged allegiances and affiliations within the collectivity. In order to accomplish this, the most intimate and sensitive aspects of one's life had to be exposed and held up to public view. At the same time, the scale was small and intimate, a strange mixture of non-kin familialism and ruthlessness. The individual had to do nothing less than destroy what he or she was and reconstitute both self and society. This produced a certain requisite austerity, as well as both the cool, impersonal, ruthlessness of a "good communist" and an intensity of friendship amounting to a kind of love. Yang Shangkun put it very well at the time. "I feel that the relationship between we [sic] party members is the noblest and purist friendship. It is built on a common view of the world and on certain political principles. It is a kind of class love, comradely love, and the great love of collectivism. It cannot be compared with secular 'friendship.' Our friendship is constructed on the basis of the party's principles without which such friendship cannot exist."[3]

This passage suggests that exegetical bonding, while it is an engagement with words and ideas in a context of immediate social learning, results in an emotional and symbolic intensity that includes the consciousness of self in terms of others. The result of exegetical bonding then is prescriptive illumination. Its higher purpose is enlightenment by the transcendence of ordinary understanding. The act of realizing transcendental understanding results in a kind of bonding. Through a personal *Aufhebung,* one reaches a new plane of interaction intertwined with discourse itself. Selected words serve to recode the self in terms of shared signifiers that are highly charged, and that become the unique property of the membership as a whole. By this means too, every ordinary aspect of life is imbued with intersubjective consciousness. As Liu Shaoqi put it in one of the documents reprinted for rectification:

> We are therefore opposed to individual heroes and exhibitionism, but not to a progressive attitude, for this is the Communist Party member's most precious quality. But a progressive attitude which is proletarian and Communist and one which is individualistic are two different things. The former searches for truth, upholds the truth, and fights most effectively for the truth; it is characterized by unlimited progress and advancement. The latter turns its attention to the individual, is of an extremely limited nature, and has no future. For the sake of individual interests, it often consciously destroys, conceals, or perverts the truth. Our comrades must therefore understand that the true Communist leaders and heroes are anything but individualistic leaders and heroes.[4]

What Mao and his associates did during the Rectification Campaign was to require the learning of a meta-language embodied in key texts, which, once learned, provided a logical grid for the collective interpretation of experience and the generation of symbolic capital. This meta-language, full of prescriptive and explicit codes (three principles, eight points, five changes); was made formulaic. It became a kind of "memory palace" in itself.[5] But there was no mistaking its import: to intervene in and direct the ways in which people would encounter, mediate, and share knowledge and experience in order that identities would be redefined and the discourse community become one's primary affiliation. In this sense, political affiliation becomes more important than any other bonding attribute, whether it be ethnicity, language, religion, or race.

This is why we can consider the Yan'anites an elect group, a band with distinct, shared characteristics. Rectification was a method unique in the degree to which it sought to penetrate the world as it appeared to be and to reshape it as a "true" world that conformed to a logical image; indeed, rectification was nothing less than a secular political religion. We have called Yan'an the moral moment of the Chinese revolution. If this is so, the Rectification Campaign was the moral moment of the moral moment.

For all that, people reacted differently to it. While most believed the campaign was necessary, it came as a shock that disturbed many outside observers and shattered the illusion that Yan'an was a peaceful, populist, and peasant revolutionary democracy. But rectification signified different things to different people. For some who looked back to pre-rectification Yan'an with nostalgia, the campaign represented the loss of innocence about the true reality of Yan'an,[6] an innocence already badly eroded by both the anti-Trotskyite campaigns that began in 1937 and the beginning of the move to assert Mao Zedong's thought as the movement's doctrinal orthodoxy that began in 1939. For Mao and those close to him, it was essential to build up symbolic capital out of reserves of moral power and by controlling impulses, to both unify the common understanding of revolutionary purpose and impose discipline. To understand was also to obey.

Rectification represented what might be called the hermeneutical transformation of texts as social facts into things in themselves embodying the party line. Exegetical bonding was the way to internalize this line and reshape interpretative capacities. It produced standards of conduct that by its own definition had to be exceptional. Indeed, exceptionalism was built in from the start, to the point that those who were rectified felt that in giving up the residue of their private doubts, they transcended themselves both morally and politically, as communists. By this means, the opportunities for conflicts in interpretation were reduced at the same time that people were called on to take an active part in interpretation.

One purpose of such interpretive coding was to ensure that party members behaved in a predictable way no matter how varied the circumstance or environment in which they operated. The discourse locked all administrative units together, whether in Yan'an, in other base areas, or behind enemy lines. Rectification also occurred at a time when the communist-held base areas (other than the Shaan-Gan-Ning) were coming under increasing pressure from the Japanese invaders. To resist this and to protect against GMD encroachment in subsequent years, Mao had to make sure that the party and its army would fight as a coherent force. The apparent success in the struggle against Japan and the sacrifices that were made after the GMD imposed its blockade helped Mao by creating a sort of moral momentum. Following the disasters that had preceded and accompanied the Long March, these were considerable successes, which many in the party came to identify with the correct policies implemented by Mao. In turn, this provided Mao and his supporters with the necessary confidence to believe that a symbolic mobilization would, through an elaborate combination of textual analysis, study, and self-criticism within the immediate circle of intimates, generate a public sphere of more or less like minds, a kind of Rousseauean general will. But to ensure that this general will had sufficient bite, the Rectification Campaign had within it a movement called, significantly enough, the "Rescue Campaign." It was a brief but terrifying episode designed to "rescue" people from themselves, especially if they came from the white areas. This group of people were thought to be especially imbued with bourgeois attitudes. In addition, the Rescue Campaign attempted to root out spies and agent provocateurs who, it was feared, had penetrated the party and the core Yan'an. This campaign caused such a great fear to spread throughout Yan'an and was potentially so undermining that Mao had to take exceptional steps to bring it to an end with an official apology.

The Rationale

The expansion of party membership after the start of the Sino-Japanese War (1937) and the presence of Yan'an as a place of resistance to the Japanese brought with it a variety of problems. Many intellectuals and patriots had come to Yan'an to wage war against Japan rather than because they were attracted by the theories of Marx and Lenin and the communist organizational form. The "storm membership drives" in the early years of the anti-Japanese war meant that many new recruits had been admitted into the party without proper screening. Zhang Ruxin, noting the composition of the Central Research Institute in Yan'an, remarked that the vast majority of new party members were "petty bourgeois, young intellectuals." Some 74 percent of the members of the institute had joined the party after the start of the Anti-Japanese War, 79 percent were twenty to thirty years old, and 82 percent were urban "intellectuals." According to Zhang, this group of "intellectuals" was particularly susceptible to the influence of "individualism" and "dogmatism" since they still possessed a petty bourgeois worldview.[7] According to Huang Huoqing, the problem in the party as a whole was just as acute. Of the party's eight hundred thousand members at that time, 90 percent were recent recruits, many of whom with a petty bourgeois background.[8]

Mao Zedong and his supporters felt that many of these new recruits were not well versed in Marxism-Leninism in its sinified form or clear about the party's ultimate aims. If the CCP was to remain a coherent, fighting force, a high degree of ideological orthodoxy would be necessary. As is clearly seen in the case of Wang Shiwei, Mao and his supporters were worried that the intellectuals would rupture the discourse, change the codes, desituate Mao's theories, and rearrange the narrative of significant events. This would undermine the exemplary behavior he sought to promote. In a sense, Mao profited from the economic and military accomplishments of the Yan'anites: these accomplishments kept the intellectuals from focusing on the darker side of Yan'an.

As we have seen, the history of the CCP during the thirties had been marked by bitter internal struggles that had, on occasion, spilled over into fratricide. Since the dismissal of Chen Duxiu and the August 7 Emergency Conference (1927), adherence to the correct ideological line came to legitimize policy, and understanding of the line was a necessary condition for leadership. Debate in the party became governed by the manipulation of ideological symbols with the result that genuine debate about policy disputes declined. Policy difference became synonymous with line struggle.[9] If most party members could be persuaded to rally to a new orthodoxy, the risk of such violent inner-party struggle would be substantially diminished. Mao's capacity to interpret apparent defeat as merely a temporary setback in a process of history that was moving inexorably forward, combined with his capacity to make sense of the rapidly changing world, was reassuring to other party leaders. In turn, this helped him enhance his status as the revolution's supreme leader and interpreter. In particular, his reinterpretation of the party's history offered a logic and order that many believed would end the killing within the CCP. This must have been reassuring to those who had suffered as a result of the changing lines of the thirties.

Increasingly, Mao came to believe that even after winning his four struggles, the task of reconsolidation and the concentration of all four modes of power into a single cosmology—territorial, military, intellectual, and theoretical—would require an exceptional effort directed from the top in the name of those at the bottom. The discourse would provide a source of allegiance for party members by linking their precarious individual situations to China's degradation at the hands of the imperialist invaders and the warlords, who were viewed as products of China's feudal system. In order to unify the discourse and ensure that everyone spoke the language, a process of exegetical bonding was required. This process would eliminate any vestige of individualism, or what we might refer to today as the kind of methodological individualism that more "normal" politics comprehends. The goal was to create a seamless web of discourse out of which a community would be created according to the rules of collective individualism, a community in which self-enlightenment and knowledge would enhance each individual's sense of well-being and enable each person to believe that his or her own person was enhanced by the collectivity.

Of particular importance for the party as a whole, and for the individual in particular, was the notion of "overcoming." Designed to enable people to overcome a variety of specific inadequacies (from simple literacy to theoretical understanding) both conceptually and practically, overcoming encompassed all kinds of specific and theoretical knowledge (from fixing radios to military tactics). This was part and parcel of the process of the individual's reclaiming the patrimony, an act of self-possession made possible both through individual effort and the institutions provided by the community. Thus, peasants "overcame" illiteracy, children "evolved" into thinking adults by learning the basic principles of communism, and those with middle and high school education could go on to the "universities."[10]

Mao sought to combine the "overcoming" by the individual with that of the movement as a whole through the process of retelling the history of the communist movement. When Mao began this process of reordering, his enemy in the sphere of theory, Wang Ming, had already been defeated politically. However, Wang could still utilize his expertise in the sphere of ideology. His threat was all the more potent because many of the Russian Returned Students were in influential positions in the training system. This could allow Wang to claw back ground through the training of party cadres. Thus, for Mao to gain control over ideological reproduction it was necessary for him to control the discourse of the "Academy." This, in turn, entailed a shift from mouthing Marxist-Leninist texts to accepting a theory grounded in "Chinese realities." First Mao had to define this theory; then he had to select the corpus of texts for study and internalization.

The construction of a "Maoist party history" was an integral part of this process.[11] It had to do more than simply order and retell the past. Mao sought to channel that history and place himself in the central role. This would provide him with the legitimacy necessary to secure an unchallengeable leadership position. Mao as supreme leader and correct interpreter of the past would become the ideological authority defining the present and the future orientation of the revolution. Mao's correct interpretation of history would be used to convince party members of his correct thought.

In linking theory to revolutionary practice in this way, Mao undercut the theoretical pretensions of Wang Ming and the students who had returned from the Soviet Union by labeling them "dogmatists." He claimed they derived their theories from books and not from the practice of the Chinese revolution. By contrast, Mao staked his right to leadership on the claim that he had applied the theory of Marxism-Leninism to the concrete realities of the Chinese revolution. After his none too successful diversion into Marxist philosophy in the winter of 1936–37, Mao concentrated on promoting himself as a theorist who had fully understood the course of the Chinese revolution. At the party's Sixth Plenum (October

1938), Mao launched his drive for a sinified form of Marxism-Leninism, claiming that there was no such thing as an abstract Marxism. Marxism had to take on a national form and be presented in a new, lively Chinese style that ordinary people could appreciate.[12] Persistence in peddling "abstract Marxism" amounted to having a dogmatic perception. In launching the Rectification Campaign, Mao noted the following:

> Our comrades must understand that we do not study Marxism-Leninism because it is pleasing to the eye, or because it has some mystical value, like the doctrines of the Taoist priests who ascend Mao Shan to learn how to subdue devils and evil spirits. Marxism-Leninism has no beauty, nor has it any mystical value. It is only extremely useful. It seems that right up to the present quite a few have regarded Marxism-Leninism as a ready-made panacea: once you have it, you can cure all your ills with little effort. This is a type of childish blindness and we must start a movement to enlighten these people. Those who regard Marxism-Leninism as religious dogma show this type of blind ignorance. We must tell them openly, "Your dogma is of no use," or to use an impolite phrase, "Your dogma is less useful than excrement." We see that dog excrement can fertilize the fields and man's can feed the dog. And dogma's? They can't fertilize the fields nor can they feed a dog. Of what use are they?[13]

At the start of rectification, Mao also confirmed that the study of party history and line was crucial to an understanding of the present. An appreciation of the "correct party line" lay at the core of the movement. This confirmed the fact that theory had to be rooted in the Chinese soil. As Mao commented, the "backside had to be attached to China's body." Otherwise one would wander aimlessly with nowhere to sit down.[14]

Thus, there was more to the construction of a "correct" party history than providing a framework for party members to relate to. It was intended to end alternative discourses within the movement. Disagreement with the Maoist view of party history would be tantamount to committing a mistake in "line." Rectification was not just a peaceful proselytizing event but entailed the eradication of alternative intellectual responses to party rule, no matter whether the challenge came from Wang Ming and his supporters or from those intellectuals, such as Wang Shiwei, who represented the cosmopolitan trend of the May Fourth Movement within the CCP. The construction of a "correct" party history and the presentation of Mao Zedong Thought based upon it disguised the ruthless Mao who pursued ultimate power. The creation of this single discourse eliminated the pluralism of ideas that had temporarily replaced the monism common-place in the Chinese polity.

The linking of the individual story to that of the movement as a whole and the emergence of Mao as the savior reveals the true nature of the three stories in Chapter 3 in terms of their epic components. The long story was not only about the loss of the double patrimony; it was also an epic of failed modernization where others, particularly Japan, succeeded. It created a historical space for an alternative way, not yet discredited: the promise of disjunctive opportunity that Soviet Russia came to represent immediately after the October Revolution. This was the way to transform the system from above in the name of those below, with the state using revolutionary symbolic capital to unleash, transform, and mobilize the entire society not only for modernization but also for a higher moral community. The long story connected failed modernization to the transformational developmental project, and Yan'an was the point of transition.

In the intermediate story, the message is not only that modernization has failed, but also that the most recent instrument of its failure is the GMD. It was argued that the developmental route favored by the GMD would exacerbate difficulties and contradictions, and would substitute fascism for the kind of "democracy" Yan'an defined and the kind of socialism it embodied in its utopic project. In this respect, the GMD incorporated the failed modernization of the long story and as such represents failed nationalism.

Such failures personalized the struggle over legitimacy. Both the GMD and the CCP accepted the legitimacy of Sun Yat-sen as the correct nationalist leader of modern China. Whether Chiang Kai-shek or Mao was the true justified successor became crucial in light of previous failures. The issue of *line* of succession and thus the fulfillment of the testament and Sun's "Three Principles of the People" is also the issue of how China will be reconstituted—the large project of a revolution of rival claims. It was because of this mutual acceptance of Sun Yat-sen and his Three Principles that a united front was at all a possibility. However, precisely because so much was at stake, the "united" front was united in what it opposed (the Japanese invader) but was fatally divided over what it supported. Hence, the real significance of the intermediate story is the united front with all the ambiguities that involved, and the curious intimacies of association and break.

However, Mao begins the process of exegetical bonding with the short story. Here personal experience could most easily be reinterpreted to merge with grand design. The short story is a record of the incorrect applications of Marxism that have resulted in failed "lines." In turn, these "lines" have brought the party untold disasters. The retelling of these failures within the framework of the larger stories erodes the alternatives to Mao's theory and strategy so seriously that they have no basis on which to stand. In this sense, time was on Mao's side because the defeats suffered by the CCP under his predecessors gave his ascent to power the feeling of the miraculous. Hence, the short story is really about the miracle of Mao, the Long March providing the fitting occasion for his ascension. Parodic negativity was built into rectification both as history and experience and was brought down to the level of each individual by means of self-purification. The larger epic components took on an immediate relevance in the personal context.

In turn, the process of rectification shifted the entire weight of these negative parodies onto the individual through a combination of learning and education, which lift the individual to a level where he or she becomes responsible for knowing better. Accusatory practices were thus justified. Those who fail also fail themselves. In terms of the larger discourse, those who fail were clearly insufficiently educated. Hence the need for further study. Those who have studied further should have purged themselves of leftover sensibilities of liberalism and other bad tendencies. If not, they need to purify themselves further. Education goes hand in hand with purging and purification; these are the three routes to higher truth and to moral and intellectual enlightenment, which people themselves desire. It is only by means of this process that revolutionary and Maoist norms could be internalized in each individual.

If Yan'an marked the culmination of the three stories with time converted into space, then the core or utopic Yan'an became not only the moral moment of the revolution, but the immediate focus of the revolution itself. By transforming Yan'an into a collective community within the larger revolutionary frame, the here and now became the precondition for later success.

Mao's republic occupied the physical space of Yan'an. But as a discourse community, it had itself to go through a decisive transformation at the core. Within the core, this was all the more urgent at the highest centers of instruction. This transformation, hints of which began in 1939, occurred from 1942 to 1944 with the Rectification Campaign. It was the moment of collective truth, a truth in the discourse, both particularly Chinese and universal. It was timeless in form, but served as the transition point for the next stage.

Each person took his or her place not as an individual but as a signifier for a system; a person's every word, act, and posture conveyed more than one could by oneself. The individual became a soldier in an army of truth. Yan'an life became even more rigoristic than before, more Spartan and disciplined. Internal and external crisis were each to be met, not in their own terms but by those imposed on the situation. Knowledge became situated knowledge, a kind of placement process in which the discourse took on a life of its own.

If the principles were timeless, time did not stand still. It was measured in immediate tasks and episodes. Meetings became events. Texts replaced shifts in time; shifts in interpretation situated the texts by means of performance, orality, literacy, and writualization, and in this way a *habitus* was formed. Nothing could be taken for granted. The campaign orchestrated exegesis, thereby bonding people to one another within their units and within Yan'an more generally, a process that went hand in hand with the deliberate production of symbolic capital. This capital, while the property of all, was also the unique trust of Mao Zedong.

Exegetical bonding required mobilizing all the institutional facilities and intellectual resources of Yan'an. The original purpose of the education system was shifted. It had functioned as a mechanism for reassignment, forging new loyalties by means of the unit *(danwei)* system, and had trained thousands of cadres for assignment elsewhere in the Border Region, in the other base areas, or behind enemy lines. Now it was to become the venue for concentrated textual learning and exegesis. It was the educators' turn to be educated. The training went beyond discipline to a complete view of the revolutionary life. Education was designed to change the principles and norms one lived by as well as one's conduct and behavior. These changes would be judged and evaluated by a complex system of screening and observation. Not only was every person readily identifiable, but each was simultaneously observing and observed. How to make such scrutiny responsible was one problem; how to prevent it from becoming corrupt was another. We have already described how the Border Region as a whole was organized and structured. Each person occupied roles functional to the activity being performed so that as an economic unit the region could be made to yield sufficient surpluses to support the core Yan'an and its activities. In terms of party roles especially, a heavy premium was placed on the normative meaning of revolutionary action. The best way to consider the Shaan-Gan-Ning Border Region is as a structural network in which instrumental activities were endowed with a consummatory dimension.[15] There were various ways in which this endowment was secured, but "education" was the most important. A full range of institutions was devoted to education; rectification was an intensification of this process.

The techniques for popularizing the newly emergent Maoist party history and discourse became the hallmark of later CCP campaigns. First, the objectives of the campaign and the contents of study were identified by Mao and his supporters. Second, texts and materials were chosen for study by the target group. These materials contained both positive and negative examples and were geared to reinforcing the thrust of the leader's policy. Third, the study itself was organized and its stages decided upon. Small groups for discussion of the texts formed the backbone of the study system, accompanied by lectures from key figures and publications in party journals explaining the correct interpretation of the texts. People in the study groups were called on to think of concrete examples from their own experiences to illustrate the thrust of the campaign's message. On the basis of this, individuals were to evaluate their own, and others', past behavior. Acceptance of the new discourse would provide both a sense of relief at having "passed the test" and pride at being admitted into the new order. Finally, the campaign would enter a summation stage, when particular targets (already decided upon by the leadership at the beginning) would be identified. The rewards for those who accepted "unity of thought" were accompanied by the threat of terror or exile for those who refused to accept the new line.

Preparation of the Texts

The basis for rectification was laid when Mao began the campaign among senior cadres to study party history, particularly the history of the party since the Fourth Plenum of January 1931. It was at this plenum that Wang Ming and his supporters, aided by the Comintern representative Pavel Mif, gained control over the party apparatus. Although Wang had sat out most of the subsequent period in Moscow, Mao blamed him for sponsoring a "leftist" line that had brought disaster to the party, culminating in the loss of the Jiangxi soviet and the march into the wilderness. As far as Mao was concerned, this line had proved even more disastrous than that of Li Lisan, which it had displaced. Order amidst this chaos only began to be restored at the Zunyi Conference (January 1935) when Mao emerged to take power, rejected the "incorrect line," and brought new direction to the party.[16]

As noted earlier, Zunyi was only a first step in Mao's ascent to power, it was by no means irreversible, and at the time only the military line was rejected, not the political line. However, as early as October 1939, Mao was busy declaring that the Zunyi Conference had set the party on the road to Bolshevization and laid the foundations for forming the united front against Japan.[17] It was not easy for Mao to get the veteran cadres to accept this shift to wholesale denunciation of the plenum. It was still widely regarded as legitimate and as having played a crucial role in terminating the Li Lisan line. Many senior cadres had been involved in the events and may have been unhappy to see their own positions potentially undermined by criticism of the plenum. Finally, there was the Comintern to be considered. The Fourth Plenum had been convened under the auspices of the Comintern, and its decisions and the leadership elected were said to have been in line with the Comintern's wishes. The problem of the Comintern disappeared in May 1943 when it was dissolved, and cadre resistance was eroded by the exegetical bonding that took place when the study of party history was broadened into the Rectification Campaign. By the time party history was returned to, the nonacceptance of Mao's viewpoint had been identified with incorrect thought. If this was not enough to make the cadres accept Mao's history, the treatment of Wang Shiwei and Kang Sheng's Rescue Campaign of 1943 made it clear there were penalties for those who held out.

The first major document to be studied by senior cadres was the *History of the Communist Party of the Soviet Union (Bolshevik): Short Course;* it was followed by edited collections of documents covering CCP history from its foundation to the present. The *Short Course* provided impetus to the idea of compiling an official party history. While the publication of this work marked the triumph of Stalin in the Soviet political system, its translation into Chinese was used by Mao Zedong to assume ideological hegemony based on a "correct" history of the party's past. The book served as a model for the study of party history, and its Conclusion was one of the twenty-two pieces of required reading for the Rectification Campaign as a whole. The *Short Course* was held up as a fine example of linking Marxist theory to a particular situation—in this case, the Russian Revolution. In this sense, Mao used it to preface his attack on dogmatism. Speaking in May 1941, Mao Zedong praised the work as the "highest synthesis of the world communist movement in the last 100 years, a model for the union of theory and practice; in the whole world, this is still the one comprehensive model."[18] Translation work was begun quickly, and in November 1938, Chapter 7 and the Conclusion were published in the weekly *Jiefang* (Liberation). It is claimed that by March 1941 some one hundred thousand volumes were in circulation.[19]

This Soviet model, which indicated how Marxism-Leninism had been applied to the case of Russia, was quickly followed by the dissemination of materials outlining the process of the Chinese revolution. Mao Zedong himself took an active role in editing the Chinese materials to be used in the study. His first work was to supervise the editing of a collection of documents covering party history from its origins until the present. The collection was to "form the basis for clarifying the political, organizational, and ideological line after the Fourth Plenum."[20] Research was to focus on specific meetings or events, and senior cadres were called on to summarize their own experiences.[21]

The most important collection of materials for cadres to study were the two volumes *Before the Sixth Party Congress* and *After the Sixth Party Congress,* the latter being the most important.[22] These materials were compiled from July to mid-August 1941 following a Politburo decision that put Mao Zedong in charge of the work.[23] Circulation of this initial collection was useful preparation for the September 1941 Politburo meeting; one CCP historian has claimed that discussions could not have proceeded so smoothly without the materials as they disarmed various senior cadres and helped them "realize their mistakes."[24]

After the Politburo meeting, responsibility for editing came under the Committee for Clarification of Party History (set up by the Secretariat in October 1941), with Mao still possessing final responsibility. The published collection formed the core of materials for study by senior cadres. According to Mao, this study of party history was intended to improve current policy and to ensure that the line was correct.[25] *After the Sixth Party Congress* was formally published in December 1941; it contained some 550 documents covering the period from July 1928 until November 1941. The materials were drawn from Central Committee resolutions, directives, announcements, telegrams, articles, and speeches by various leaders. The collection also provided the basis for the first versions of the *Selected Works of Mao Zedong.* The second volume, *Before the Party Congress,* was published in October 1942. The work contained some 200 documents covering the period from March 1922 to June 1928. The materials contained in the two volumes affirmed that the emerging narrative of Maoist party history was correct. Further, the speeches included displayed Mao and key supporters, such as Liu Shaoqi, as being better equipped to lead the party than Wang Ming. Because the materials covered such a broad range of issues, a shorter selection of 170 documents was published under the title *The Two Lines (Liangtiao luxian)* when the movement to study party history entered its final phase in late 1943.

Once the movement to study party history was broadened into the Rectification Campaign, eighteen documents were selected for study, although this was quickly increased to twenty-two. As the campaign spread out from the center to other base areas and regions, these twenty-two documents were published in book form under various titles such as *Zhengfeng wenxian* (Rectification Documents).[26] For the first time, it was officially recommended that works by Mao Zedong himself form a core component of the study materials. Of the initial eighteen documents proposed for study, seven could be directly attributed to Mao.[27] Only two works by Soviet writers had been included, although the four added on April 16 were all by Soviet or Comintern writers (Lenin, Stalin, and Dimitrov). In addition, the four Central Committee resolutions included were in all probability drafted by Mao; the reportage by Kang Sheng amounted to little more than interpretations of Mao's speeches that had launched the Rectification Campaign. While this marked a considerable increase in Mao's influence, it did not necessarily suggest sole control over the movement. However, the fact that only two Soviet documents were included among the initial eighteen showed that the CCP had clearly decided to determine its own future.

Organizing the Cadres

Before the texts could be studied, the cadres had to be organized. Shortly after the Sixth Plenum, where Mao had made his plea for sinification, he began to pay attention to the education of senior cadres. On December 13, 1938, on behalf of the Secretariat, Mao stated that it was necessary to step up the study of Marxism-Leninism and China's revolutionary history and that preparatory work should be finished by January 25, 1939.[28] Subsequently, on February 17, 1939, the Central Committee decided to establish a Cadre Education Department with Zhang Wentian as head and Li Weihan as his deputy.[29] The task of this department was to mobilize cadres for the study of Marxism-Leninism and revolutionary history and to discuss methods of study.[30]

Serious study by senior cadres began in May 1939 with consideration of the *Short Course;* this was basically completed by March 1941.[31] In June 1940, middle-level cadres began their study, also finishing in March 1941. In all, 2,118 people participated in this study in Yan'an.[32] Gradually, the framework was broadened to include the study of the concepts of line and rectification for a three-month period of cadre training beginning on March 15. Getting to senior cadres outside Yan'an was an important prerequisite for launching rectification throughout the party as a whole. These cadres would be called on to deliver keynote speeches at the Party School and other institutions, and would interpret key developments and texts.

At a Politburo meeting that began on September 10, 1941, the crucial decision was taken to open out the movement into a campaign to rectify work style.[33] Meeting participants discussed the question of how genuine party unity could be achieved and, to this end, two major issues were debated. First, they discussed how cadres could learn to link Marxist-Leninist theory with the actual situation in China. Second, they decided the "correct" interpretation of party history and the political line during the 1927–1937 period.

Mao's speech to the meeting outlined the key themes of the Rectification Campaign. He denounced the Li Lisan line and the "left" opportunism of the later Soviet period (Wang Ming) as examples of subjectivism, claiming that the latter had inflicted the greatest damage on the movement. He felt that despite the correctives introduced at the Zunyi Conference, "subjectivism" in the ideological sphere still influenced work in Yan'an. Mao traced this subjectivism to three factors: "leftism" in the Chinese tradition; the people such as Bukharin and Zinoviev, whose "foreign traditions" had influenced the movement; and the petty bourgeois nature of China, which derived from a lack of scientific development. Concluding his speech, Mao outlined the methods that would be used in rectification, such as focusing on the serious threat posed by subjectivism, clarifying the difference between Marxism and "dogmatic Marxism," exposing the qualifications of those whose theory was divorced from practice, and dealing with sectarianism.[34]

In line with Mao's comments to the meeting, the education of senior cadres was stepped up and formalized further. On September 26, 1941, the Secretariat published a decision on organizing study for senior cadres.[35] The decision outlined the objectives and scope of the study, the number of those who should participate, the method and the contents of the study, and the relationship between the central and the local study groups. It called for the participation of some three hundred cadres drawn from the Central Committee, the central departments and bureaus, the regional or provincial party committees, and leaders of the Eighth Route Army and the New Fourth Army. One-third of those engaged in study would be in the Yan'an area. The first class was to last half a year and study two topics: the theory and method of Marxism-Leninism, Engels, and Stalin; and party history. After this preparatory six months, the relationship between the two topics was to be explored as a way to overcome the problems of subjectivism and formalism. Mao Zedong was to head the Central Committee

Study Group with Wang Jiaxiang as his deputy. All the other study groups came under the jurisdiction of this central group. The groups themselves were further subdivided into small groups. The Central group was to select materials for study, summarize the study experience, and respond to questions.

On October 4, 1941, Mao Zedong and Wang Jiaxiang called for small groups to be organized within the senior study groups to study Leninist theory and the political line since the Sixth Party Congress. By the end of 1941, these groups were expected to have studied Dimitrov's report to the Seventh Congress of the Comintern (1935)[36] and the documents in the collection *After the Sixth Party Congress*. This preliminary study was seen as preparation for deeper research in the coming spring. Mao and Wang recognized that not all areas might be able to lay their hands on the relevant documents. If documents could not be found, people could report on them from memory. However, Mao and Wang stressed that in this initial phase of discussing the past, the question of particular individuals was not to be brought up.[37] This would come in the last phase of the campaign.

The next most important preparatory step was the reorganization of the Central Party School that together with the Central Research Institute would form the focal point of the Rectification Campaign. Not only was this the prime institution for party training, but the expected delegates to the Seventh Party Congress were among the thousand students to be enrolled during 1942. Some of our informants suggested that Mao never intended to convene the Congress so early as he knew there was still residual opposition to his ideas. His intention was to bring the delegates to Yan'an early to ensure that they first underwent an intensive period of education.

The December 1941 Politburo decision on Yan'an cadre schools pointed out that their main problem was "the discrepancy between what is studied in theory and applied in reality, and the grave errors of subjectivism and dogmatism."[38] To resolve these problems, the decision stressed the need for students to learn how to apply Marxism-Leninism to the practical problems of the Chinese revolution. This required further study of China's own history.

Rectification Launched

With the texts compiled or being edited and the reorganization of study completed, in the early months of 1942 the education movement for senior cadres was broadened out to rectification for the party as a whole.

The signal for this widening of the movement was given in two speeches by Mao on February 1 and 8, 1942, to the Central Party School in Yan'an.[39] These two speeches identified three mistaken tendencies within the party: subjectivism, sectarianism, and formalism. Mao's comments were critical of two groups in Yan'an: first, the intellectuals, who had recently come to Yan'an and lacked practical revolutionary experience; and second, and initially more important, Wang Ming and the Russian Returned Students. This movement combined Mao Zedong's attempts to present himself as the revolution's foremost source of theoretical wisdom with a drive to end the intellectual diversity in Yan'an by proposing obedience to a new orthodoxy. The party under Mao would provide the direction for the revolution, and the role of its intellectuals would not be to examine it critically but to proselytize it faithfully.

On February 1, Mao asserted that recently the party's general line had been correct, but that problems remained because "progress" on the theoretical front had been "extremely inadequate." Mao saw subjectivism as the core of the problems, and he defined two types, dogmatism and empiricism, dogmatism being the worst. However, since one's "immediate perception" was limited, only through theoretical study could experiences be raised to "the level of reason and synthesis, the level of theory," a line of attack clearly directed against Wang Ming and his supporters. In an even more obvious reference to Wang, Mao claimed that it would be irresponsible to call oneself a Marxist if one had only studied the Marxist classics and had not used them as the basis for understanding China's specific conditions and to "create our own specific theory in accordance with China's practical needs." China needed the kind of theorist who could apply the standpoints, concepts, and methods of Marxism-Leninism to China's actual problems. "The arrow of Marxism-Leninism," to use Mao's classic phrase, "must be used to hit the target of the Chinese revolution."

In the second part of the talk, Mao turned to the problem of sectarianism. He criticized those party members who put their own particular interests above the party's. Subjugation of one's own interests to those of the party would ensure unity of action and help the party achieve its "fighting objectives." This led Mao to argue that while the party needed democracy, it needed centralism even more. For Mao, the spirit of unity was necessary for "the people of the entire nation." Only if this was achieved would it be possible to defeat the enemy.

Finally, Mao put forward the principles to be observed when attacking erroneous tendencies. Criticism of the past was to serve as a warning for future actions. Mao likened the process to a doctor curing a disease: the objective was not to kill the patient, but to cure the symptoms so that the diseased party member would be able to become a good comrade once again. This would have helped reassure senior cadres who were wary of the adverse consequences of rewriting party history—a fear well justified if they thought about what had happened in the Soviet Union under Stalin.

In his talk on February 8, Mao took up the issue of party formalism in a clear attack on Wang Ming and the returned students. According to Mao, those guilty of subjectivism and sectarianism used party formalism as their propaganda tool and form of expression. These three incorrect tendencies within the party Mao traced to a petty bourgeois mentality that had penetrated the party from society at large. In his attack on party formalism, Mao highlighted the problem of "foreign formalism." He claimed that although the eradication of "foreign formalism" and "dogmatism" were called for at the Sixth Plenum of the Sixth Central Committee, "some comrades" were still advocating them.

This was followed by further, concrete measures to prepare the Central Party School for rectification. On February 28, 1942, the Politburo passed new regulations for study at the school terminating the existing curriculum.[40] For the remainder of the year, study was to focus on party line, and all study was to be in line with the spirit of the campaign to oppose "subjectivism and dogmatism." The Politburo had decided that the first reorganization of the school had been unsuitable as it had resulted in classes to study foreign history and Chinese classical history. The objective of the new reorganization was to ensure that study at the Party School should coincide entirely with the principles of rectification as "laid down by Mao Zedong." The reorganization was to be completed by the end of March.

The decision also brought the Party School directly under the leadership of the Secretariat of the Central Committee. Mao Zedong was put in control of political work with Ren Bishi appointed to oversee organizational matters. Day-to-day administration was in the hands of Deng Fa (principal), Peng Zhen (head of education and responsible for political education),[41] and Lin Biao (responsible for military affairs). These three were to organize a new management committee for the school.

Finally, the senior class of the Academy of Military Affairs was to be merged into the Party School. The number of students from various organs in Yan'an and senior cadres from the various schools was to be limited to between 300 and 400. On March 11, 1942, the Party Center issued regulations guiding the recruitment of students to the school.[42] Those from organs directly under the Central Committee or party, government, or mass cadres from outside were to be investigated and approved by the Central Organization Department; those from organs under the Military Commission or military cadres from outside were to be investigated and approved by the military's General Political Department; and cadres from the Border Region were to be investigated and approved by the Northwest Bureau.[43] The criteria used by each system for checking candidates' thought and political background were to be uniform. However, as the Central Organization Department and the General Political Department would not be able to make a full investigation, those admitted would have to be investigated once more by the Party School itself. On March 20, 1942, Mao's direct influence over the Central Party School was strengthened further by the Politburo's decision to name him Principal. Peng Zhen was to serve as his deputy. Mao had now identified the movement's first set of targets and established an organizational structure for study with himself in control.

Through the remainder of 1942, the scope of the movement was broadened gradually and resistance to proper study in the Rectification Campaign was challenged. On February 28, the Central Committee issued a resolution dealing with those cadres who could not attend the party schools. This resolution pointed out that although the call had been made in 1938, the training of the 90 percent of cadres who could not attend party schools had not begun in some localities and departments. To give them a proper education, the propaganda department under Kai Feng was called on to devise procedures for party, military, and political organizations to "carry out the education of cadres on the job."[44]

On April 3, 1942, the Propaganda Bureau published its important report on the Rectification Campaign. This report raised the campaign to a new level by providing precise timetables and the list of eighteen key texts for study. The report highlighted the resistance to carrying out the movement properly, claiming that "very few leading organs" had properly prepared and planned discussions. The documents were to form the core of the study with participants not only reading them but taking notes and debating them in small discussion groups. Where necessary Central Committee members or workers from the Propaganda Bureau were to be dispatched to make reports to the study groups. The circular stressed giving equal weight to "guidance from above" and to the "development of democracy." It noted that the Central Committee had stipulated a three-month period of study by all organizations with the exception of the party schools, where the period was only two months. This was to be followed by a period of investigation, criticism, and self-criticism. During the final stage, conclusions, reports, and recommendations were to be made.

On June 8, 1942, the Propaganda Bureau issued a supplement to the April directive on how the Rectification Campaign had proceeded to date and how it was to be developed.[45] To help study, the directive put forward a number of supplementary measures. The Center was to set up a General Study Committee to guide all study in Yan'an. Each department and unit was to set up a study branch. The General Study Committee was to be headed by Mao Zedong with Kang Sheng as his deputy. The appointment of Kang Sheng foreshadowed what was to come with the Rescue Campaign. Daily monitoring of the study was in Kang's hands, the man who was in charge of the communists' secret service operations.[46] In fact, in August 1941, just before the Politburo decided to push ahead with the Rectification Campaign, Kang was appointed Chair of the Cadre Investigation Commission, which was entrusted to vet the political attitudes of cadres.[47] Rectification and the investigation of cadres' backgrounds were being linked. This link became explosive during the Rescue Campaign in 1943. The General Study Committee was to convene a study meeting for senior cadres in Yan'an either weekly or fortnightly. Apart from the General Study Group, three other groups were set up at the center to oversee the work in the various administrative systems *(xitong)*. All were headed by Mao supporters.[48]

All who could read were to participate in the study movement by attending small groups. According to the June 8 document, 17,098 people were participating in the Rectification Campaign in Yan'an. The directive concluded that it was "extremely" necessary for the whole party to study the twenty-two documents. Indeed, in order to meet this objective, other study in cadre schools was to be stopped temporarily in order to meet this objective. To facilitate study, work hours were reduced. For example, in Yan'an, mornings were set aside for such study. However, the directive made it clear that this could only be arranged in accordance with local conditions. It was not to be forgotten that a war was being fought! Finally, the study period was to be increased from four to five months, again in accordance with local conditions. It was expected that this new organization would enable some ten thousand people to join the study.

A number of problems arose in the study movement; these were highlighted in a *Liberation Daily* editorial of June 5, 1942.[49] Among the problems singled out were the tendency of focusing on particular words and sentences in the documents rather than seeking to understand them as a whole, not engaging in self-examination, trying to hide from rectification, not criticizing one's own faults while attacking others, and senior leaders' not paying enough attention to the study. In summarizing experience with rectification to date, the editorial noted that the "most important factor" was leading cadres. It was claimed that only if they studied seriously could the movement be carried out properly. In essence, the thrust of these criticisms was that study had to be taken seriously. It would not be sufficient to pay lip service to study; this would not mean a genuine acceptance of the new discourse.

Study of the documents was combined with consideration of specific events or meetings and personal experience. This method, known as *qifa,* sought to move individuals from close personal experiences that were readily understandable to acceptance of the master narrative constructed by Mao. As Peng Zhen announced, study of the documents was intended to lead to a self-examination *(fanxing)* of every individual's work, thought, and life history. This process was in turn to form the basis for investigation of the departments in which one worked or with which one was connected. This would result in rectification of "erroneous tendencies."[50]

Starting in February 1942, the whole Central Party School was mobilized for study of the twenty-two documents. School meetings were held and were addressed by senior leaders who set out the new discourse. Wall posters and a study newsletter were used to promote it. At the school, discussion groups were made up of a minimum of three and a maximum of ten members. These groups were also addressed by senior leaders to ensure that they knew what the correct interpretation of the documents should be. Participants had to write up profiles on their thoughts, life histories, reading notes, and notes on self-reform. These notes and those taken during discussions were checked over by the school leaders, and individuals were helped to correct their notes through criticism. To help the participants even further, the *Liberation Daily* published sets of notes that could be used as examples.

This first phase ended in late June and early July with ten days of examination for all students. Showing his meticulous concern for rectification Mao is said to have personally approved the exam questions.[51] The questions dealing with dogmatism show how the grasp of the general concept was to be linked with one's own personal experiences: What is dogmatism in the party? What are the most serious instances [of dogmatism] you have encountered? Have you already opposed mistakes of dogmatism in your study and work? If such mistakes have been made, in what ways have they been manifested?

These same mechanisms were used in other work units. Thus, for example, in late July 1942, the Northwest Bureau held a meeting to draw conclusions from the Rectification Campaign. It set three questions for examination in the middle- and lower-level study groups. First, participants were asked whether study of the rectification documents had caused them to recognize any shortcomings in their own work. Second, participants were asked if they had encountered subjectivism. Third, they were asked how they thought shortcomings in their own study or that of their study group could be overcome. At the same time, the bureau asked for reports to be compiled and sent on to the higher authorities. These reports were important as they were to point out who were the best and worst participants in the study as well as what were the best and worst organizations.[52] Earlier, the bureau had announced that the notes and speeches by participants in the study would form the basis for understanding each comrade's thought and his or her transformation.[53]

This same method was used when the time came for summing up the study of party history. In mid-May 1943, the *Jiefang ribao* reported that cadres in the Suide district were devoting three weeks to a thorough study of the documents on the history of the party in the Northwest.[54] Two-line struggle was stressed in this process of study, and cadres were expected to review their own work in light of this. They were to study whether they had committed errors of line, especially in the period since the united front against Japan had been launched. The paper claimed that this soul-searching had led to some cadres reporting to the party problems in their history or thought that they had never told anyone else before.

Zhang Baichun, who experienced the campaign at Kangda, felt initially that rectification and its main themes did not concern him. He had never studied and thus, in his view, could not suffer from subjectivism. He did not have any friends or relatives and thus did not feel that dogmatism was relevant. Finally, as he never wrote articles, he could not see how party formalism was relevant to his life and work. However, he claimed that study made him realize that all these "isms" did indeed apply to him. Subjectivism applied to one's thought and work methods; party rectification did not relate to family and friends but to relations within and outside of the party; and party formalism could apply equally to speech as to the written word.[55]

Confessions of bad thought could be quite personal. Dou Shangchu admitted that his thought contained so many faults that one session would not be enough to go through them all. In particular, he felt that his attitude to marriage had been transformed through rectification. Before study, he had not seen this as being an issue that was of interest to the party. He claimed that previously he had three conditions for a prospective wife "first, it must be a human being, second, it must be alive, and third female." His ideal was a women who would stay at home. However, the leader of his study group had shown him that he must also take the political situation into account when choosing a partner. Regimental commanders such as Dou, when looking for a wife, were to make sure of three other conditions: first, the prospective partner should have no problems politically; second, the couple should love one another; and third, the woman had to be a party member.

The Discourse Accepted

Public acceptance of the new discourse also applied to the senior leaders who were deemed to have now fallen afoul of the new party history. This was particularly the case for those who were criticized for following either Li Lisan (such as Zhou Enlai) or Wang Ming (such as Bo Gu). In particular, while making speeches cum confessions, senior leaders sought to highlight differences between themselves and Li and Wang, and affinities with Mao. Zhou was entrusted with clarifying line and policy throughout the twenties and especially at the Sixth Party Congress, held July–September 1928.[56] The identification of Mao Zedong with correct policy options was apparent in Zhou's talk. He highlighted Mao Zedong as the party's "representative" who realized that as a result of the May Thirtieth Movement, the revolution was turning into a revolutionary peasant war. In his account of the Sixth Party Congress, Zhou contrasted the failure of the Congress to recognize the importance of armed struggle, to build up the party, and establish its own regimes with the correct development of Mao's thought on these issues. Zhou proceeded to note that the Congress decisions carried more weight because Mao "had not yet become leader of the party as a whole," a fact that was the "party's misfortune."

At a Politburo meeting on November 17, 1943, Zhou, who had been close to Bo Gu, an associate of Wang Ming's, was at pains to outline their differences at Zunyi.[57] Zhang Wentian explained how he had linked up with Mao and Wang Jiaxiang to oppose the three-person military group (Bo Gu, Otto Braun, and Zhou Enlai). He noted that "contradictions" with Bo Gu had led to Zhang's gradually being squeezed out of the leadership, a process that accelerated after the Fifth Plenum. While Zhang noted that he was quickly converted to Mao's view during the Long March, he admitted that he had not accepted fully that the old political line was incorrect.[58]

For Mao, it was especially important to extract confessions from Bo Gu and Wang Ming, and it was of prime importance that both be seen to accept Mao's line. At a Politburo meeting on November 13, 1943, Bo acknowledged that his military plan for the Long March had been incorrect and also that it had not been discussed by the Politburo. Further, he accepted that Mao Zedong had saved the party and the army at the Zunyi Conference. However, it appears that Bo did not refer explicitly to any mistake in political line.[59]

In his speech to the Seventh Party Congress, Bo offered what amounted to public self-criticism. He accepted that the tendencies of dogmatism and sectarianism came together around the time of the Fourth Plenum, the time at which Wang Ming and he took power. He highlighted policy in the white areas as being opposed to Liu Shaoqi's correct line and the campaign against Luo Ming as having been directed against Mao's correct policy in the Soviet areas. As for himself, he claimed that he did not realize his faults at Zunyi, as far as political line was concerned, and that he persisted in the mistaken line until the end of the year.[60]

Gaining Wang Ming's approval was more difficult; according to Wang's own account, he refused to accept the newly emerging Maoist party history.[61] However, this is ambiguous. He had not participated in discussions about the resolution on party history because of illness but was sent drafts on three occasions for his perusal. In addition, members of the Presidium discussed the issue of his "mistakes" with him.[62] Finally, Wang Ming wrote a letter to the Seventh Plenum accepting the "Resolution on Some Questions in the History of Our Party," stating that he recognized his errors and that he accepted the criticism that his work *The Struggle for the Further Bolshevization of the Party* contained "leftist" errors.[63] Wang's acceptance showed Mao's total triumph and let other party members see that there was indeed unity within the party—unity based entirely on the terms set by Mao Zedong and his supporters. Wang Ming's reward was to be elected together with Bo Gu to the Central Committee of the Seventh Party Congress.

The convocation of the Seventh Party Congress in April 1945, and the preceding plenum, represented the public triumph of Mao's discourse within the party. The resolution on party history adopted by the plenum served to demonstrate the correctness of Mao's principles and line over his opponents throughout the crucial years of the early thirties. The Congress itself was a tribute to Mao and his leadership; it was now clearly his party. Even the new constitution that was adopted and Liu Shaoqi's report highlighted the dominance of Mao's position as the fount of wisdom concerning the Chinese revolution. The new party constitution reflected the stress on Mao Zedong Thought, stating that together with Marxism-Leninism it provided the guiding principles for all party work.[64] Liu praised

Mao Zedong Thought as the "most important historical characteristic of our current revision of the party constitution." Mao's thought, according to Liu, was "communism and Marxism" as applied to China; it integrated Marxist-Leninist theories with the practice of the Chinese revolution. Further, it was the "development of Marxism with regard to the national-democratic revolution in the colonial, semi-colonial, and semi-feudal countries of the present period." In fact, Liu traced the development and maturing of Mao Zedong Thought from the founding of the party in 1921. With a flourish, Liu announced that "our comrade Mao Zedong is not only the greatest revolutionary and statesman in Chinese history but also the greatest theoretician and scientist."

While the twenty-two documents might have provided the focus for rectification, gradually a Mao canon was developed that bore the title of his own selected works.[65] As the study movement spread out from the core in Yan'an, Mao's work increasingly became the focus of study for lower-level party members, replacing the various documents of the Central Committee and other senior leaders. According to the senior party historian, Gong Yuzhi, the basis for the compilation of the first and all subsequent editions of Mao's selected works was the collection *After the Sixth Party Congress (Liuda yilai),* which had been used by senior cadres in Yan'an to study party history.[66] Mao had played the major role in its editing and the selection of its texts.

According to Gong, five original editions of the selected works were edited before 1949.[67] The other base areas administered by the CCP edited these collections or reprinted them as essential study reading materials in the period 1944–1948.[68] The first official version of Mao's works was not published in the Shaan-Gan-Ning but in the Jin-Cha-Ji (Shanxi-Chahar-Hebei) Border Region in May 1944.[69] It was commissioned by the region's military commander, Nie Rongzhen, to aid cadre study in the Rectification Campaign in the base area. Now the materials for study had changed from twenty-two documents including a significant number by Mao to twenty-nine pieces all authored by Mao. Once rectification spread out from the core in Yan'an, the wisdom of one man was now substituted for that of the party as a whole.

The Inquisition

The emphasis on confession leads to one of the strangest, and at the time most disturbing, moments in the entire history of Yan'an. This was the so called "Rescue Campaign." While no one knows exactly how long it lasted (estimates vary widely), there is no doubt that its object, to route out spies and "rescue" people from secret lapses, had an enormous impact. Its object was to get people to confess and to use their guilty knowledge as a point of entry into the process of confession. The campaign was largely the responsibility of Kang Sheng, with Chen Boda very much a part of it.[70] It revealed the vicious path to communist killing communist that rectification might have taken if senior leaders, particularly Mao, had not reined in the campaign before the damage was too great. In retrospect, it marked a turning point and was a forewarning of the vicious personal attacks that would consume many after 1949.

The rationale of the Rescue Campaign was a reinterpretation by Kang Sheng of the spirit of the April 3, 1942, Propaganda Bureau circular. As noted earlier, this called for democracy and guidance from above to govern the process of rectification. Kang stated that this circular, and the initial phase of rectification, had been intended to "expose" evil tendencies.[71] "Exposure" was not a term used in the original vocabulary of rectification. However, Kang Sheng felt that the movement had "exposed" many examples of "counterrevolutionary ideological poison."

In particular, Kang mentioned Wang Shiwei, who he placed at the center of a conspiracy concocted by the "Five Member Anti-Party Clique" (Wang, Pan Fang, Zong Zheng, Cheng Quan, and Wang Li). For Kang, what had begun as an ideological struggle had turned into one against counterrevolutionaries. All five were resistant to rectification, outraged by it, and expressed their views in strong terms. As we have already seen, Wang Shiwei was particularly unrepentant. Such people and other "traitors" hidden in Yan'an would have to "confess."

Kang describes the confession as a form of repentance that would bring the individual back into the fold, a cathartic cleansing of one's sins:

Why does the Communist Party make so much effort to rescue you? Simply because it wants you to be Chinese, and not be cheated into serving the enemy. Those of you who have lost your way, be conscious, take a firm decision, repent to the party, and cast off the special agent's garb, cast off the uniform of the fifth column, put on Chinese clothes, and speak about the deception, the insults, and the injuries you have suffered, and confess to the crimes you have committed. The Communist Party welcomes those of you who have lost footing to become Chinese and oppose Japan and serve the country . . . We were concerned about you, afraid you will commit suicide . . . When a person confesses to the party we immediately remove the evidence about him, remove his name from among the ranks of special agents and we are happy that he has become conscious. The Communist Party has saved another person!

There was a sting in the tail as Kang Sheng added, "Finally, I warn those people who do not wish to confess, we have maintained a lenient policy, but leniency has a limit."[72]

The discourse of confession creates its own forms of power. For confession requires someone to confess to. Hence power in an ostensibly egalitarian community adheres to those who not only have knowledge but also are manifestly pure enough to listen and pass judgment on their weaker brethren, and to decide when confession and self-criticisms are sincere, whether abasement has been sufficiently deep, and where the rooting out of blemish and stain have transformed the character and persona of the one being rectified. It was here that Kang Sheng proved himself indispensable.

He was by all accounts a remarkable figure. Born in Shandong province, he was a longtime friend of Jiang Qing. Indeed, some have suggested that at one time she had been his mistress, that it was he who insinuated her into Yan'an in the first place and into Mao's good graces in the second.[73]

Kang had been trained in Moscow in NKVD methods at the height of the purges. Although he was associated with Wang Ming in Moscow, and arrived with Wang in Yan'an on November 29, 1937, Kang quickly separated himself from him. Kang was a highly cultivated man, a connoisseur of the arts and literature, and generally a person of refinement and taste. He collected ancient Chinese objects d'art, especially Song pots. Many people admired his literary style and enjoyed the ruthless vigor of his attacks against chosen enemies; not a few of those interviewed indicated that women in particular admired him.

For some, however, Kang represented the dark side of Yan'an, the evil force, the person who became the lord high executioner, "Mao's pistol."[74] He looked the part. He wore a shiny black leather jacket (Soviet style), black breeches, and boots, had black hair and a black mustache, rode a black horse, had a black Alsatian dog, and carried a riding crop. He kept to himself and lived alone, some distance from neighbors. His apparent purpose in life was to make people confess, whether or not they had committed the crime of which they were accused.

Kang described his methods in his account of dealing with the so-called "Five Member Anti-Party Clique." He reported[75] what he had said to Yu Bingran's wife:

"Why do you have to be the one sacrificed? Where on earth is there such a wife like you?" He succeeded in persuading her to admit that it was Yu who had asked her to confess. That is how we exploited the contradiction between Yu and his wife. Later on, we enlarged that contradiction. That was how we struggled against Yu. Eventually we arrested Yu, who confessed to the whole process. Then we attacked Cheng and Wang. That was the second round circle. After the seventy-two day meeting [to criticize the "clique"], Cheng and Wang attacked us again. He [? Cheng or Wang] wrote a letter in which he told the truth. He said: "I admitted that I was a Trotskyite at the meeting. In fact, I am not. If in the future this is found out, it should be cleared." He was telling the truth. We knew that he was a GMD member. But we merely labelled him with a counterrevolutionary hat and kept ignoring him until after Yu confessed everything. After that, we got some materials to work him over with again! We arrested Pan and Zong on April 1. That was another round of attack in the struggle. Another triangle . . .[76]

The central object of Kang's method is exposure by means of incriminating "triangles" in which "contradictions" are used to define plausible conflicts in terms of necessary guilt. Precisely because he was so well educated, Kang was able to identify particular words as revealing expressions of guilt. For example, he "decoded" a letter to Mao written by Cheng Quan a few days after Mao's attack on the "eight-legged essay." When Kang discovered the letter was itself written in the style of the "eight-legged essay" he was furious. "That bastard's [literally, "bastard turtle's pawn's"] hatred towards the party was beyond our expectations. It seems that all the legs in his eight-legged letter were connected like the chapters of a novel . . . The first line goes something like 'sound, color, dogs, and horses.' 'Sound' refers to a gramophone, 'color' refers to beauty, 'dogs' refers to raising dogs, and 'horses' refers to riding horses [leisure activities]." The outrageous meaning? "Big cadres walk by ostentatiously."[77] Linking this to the second leg, Kang Sheng draws out the meaning "High cadres and low-ranking cadres are mutually antagonistic."

Wives, friends, and associates all became parts of the incriminating triangle. Sooner or later a confessional breakthrough would occur, and the noose would tighten around the victim's neck.

This process of exposure and confession was not limited to a few people in Yan'an. Many of the victims of the campaign came from the white areas, as they could provide no evidence that they were not engaged in counterrevolutionary activities. (In fact, Kang Sheng seems to have had something of a Mata Hari obsession as far as women from the white areas were concerned.) Virtually everyone, high or low within the core Yan'an went through exposure.[78] Yet it turned out that virtually no spies were caught in Kang Sheng's nets. Kang himself later admitted that less than 10 percent of those who had "confessed" were actually spies or enemies.[79] The Rescue Campaign had such a devastating result that when Mao finally called off the campaign it was said that he did so "with hat in hand" (with many apologies).

The Rescue Campaign bared the knife inside of rectification. The lesson was unmistakable. Mao clearly wanted Kang Sheng to do what he did, and stopped the campaign only just after it had had the desired effect, and after a number of people had been killed (estimates of victims vary from three to one hundred) and a number of others had committed suicide. In a small, intimate community, word of the campaign traveled quickly and sent shock waves in every direction. After the Rescue Campaign no one doubted where power lay and the consequences of standing up to it. No wonder, then, that those who had gone through the confessional process came to see the evil of their faults and the promise of the right way. They had little choice.

Reenactment as Redemption

Both the Rectification and Rescue Campaigns show how the new discourse was intimately linked to the confession, and how both were mixed up in the everyday concerns of many of the individual participants. This combination of education as both a structure and a venue for textual exegesis, reinforced by the system of discussion in intimate small groups often linked to the *danwei,* created opportunities to explain and proclaim one's sentiments. But it also makes possible what Ricoeur calls a "phenomenology of confession" and what he further describes as "reenactment of evil."[80] The term "phenomenology" is entirely appropriate since what is involved is an evolution of intentionalities, their articulation, and the eradication of "bad" ones in favor of the "good." It involves an excruciating process designed to get past dissimulation. Indeed, so taken for granted was it that people would dissimulate in their initial self-criticism that the charge of insincerity virtually prefaced a much more elaborate program of criticism. So considered, the rectification process takes education one step further in the direction of individual overcoming. Where education involves the overcoming of ignorance through knowledge, rectification involves overcoming resistance. One realizes oneself through the deepening shame of the confession, which leads to subsequent purification and gratification. One begins with stain and blemish, the purging removal of which is essential for enlightenment, not only for the self but also for the collectivity, lest others become contaminated and polluted. Indeed, the notions of pollution and purification are endemic in rectification.

Put these together and they constitute a moral grammar, a language, and, in their totality, a discourse. The adherence we have called a discourse community. As Ricoeur points out, confession produces its own language ("Oh Lord, how I have sinned"). One might say that if one part of the discourse of Mao Zedong Thought involves the sinification of the Marxian dialectic and its translation into a praxis of adaptation, the confessional process also produces *sin*ification—an imposed rather than an original sin. Sinification and *sin*ification together constitute the basis of the discourse, with rectification the heart of the internalization process.

Evidence and accounts by participants show that rectification had a powerful effect on many. The process of exegetical bonding took place in the small groups that were organized to study and absorb the texts. The process was performative. It made the words and thoughts into actions more powerful than ordinary actions. To utter the right word is to establish a certain finality. This process, along with educational prescriptions, enables one to know what words to utter and think. By this means individuals can reconstitute themselves. Hence the virulence of the attack on Wang Shiwei, who refused to play by the "rules of the game." We might call rectification the "deep theory" equivalent to Geertz's "deep play."[81]

What is different from the parodic quality in deep play is the parodic negativity in deep theory. The former reflects underlying structures and meanings, reciprocities of desire and regulation as they exist in a given culture and society, while the parodic negativity of the latter is designed to caricature precisely these underlying structures, meanings, and reciprocities of desire and regulation and, by so doing, create a theory of transformation to enable people to become self-conscious about what is normally taken for granted, and conscious of themselves as the people who hitherto took them for granted. One might say that the juxtaposition of the three stories in relation to Mao's theories (the twenty-two texts in particular) projects the process of soul-searching onto the clearly visible public screen of the rectification arena. Further, no one is allowed to quiver and die. The performative has a life of its own.[82]

9

FOUCAULT'S PARADOX
AND THE POLITICS OF
CONTENDING DISCOURSES

※

We have applied discourse theory and a logocentric model together with the ensemble of concepts outlined in Chapter 1 to Yan'an both as a historical case and a political phenomenon. They have been combined as a single praxeology. We have also seen how in Yan'an Mao selected facts to represent truths, using facts as metaphors based on historical similarity and metonymies based on theoretical contiguities.[1] His was the dialectic of the higher logic behind the fact. For Mao, this was what truth was all about. But if it was rationalistic in form, it was also pragmatic in consequence.[2]

Situated between pragmatism and logocentrism, Mao's theory is closest to the second, while his practice comes closer to the first. But when it came to such things as exegetical bonding, learning the discourse, the creation of symbolic capital, Mao instrumentalized the logocentric course and the closed view. Truth was above all a praxis of logical necessity.

The great advantage of a dialectical method is that it allows one to move back and forth between two poles in a curious game in which who wins does so because the right principles have been invoked while the losers lose because they are without principles. We have seen how in Yan'an the losers were denounced as putchists, opportunists, adventurists. Working out the correct interpretation thus engages one in theory, while in fact one is gauging the consequences in advance of a particular favored truth or line. When measuring the consequences is a matter of how to realize both short- and long-term goals, being analytically and historically correct requires one to pay very close attention both to how one considers the historically necessary consequences of China's forces and relations of production, and how those forces and relations are expressed.

The question of leadership in China was, from the beginning, bound up with the political problem of how to apply this dialectic. Today it means trying to find some dialectical midpoint between both a logocentric pragmatism and a pragmatic econocentrism. In Yan'an it meant identifying fundamental social contradictions that, stated first in the abstract then located on the ground, became identifiable cracks or fault lines in China's political and social structure. Once they were made visible, one could determine strategies to deal with them. Each fault line became a point of manipulative exploitation. The point was to widen the crack until it became a disjunction so great that there was no alternative to the revolutionary way. In effect, the theory so devised within the framework of the discourse came to define the overall trajectory of the Chinese revolution itself.

If one believed in advance that this would be possible, and virtually all communists of whatever faction shared some such notion, then it was crucial to be right. It was more crucial than winning victories on the battlefield. For, in the end, the general truth would prove itself in the disjunctive event and the moral moment. Power meant the ability to define the correct line. This tendency became dominant after the removal of Chen Duxiu as party leader in 1927. This was the first time that a party leader had been removed, and it proved a traumatic event for most of those involved.[3] Chen had been like a father to many of those involved in his dismissal; as the movement's patriarch he had brought many of them into the party and had raised them in it. In the Chinese tradition, one did not turn on one's father, so Chen's opponents needed a powerful rationale to justify their act. Chen's removal was legitimized not only through criticism of his "mistakes" but also through the invocation of ideological symbols. Adherence to the correct ideological line came to legitimize policy, and understanding of the line was a necessary condition for leadership. Initially, this had the effect of strengthening Comintern control over party leadership, as the Comintern was thought to possess a "higher wisdom." This shift signaled the end of genuine wide-ranging debate within the party, as ideological correctness became the key element for control, leadership, and cohesion within the CCP.

Yet because the political situation was extremely fluid, one could be right for a while and then terribly wrong. Locating the fault line and exploiting it was, under the circumstances, far more easily said than done. Hence, in the name of revolutionary praxis, the strategies, tactics, and indeed, what constituted the "correct" line kept changing. Especially in the early days, neither the Comintern representatives nor the Chinese communists themselves, despite the massive outpouring of documents and continuous discussions on the subject, could agree on what a correct line might be, at least not for very long. The search itself generated both vulnerabilities and opportunities for power.

Perhaps the greatest problem was how to define the revolutionary class. Marxism, as distinct from putchism, favors (in theory at least) revolution from below. That, in turn, requires a dynamic, transforming class agent whose functional utility is the creation of economic capital, the appropriate returns of which are frustrated by hegemonic class and/or political powers. This contradiction produces its own form of higher consciousness, which, when released from a certain deferential inhibition, explodes the boundaries of the system and all the limitations imposed by it. It does so with the force of necessity. The result provides a condition of justice embedded in the logic of the revolutionary transformation—the principle of returning to the producers the value of what they have produced. Material justice in a social universe enables a higher consciousness, a new mutual sensibility through the socialization of the means of production.

There was an example to follow. The Chinese, early GMD members as well as communists, were deeply influenced by the Bolshevik revolution. Here was a concrete example of transformational change that did not require passing through all the necessary stages laid down by classical Marxists. The problem was that the class conditions favoring the formation of a dynamic revolutionary class were far less appropriate in China than in Russia. It was partly in emulation of the role of the Soviet communist party and partly the enhancement of that role that was Mao's preoccupation. In these terms, Yan'an became a state in miniature. However, if this enhanced role was not simply to be based on naked power, it required something else, a claim to a higher consciousness. This was what made the party attractive. For the primary feature of the party acting for a class (or in the name of a class) is that one can leave the class itself, remaining of it rather than in it. Since the class cannot act for itself, others can act on behalf of it.

In the specific conditions of China, it is the peasantry, more than any other, that represents this critical class. While not capable of being revolutionary it is frequently insurrectionary. The task became to mobilize its insurrectionary elements and use them for revolutionary purposes. Although the peasants could not be the revolutionary class of the future, at least they could get rid of the past.

However, this peasantry had special qualities. It was the class that had been dispossessed. Thus, it served a general moral purpose. It was the class of visible anguish and suffering. Such circumstances represented the general condition of loss prevailing in China. The peasants were collectivized victims within a China that was itself a surrogate victim of imperialism. The peasants, not the proletariat, constituted the moral center of the Chinese revolution. They defined "what is to be done"—to restore the lost patrimonies.[4]

The special position of the peasantry in Mao's narrative of the Chinese revolution gave it a redeeming as well as a transformational role. It also defined the CCP's unique role as the redeeming historical agent. In this sense, and especially when loss is the basis for a revolutionary narrative, the end is in the beginning. Loss defines what needs to be done and produces the space for the party as historical actor.

Yet this changes the very nature of Marxism. When the struggle over correct lines began to shift from a mainly military to a more philosophical one, Mao reinvented himself as the agent of history. He became the focus of his own story. He enabled individuals within the party to transcend themselves. Hence, too, the central importance of education and, with it, cadre intellectuals. Every revolution needs educated people in possession of higher truths, communist ones more than any other.

How ruthlessly does one pursue revolutionary principles? Both in the Soviet Union and in the CCP, it was recognized that if material conditions were not ripe for a socialist revolution, a nationalist or bourgeois start had to be made. Thus, one had to make *a* revolution in order to make *the* revolution. In China, a general revolutionary situation already existed. The question was when and how to pursue, and how to recognize, the conditions for a genuine transformation to socialism. On this point Mao was shrewdly inconsistent, devoutly adhering to the necessity of *a* revolution by following the strategy of the united front, while assuming that a "revolutionary tipping point" would occur when the military situation made it feasible.

It was awareness of this duplicity that made Chiang Kai-shek hold back his best forces instead of willingly committing them to combat against the Japanese. The result was to jeopardize the nationalism of the GMD. It allowed the CCP, in the name of pursuing the anti-Japanese war and nationalism, to preempt the claims to power made by Chiang Kai-shek.

Principle and strategy aside, the CCP was attractive because it offered the promise of a fresh alternative to the prevailing alternatives: liberalism, monarchism, constitutionalism, parliamentarianism, neotraditionalism, and fascism. From the start, the CCP made visible efforts to move to an alternative revolutionary route based on an inversionary discourse fundamentally at odds with conventional thought. It was a view quite distinct from Confucian or conventional nationalist ones. It proposed a philosophical break and a new beginning. Through verbal and semantic transgressions, all conventional boundaries—family, clan, class, and religion—were ruptured and were replaced with communist alternatives.

Less clear was the question, which communist alternatives? The debate over the answer also became a question of the discourse itself, at least until Mao assumed full power. When Mao put an end to the contentions, exegetical bonding began. Communist parties have an insatiable appetite for meetings. They also see significance in virtually every act: this mobilization, that strike, this campaign, that strategy. Hence theory was connected to continuous discussion both above and under ground. In the early days, moreover, underground activity was more important than overt action. Hence learning was always undertaken in a universe of continuous engagement, of danger, high risk, violence, and terrible punishment. Moreover, and not surprisingly, there were betrayals galore, and many lapses from grace.

One might say that there were two intersecting fields of force. One was based on the relationship between the CCP and the GMD, and the complexities of the united front in particular. The second was within the party. The two fields helped situate and center Mao, first as the heir to power after Sun Yat-sen, second as the putative descendent of Marx through Lenin and Stalin. As the chief agent, Mao was able to refract and generate a field of force, at the epicenter of which he becomes a teacher. Of course he is an exceptional one, and he uses every bit of artifice to play the role. The way he does this becomes increasingly dramatic, especially in a Yan'an that serves as a natural agora, a representation of public space, a stage with platforms and podiums. It is in the agora that Mao's discursive power manifests itself, first in orality and then in text, uniting addresser and addressee, writer and reader. By the same token, the different fields of force are singularized into standard lexical fields, a "sociability of words" as Fernandez calls it, manifesting concreteness in territoriality and with an increasingly mythopoetic intensity.[5]

Lexicality both defines the field of force discursively and establishes a cosmocratic center to be filled by the one with the best claim to occupancy. It is here that the battle of texts becomes important within the party. In this case, Mao's struggles within the second field of force, within the party, broke down the loyalty of soldiers to officers by unifying the relationship between addressee and addresser. Where there were listeners and speaker, there were now readers and writers, and within the context of education new clienteles formed. It is in this way that discourse communities are organized. And it is in the lexical intersection of fields of force that discourse communities are created and symbolic capital generated, in this case from on high in the name of those below.

Mao was more careful than all the others, especially Wang Ming (who relied on the Comintern) and Li Lisan (who relied almost exclusively on his own judgment). Mao consistently paid homage to "the below." He manipulated the intersections of the two fields of force lexically and strategically in order to win power. He made joining the revolution the act by which one entered both fields of force simultaneously. Once inside, further action was required; revolutionary principles, as expressed in revolutionary actions, had to be internalized. One did not simply join a congregation. One was called up to prove oneself continuously. Old members had to get rid of possible contaminating previous associations. New members were required to reenact the foundation of the party in their own lives. Rupture and break combined with renewal made up the overall pattern. Individualized and repeated, it bonded people and allowed them to share experiences. One could distinguish insiders from outsiders by their bearing alone. There was no such thing as an "ordinary" membership. Only deep affiliation would do. Only in this way can a discourse community become real, and events within it become drenched in symbolic significance.

In this way, the party provided an identity more compelling than any other. It transcended nationality, family, clan, religion. Moreover the method of transcendence became, over time, more and more systematic. Exegetical bonding became coterminous with rectification.

But rectification was not a thing in itself. It had to be taken as part of that larger field of force that consisted of negative reciprocities and violent exchanges, the long-term armed struggle against both the GMD and the Japanese. Lexical performances in a life and death struggle take on properties of the real very quickly. Moreover, life and death situations of violent encounter are precisely the subject matter of mythopoetic text-dramas. In these text-dramas, which embody fictive history, time is reperiodized according to frames of meaning, and fictive truths are experienced as myths. The explanation of these myths opens the way for the logical truths of the texts.

Conversion from one set of truths to another is also an occasion for a text-drama. The cosmocrat recounts, reviews, and enunciates in the telling (orality) according to narrative rules and from on high, using a podium, platform, stage, or forum. There is accompanying sign language (flags, slogans, calligraphy) as well as sound language (the clumping of military boots, the clink of equipment, clapping, laughter, the singing of revolutionary songs). The cosmocrat, alone or surrounded by the starred cohort, gives voice. The audience, including commanders and commissars along with others, listens. Replicated again and again, each such occasion becomes an event in itself. Each reenacts, and many celebrate, previous events. Memory is built up in the repetition of these totalizing occasions. They are part of the context for studying the text. To read the text is to relive the circumstances and conditions of its origin.

With the message acted out in public forums, meetings, congresses, and plenums, and disseminated by means of the remarkably elaborate educational system and the increasingly well developed network of theatrical, literary, musical, and other modes of cultural communication, addressees are by no means passive listeners or observers. Furthermore they must apply what they have learned to such concrete activities as contributing to production campaigns, fighting, or working behind enemy lines. Periodically, they pore over the texts in a highly structured and disciplined fashion so that every act is seen to engage the logic and theory contained in the texts.

These processes enable us to speak of Yan'anites as a chosen people, a people of the texts, and to describe Yan'an as a closed system operating in an open universe in order to produce a closed universe with an open system—that is, the final and unspecified condition of the higher freedom embodied in all forms of Marxism: the communism of the last instance and the final justice of the returned social product.

By the same token, individualistic or liberalistic tendencies are eschewed in the closed system, replaced by a heightened sense of self-ness, self-esteem, a belief in individual potential, indeed potency. These qualities can be conferred only through membership. Without this, it is impossible to realize the required state of mind. And without that state of mind one is lost, not found. Again, within the closed system, the process of self-revelation continues for each person until the decisive self revelatory experience, which is also a moment of *joussiance*. At that point, the transference of the text to the self is complete. The self is itself transformed permanently. At that point too one should arrive at a point where there is no need for further rectification. Unfortunately, the closer one reaches this point the more it recedes.

Indeed there is no last instance. Despite the monopoly of power offered by the role of teacher-cosmocrat, the field of force around it requires a demonology and a continuous drama of sacrifice and exorcisim. It is not enough to be voice and author, moral architect and spokesperson, calligrapher and poet; one must also be able to engage in ritual murder. Mao is able to play all parts equally well, moving with ease from one to the other. Narrating the stories and writing the texts, he makes himself part of the process. Everything associated with his person also becomes significant—the long hair, the long fingers, the baggy clothes, the earthy expressions, the fact that he scratches himself with the same fingers that hold the brush, the "unselfconscious" teacher honoring of himself. But, as his official photographer pointed out, for all Mao's pretending to dislike having his picture taken, he was very careful to arrange himself to project just the image he wanted.

His modesty consisted of a certain demeanor and the assertion of deference to the higher wisdom of the people. As author he claims to do little more than give voice and logical shape to what the people already know but are unable to articulate for themselves. Thus, all one needs is to locate the logic of their situation, a logic that is there. Once that knowledge is identified, the people will understand immediately.[6] The Chinese people may be "poor and blank," as Mao often said, but they are not empty. The danger of incorrect lines is not only strategic blundering but a blinkered unity of people and movement.

Mao practiced what he preached. He is the leading example of the maxim "From the people to the people" in the special sense that his texts illustrate the process of leveling down and up. Each text contains something for everybody, from earthy barnyard humor to abstraction, from aluusions to the classics and folklore to simplified connections between universals and particulars. The writing is as stylized as the "eight-legged essay" that Mao abominated (but secretly, one believes, admired). His own essays are, moreover, designed to be read up and down. Read down, they consist of linked admonitory terms that form an unmistakable litany. Certain key "guilt" words—words that signify something someone is guilty of—are repeated again and again. They form a disciplining grid that, whether spoken or read, constitutes its own staccato, or drum beat. This grid leaves little room for ambiguity. It makes for easy summary translation into two lines, or three points, or eight rules.

Read across, discursively, and one finds events, stories, narratives, classical allusions, anecdotes, theoretical formulations, logical principles, and exhortations, all held together by revolutionary sequencing in which the goal does not impose a time limit on the more immediate tasks to be accomplished, while the accomplishment of immediate tasks brings the longer-range goals into greater proximity.

Most of all, as we have said, it is through the educational system that the texts become serviceable. The institutional structure of education serves as an organized basis for affiliation and a venue for the conversion into discourse. Education, crucial to the discourse community, represents the condition of possibility for exegetical bonding, the building up of the discourse community, and the production of symbolic capital.[7]

These three, exegetical bonding, the discourse community, and symbolic capital, are the necessary ingredients for collective individualism. Take away any one, and it quickly converts into methodological individualism. Retain the three and the individual gains through the collectivity, and the collectivizing act is learning. In Yan'an this learning was carefully controlled, the pedagogy explicit. Nothing was left to chance.

The results were an enhanced interiority of vision and thus a net gain for individuals and a dead loss for individualism. The original act of conveying one's individualism, one's original sense of the vulnerable self to the collectivity, brings returns in the form of the collective self and the affirmation of power for principled ends. By this means the self is transcended.

Finally, these qualities are locked in place, or reinforced, by the principle of affiliation (the *danwei*). This *danwei* generated and maintained within the core community a high degree of intimacy between members. Within the unit, the primacy of the small group reinforced both the discourse and the self–other connections, and so established the immediacy of mutual obligation—all in the context of everyday activities, especially care of the body (washing, defecating, being sick) and the exchange of experiences. "Exchange of experience" was carried on with the strong discipline, much of it military, that prevailed in the *danwei*. Another kind of self-discipline led to extreme sexual impoverishment and, for the majority, total sexual abstinence. Desexualized dress and shapeless uniforms underscored the essentially comradely nature of association. There was also a strong emphasis on military exercises, sports, and training to withstand physical hardship.

The primary group was replicated in all other bodies connected to the larger structure of party and army, wherever people were posted. In all units, one found the same fictive truths, the same discourse, the same priorities, and the same sense of accomplishment (which, at a minimum, was perpetual surprise at their own survival, individual and collective). That long, serpentine journey of the ever more purified Long Marchers never lost its miraculous quality. The retreat into the caves created a brotherhood. The dissemination and spread of both unit organization and texts from that revolutionary redoubt rendered the enemies at the gates more vulnerable than their military power would suggest.

These are the ingredients that came together in Yan'an, Mao's republic, and suggest to us a form of revolutionary Platonism. Unlike Plato's, of course, Mao's republic was improvised on the ground and was only later generalized into a model political system with its own internal, principled logic. And, in contrast to Plato's, Mao's republic had the intellectuals, in theory at least, learning from the peasants and workers. Beginning in such an improvised, down-to-earth way, Yan'an gave the illusion of possibility; but in the beginning, it did not create the conditions for its own possibility any more than Plato's republic did. Like Plato's, Mao's republic represented an ideal that could universalize itself as an abstraction. But no one could figure out what appropriate institutional mechanisms would convert the timelessness of the principle into permanence on the ground. The attempt to find appropriate structural mechanisms led the CCP into desperate zigzags of policy, from the application of Soviet economic policies to the Great Leap Forward to the Cultural Revolution. Mao sought to hang on to the desired norms and behavior by preserving the power of symbolic capital, when in fact it had begun to erode even before he came to power.

After Mao came to power, the sudden and critical need for economic capital took precedence over everything else. Despite genuine efforts to promote moral rather than economic incentives, it turned out to be impossible to use symbolic capital to create economic capital. The first whiff of the latter made the former disappear like smoke.[8] This highlights one of the fundamental flaws in developmental Marxism: there is no radical socialist structure that does not corrupt the principles it is supposed to represent.[9]

The Morphology of a Discourse Community

If the original significance of Yan'an was its revolutionary Platonism, its long-term consequence has been as the legitimizing myth of the revolution. A few of the old Yan'anites, not formally but effectively still in power, use the myth to justify their opposition to any final break with the past, even though everyone knows that Yan'an has now disappeared beyond the horizon of living history. There will be no fresh start as long as they can prevent it. Certainly there will be no drastic change in the political discourse.[10] Today, Yan'an remains important chiefly as an obstacle to fresh political thinking rather than because of any virtue it might retain on its own. Among those who made the decision to send the military into Tiananmen Square June 3–4, 1989, the old Yan'anites figured prominently. It was perhaps their last, violent, dying spasm, one that revealed their bankruptcy and their inability to accept the political and social consequences of the economic reforms they had sponsored.[11]

This raises a more general point about such utopic endeavors. Even at Yan'an's high point, when it appeared to be an effective political system in which logical and moral principles, internalized in exemplary conduct and socialized in role performance, were institutionalizing the norms and principles, it was anything but a political system. What made the system work was the belief that the heady broth of myth and logic in Yan'an constituted a higher truth. It generated the kind of symbolic capital that is rare in politics and even more rarely endures as long as it did in Yan'an.

Perhaps this was able to happen precisely because Yan'an evolved out of a kind of bricolage. What Yan'an shows is how discourse communities form and how Mao as *bricoleur* used selected events—the Opium War, the Taiping Rebellion, the Sino-French War, the Sino-Japanese War, the Reform Movement of 1898, the Boxer Rebellion, the Revolution of 1911, the May Fourth Movement, the May Thirtieth Movement—as surrogate raw materials for his three stories. The stories were repeated so often that they took on the character of a ritual incantation. The logical structure following from it took the form of class deformations in Chinese society (colonial, semicolonial, and semifeudal) and gave the revolution its immediate structure and aims: to go through a nationalist-capitalist phase to a socialist-communist outcome by means of the right strategies for war and revolution, the united front and the destruction of the old order.

As Mao explained in "The Chinese Revolution and the Chinese Communist Party," while the character of the Chinese revolution at the time was bourgeois democratic rather than proletarian-socialist, there was plenty of space for innovation. Mao continues:

> However, in present-day China the bourgeois-democratic revolution is no longer of the old general type, which is now obsolete, but one of a new special type. We call this type the new-democratic revolution and it is developing in all other colonial and semi-colonial countries as well as in China. The new-democratic revolution is part of the world proletarian-socialist revolution, for it resolutely opposes imperialism, i.e., international capitalism. Politically, it strives for the joint dictatorship of the revolutionary classes over the imperialists, traitors and reactionaries, and opposes the transformation of Chinese society into a society under bourgeois dictatorship. Economically, it aims at the nationalization of all the big enterprises and capital of the imperialists, traitors and reactionaries, and the distribution among the peasants of the land held by the

landlords, while preserving private capitalist enterprise in general and not
eliminating the rich-peasant economy. Thus, the new type of democratic
revolution clears the way for capitalism on the one hand and creates the
prerequisites for socialism on the other.[12]

In this form, the myth of the long story provides for the logic of its
history, defining present tasks under conditions in which time and history
are on the side of the CCP. Thus, the myth can afford to be somewhat
flexible without compromising its principles. It can tolerate rich peasants,
for example, and small private capitalism, but not the system that prevails
more generally and that supports the GMD. In short, the task is defined
as a revolution in the revolution involving nothing less than the transformation of Chinese society.[13]

By this means Mao can interpret the united front in terms of socialism
in a perspective of world historical change while at the same time locate
within the intermediate story the point of revolutionary disjunction or,
better, the second revolution inside the first. This involves the creation of
a party center as the revolutionary nucleus out of which the party will
pursue the dissolution of the united front itself and with it the GMD.

Similarly the events of the intermediate and short stories have the effect
of pursuing both lines, the one of cooperation and conflict with the GMD
and the other the conflict and revolutionary purity within the CCP. These
two overlap in their respective fields of force, in simultaneous struggles.
Here the incantational events include the Nanchang and Autumn Harvest
Uprisings, the Jinggang Mountains, the establishment of the Jiangxi base,
and the Long March. All illustrate the remarkable capacity of the CCP for
survival against the vastly superior forces of the GMD, yet also illustrate
the need for cooperation with it. Negotiating these two quite contradic-
tory policies requires, indeed, finding the correct line.

Once the correct line is found and a system contrived for it, the
transition from bricolage to a mythologics is complete, and with it the
discourse is formalized. But while this second stage or phase is more
abstract, events obtrude directly into it, especially the intensification of the
blockade against Yan'an by Chiang Kai-shek and the stepping up of the
Japanese War. The mythologics is crystallized in the form of the power
struggles between Mao and Zhang Guotao, Liu Zhidan, Wang Ming, and
Wang Shiwei. Each struggle is an occasion used by Mao to transform
stories into texts in a context of internal struggle.

The struggle itself gives a definiteness to the correct line and the larger
corpus, now named Mao Zedong Thought. This struggle increasingly

depends on intellectuals, who become responsible for restructuring society by means of the educational system and cultural dispersion. In turn, they need proper instruction so that in exercising their responsibilities they contribute to, rather than erode, the necessary conditions of a discourse community.

The final step in the progression from bricolage to mythologics, to legitimizing the myth of the revolution, requires the ritualization of symbolic capital, namely the sacralization of the texts and the institutionalization of the beliefs. At this point Mao's speeches are edited and modified by Chen Boda and others to become the honored transcripts of the revolution. This process, which became most visible from 1942 on, especially during the Rectification Campaign, actually began much earlier. There were signs of things to come as far back as 1937, in Chen Boda's New Enlightenment Movement. "Unfortunately," Chen observes, "China's Marxist philosophers have so far not been successful in integrating their foreign theory with Chinese reality. The time has come for a greater effort to evaluate the broad dimensions of China's cultural legacy on the basis of dialectical materialism."[14]

While such admonishments, especially in the context of the struggle between Wang Ming and Mao, stimulated some of Mao's most important texts, they also represent the takeoff point for Mao's own cosmocratic evolution. As Raymond Wylie put it:

On June 22 [1937], *Liberation,* the CCP's new central organ, published its first portrait of Mao. A comparison of this with the portrait of Zhu De published in the same journal on June 16th indicates Mao's growing preeminence. Though the two portraits, both woodcuts, were done by the same artist, the treatment of the two leaders is radically different. Both Zhu and Mao are shown full face, but the background in the Mao portrait—marching columns with flags flying—is more dynamic than the one of Zhu. In addition, Mao's face is strikingly illuminated by the glowing rays of the sun, a motif that has associations with the emperor in traditional China and was to become the hallmark of the later cult of Mao. Finally, whereas an empty space beside Zhu's portrait is filled with decorative lines, a similar one below Mao's portrait is filled with a quotation from Mao calling for the "complete liberation of our nation and society." The marching columns, the rays of the sun, the apt quotation—all these indicate that the cult of Mao was definitely in the making by June 1937.[15]

This evolution took only a few years. Shortly after his arrival in the region, Mao changed roles. Moving from an Odysseus figuring in his own protracted war to a Socrates generating his own political system using a dialectical method and derived truths constitutes a kind of ascent. In the course of this ascent, Mao unites Chineseness with Marxist internationalism, extending his model republic in concentric circles: the region, China, the colonial world.

The effort is also a metaphor for China as a whole in its groping with how to digest the very different and free-floating cultural and historical strands both internal and external—westernization, modernization, liberalization, and democratization, not to mention liberalism, Marxism, Trotskyism, and Stalinism. It is Mao who reorders these in the role of self-educated sage who, in his life as a wanderer, learned which facts to use as truths by employing all the cunning of an Odysseus.

It is as Odysseus too that he defines the lost patrimonies by locating the lost souls. Using metaphors of illness and the need to restore health to China and its people, and using metonymies that represent the logic of revolution, Mao provides the retrieval of loss, the millennial project that validates the revolution, and, most important, the necessity for revolution in and of itself. Mao, in this sense, is alive to the importance of violence as a necessary connection between his revolutionary logic and the realization of millennial goals.

By so doing he simultaneously personalizes and universalizes. If virtually everyone agrees that he did not create Mao Zedong Thought by himself, almost everyone returns to Mao as the logical and moral architect of the Chinese revolution, the Socratic figure for whom truth as the underlying reality of history can be discovered by means of a dialectic, and, once discovered, serve as the basis for the community.[16] His narratives and his metaphors, his metonymies and his texts, are situated in events and circumstances as illustrations of larger systemic processes, creating a logic that exposes capitalist imperialism in particular. However, once this exposure has occurred, the loss must be converted to a gain. China and the Chinese must transform themselves in struggle, each episode of which serves as a metonymy for a theory of revolutionary disjunction and transformation.[17]

For all Mao's logic, however, the millennial future remains vague. What is far more important is what the revolution is against, rather than what it is for. This fact is both its major strength and its fatal flaw. Hence Yan'an can be regarded more than any other border region or base area as the center for the double revolution, nationalist and socialist. But it cannot offer a concrete blueprint for what will follow. And it is at this point that the search for some way to hold the normative and the behaviorial in place while experimenting with appropriate structures for the long pull becomes the crucial political problem. At the same time, Mao's revolutionary Platonism becomes reified, as timeless in its moral durability as Plato's republic.

To be effective, such a system must become, represent, and constitute symbolic capital in and of itself, as distinct from generating it, which was the purpose of the original bricolage and the mythologics that was constructed. Indeed, the major crisis of authority that China confronts today is, in large part, a consequence of the transition of Yan'an from an interior mythologics to a legitimizing myth used to justify the present system. This has not worked—indeed, could not work—for reasons that have as much to do with the fragile quality of symbolic capital as with the programmatic solutions favored by the Chinese leadership after taking power in 1949.

To summarize, the steps from bricolage to mythologics to legitimizing mythology represent not only the evolution of principles but also the transformation of Mao himself into a sole philosopher-king in a system that as it evolves, transcends the conditions of its own possibility. It becomes more like Plato's republic rather than less. What began as bricolage evolved into a discourse community and in turn became a set of abstract principles that could never be realized, although not for lack of trying.

Revolutionary Platonism and the Political Concrete

The evolution was accompanied by the continuous augmentation of symbolic capital. In this context, our use of the term derives less from Bourdieu than a somewhat idiosyncratic reading of Plato's *Republic*.[18] Three quite different kinds of symbolic capital are employed by Plato. He describes myth as reinforcement, as it relates to logic, explicitly laid out in the myth of Er: myth takes over where logic leaves off. He describes a functional myth of the harmonious social community, in which the contributions of each class to the republic might be said to represent necessary values without which the state would not survive. Finally, there is the myth of discursive truth and its complex relationship to art, literature, and music, and their role in the formation of character and in relation to logical understanding. These three aspects combine in the dialogue to form their own discourse community, the whole becoming a utopic synthesis and a normative, structural, behavioral model.

As deployed by Plato, this combination of ingredients constitutes the classic mythologics, the consequences of which include civility, the effects of discursive practice on citizenship (namely, living in a "city"), and the logic of a justice that learns from, and transcends, the collectivized interpretation of experience. Collectivization occurs through the practice of dialectics, controlled always by the superior logic of Socrates. By a logical *Aufheben,* the city embodies that form of transcendental knowledge that produces individuals who are able to realize their own potential.

Plato's dialogue is not innocent. He acknowledges the necessity to show balanced reciprocities of class, and sets the exchange of cultural objects and meanings within a logical frame. The purpose of the model is, in effect, to start the political world all over again. To read the *Republic* is to understand what a truly subversive act Plato proposes, a rupture between what the world is and what it ought to be. The end result is political knowledge that is timeless and universal, in contrast to that based on the transitory and epiphenomenal.

Indeed, Plato remains the most original political thinker of all. He is the one who posed the political aspects of moral discourse with the greatest clarity. As Stephen Halliwell put it, "The major theme of the *Republic* is the nature of justice, which comes to be interpreted as the central value in both the unity of human societies and the harmony of individual souls. This parallelism between the city and the soul, the social and psychic, forms one of the bonding *leitmotifs* and it allows the scope of the dialogue to encompass great questions of politics, psychology and morality."[19]

Plato's ingredients reveal the intrinsic enterprise of Mao's republic, which despite its situatedness in a revolutionary moment in China's history represents in Mao's hands something as ruthlessly ambitious as Plato's own project. However, Mao's conditions, because they were real, were much more daunting. And Mao is no Plato. His imagination and theoretical skills were more limited. This may be why he succeeded where Plato failed; at least Mao was able to displace more sophisticated Marxist theorists.

One finds in Mao's corpus a great concern with all aspects of the soul in general, but not with individual souls. He is similarly concerned with education and culture. Both Mao and Plato address the social questions of art, representation, and reality from the standpoint of the nature of truth and illusion. There are several important differences, of course. Plato grounds his republic in a logical, discursive conversation between two individuals. Mao begins his with military strategy in a situation of revolutionary war. He has a double demonology: Chiang Kai-shek and the nationalists on the one hand, and his four opponents in the party on the other. How he deals with both sets him apart from mainstream communists as well as nationalists in a ballet of force. Mao, like Socrates, centers himself within a small band of intimates who are originally more or less reluctant, but who are convinced by a superior logic. Where they part company is in terms of realization. Mao's logic, as it evolves, is derived from events and situations that are used as interpretative materials, mythic and logical, in narratives and texts. These Plato eschews entirely.

An even more important difference between them is that Plato "invents" Socrates while Mao invents himself. No other inventions have quite the same flesh and blood as Mao's. Perhaps because of Mao's preoccupation with events and circumstances, there was all too much flesh and blood on the ground. Socrates drinks the hemlock and sacrifices for all of us—becoming the precursor for later sacrificial figures such as Christ. However, Mao's ambition was even greater. It was to define destiny in terms of himself—to become, as Nicholas Kristof put it, the first atheist to become god.[20] Not even Socrates aimed that high.

There are also, of course, many interesting differences between the two republics, and some ways in which they are entirely opposite. One difference is the emphasis on equality in Mao's republic, although even in Yan'an the functional hierarchy was easily as elaborate as that of Plato's. But the boundaries around class were less fixed or hard in Mao's case. Analytically too there are major differences. Mao begins as a *bricoleur,* his logic begins with a series of mythic narratives that create a space for the logic. Plato begins with a rationalistic dialogue that winds up with a numerology and the myth of Er, the latter a final representation of justice in the rewards deserved by souls after their death in a universe as fixed and balanced as the stars. The end product for Mao is less fanciful but no less precise: socialism as a promise of timeless equity, a perpetual harmonization of benign contradictions. Both Mao and Plato create a discourse community around the appreciation of higher truths. In both creations the results come to the same thing, the reinforcement of belief where logic leaves off—a mythologic.

In both, education is the key to a functional hierarchy and fulfillment is a consequence of work, with each class contributing to the well-being of all. In Mao's republic, classes never disappear entirely, as they do in Marx's notion of the liberated "species-being." What prevails are benign contradictions, rather like Plato's mutualism of classes (rather than a mutuality of individuals). Finally, and most important, although Mao begins as a mythmaker, he enters into his own narrative to emerge as the personification of logic. Plato's Socrates begins with logic and ends in a mythic sacrifice. In both cases, there is drama and what one might call performance. Mao and Plato are both great mythmakers, the one of antiquity, the other of modern radical nationalism. Here the comparison ends.

Plato's logic has the virtue of standing above history; Mao's is part of it and suffers accordingly, not only for what it did not accomplish, but also for what it did. Indeed, as Rewi Alley commented, "History was not very kind to Mao." It is as good an epitaph as any. For there are a great many in China, including some surviving Yan'anites, who would very quickly add that Mao was not especially kind to history.

However one wants to evaluate Mao, what he represents is a case that has a generalizable significance. This is especially so for ethnicity, nationalism, radicalism, revivalism, projectivism, and the uses of discourse for building communities. Moreover, what Mao accomplished, with more design than Plato, was the creation of symbolic capital. He used it to transform the raw terrain of Yan'an (the virtual surrogate of Chinese poverty) to a mobilization space. The redemptive enterprise was wedded to the revolutionary moral moment. Comparing Plato's with Mao's republic raises the interesting question of how such models can be generalized concretely, to become political realities. Both Yan'an as the ideal political system for China and Plato's republic as the model for all human communities require a complete break with past practices. Plato never addressed the question in the *Republic;* Mao's solution was a virtually complete revolutionary disjunction for China as a whole.

The problem of starting the world all over again is embedded in complete or totalizing political systems. Sartre's notions of seriality and the practico-inert lead logically to form-smashing and violence. Althusser's notion of overdetermination involves superstructural breaks or disjunctions; Foucault's concept of inversionary discourse makes the victim into the revolutionary. It is at this point that the process of mythological transformation, together with the role of exegetical bonding and symbolic capital, becomes interesting. For they involve revolutionary change as a social text. They involve, more specifically, certain themes emphasized by Ricoeur (reenactment, sin, stain, and narrative and the uses of metaphor), Lévi-Strauss (his original use of the concept of bricolage and the reconstruction of experience in the form of order-producing myths and theories), and finally Bourdieu (his notions of *doxa* and *habitus,* both of which are appropriate to what was being done in Yan'an). It is here that our model comes into play as an interpretation of the interpretation.

The single most critical consequence of Yan'an was, of course, the mobilization and organization of communist power. However, this would not have been possible without the generation and dissemination of symbolic capital. This raises the further question of the relationship between utopic communities as model political systems and the consequences they lead to in concrete political life.

From the Cave to the Square

In order to pull together the threads of the analysis in terms of contemporary politics, we move to Tiananmen, another simulacrum. Here too we find an inversionary discourse, but what this one aims for is a democratic politics, one where an econocentric rather than a logocentric discourse begins to apply. In Tiananmen we encounter Yan'an once again, this time as a residual obstacle to democratization. As the legitimizing myth of a revolution whose discourse and meaning few remember and many would like to forget, Yan'an confronted head-on those seeking both a disjunction and a new discourse, a democratic one.[21] And just as Yan'an was a visible space, its caves and broken landscape and poverty stricken peasants having much to do with the recentering of Mao's republic, so was the encampment in Tiananmen Square.

No more sensitive spot could have been chosen for the purpose. Tiananmen Square has represented the political center of China since Ming times.[22] It represented on the ground a mirror image of heaven, radiating outwards from the square north, south, east, and west where the four great gate temples once stood. Destroyed by Mao but embalmed in memory, they frame the center, surrounding the secular power with the sacred. The square represents that ancient unity represented by the cosmos, the positions of the sun, the moon, and the constellations. Moon and sun represent the nature of human beings, male and female, *Yin* and *Yang,* binaries, a dialectic fixed and stable in principle and continuously changing in relations.

No wonder that Mao chose this space to declare the founding of the People's Republic. His proclamation, after so many years at the periphery, recentered the moral space of Yan'an at the Gate of Heavenly Peace. No wonder too that he expanded the square by furiously knocking down ancient walls, gates, and buildings, replacing them with the obelisk commemorating the martyrs of the revolution, the Great Hall of the People, the Museum of the Revolution. It was also here that Mao chose to hail the millions of Red Guards at the beginning of the Cultural Revolution; and, in 1976, it was here that chosen representatives mourned Mao's death, many returning one month later to cheer the arrest of his last, closest supporters, the "Gang of Four." The occupation of Tiananmen Square, the symbolic center of Chinese communist politics in 1989 meant that the struggle in Beijing became one for the control of the nation.[23]

Mao left enough of the old to claim a continuity of power, but tore down enough to emphasize the rupture with that past. And by refurbishing the space in Tiananmen Square Mao retrieved something of the other grand revolutionary space, Red Square, itself a replica of Jacobin Paris. In Moscow, there are also many reminders of the past still in place. Mao in effect superimposed all these layers of architectural metaphor one on the other, the original temples the four defining points of a cosmologically defined terrain, serving as sacred quadrants beyond the confines of the square itself. But whereas in Red Square, Saint Basil's Cathedral faces Lenin's mausoleum and both are in front of the Kremlin wall, in Tiananmen, Mao's tomb faces his own portrait on the Gate of Heavenly Peace.[24]

Climbing up the grand white marble steps to Mao's crypt, one views the body in a glass sarcophagus raised up in the middle of a large room. One ear appears slightly decomposed, but the hair is black, the face waxed and rouged. Wearing a green military tunic, the lower part of the body covered by a blanket, Mao is very much alone, though surrounded by the memorial rooms dedicated to his most important comrades, Zhu De and Zhou Enlai. A third, Liu Shaoqi, was restored to this pantheon after having been Mao's victim during the Cultural Revolution.[25] The building of the mausoleum was perhaps the last tribute to Mao's "participatory" democracy. Selected members of all work units in Beijing and the surroundings areas were mobilized to work on at least one shift to build the mausoleum for the "People's Emperor." Ironically, the wood boards around the building site became the first venue for wall posters criticizing the "emperor's" legacy. This somewhat unremarked event prefaced the Democracy Wall of 1978–1979.

The students who came to Tiananmen in 1989 were very young, as young as those who went to Yan'an. Like the Yan'anites, they came from all over China. Allowed to come to the square without paying the train fare, they arrived in great numbers, and camped out to make their protest visible. The authorities charged that such protests by the chief beneficiaries of the revolution was an affront to past sacrifices made by the Chinese people as a whole. But the encampment touched a raw political nerve.

In effect, the students took possession. They created within the square the simulacrum of a democratic republic. They took over the Monument to the Martyrs of the Revolution (a kind of campanile with cascading steps, the top of which the students converted into their communications headquarters); from there they broadcast their words to everyone in the square and to all other universities in China. From the highest parapet of the martyrs' memorial, announcements, programs, and agendas were announced and passages played from Beethoven's Fifth and Ninth Symphonies as well as the International. They ignored Mao's mausoleum; but between it and Mao's portrait hanging from the facade and gates of the Forbidden City they erected the "Goddess of Democracy."[26]

If neither crypt nor body were important to the students, Mao's portrait was. As an icon of power one can see it from every part of the square as it looks down unchallenged from its perch on the wall near the entrance to the Forbidden City. In the last days of May 1989, the students erected their Goddess of Democracy directly facing the portrait, challenging Mao to his face, as it were, rather than his corpse.[27] The Goddess of Democracy stood, dressed in her white robes of plaster and styrofoam, holding the torch of freedom in both hands literally under the old man's nose, her large but not ungraceful body twisted slightly, somewhat urgently, yet with a serene and triumphant countenance, challenging Mao to respond. Around her were the red flags and slogans of the movement. Below were the tents of those who were her guardians. Electrifying the crowds, shown throughout the world on television, she was an immediate target of the tanks that broke through to the square before dawn on June 4, 1989. Perhaps the most haunting image of that day is the Goddess of Democracy smashed and lying in pieces, its innocence gone and with it the hopes of a generation.

People throughout China slowly began to hear and then see for themselves the events taking place in Tiananmen. What they witnessed was the concretizing of abstractions like "social text," "magic realism," "symbolic density." Few could remain unresponsive. To be in the square was to become drenched in signifiers, saturated with metaphors. Commentators from the steps of the monument made speeches. They prepared texts. They interpreted the meaning of the unfolding events. People looked for omens of state response like fortune-tellers huddled over tea leaves.

The vast space of the square came alive with student militants in a sea of tents, red flags, slogans, and loudspeakers. They made it a mobilization space for a political revolution to come. Under the noses of the authorities there was created, more or less spontaneously, a primitive democracy, a community complete with streets and neighborhoods. Movement within remained orderly. Different sectors were cordoned off; one needed a pass stamped by someone in authority to enter.

Each neighborhood had its tents and shelters, its kitchens and eating places. Each college and university had its own space that received the visitors. Everywhere was a jumble of bedding and pots and pans. Within the tents, the flaps of which were mostly up, people read. Others passed the time talking, writing, passing out leaflets, organizing. Many of those from outside Beijing spent the day sight-seeing, but in the evenings they always returned to the square to "exchange experiences" and protect the encampment from encroachment by the authorities.

The students organized latrines and garbage disposal. Food was donated by various units, factories, and rural villages. Transport trucks, buses, cars—materialized out of nowhere. Water was provided in large trucks. Funds were collected and distributed, posters printed, news sheets distributed, an internal postal service established, monitors appointed, and tribunals for maintaining law and order created. A people's university was organized. Reading material was printed and distributed, relations between the "interior" and the "exterior" laid down, processions orchestrated and choreographed day and night.[28] Just when it appeared that the movement looked like it might falter, a hunger strike began, which aroused a great wave of public sympathy. Medical facilities sprung up and doctors, nurses, and medical assistants rushed to the site dressed in white, wearing surgical masks and caps. Areas were kept clear for ambulances.

The students hoped they had imprisoned the party-state behind the walls of the Forbidden City. They poked fun at the ritualized cosmology embalmed with Mao in the mausoleum. They elected to build their "city" in the square, ostensibly to prevent the authorities from interfering in their participation in Hu Yaobang's funeral. They also saw the funeral as a double reenactment, first of the May Fourth Movement, and second of the *Qingming* remembrance for Zhou Enlai in April 1976 that turned into a protest against the "Gang of Four" and, by extension, Mao himself. However, now the protest was against the entire political system.

It was, of course, a lesson in democracy. The groups of demonstrators who marched down the main routes and passed through the square followed the lines carefully demarcated by ropes and monitored by students wearing red armbands. Every variety of unit was represented—work, school, institute. Each carried flags and banners. Journalists demanded a free press and the end of censorship. Research workers called for greater intellectual freedom. Workers came from some of the biggest factories in Beijing. There were commons areas where people discussed the issues passionately.

All were concerned about corruption. By the late 1980s, abuse of public position and the privatization of public functions had reached extreme proportions. Chinese society had become one "on the take" where, without a good set of connections and an entrance through the back door, one found it very difficult to participate in the benefits of economic reform. It was not surprising that the student slogan "Down with official speculation" *(dadao guandao)* found a large, enthusiastic audience. With this slogan their stress on patriotism, the students appeared to many Beijing residents as a group less corrupt than any other in society. This role as the moral conscience of society was important in keeping the movement alive and drawing in broader public support. Their moral image was heightened by the launching of the hunger strike on May 13.

The situation grew more tense with the declaration of martial law on May 20. Police agents honeycombed the square. The focal point was the obelisk, the Monument to the Martyrs of the Revolution, with its tiers of steps leading towards a stone parapet. Anyone was allowed to sit on the lower steps, but to go to the parapet required a pass. At the upper level, one found representatives of the committee that represented the top leadership of the student movement. These in turn were representatives of student committees. Each university had its revolutionary center where everyone would gather, a miniaturized version of Tiananmen, with loud-speakers, wall posters, and music (the International alternating with Cui Jian) interspersed with speeches, news from the square, and organizational announcements.

At each home university were waiting crowds, many with bicycles, attentive to mobilization instructions. In the dormitories were students and, more hidden from public view, young instructors who both partici-pated in and advised on the ever-changing situation.

More than a hint of violence was present from the start. It made the moment heady, gave courage to the timid, and by heightening the sense of the present gave everyone an exemption from consequence. The stu-dents hoped that by being right they could force the state to mediate, and make the entire confrontational episode an occasion for political learning. But it is rare that those in power learn very much; or, if they do, what is learned is usually the wrong thing.[29]

In such enactments of power, when symbolic significance offends ordi-nary uses, when one presumes to make judgments about the abuses of power by the state while violating the conventional boundaries between public and private space, not only is the authority of the state violated but also conventional rules of power are thrown into contempt.[30] But through such acts, the lexical system can be changed. New signifiers are formed. Each act of daring has words to go with it; each word becomes perfor-mative in the acts of daring. When crowds of young women and men begin to make statements that flaunt authority, both in the meaning or content of the words themselves and also in the tone, the use of the hand, the stance, the bullhorn, the shouting against the sky—in short, in those performances that combine a magic realism with an interior luminosity of the sort Victor Turner describes in *The Ritual Process*—then a new discourse and a new form of symbolic capital become possible.[31] Radical in just this way, Tiananmen proclaimed its own sovereignty far more explicitly than Yan'an ever did. It claimed and hoped for a political exemption that in the end it did not receive.

Though it lasted only for a brief moment, Tiananmen retrieves a history of Chinese student rebellion and university organization that included the May Fourth Movement, the China spring of 1979, and the student protests of 1985, 1986, and 1987.[32] The protests constitute a history of setbacks; in the eighties, they led to the downfall first of Hu Yaobang and subsequently Zhao Ziyang.[33] But like the Yan'anites, which they finally displaced, the students in Tiananmen, although they failed again, offered empowering insight, self-validating vision, and strong beliefs that defined those "inside" and those "outside," the latter prisoners of conventional views and prevailing orthodoxies. The establishment leaders, heads in the sand, noses to the grindstone, generated their own form of false consciousness, which it was up to democracy to explode.

Creating a new discourse community under such circumstances was a dangerous game, and everyone knew it. Most of the students hoped that the power they represented would lead the authorities to negotiate. However, the more their discourse challenged conventional codes, the higher the stakes. If their object was to mobilize intelligence against power in a generational revolt, then for the state such polarization had to be asymmetrical. Power was on the government's side, but their right was challenged. Right was on the students' side, but their power was dismissed. Entering into genuine dialogue would mean recognizing autonomous organization in society, something that was anathema to the Yan'anites. To win, however, the authorities knew that at some point they would have to return the space to its original purposes, clear the square, and restore its functionality.

The only question that divided the leadership was whether to use mediation or force. The decision they made and the tragic events that followed are well enough known and do not need to be recapitulated in detail here. Lightly armed units of the army poured through the gates of the Forbidden City. Army columns, heavily armed with automatic weapons and tanks, came down from both east and west entry points to the square along Chang'an Avenue.[34] Other units came out of the Great Hall of the People on one side and the Museum of the Revolution on the other. Bulldozers and huge scoop trucks swept the streets and pushed away the tents and the people in the square like so much rubbish. How many were killed on their way to or from the square no one knows exactly. At the Italian hospital around the corner from the square, bodies piled up. The next day the nurses pretended to know nothing about it.

Today Tiananmen Square is bereft of the exuberance, vibrancy, spirit, and courage of the many young people who asked their government to begin a process, to start a dialogue, and who were instead met with machine guns and tanks.[35] In the David and Goliath confrontation that followed, the forces of order regarded themselves as surrogates for the state. But the students came to regard themselves as surrogates for society. The struggle came to be society versus the state. The state won, for the time being, and in the immediate aftermath tanks, clustered in groups of five, stood guard over the silence of Tiananmen Square, the "fifth modernization"—democratization—aborted. Today, no matter how filled with tourists or people doing their business in the ordinary course of events, Tiananmen Square remains the place where, in defense of *guanxi* socialism, the Chinese authorities massacred the aspirations of their young and lost an opportunity for peaceful change.

From a Logocentric to an Econocentric Model: The Decline of Symbolic Capital

Chen Kaige is a filmmaker. In 1988, he made a film called *Yellow Earth (Huang tudi)* about a village on the shores of the Yellow River in the Shaan-Gan-Ning Border Region. The film, set in the late 1930s, is also about Yan'an, but not in the way one might expect. Yan'an is present by its physical absence. As portrayed in the film, the life of this village has not changed for as long as anyone can remember. The party intervenes once; the consequences are terrible, although their intentions were good. In the story, a representative of the party shows up one day in the figure of an Eighth Route Army soldier cum literary worker (not even a "real" party worker). He has been sent to various villages to collect authentic peasant songs for folkloric singing and drama troupes. In the village nothing is as he expects. Life is a struggle, but not a struggle against rapacious landlords. Everyone is poor. There is no class struggle, only struggle against the river. Sheer survival against flood and famine in an unyielding land is what life is about. Nature is the enduring enemy. The soldier-cultural worker has an idealized view of peasants. He expects them to celebrate their survival in the midst of such harshness in local songs. In search of such songs, he meets and becomes infatuated with the older sister of a goat herder, the young boy himself possessing a natural intelligence. The soldier asks the boy to sing a peasant song for him. The boy obliges and shocks the soldier-cultural worker. This is what he hears:

> When the pomegranate flowers, the leaves start showing,
> My mother sold me off to him, without me knowing.
> All I ever asked for, was a good man to wed,
> But what I ended up with was a little piss-in-bed.
> When you piss, I'll also piss,
> Curse you, you can piss with me.
> In spring next year, when flowers blossom red,
> Frogs will start croaking, under the bed.
> Right to the East Ocean, flows a river of piss,
> To the Dragon King's palace, under the sea.
> The Dragon king laughs, as he hears the piss:
> This little piss-in-bed is in the same line as me.[36]

The soldier replies with a eulogy typical of idealized party songs.

Having heard of the new world being created in Yan'an, the girl demands to be taken with him. The soldier is incapable of making the decision, but he promises "to reflect her opinions to the leadership," a line familiar to all victims of bureaucratic vacillation in China. The girl is devastated and decries the new world for replicating the old with its lack of spontaneity, its rules and regulations and hierarchy. She waits a long time for the decision. Deciding to go herself, she starts across the Yellow River. She drowns in her attempt to find out for herself about the new world.

Yellow Earth set off quite a debate. Old Yan'anites, such as Wang Zhen, were greatly upset by it. What to do about the film was the subject of considerable controversy. In the film, where Yan'an is not totally irrelevant, it simply meddles in people's lives, ending in disaster.

The film has a number of subtexts. One is the complete disappearance of symbolic capital. The film renders it an illusion. Certainly insofar as symbolic capital existed it had already begun to disappear before Mao proclaimed the People's Republic in Tiananmen Square on October 1, 1949. Indeed, the film casts doubt on the whole Yan'an enterprise and undermines it as the legitimizing myth of communist rule. It implies that indeed Yan'an never had any real relevance in the lives of ordinary people except by imposition. It implies too that ritualized, reenacted, an object of obligatory genuflection and obedience, Yan'an was in its own time a parody of itself (as Wang Shiwei would have had it). For one moment during the Cultural Revolution—it was not, and then it became a monster.

Yellow Earth suggests that symbolic capital was pure fantasy. And of course it always is. It is precisely this aspect of politics that is so little studied; yet we all know that fantasy can have enormous power. In this book we have tried to show how and under what conditions and circumstances such fantasy can appear to be the clearest reality, and how an inversionary discourse can turn fantasy and reality upside down. In fact, the fantasy aspect of politics is always with us, and plays a fluctuating and elusive role even in the most rationalistic of theories. Political fantasy, then, will turn up again and again, and in many guises. Its inspiration may be political or religious. When fantasy takes the form of symbolic capital it is capable of producing fantastic consequences.

By the same token, symbolic capital cannot last. It gives way particularly when political priorities shift from moral moments and exceptional events to the duller, slogging requirements of generating economic capital. Insofar as economic capital means modernization and development, a quite different set of possibilities becomes significant. Models are required invoking discourses based on systemic relationships between needs, wants, priorities, preferences, and interests rather than principles. This discourse, which Mao found abhorrent, is what is struggling to be heard in China today. Under the surface of a conformist collective individualism, methodological individualism has been reasserting itself. Individuals increasingly believe that they have more to gain through the pursuit of their own self-interest and everything to lose if they try to draw down benefits from the collectivity. Revolutionary goals have disappeared, and behavior is entirely separated from the erstwhile norms and principles of the revolution. The myth of Yan'an in the hands of the old guard has become a stick with which to beat people.

No matter how brightly symbolic capital burned in its moral moment, and no matter how bright the moral moment of the revolution, for the younger generation at least, it is a rather bad joke. There is no psychic benefit to be drawn from collective individualism, only fear, or a certain passive acquiesence. If collective individualism depends on individuals drawing down more benefits from the collectivity than they convey to the collectivity, any such possibilities have long since disappeared. The

Yan'anites promised that the result of the transaction would enable the collectivity to generate more benefits than the summation of all individuals acting on their own behalf or pursuing their own self-interest. In the context of the moral moment that was true. Today that is entirely gone.

There are larger implications to all this. Every socialist system is based on some variant of collective individualism. But clearly as a permanent political condition it will not work, for normative, structural, and behavioral reasons. This does not necessarily mean the end of socialism. But it suggests that any transition from a model political system, utopic in scope and conceptually closed, especially where symbolic capital is to be applied to the enlargement of economic capital, will produce a moral vacuum. No modern socialism, other than social democracy, has come to grips with that. Marxism and socialism are inversionary discourses good for criticizing and exposing the deficiencies of capitalism. But they have no good solutions to the problems they expose. And their history in the form of hegemonic or dominant discourses, as expressions of power, has led to their demise virtually everywhere.

The more heroic the original revolutionary circumstance, the more the life goes out of the discourse. The metaphors and metonymies hide more than they reveal. The truths people know go officially unrecognized. The discourse not only loses its interpretative force, it becomes punitive. Further incantations of myth and logic quicken a performative decline. The mutuality of meaning that had constituted boundaries of discretion and obligation, constructed out of tropes, metaphors, and metonymies, becomes a mutuality of lies, deceptions, pretences. Any lingering symbolic capital disappears totally, with a speed and rapidity that confounds its adherents, leaving cynicism and corruption in its wake.

Between Yan'an and Tiananmen lies an entire world of events. The most significant turning point was the Cultural Revolution, that explosive effort to restore symbolic capital as the condition for further modernization. The Cultural Revolution was, among other things, a reenactment of Yan'an in general, but of the Rectification Campaign in particular. It was intended as a return to exegetical bonding and the renewal of symbolic capital. What it resulted in was *guanxi* socialism.[37]

Guanxi Socialism

Today, in the aftermath of Tiananmen Square, all is superficially quiet. Beijing is calm and the general population passive. At the top sits the party-state, whose leaders are fearful of losing control and even more fearful of each other. All have been betrayed and have betrayed others. Bitter interfamilial and virtually dynastic infighting is going on for the succession. The result is government by intrigue, confused in purpose, corrupt in practice. The party is in disarray. Its ostensible leadership is utterly pedestrian.

Those in power are old, yet they are fearful of relinquishing power too soon to the lesser lights they appointed, who are so totally lacking in vision.[38] The old leaders see nothing but the prospect of chaos in alternative doctrines. Most of all, they believe that those favoring democracy take too much for granted and fail to understand the destructive impulses operating in Chinese society. This explains the force with which they put down the students and their demands. They want to eradicate the possibility of an alternative discourse.

They also fear what the students see all too clearly: that reforming the system in order to generate economic capital and relaxing coercive controls without genuine democratization have resulted in *guanxi* socialism *as a system in itself,* situated between a failed Maoism and a stillborn democracy. It is the worst kind of parody of both. It is a parody of socialism in which the economic market has come back as the intersecting point of hierarchy, where wealth and power accrue to the advantage of those in the party or the bureaucracy. It is a parody of democracy because while a market of sorts is operating, it is under political conditions so highly restrictive that no semblance of either genuine freedom or political accountability is possible. Instead what is working is a system of state, society, party, and bureaucratic reciprocities based on networks of favor, kinship, friendship, and association.

The chief characteristics of *guanxi* socialism are public enterprises controlled by the state but that in practice are fiefdoms more or less plundered by those who run them, and a market system in which goods and services are less important than power and prestige. The combination of party appointment to controlling positions and a dual economy creates a hybrid economic formation that one might refer to as "nomenclature capitalism." The real basis of exchange is secrets and privileged access to key information. Information is so layered in China and access so dependent on position and connections that it amounts to secrets that can be bought, sold, and bartered. This governs exchange between and within private and public sectors. Sometimes the exchange is for money, but as often as not it is for power. *Guanxi* socialism is a system in which everything is a secret and every secret is for sale. The market for secrets is based on the degree to which an item of information is important. The more important the information, the more expensive the secret. Whatever one's estate, high or low, everyone is adept at getting some salable secret information, which, carefully guarded, is the basis of social exchange. Indeed, it is a system in which use value and exchange value are more closely calibrated than in any market system.

The higher up the hierarchy, the more privileged the information and the higher its exchange value. A vice-president of the Chinese Academy of Social Sciences may use research funds to start a private computer company, but the key to its success is really the purchase of information carefully withheld until the price is paid, information about who in the party will react and how, and with what consequences, financial and legal. Information in the form of secrets must be purchased if one wants an apartment, or to move from one city to another, or to rise in the party-state bureaucracy. Professors have secrets about how to get, and who will get, fellowships, and how to be appointed to serve on government commissions or go abroad. The clerk in a library will suddenly know how to find an otherwise unavailable book or document. A mechanic, the only person who knows how to fix the photocopier, will be unavailable until something is given in return. Come back tomorrow, but with a reward. It is not mere bribery, which to some degree is everywhere, especially at the fringes of the market.[39] It is the market itself, with its own formal properties of obligation.

Every scrap of information is scavenged from every kind of situation, and once it is placed in someone's keep, it becomes that person's private property. Power is access to secrets and control over information. This is the present role of knowledge in China, to create and sustain a secrecy exchange. As long as such an exchange fits with existing and asymmetrical reciprocities it can, paradoxically enough, sponsor a liberalization of sorts (especially in the economic sphere, where buying secrets is part of the exploding economic growth) and an expansion in the forms and values of *guanxi*.

Thus, *guanxi* socialism is the system which in the name of (economic) liberalization has come to prevail in China today. It is as much what the students in Tiananmen were against even though they are the principal beneficiaries of the present system. But it is the abuses produced by *guanxi* socialism, and their costs, political and human, on which the students focused their anger. One of the startling consequences of this situation in a post-Tiananmen China is the revival of Mao as a talisman, a symbol of lost virtue. Indeed, the real problem of democratization in the future will not be socialism but how to deal with the pervasiveness of the *guanxi* that will survive it. The danger is that the secrecy market will remain the real one, that the market will only ostensibly be open. No doubt the wily old men who rule China see this problem very well. They have also accepted the need to increase economic capital, namely to expand the market. Indeed, as Deng Xiaoping made clear after his visit to South China in early 1992, continued economic reform is vital for the party's continued legitimacy. He claimed that if China's economic reforms were reversed, the party would lose the people's support and "could be overthrown at any time." He ventured the view that, without the reforms, the party would certainly not have survived the trauma of June 4, 1989.[40] However, Deng and his supporters have no good solutions; suggesting that reform should not move like "old women with bound feet" is not enough. Since 1989, the situation has been particularly paralyzing since whatever else happened, it was made abundantly clear that, legitimacy myths to the contrary, the moral monopoly of Yan'an is totally gone and the party-state is the oppressor of society. The representatives of the "people's" republic have become a class for themselves. They recognized that what happened in the square was not a random show of youthful defiance of the state but an effort to strip away the pretences on which their power rests, to take away their authority and underscore their bankruptcy. While not defining what kind of democracy was desired, the protesters called for a new beginning. Indeed, the challenge was not only to authority but also state sovereignty. Tiananmen Square became a venue not only for events of confrontation but also for the interpretation of their significance against a backdrop of *guanxi* socialism, the product of Deng's last play.[41]

A Journey without Maps

The students wanted nothing less than the opening up and liberalization of norms according to principles of freedom and the law, to transform structures in terms of not only an economic market (already accepted by the regime) but also a political one, with institutions of representation and accountability such as political parties and courts, and finally, perhaps the most shocking, the privatization of behavior. In short what they wanted was a "choice" system rather than a tutelary one. We are left with an interesting puzzle. Clearly China is embarking on piecemeal reform and groping its way towards some kind of solution to the problem of what kind of political system should be allowed to develop. Clearly, the emphasis is to generate economic capital while preventing any kind of symbolic capital forming around the ideals and principles of democracy, and favoring piecemeal solutions. Given the preceding analysis, this could not help but be true. However, it raises the alternative question of whether, in a country so vast, and where *guanxi* are so pervasive, whether or not a more democratic system would quickly founder without some larger commitment to democratic principles on the part of people generally. Such principles may not be very abstract. They ought to involve some respect for human rights and basic freedoms. People would have to feel the need for these principles to the point where their absence would seem intolerable.

It was that sense of an intolerable absence plus the intolerable presence of a neofeudal party-state held together by *guanxi* socialism that led to Tiananmen Square. In the square, a new kind of symbolic capital was created, at least for the moment. Indeed, if American, or British, or French experience is any guide, symbolic capital and the moral moment plays a significant role in making democratic principles stick, and making constitutional rules come alive in institutional practices.

Indeed, in this sense, if symbolic capital is utterly vulnerable to economic capital, the latter is vulnerable to corruption and inequality, unless they are limited by principled notions of justice, equity, and choice. The choice between *guanxi* socialism and *guanxi*/nomenclature capitalism is not very appealing. The latter, moreover, would realize the worst fears of the present leadership, and in the end no doubt would lead to chaos and disorder. In this respect, China has a good deal in common with other erstwhile socialist systems. All need to develop a market system in place of a command system, and democratization as a method of accountability.

Today the problem for democrats is the same as it was for communists a few years ago, namely to find those structural relationships that will sustain democratic principles and internalize them in appropriate conduct, the self discipline and restraint necessary to make choice work instead of plunder.

A number of Asian countries are engaged in precisely such an evolution—Taiwan for one, South Korea for another. It is a difficult transition to make. What all suggest, however, is this. Requirements for high growth are high information, declining coercion, less hierarchy, and more accountability by means of representative institutions and a marketplace in which priorities of goods and services in the economic sphere are balanced by needs and wants in the political. This requires political parties in active competition, through which greater information becomes available, with votes in the political marketplace equivalent to money in the economic. The Chinese are trying to emulate these other countries by loosening up the economic marketplace while restricting the political in the hope that technical and interest-group information will become more freely available but populist information will be suppressed. This lies behind the enthusiasm among some younger Chinese leaders for neoauthoritarianism or neoconservative rule.

No one, however, has a clear picture of how to make the full transition without losing control. Present evidence from the former Soviet Union has no doubt convinced the Chinese leadership that too rapid a transition would be a disaster. But even earlier, when the question of democratization was posed by the students in Tiananmen Square, the state postponed the answer.[42] However, the disintegration of the Soviet Union and the collapse of the Communist Party of the Soviet Union have convinced most of the Chinese leadership that it cannot sit quietly and do nothing. The question remains of what to do.

It is precisely in the transition from symbolic to economic capital that revolutionary regimes become coercive. Insofar as they are successful in initiating economic growth, they reach limits imposed by coercion itself. That is, it is a requirement of high-growth systems that innovation and other forms of information—technical, interest-group, and popular—be available. The more a system relies on economic capital, the more information it requires. The more economic growth it gets, the more pluralism it will generate. Interests multiply and principles are converted to them. Hence the Chinese dilemma. Pluralistic interests and technical knowledge within a framework of a double market, political and economic, constitute a discourse all right, with a pedigree quite opposite to that of Mao's. This discourse involves political systems, but of a non-Platonic, open-ended sort, in which methodological individualism rather than collective individualism is the operative principle.

What is now necessary in China is a new period of bricolage. This would involve a search for the pieces of an authentic democracy that would retrieve the traditions of the May Fourth Movement with its emphasis on science and democracy, and possible alternative ways to make the transition from the principled venue of the lost Yan'an ideal, through the present intolerable *guanxi* socialism, to the institutional democracy that must succeed it. The institutional problem is enormous, for some way needs to be found to prevent a fledgling democracy from being ground down or overwhelmed by a public that is on the whole politically ill-informed, and by the voracious appetites for corruption that a more politically relaxed environment can easily encourage.

Other questions come crowding in. Is there something intrinsic in the system of socialism that prefigures its failure? Is the example of the failure of socialism in the former USSR and in the countries of Eastern Europe definitive? That is, do they show that Marxism as a discourse is so analytically flawed that any political system enacted in its name is doomed from the start? In the light of such notions of the basic flaw, should liberalism, capitalism, the welfare state, or social democracy be newly appreciated? Are they less flawed than Marxism, both as discourses and as systems?

And in these terms how should one evaluate the undeniable successes of the Chinese communist system, most particularly its "iron rice bowl" policy of basic and minimal welfare for all such that even in the freeing up of enterprise zones for capitalist production, the state sector still retains workers in a labor-intensive and uneconomic system in which capitalism increasingly pays for socialism? In the shift to rural family farming a great leap in economic capital has been unleashed, which stimulates demand for goods and services but also stimulates the bureaucracy to emphasize the *guanxi* side of *guanxi* socialism. One must ask how long the public enterprises can continue to lose money precisely to avoid laying off unproductive labor or marginalize significant sectors of the labor force.

Looking back, one can say that while Yan'an accomplished the impossible in terms of the revolution, its very accomplishment throws in doubt the question of belief itself—any belief—as the basis for power. This does not mean that the only alternative is an interest and bargaining politics. It does mean that systems in which diversity and pluralism become the essential elements in a political process require equity principles embodied in a legal constitutional framework. It was Karl Popper who long ago made the point that the collective society based on utopian engineering, no matter how rewarding aesthetically, is in the end a closed society.[43] Mao's effort was to open society as it was to its own potentialities, to what it might become. By doing so, he ensured that it would become closed, even hermetic.

The question, then, is not whether democracy, but what kind. Clearly any democratic alternative in China will have to accept very special obligations. Can one assume that normal institutional mechanisms will work where the inheritance of *guanxi* is so strong, where the population is so huge, where even a slight rise in unemployment involves millions, and where the population nurses multiple forms of anger? Something like the "iron rice bowl" policy will have to be continued. The large and inefficient public sector will have to remain in place if only to prevent marginality, chronic unemployment, and the creation of a huge class of functionally superfluous people.

The hope is that the growing collective and private sectors will gradually wean away the workforce. As things stand now, however, many of the new entrepreneurs in major cities depend on the public sector to meet their basic needs. Many of the new businesspeople in Beijing, with their mobile phones and beepers, have an "official" job in a state enterprise or the academy that provides them with their basic salary, housing, and welfare benefits (the latter two not being offered by the collective, private, or foreign sectors). The work demands are sufficiently low that they can apply their entrepreneurial skills in a second job within a relatively safe level of risk. Business failure would not mean loss of home and livelihood but merely a temporary retreat into the state sector *danwei* (work unit) to rethink and perhaps try again. Occasionally the state sponsors the development of new collective or private companies. The military, the heavy industrial sector, universities, party newspapers, and academies are all involved. The profits are either siphoned off into individual pockets, are reinvested, or are used to cover the social overhead of the parent state-run unit. In some ways, the enterprise is substituting for certain functions of the state sector. Whereas before, when invited for a meal, protestations would be brushed aside with "The state is paying," now it is often "Don't worry, it's on the company."

But like all big questions, which institutional conditions and instruments will work effectively in a nation of some 1.2 billion people remains moot. When one sees the fatal flaw in an opposing system, the temptation is to affirm one's own. But ordinary life is never so tidy and neat as to allow itself to be fully recast in one logical system or another. Today the favored alternative to Marxism is in rational actor models, game-theory political systems, trade-offs and pay-offs, and methodological individualism. Indeed, the proliferation of methodologically sophisticated market models in the field of political development is itself part of the system of political belief that seeks its own reality in highly contrived and arbitrary assumptions and principles. There is nothing intrinsically wrong with this, except that it needs to be seen for what it is and not something so self-evidently "real" as to constitute some underlying truth.

Underlying truths are dangerous in politics. Yet one cannot live without them. For the paradox is that the value of much of what passes for political philosophy is that when transformed into a cause, it becomes the stuffing for doctrines and ideologies. Especially under conditions that appear to some intolerable, and where a political morality is indissolubly wedded to a logic of outcomes, it becomes the most compelling way of thinking one's way past current predicaments. This capacity is both dangerous and creative. It enlists imagination and provides for leaps of endeavor.

Looking backwards into the future, one sees then both the illusion and the promise of Yan'an in more universal terms. In many societies, rationality, myth, and a certain systemic tidiness are reduced to formulaic statements. The dialectic as a method is itself a form of engagement, especially between the thing and what is represented, the person and the mind. The more one regards it, the more dangerous it appears. Yet without something like it, or without Marxism as both an inversionary discourse vis-à-vis capitalism and liberalism and as a myth of the working class or the peasantry, would the course of China's history have been more benign and its circumstances, overall, better? This is a question without an answer. Views of such matters regarding both the French and Russian revolutions have been revised so much as to cast doubt on the whole radical enterprise in China. This is particularly easy to do because Marxism is so universally discredited today.

However, if one goes back to the circumstances of the time, the overwhelming problems China faced, the fact of imperialism and Japanese intervention, not to speak of the political character of the GMD, it is difficult to accept a revisionist position. To ask what might have happened if the communists had not come to power does lead to some rather interesting speculations. Judging from other experiences, it is most probable that the country that resulted would have resembled somewhat the relatively large and potentially rich countries of Latin America—mired in problems so overwhelming that despite, and indeed, because of growth and development they go from democracy to military dictatorship with disheartening frequency, and where contempt for the state is at the same time deserved and disastrous. Given this, it is hard to feel much nostalgia for what might have been. The route China followed had some unique horrors, but the alternative would probably have resulted in more commonplace but no less unattractive ones.[44]

This raises the more general question of a world without socialism. Will this facilitate a reversion to ethnicity and primordial conflicts over race, religion, language, and similar Ur-affiliations? Will there be a revival of extreme nationalism, some of it tinged with fascism or corporatism? And in the absence of feasible socialist or social democratic alternatives will an unbridled turn to capitalism lead to greater rather than less polarization between rich and poor, and in ways even more extreme in less advanced countries than those such as the United States, where such polarization is growing more extreme? Given this, how can one compare faulty capitalisms with faulty socialisms?

China still must find some concrete way to answer these questions. Where does China go after Tiananmen Square? The students pointed out one direction. The Chinese leaders chose to resist it. Will it take another revolution to change the system? Tiananmen Square is now the simulacrum for one. It has all the ingredients for symbolic capital and a new discourse; it has retrieved myths galore and has developed a transcending logic. There are in exile more than one Odysseus with Socratic potentialities, who are busily learning the logic of democratic politics. The present regime is making every effort to pretend that what happened in Tiananmen Square never happened. Perhaps, and as far as some are concerned, and for the time being, they have succeeded. But Tiananmen and the forces that produced it are there, just under the surface of visible political life. When all is said and done the choices for China, although hard to make, are fairly simple: an appropriate form of democratic socialism or democratic capitalism, each based on market principles in political as well as economic life; or some form of corporatism. China is still in a position to make those choices. Its great advantage is that whatever its difficulties, unlike the former Soviet Union, its economy is not in a shambles. People know what a market is and how to make it work. But China is coming up against some fundamental political contradictions. The present situation can only be temporary. Whether the next generation of Chinese political leaders will accept the challenge to opt for a more normal and democratic politics will make all the difference, both to China and to the rest of the world.

We have delineated the transformation of the CCP from a political movement into a discourse community. We have shown how in the process boundaries and affiliations were formed, both on the ground and in the mind. We have suggested that these resulted from a desperate desire, a need, to rethink one's circumstances and to interpret and transcend tragic conditions. Such thinking, the supremely political activity, is a way of making order out of random dangers and defining necessity out of a logic of order. If our analysis is correct, concern with such matters should enable us to understand better how, in the practice of such political interpretation, myth and logic come to depend on each other, the one as metaphor, the other as metonymy. To the degree to which events are narrativized they are also given a logical and historical pedigree, a double signification that in itself represents a dialectic—not the Marxist kind of dialectic, of course, nor the Maoist, but a kind that produces fictive truths from which a logic is inferred. This is why we say that the mythic narrative formed out of storytelling establishes the conditions of possibility for a logical theory, and the logical theory establishes the conditions of possibility for mythologizing events.

But an even larger issue emerges from this discussion. One might call it "Foucault's paradox." The inversionary discourse that appears offers an unlimited prospect of freedom and proposes to free people from constraints of power, to break the hegemony of the discourse through which it is represented; but it, in turn, becomes hegemonic, all the more as it cleaves to its original intent. The result is something like the *tragi-rocambolesque* in politics. If the storytelling is about loss and disorder, and the theory building is about a projected state of justice that creates its own moral self-sufficiency, ultimately the system becomes vulnerable to the discrepancies of life itself, which distance participants from the original events. In the end, the details of the original discourse begin to be seen with humor, and, most devastating of all, are perceived with irony.

Despite the high drama, the sheer theatricality of Yan'an as a simulacrum, the society of Yan'an now appears as something of an absurdity. The insistence on the heroic and glorious always teeters on the edge of the ridiculous and the fantastic. But even most of those who recognized at the time that the other side of purity and danger is hypocrisy and manipulative control were swept along by the high drama of revolution. No one could have survived if he or she had pointed out that Yan'an was its own theater of the absurd.

Even on an individual level Foucault's paradox is significant. The more one was required to play his or her part with passion and intensity, the more each person became haunted with the possibility of humor that rendered doubt. It is one thing to surrender part of the self to the community. It is another to be able to ward off humor and irony. And the authorities in Yan'an recognized, as authorities do today, that irony is always the last, best political defense of the self.

Yan'an, to the degree that it theatricalized all aspects of daily life and gave it heroic proportions, and to the degree that it provided each man and woman many parts to play, generated irony in the act of exorcising it. For behind all the masks that each person wore and the roles each person portrayed, there remained all those secret selves unknowable to anyone else. In this sense, despite appearances to the contrary, there was humor in Yan'an and the *rocambolesque* of a sort that always troubles those in power and that is the saving grace of us all.

APPENDIX

NOTES

INDEX

APPENDIX: CADRE SCHOOLS IN THE SHAAN-GAN-NING BORDER REGION, 1935–1945

School	Date founded	Initial principal	Location
Shaan-Gan-Ning Red Army Military Affairs College	Oct. 1935	Wu Daifeng	Wayaobao
Central Party School	Dec. 1935	Dong Biwu	Wayaobao
Chinese People's Anti-Japanese Military and Political University	Jan. 21, 1937	Lin Biao	Yan'an
Lu Xun Normal College	Feb. 2, 1937	Wang Zhiyuan	Yan'an
Shaan-Gan-Ning Border Region Party School	July 1937	Zhu Xumin	Yan'an
North Shaanxi Public School	Sept. 1937	Cheng Fangyu	Yan'an
College for the Family of Eighth Route Army	Nov. 1937	Li Zhen	Yan'an
Anti-Japanese Soldiers Motor College	June 1, 1937	Liu Ding	Yan'an
Lu Xun Academy of Arts	April 1938	Sha Hefu	Yan'an
Academy of Marxism-Leninism	May 1938	Zhang Wentian	Yan'an
Branch of North Shaanxi Public School	July 1938	Li Weihan	Xunyi
Border Region Middle School	Sept. 1938	Cai Ziwei	Yan'an
Shaan-Gan-Ning Border Region Agricultural University	April 1939	Zhu Kaiquan	Yan'an
Workers' College	May 1939	Zhang Jie	Yan'an
Chinese Women's University	July 1939	Wang Ming	Yan'an
Shaan-Gan-Ning Border Region Normal School	Aug. 1939	Zhou Yang	Ansai
Shaan-Gan Ning Border Region No. 2 Normal School	March 1940	Xi Zhongxun	Xinzheng
Shaan-Gan-Ning Border Region No. 3 Normal School	May 1940	Bai Dongcai	Dingbian

School	Date founded	Initial principal	Location
Zedong Young Cadres School	May 1940	Chen Yun	Yan'an
Administration College	July 1940	Lin Boqu	Yan'an
Longdong Middle School	Sept. 1, 1940	Ma Wenrui	Qingyang
Eighth Route Army Military and Political Academy	Sept. 1940	Wang Jiaxiang	Yan'an
Chinese Medical University	Sept. 1940	Wang Bin	Yan'an
Academy of Sciences	Sept. 1940	Li Fuchun	Yan'an
Mizhi Middle School	Sept. 1940	Ma Jichuan	Mizhi
Suide Middle School	Feb. 1941	Huo Zhongnian	Suide
Xin wenzi Cadre School	April 1941	Wu Yuchang	Yan'an
Military Art College	April 1941	Mo Wenhua	Yan'an
Japanese Workers and Peasants' College	May 1941	Lin Zhe	Yan'an
Yan'an University	Sept. 1941	Wu Yuchang	Yan'an
Minorities Academy	Sept. 1941	Gao Gang	Yan'an
Fuxian Normal School	Sept. 1941	Qin Lisheng	Fuxian
Military Affairs Academy	Nov. 1941	Zhu De	Yan'an
Shaan-Gan-Ning Border Region Local Arts University	March 1942	Ke Zhongping	Yan'an
Northwest Bureau In Service Cadres Continuation School	April 1942	Li Zhuoran	Yan'an
Sparetime Law College	April 1942	Zhang Shushi	Yan'an
Russian College	Aug. 1942	Zeng Yangquan	Yan'an
Northwest Party School	Autumn 1942	Xi Zhongxun	Yan'an
Yan'an Normal School	Spring 1943	Liu Duancai	Yan'an
Yan'an Middle School	Spring 1944	Huo Zhongnian	Yan'an
Yan'an Foreign Languages College	April 1944	Zeng Yongquan	Yan'an
Sanbian Public School	May 1944	Lu Qinliang	Yan'an
Korean Revolutionary Military and Political School	Feb. 1945	Jin Baiyuan	Yan'an
Artillery School	Feb. 1945	Guo Huaruo	Yan'an

Source: Fang Chengxiang and Huang Yaoan, eds., *Shaan-Gan-Ning bianqu gemingshi* (The Revolutionary History of the Shaan-Gan-Ning Border Region) (Xi'an: Shaanxi shifan daxue chubanshe, 1991), pp. 620–624.

NOTES

✳

Preface

1. This subject—the role of subversive books in the French revolution—is explored in Daniel Roche and Roger Chartier, eds., *Livre et Révolution* (Paris: Aux Amateurs de Livres, Mélanges de la Bibliothèque de la Sorbonne, No. 9, 1987).

2. Robert Darnton, "Philosophy under the Cloak," in Roche and Chartier, *Livre et Révolution,* p. 121. See also Terry Eagleton, *Literary Theory* (Minneapolis: University of Minnesota Press, 1983), p. 131.

3. See, for example, Roland Barthes, *Image, Music, Text* (New York: Hill and Wang, 1977).

4. David E. Apter and Nagayo Sawa, *Against the State: Politics and Social Protest in Japan* (Cambridge, Mass.: Harvard University Press, 1984).

5. Both of us were in Tiananmen Square the night of the massacre. What transpired there offered a unique perspective from which to view the past and interpret the changes between past and present. Throughout our discussion we play off the present against the past, and we conclude with a brief discussion of the events in Tiananmen Square.

6. The use of Western classical figures to universalize certain phenomena is not, of course, alien to the China field. One excellent example is the use made by Leo Lee in analyzing "hero-types" among the romantic generation of Chinese writers in terms of "Wertherian" (passive-sentimental) and "Promethean" (dynamic-heroic) characters. Leo Ou-fan Lee, *The Romantic Generation of Modern Chinese Writers* (Cambridge, Mass.: Harvard University Press, 1973), especially pp. 279–293.

1. Toward a Discourse Theory of Politics

1. These too were derived in the context of a field study. See David E. Apter and Nagayo Sawa, *Against the State: Politics and Social Protest in Japan* (Cambridge, Mass.: Harvard University Press, 1984).

2. See James Clifford, *The Predicament of Culture* (Cambridge, Mass.: Harvard University Press, 1988), pp. 21–54.

3. See Edgar Snow, *Red Star over China* (New York: Vintage Books, 1947), and Mark Selden, *The Yenan Way in Revolutionary China* (Cambridge, Mass.: Harvard University Press,

1971). For the relationship between Yan'an and the subsequent evolution of Chinese politics see Edward Friedman, Paul G. Pickowicz, and Mark Selden, *Chinese Village, Socialist State* (New Haven: Yale University Press, 1991), Chapters 2–4.

4. Such terms are subject to interpretive arbitrariness, false definitiveness, and specious closure. Our intention is to use them rather like different lenses fitted to the mind's eye, each contributing something different to the way we see the construction of power—how people create it, convey it, and become victims of it. We are also aware of the interpretive dangers described by James Clifford: see his "On Ethnographic Surrealism," *Comparative Studies in Society and History* 23 (October 1981): 539–564.

5. See, for example, Kenneth J. Arrow, *Social Choice and Individual Values* (New Haven: Yale University Press, 1978). See also Robert A. Dahl, *A Preface to Democratic Theory* (Chicago: University of Chicago Press, 1956); Anthony Downs, *An Economic Theory of Democracy* (New York: Harper, 1957); and Steven Lukes, *Power* (London: Macmillan, 1974).

6. See Jon Elster, "Marxism and Methodological Individualism," in Pierre Birnbaum and Jean Leca, eds., *Individualism* (Oxford: The Clarendon Press, 1990). See also Elster's *Making Sense of Marx* (Cambridge: Cambridge University Press, 1985), and Donald P. Green and Ian Shapiro, *Pathologies of Rational Choice* (New Haven: Yale University Press, 1994).

7. See Bernard Yack, *The Longing for Total Revolution* (Princeton: Princeton University Press, 1986), and Paul Ricoeur, *The Symbolism of Evil* (Boston: Beacon Press, 1967). See also David E. Apter, "Democracy and Emancipatory Movements: Notes for a Theory of Inversionary Discourse," *Development and Change* 23 (July 1992): 139–173.

8. See Guy Debord, *La société du spectacle* (Paris: Gerard Lebovici, 1987).

9. See Benedict Anderson, *Imagined Communities* (London: Verso, 1983).

10. See Hannah Arendt, *On Revolution* (London: Penguin Books, 1977).

11. See Jean Baudrillard, *Simulacres et Simulation* (Paris: Galilée, 1981).

12. In this vein, for example, one might treat elections as spectacles of good and evil akin to Barthes's wrestling match. Roland Barthes, "The World of Wrestling," in *Mythologies* (New York: Hill and Wang, 1972), pp. 15–28.

13. Discourse theory begins with Plato and in the agora. He relied on a dialectical method to find truths behind forms, and by doing so provided the conditions for unifying the individual with the collective rationality. In Yan'an, too, truth was dialectical, waiting to be carved out of the forms that disguised it. A form of primitive communism with Chinese characteristics, Yan'an invested everyday life with meaning-full values. If to be part of Yan'an was to be different from the China that was, it was also to be an agent and participant in the China that was becoming.

14. See Jürgen Habermas, *The Theory of Communicative Action* (Boston: Beacon Press, 1981), vol. 1. See also his earlier work, *Communication and the Evolution of Society* (Boston: Beacon Press, 1979).

15. For Bourdieu symbolic capital involved the precisely valued exchange of non-economic objects in a system of balanced reciprocities. For us it consists of a fund, or moral capital, generated by a conveyance of individual experiences to one collectivized in myth

and logical discourse, to be drawn down by the individual from the collectivity. It is crucial to the power of a discourse community, making it a party or, better, an army of truth.

16. We use such ideas with both caution and diffidence, since they derive from other fields and were designed for different purposes. We use "structural" to refer to the way people create order out of experience and transform an ordering in the mind into an ordering on the ground. "Phenomenological" refers to the social reconstruction of reality from the perspectives of those involved, the empirical retrieval of formative experiences and original intentionalities. In turn, a "hermeneutics" of power refers to the transformation of discourse from orality to authoritative texts, a process of *writ*ualization in which certain writings become hegemonic and totalizing.

17. The triumph of the market principle over socialist alternatives and the return to democracy being tried in many countries may prove to be less than all-encompassing. Too much stress on the econocentric model may prevent us from taking sufficiently seriously forms of power that arise out of violence, confrontation, and engendering inversionary discourses.

18. The term is particularly associated with the work of Pierre Bourdieu. See his *Outline of a Theory of Practice* (Cambridge: Cambridge University Press, 1977). For a more detailed analysis of Bourdieu's usage and ours see Chapter 4.

19. In this context, see Michel Foucault, *Discipline and Punish: The Birth of the Prison,* trans. Alan Sheridan (New York: Vintage Books, 1979).

20. See Hayden White, *The Content of the Form* (Baltimore: The Johns Hopkins University Press, 1987), pp. 50–51.

21. Sidney Rittenberg and Amanda Bennett, *The Man Who Stayed Behind* (New York: Simon and Schuster, 1993), p. 73.

22. This was recounted to us by one veteran revolutionary who had worked for the party in Chongqing before being forced to flee.

23. This also affected Sidney Rittenberg. He saw Yan'an not just as a place "where people were trying to live virtuous lives. It was the crucible in which the New China would be forged, and with it, the new world." Rittenberg and Bennett, *The Man Who Stayed Behind,* p. 73.

24. See Erving Goffman, *Interaction Ritual* (New York: Doubleday Anchor Books, 1967).

25. This cellular structure was not unique to the CCP but in somewhat different form always embedded in Chinese social practice. See Vivienne Shue, *The Reach of the State: Sketches of the Chinese Body Politic* (Stanford: Stanford University Press, 1988).

26. For a more general discussion of this model see Apter, "Democracy and Emancipatory Movements."

27. *Sendero Luminoso* in Peru is one example where Yan'an rather than the October Revolution is the exemplary case.

28. See Michel Wieviorka, "Les Maoistes Français et l'hypothèse terroriste," *Esprit* (October–November 1984): 133–145. Such major figures as Julia Kristeva, Jean-Luc Godard, Raul Vaneigem, and the followers of Gauche Prolétarien became passionate

admirers and defenders of Mao in the late sixties and early seventies in France. See Patrick Combes, *La littérature et le mouvement de Mai 68* (Paris: Seghers, 1984); and Maria-Antonietta Macciocchi, *Daily Life in Revolutionary China* (New York: Monthly Review Press, 1972). See also a collection of articles on China in *Les Temps Modernes* by Charles Bettleheim, Marco Maccio, Victor Nee, and Don Layman, and the Comité Travailleurs-Soldats (August–September 1970): 193–331.

29. See Stuart R. Schram, *The Thought of Mao Tse-Tung* (Cambridge: Cambridge University Press, 1989).

30. We take the use of the term *narrative* from Jerome Bruner, who we believe got it right. Jerome Bruner, "The Narrative Construction of Reality," *Critical Inquiry* 28 (Autumn 1991): 1–21.

31. See Fredric Jameson, *The Prison-House of Language* (Princeton: Princeton University Press, 1972).

32. See in particular Paul Ricoeur, *The Symbolism of Evil*. See also his *Lectures on Ideology and Utopia,* ed. George H. Taylor (New York: Columbia University Press, 1986), and *The Rule of Metaphor* (Toronto: University of Toronto Press, 1979).

33. See in particular Clifford Geertz, *The Interpretation of Cultures* (New York: Basic Books, 1973).

34. Of course we are aware that the theoretical demands these categories make require more than we can really deliver. We can only approximate from interview materials and pieced together descriptions what it is that people expressed when they lived it and how they interpreted what they experienced. And of course the concept of discourse can include everything from talk of a hubbub sort to more formalized and hortatory speeches by political leaders. How to treat writing as it evolved out of "orality" (as the term has been used by Goody) into "textuality" would also require the close reading of original materials, much of which remains unavailable. See Jack Goody, *The Interface between the Written and the Oral* (Cambridge: Cambridge University Press, 1987).

35. For example, the CCP drew parallels with the triumph of Lenin over Kerensky, and the Russian communists over the Social Revolutionaries and the Mensheviks.

36. Lu Xun, *Diary of a Madman and Other Stories,* trans. William A. Lyell (Honolulu: University of Hawaii Press, 1990).

37. People will always define and interpret Mao's role differently. Some, struck by the evolution of his power, compare him (as did Mao himself) with the first Ming emperor, who rose from peasant origins to found the dynasty. Others, more concerned with his dialectics and his Marxism, regard him as Lenin and Stalin rolled into one. But it is not so much the many-sided quality of Mao as a persona that intrigues us as how much he remains an enigma. In his lifetime he was now close to his followers and then utterly remote and above them, distancing himself, then breaking the distance and jumping the generations, to become at the end of his life more avatar than real-life figure.

38. No wonder Mao had no use for the intellectuals, whether of the May Fourth or the communist variety. He had just enough classical education to manipulate the old symbols but not enough to win the respect of the old intelligentsia, and just enough Marxism to deploy it as a kind of superior insight, but without any depth of theoretical

understanding. Indeed, there is no evidence that he ever read *Das Kapital*. As for economics, he used to say that he was more interested in the relations of production than the forces
of production. His notion of dialectics was limited to class struggle and the more conspiratorial implications of the term.

39. Roland Barthes, *The Pleasure of the Text* (New York: Hill and Wang, 1975).

40. All the interviews have an element of what Frederic Jameson has called "magic
realism." See his "On Magic Realism in Film," *Critical Inquiry* 12 (Winter 1986): 301–325.

41. An intellectual was loosely defined as anyone with middle or secondary school
education or above. Yan'an was not regarded by the "real" intellectuals (that is, the best
writers, artists, and thinkers) as genuinely "intellectual." Moreover, they did not consider
Mao and his comrades in this category, but rather as rustic and self-educated. For an account
of the intellectuals' critiques of the Communists and the Nationalists see Suzanne Pepper,
Civil War in China: The Political Struggle, 1945–1949 (Berkeley: University of California
Press, 1978), pp. 132–229.

42. We went as far as we could to accomplish these tasks. But our research was abruptly
terminated by the crushing of the student-inspired protests of 1989. Afterwards, it was no
longer possible for us to continue. Even before the events of Tiananmen Square, we had
been watched, followed, and monitored by the secret police. The fact is, Yan'an remains
a highly sensitive subject. Initially enthusiastic, the Chinese authorities (who had probably
hoped that we would do for Yan'an what Harrison Salisbury had done for the Long March,
namely give it a bit of burnish and gloss appropriate for modern heroic literature), changed
their attitude as we began to probe the darker side of the Yan'an experience. This darker
side has been repressed until relatively recently. Today the spate of books, testimonials, and
memoirs that commemorate and ritualize the experience the authorities hope will succeed
in embalming Yan'an in much the same way as Mao's body is embalmed in the Mausoleum
in Tiananmen Square.

43. For a collection of essays looking at this movement from different perspectives see
Tony Saich, ed., *The Chinese People's Movement. Perspectives on Spring 1989* (Armonk, N.Y.:
M. E. Sharpe, 1990).

44. This had been the case even earlier. See Friedman, Pickowicz, and Selden, *Chinese
Village*.

45. Our assumption is that a political system cannot sustain innovation in technique
and design without listening to the interests of those whose job it is to transform design
input into productive output. Moreover, the more advanced the society becomes, and the
more complex its base in terms of social structure and role, the more pluralized the interests,
and the more instrumental the needs, the more important it is to have a politics that can
mediate rather than control—in short, what we have called elsewhere a reconciliation
system. Moreover different kinds of information (technical, specific interest, and popular)
imply a different form of obligation. How to square them off within a mediating political
framework is the problem facing not only China but many other developing countries.
For more generalized theoretical statements of these assumptions see David E. Apter, *The
Politics of Modernization* (Chicago: University of Chicago Press, 1972), *Choice and the Politics
of Allocation* (New Haven: Yale University Press, 1971), and *Rethinking Development* (New-

bury Park, Calif.: Sage, 1987). On China, see Tony Saich, "Modernization and Participation in the People's Republic of China," in Joseph Y. S. Cheng, ed., *China: Modernization in the 1980s* (Hong Kong: The Chinese University Press, 1989), pp. 39–68; and "The Reform Decade in China: The Limits to Revolution from Above," in Marta Dassu and Tony Saich, eds., *The Reform Decade in China: From Hope to Dismay* (London: Kegan Paul, 1992), pp. 10–73.

46. Indeed, the legacy of the Cultural Revolution discredited the party, chastened the army, and produced a remarkable cynicism among the younger generation. The effort to liberalize had nothing to do with what we think of liberalization. Efforts at economic reform required that coercion be reduced, but did not foster democratic participation. What was wanted was technical information, innovation in industrial design, at best a hesitant kind of economic market without too much private enterprise and not much of a political marketplace. Entrepreneurship over bureaucracy was encouraged in order to enhance, rather than undermine, the power of the state.

47. See, for example, The Ideology and Theory Department of the *China Youth Daily,* "Realistic Responses and Strategic Options for China after the Soviet Events." However, its stress on patriotism replacing Marxism as a form of legitimation did draw criticism from some of the Yan'anites. For a translation of this document and criticisms of its approach see "Realistic Responses and Strategic Options: An Alternative CCP Ideology and Its Critics," David Kelly, ed. and trans., *Chinese Law and Government,* forthcoming.

2. Four Struggles

1. It is by no means clear, for example, that the "Wang Ming line" and Mao's own views on such questions as the united front were so different. Both had to operate within the general line of the Comintern. See Shum Kui-kwong, *The Chinese Communists' Road to Power: The Anti-Japanese National United Front (1935–1945)* (Oxford: Oxford University Press, 1988) and Kristina A. Schultz, "Wang Ming's Vision: 1930–1935" (unpublished Master's thesis, Harvard University, January 1989).

2. See Li Jui (Li Rui), *The Early Revolutionary Activities of Comrade Mao Tse-tung* (White Plains, N.Y.: M. E. Sharpe, 1977) for the early years. See also Benjamin Schwartz, *Chinese Communism and the Rise of Mao* (Cambridge, Mass.: Harvard University Press, 1979), Chalmers Johnson, *Peasant Nationalism and Communist Power* (Stanford: Stanford University Press, 1962), Lyman P. Van Slyke, *Enemies and Friends, The United Front in Chinese Communist History* (Stanford: Stanford University Press, 1967), Mark Selden, *The Yenan Way in Revolutionary China* (Cambridge, Mass.: Harvard University Press, 1971); Jerome Chen, *Mao and the Chinese Revolution* (Oxford: Oxford University Press, 1965), Shum, *The Chinese Communists' Road to Power,* and Tony Saich, *The Rise to Power of the Chinese Communist Party: Documents and Analysis, 1920–1949* (Armonk, N.Y.: M. E. Sharpe, 1994) (with a contribution by Benjamin Yang).

3. The meeting became a key point in the later reconstruction of Mao's history of the party. The official resolution on party history adopted in 1945 claimed that a new central

leadership came into being at the meeting headed by Mao Zedong and that this amounted to "an historic change of paramount importance." See "Zhongguo gongchandang zhongyang weiyuanhui guanyu ruogan lishi wenti de jueyi" (Resolution of the CCP Central Committee on Some Historical Questions) in The Secretariat of the CCP Central Committee, ed., *Liuda yilai: Dangnei mimi wenjian* (Since the Sixth Party Congress. Secret Internal Party Documents) (Beijing: Renmin chubanshe, 1952), vol. 1, pp. 1179–1200. An English translation can be found in *Selected Works of Mao Tse-tung* (London: Lawrence and Wishart, 1956), vol. 4, pp. 171–218. For details of the meeting see Benjamin Yang, "The Zunyi Conference as One Step in Mao's Rise to Power: A Survey of Historical Studies of the Chinese Communist Party," *The China Quarterly* 106 (June 1986): 236–239.

4. In an interview in Beijing in May 1988 with Zhu Jingli, the widow of Wang Jiaxiang and one of the doctors who had tended Wang Ming, this tall, still elegant woman spoke of Wang Ming with contempt. Her lip curled and she spoke with real venom of how Wang Ming's fat white flesh filled her with disgust when she gave him injections. Her hatred of Wang was clearly apparent.

5. Chang Kuo-t'ao, *The Rise to Power of the Chinese Communist Party, 1928–1938* (Lawrence: University of Kansas Press, 1972), vol. 2, p. 409.

6. Zhang had become Secretary of the newly founded E-Yu-Wan Sub-Bureau of the CCP Central Committee in April 1931.

7. See the letter from the Party Center to the Provincial Party Committee of the E-Yu-Wan Soviet Area dated March 15, 1933, in Yu Jinan, *Zhang Guotao he "wode huiyi"* (Zhang Guotao and "My Memoirs") (Chengdu: Sichuan renmin chubanshe, 1982), p. 177.

8. See, for example, "Zhang Guotao zai hong sifangmian jun dangzheng gongzuo dahui shangde zhengzhi baogao" (Zhang Guotao's Political Report to the Conference of the Fourth Front Army of the Red Army on Party and Political Work), November 2, 1934, in Sheng Renxue, ed., *Zhang Guotao wenti ziliao* (Materials on the Question of Zhang Guotao) (Chengdu: Sichuan renmin chubanshe, 1982), pp. 392–428. As with Mao in Jiangxi, Zhang Guotao chopped and changed his policy to suit changing circumstances.

9. See the Military Council's combat plan of January 20, 1935, concerning crossing the river, and the telegram of January 22 from the Politburo and the Central Military Council to the Fourth Front Army concerning the main forces of the Red Army entering Sichuan, in *Hongjun changzheng zai Sichuan shiliao xuanji* (Collection of Historical Documents on the Red Army's Long March in Sichuan) (Guiyang: Guizhou renmin chubanshe, 1983), pp. 53–55 and 57 respectively.

10. For an excellent account of Mao's confused stumblings to find a correct strategy and a way out of Northern Guizhou that is in marked contrast to the official party histories on the immediate post-Zunyi period see Benjamin Yang, "Ins and Outs: Changes in the Military Line After the Zunyi Conference" (paper delivered at the conference New Perspectives on the Chinese Communist Revolution, Amsterdam and Leiden, January 1990).

11. In his memoirs, Zhang records that he moved immediately to cross the Jialing River in response to the Central Army's maneuver. However, this was not true. Chang Kuo-t'ao, *The Rise of the Chinese Communist Party,* vol. 2, pp. 366–367.

12. Zhang Guotao, "Zhonghua suweiai gongheguo xibei lianbang zhengfu chengli xuanyan" (The Declaration of the Northwest Federal Government of the Chinese Soviet Republic), May 30, 1935, in Sheng Renxue, ed., *Zhang Guotao wenti ziliao,* pp. 449–452.

13. This meeting was at Lianghekou and was probably attended by Mao Zedong, Zhang Wentian, Zhou Enlai, Bo Gu, Zhu De, Wang Jiaxiang, Liu Shaoqi, Kai Feng, Deng Fa, Liu Bocheng, Li Fuchun, and Zhang Guotao. Possibly Otto Braun and Xu Xiangqian were invited to attend. Deng Xiaoping was present as minute taker. Less probable is that army corps leaders such as Peng Dehuai, Yang Shangkun, Lin Biao, and Nie Rongzhen were present. See Benjamin Yang, *From Revolution to Politics: Chinese Communists on the Long March* (Boulder: Westview Press, 1990), p. 144.

14. "Zhonggong zhengzhiju jueding guanyu yi, si fangmianjun huihou de zhanlüe fangzhen" (Politburo Decision Concerning the Strategic Policies after the Reunion of the First and Fourth Field Armies), June 28, 1936, in The Central Party Archives, ed., *Zhonggong zhongyang wenjian xuanji* (Selected Documents of the CCP Central Committee) (Beijing: Zhonggong zhongyang dangxiao chubanshe, 1982–1991), vol. 9, p. 482.

15. The meeting was attended by Politburo members Zhang Wentian, Zhou Enlai, Mao Zedong, Zhu De, Bo Gu, Zhang Guotao, Deng Fa, and Kai Feng. Apart from Zhang Guotao, other Fourth Front Army participants were Chen Changhao, Xu Xiangqian, and Fu Zhong. Wang Shoudao was present as minute taker. Yang, *From Revolution to Politics,* p. 151. Importantly, Xu, Chen, and Zhou Chunquan from the Fourth Front Army obtained Central Committee membership, while He Wei and Li Xiannian were made alternates.

16. "Zhongyang guanyu yi si fangmianjun huihe hou de zhengzhi xingshi yu renwude jueyi" (Resolution of the Central Committee on the Political Situation and Tasks Since the Meeting of the First and Fourth Front Armies), August 5, 1935, in The Secretariat of the CCP Central Committee, ed., *Liuda yilai,* vol. 1, pp. 683–690.

17. Wang Jianying, *Zhongguo gongchandang zuzhishi ziliao huibian* (Collection of Materials on the Organizational History of the CCP) (Beijing: Hongqi chubanshe, 1981), p. 236. Shortly after July 18, the top military leadership was reorganized. The Front Headquarters was to be run by supporters of Zhang Guotao. Xu Xiangqian was appointed General Commissar, and Chen Changhao Political Commissar. (Thanks to Zhang Meng and Michelle Chua for their help in sorting out the details of the conflict between Mao and Zhang.)

18. Mao's telegrams to Zhang Guotao concerning tactical movements were probably intended both to take away Zhang's autonomy and to test the loyalty of these leaders.

19. The left route was to march from Zhoukeji toward Aba and the right route from Maoergai to Songpan. The left route army departed on August 15 and arrived on August 20. The right route army departed on August 18 and arrived at Baxi and Banyou at the end of the month.

20. This account is based on comments of Mao Zedong to a meeting in Yan'an in March 1937. See Military History Research Department of the Military Academy of Sciences, ed., *Zhongguo renmin jiefangjun zhanshi* (Military History of the Chinese People's Liberation Army) (Beijing: Junshi kexue chubanshe, 1987), vol. 1, p. 274. However, the

precise contents of the telegram are disputed. According to Xu Xiangqian, the telegram did not imply that Mao should be detained but simply stated Zhang's continued opposition to the move north. Others said the text was sufficiently ambiguous in wording that a suspicious Mao could have interpreted it in a number of ways.

21. For the letter disseminating this information to party members see "Zhongyang wei zhixing beishang fangzhen gao tongzhi shu" (Letter of the Party Center Informing Comrades about Implementing the Policy of Moving North), September 10, 1935, in The Central Party Archives, ed., *Zhonggong zhongyang wenjian xuanji,* vol. 9, p. 504.

22. Other memoirs state that this was a subsequent change in Chen's words. These sources state that Chen had simply asked what should be done now, to which Xu had replied that it was probably too late to do anything.

23. This decision was only to be circulated to Central Committee members. See "Zhongyang guanyu Zhang Guotao tongzhi de cuowu de jueding" (Decision of the Party Center on the Mistakes of Comrade Zhang Guotao), September 12, 1935, in The Central Party Archives, ed., *Zhonggong zhongyang wenjian xuanji, neibuben* (Internal Volume), vol. 9, pp. 505–506.

24. See Yang, *From Revolution to Politics,* pp. 191–192.

25. The names of the members of these organizations have never been published, because it would compromise many of China's later top leaders. American journalist Harrison Salisbury writes that he was informed that the list included Zhu De, Peng Dehuai, Lin Biao, and Wang Ming. Harrison E. Salisbury, *The Long March: The Untold Story* (New York: Harper and Row, 1985), pp. 311–312.

26. The telegram can be found in The Political Academy of the Chinese People's Liberation Army, ed., *Zhonggong dangshi ziliao* (Materials on CCP History) (Beijing: Jiefangjun chubanshe, 1982), vol. 7, p. 193.

27. "Guanyu Zhang Guotao tongzhi chengli dier 'zhongyang' de jueding" (Resolution Concerning Comrade Zhang Guotao Setting Up the Second "Central Committee"), in ibid., p. 193. The decision was issued in the name of the Politburo.

28. Yang, *From Revolution to Politics,* pp. 211–213.

29. "Zai 'zhongyang' zongdui huodong fenzi huishang baogao" (Report to the Conference of Activists Among the "Party Center" Ranks), June 6, 1936, in Sheng Renxue, ed., *Zhang Guotao wenti ziliao,* pp. 580–591.

30. It is not known whether such an agreement was ever actually made, but if it was it would have placed party power in the hands of Wang Ming, something that would not have pleased Mao Zedong.

31. It may have been in response to this that on July 5, 1936, the Central Military Commission sent a telegram ordering the Second Front Army of the Chinese Workers-Peasant Red Army to be set up, with He Long as Commander-in-Chief and Ren Bishi as Political Commissar. In September 1935, the Central Committee had formed the Chinese Workers-Peasant Red Army (Shaan-Gan Detachment) with Peng Dehuai as Commander and Mao as Political Commissar.

32. The details are taken from the Military History Research Department of the Military Academy Sciences, ed., *Zhongguo renmin jiefangjun zhanshi,* vol. 1, pp. 343–357.

33. See his telegram of September 13. It seems that Zhu De and Chen Changhao opposed him while Xu Xiangqian sided with him.

34. "Zhongyang zhengzhiju guanyu Zhang Guotao tongzhi cuowu de jueding" (Politburo Decision Concerning Comrade Zhang Guotao's Mistakes), March 31, 1937, in The Central Party Archives, ed., *Zhonggong zhongyang wenjian xuanji, neibuben,* vol. 10, pp. 162–165.

35. For the expulsion order see "Zhonggong zhongyang guanyu kaichu Zhang Guotao dangji de jueding" (Decision of the CCP Central Committee Concerning the Expulsion of Zhang Guotao from the Party), April 18, 1938, in Secretariat of the CCP Central Committee, ed., *Liuda yilai,* vol. 2, p. 154. For the inner-party report see "Zhongyang guanyu kaichu Zhang Guotao dangji de dangnei baogao dagang" (Outline of the Central Committee Inner-Party Report Concerning the Expulsion of Zhang Guotao from the Party), April 19, 1938, ibid., pp. 155–158.

36. There were certain elements in the game. It was necessary for the Red Army to cooperate and not to be destroyed. Hence one rule accepted by all was unite or be destroyed. A second rule was that final authority must remain with the Central Committee. Zhang Guotao had tried to establish his own central committee, but this was considered apostasy. Hence, the Central Committee (with some Zhang-men added) had sole authority.

37. Edgar Snow, *Red Star over China* (New York: Vintage Books, 1947), pp. 210–215.

38. Mark Selden, "The Guerrilla Movement in Northwest China: The Origins of the Shensi-Kansu-Ninghsia Border Region," *The China Quarterly* 28 (Oct.–Nov. 1966): 63–81, and *The China Quarterly* 29 (Jan.–March 1967): 61–81.

39. See Saich, *The Rise to Power of the Chinese Communist Party,* section D, for a discussion of this point.

40. Zhu Lizhi had arrived in the region in the early autumn as a representative of the Central Committee as part of the general drive by the Party Center to reinforce its control over its scattered rural bases.

41. Gao and Liu, like many of the others were local products who could count on support from friends and relatives because of their personal ties rather than because these people shared a belief in the communist message.

42. Interview, Beijing, June 21, 1988.

43. For an account of the in-fighting in the E-Yu-Wan base see Chen Changhao, "E-Yu-Wan suqu sufande weida shengli" (The Great Victory of Purging Counter-Revolutionaries in the E-Yu-Wan Soviet), November 22, 1932, in *Hongqi zhoubao* (Red Flag Weekly) 28 (January 18, 1932): 43–57, trans. in Saich, *The Rise to Power of the Chinese Communist Party,* Document D. 5.

44. It is doubtful whether this new organ was sanctioned by the Central Committee. It was called the Delegation of the Shanghai Bureau and the Northern Bureau to the Northern Shaanxi Soviet Area *(Huju yu beiju pai zhu Shaanbei suqu daibiaotuan)* and was set up in September 1935. Zhu was secretary with the other three as members. Wang Jianying, *Zhongguo gongchandang zuzhishi ziliao huibian,* p. 241.

45. Ibid.

46. Later, it appears that Zhu and Guo tried to conceal their guilt in arranging the

arrest. The arrest order came from the Bureau they had set up. The fall guy was Zhang Qingfu ("Zhang the Corpulent"). They appointed Zhang to the Bureau, blamed the arrest on him, and subsequently arrested him. One of their associates then fed the false account of Zhang's culpability to Edgar Snow.

47. The messenger who was to deliver Zhu Lizhi's letter ordering Liu Zhidan's arrest was said to have given it first to Liu, saying, "You are the military leader, so I must give you this letter." Liu looked at the letter (it was in fact the list of people to be arrested, with his name on the top of the list). He then put the letter back in the envelope and gave it to the messenger. Liu said, "Go ahead and deliver it to Xu Haidong, the general at the front." Liu then proceeded to Wayaobao to submit himself for arrest.

48. Interview, Beijing, June 21, 1988.

49. This decision does not appear to have been ratified until November 1939.

50. Wang Jianying, *Zhongguo gongchandang zuzhishi ziliao huibian,* pp. 270, 338–339.

51. Interview, Beijing, June 21, 1988.

52. The conference was held between October 19, 1942, and January 14, 1943, and was attended by 267 leading cadres from various organizations. It was addressed by nearly all the CCP's top leaders, with the exception of Wang Ming and his supporters. Gao's two reports were "Bianqude lishi wenti jiantao" (Examination of the Question of the History of the Border Region), November 17 and 18, 1942 (Yan'an: Xibeiju, 1943), pp. 1–50, and "Gao Gang tongzhi zai xibeiju gaogan hui shangde jielun" (Summary by Comrade Gao Gang at the Senior Cadres' Meeting of the Northwest Bureau), January 14, 1942 (Yan'an: Xibeiju, 1943), pp. 1–27.

53. The details of this struggle have been analyzed most recently by Shum; we will not go into great detail here. Shum, *The Chinese Communists' Road to Power,* pp. 114–183.

54. Stuart R. Schram, *The Thought of Mao Tse-tung* (Cambridge: Cambridge University Press, 1989), p. 62.

55. This pamphlet of Wang's was originally published in February 1931 and was reprinted in Moscow in 1932 under the same title. During the campaign to study party history, Wang Ming republished his pamphlet in Yan'an (March 1940) under the title *Wei Zhonggong gengjia buersaiweikehua er douzheng* (The Struggle for the Further Bolshevization of the CCP). The full text can be found in Hsiao Tso-liang, *Power Relations within the Chinese Communist Movement, 1930–1934: The Chinese Documents* (Seattle: University of Washington Press, 1967), vol. 2, pp. 499–609.

56. Mao Zedong, "The Situation and the Tasks of the Anti-Japanese War after the Fall of Shanghai and Taiyuan," in *Selected Works of Mao Tse-tung* (Beijing: Foreign Languages Press, 1965), vol. 2, pp. 61–70. This was a speech delivered to party activists at a meeting on November 12, 1937.

57. Shum, *The Chinese Communists' Road to Power,* p. 114. Wang arrived by plane; Mao feared flying.

58. Ibid., p. 117.

59. "Wanjiu shijude guanjian" (The Key to the Salvation of the Nation), December 27, 1937, reprinted in *Wang Ming yanlun xuanji* (Collected Speeches of Wang Ming) (Beijing: Renmin chubanshe, 1982), pp. 546–554, trans. in Saich, *The Rise to Power of the*

Chinese Communist Party, Document E. 26. Only an outline of Wang's speech to the conference is available, and it consists mainly of a series of topics to be covered. Wang Ming, "Ruhe jixu quanguo kangzhan he zhengqu kangzhan shengli ne?" (How Can the National War of Resistance Be Continued and Victory Be Achieved?) in The Secretariat of the CCP Central Committee, ed., *Liuda yilai,* vol. 1, pp. 888–895.

60. "Zhongyang zhengzhiju guanyu Zhonggong zhu guoji daibiaotuan gongzuo baogao de jueyi" (Central Committee Resolution Concerning the Work Report of the CCP Mission to the Comintern), December 13, 1937, in The Secretariat of the CCP Central Committee, ed., *Liuda yilai,* vol. 1, p. 897.

61. The Politburo was made up of Mao Zedong, Zhang Wentian, Zhou Enlai, Zhu De, Zhang Guotao, Wang Jiaxiang, Bo Gu, Ren Bishi, Chen Yun, Peng Dehuai, Xiang Ying, Liu Shaoqi, Kang Sheng, Wang Ming, Deng Fa and Kai Feng. Wang Jianying, *Zhongguo gongchandang zuzhishi ziliao huibian,* p. 296.

62. Wang Ming, "Sanyue zhengzhiju huiyi de zongjie—muqian kangzhan xingshi yu ruhe jixu kangzhan he zhengqu kangzhan shengli" (Summary of the March Politburo Meeting—The Current Situation in the War of Resistance and How to Continue the War and Win Victory), March 11, 1938, *Qunzhong* (The Masses) 1, no. 19, reprinted in The Secretariat of the CCP Central Committee, ed., *Liuda yilai,* vol. 1, pp. 923–939.

63. Mao made this assertion to the Study Group on the War of Resistance in Yan'an. See Mao Zedong, "Lun chijiu zhan" (On Protracted War), in Takeuchi Minoru, ed., *Mao zedong ji* (The Collected Works of Mao Zedong) (Tokyo: Sososha, 1983), vol. 6, pp. 49–146.

64. "Zhongyang guanyu xinsijun xingdong fangzhen de zhishi" (Instruction of the Central Committee on the Policy for Movement of the New Fourth Army) and "Zhongyang guanyu jiaqiang xiangcun youji zhanzheng he chuanli youji genjudi wenti gei Jiangsu shengwei de zhishi" (Instruction of the Central Committee to the Jiangsu Provincial Committee on the Question of Strengthening Guerrilla Warfare in the Rural Areas and the Establishment of Guerrilla Bases), May 14, 1938, in The Central Party Archives, ed., *Zhonggong zhongyang wenjian xuanji,* vol. 10, pp. 512–513.

65. "Zhongyang guanyu Xuzhou shibai hou Huazhong gongzuo de zhishi" (Party Center Instructions for Work in Central China after the Fall of Xuzhou), May 22, 1938, in ibid., vol. 10, pp. 514–515. These were sent by the Secretariat.

66. Wang Ming, Zhou Enlai, and Bo Gu, "Women duiyu baowei Wuhan yu disanqi kangzhan wenti de yijian" (Our Ideas Concerning the Defense of Wuhan and the Third Stage of the War of Resistance), June 15, 1938, in The Secretariat of the CCP Central Committee, ed., *Liuda yilai,* vol. 1, pp. 946–964.

67. Wang reported this news to a Politburo meeting on September 14. The directive also approved the CCP's expulsion of Zhang Guotao. See "Gongchan guoji zhixing weiyuanhui zhuxituan de jueding" (Decision of the Presidium of the Executive Committee of the Comintern), September 1938, in The Central Party Archives, ed., *Zhonggong zhongyang wenjian xuanji,* vol. 10, pp. 574–575. See also Zhao Shenghui, *Zhongguo gongchandang zuzhishi gangyao* (An Outline of the Organizational History of the CCP) (Anhui: Anhui renmin chubanshe, 1987), p. 145.

68. Mao Zedong, "Lun xin jieduan" (On the New Stage), in Takeuchi Minoru, ed., *Mao Zedong ji,* vol. 6, pp. 163–240.

69. This was in his report of October 20.

70. "The Question of Independence and Initiative within the United Front," November 5, 1938, in *Selected Works,* vol. 2, pp. 213–217.

71. "Problems of War and Strategy," November 6, 1938, in ibid., pp. 219–234.

72. For the directive setting up the Central Plains Bureau see *The* Central Party Archives, ed., *Zhonggong zhongyang wenjian xuanji,* vol. 10, pp. 722–723. See also Zhao Shenghui, *Zhongguo gongchandang zuzhishi gangyao,* pp. 148–149.

73. On this point see Raymond F. Wylie, *The Emergence of Maoism. Mao Tse-tung, Ch'en Po-ta, and the Search for Chinese Theory, 1935–1945* (Stanford: Stanford University Press, 1980), pp. 226–227.

74. Mao Zedong, "The Role of the Chinese Communist Party in the National War," in *Selected Works,* vol. 2, pp. 259–260.

75. As a result, the event has attracted considerable interest both inside and outside of China. See, for example, Merle Goldman, *China's Intellectuals: Advise and Dissent* (Cambridge, Mass.: Harvard University Press, 1981), p. 21. See also Timothy Cheek, "The Fading of Wild Lilies: Wang Shiwei and Mao Zedong's *Yan'an Talks* in the First CPC Rectification Movement," *Australian Journal of Chinese Affairs* 11 (January 1984): 25–57, and Kyna Rubin, "Writers' Discontent and Party Response in Yan'an before 'Wild Lily': The Manchurian Writers and Zhou Yang" in *Modern Chinese Literature* 1 (September 1984): 79–102. See also Guilhem Fabre, *Genèse de pouvoir et de l'opposition in Chine Populaire: le Printemps de Yan'an* (Paris: L'Harmattan, 1990). Within China, the woman journalist Dai Qing, has done much not only to uncover materials but also to bring the matter back to intellectual attention. See Dai Qing, *Wang Shiwei and "Wild Lilies": Rectification and Purges in the Chinese Communist Party, 1942–1944,* ed. and with an introduction by David E. Apter and Timothy C. Cheek (Armonk, N.Y.: M. E. Sharpe, 1993).

76. This was to provide substance for the later charges of "Trotskyism," a charge the party now recognizes as "erroneous."

77. Kyna Rubin, "Writers' Discontent and Party Response in Yan'an before 'Wild Lily'."

78. See Cheek, "The Fading of Wild Lilies," p. 34. Wang Shiwei, "Ye baihehua," in *Jiefang ribao,* March 13 and 27, trans. in Dai Qing, *Wang Shiwei and "Wild Lilies,"* pp. 27–33.

79. Rittenberg notes that when he worked in Yan'an, he was instructed not to eat with members of his section but with "much higher level officials." This enabled him to eat meat most days as well as eggs and soup. For Rittenberg, this privilege meant not only better food but "access to top secret information." Sidney Rittenberg and Amanda Bennett, *The Man Who Stayed Behind* (New York: Simon and Schuster, 1993), p. 86.

80. The other exception was Xiao Jun, who had been less acerbic than Wang and whom Mao criticized by name in his May talks. For an account of these left-wing intellectuals and their fates see Merle Goldman, *Literary Dissent in Communist China* (Cambridge, Mass.: Harvard University Press, 1967).

81. See Mao Zedong's speech to the Seventh Party Congress, "Zai Zhonggong diqici daibiao dahuishangde jianghua", in *Mao Zedong sixiang wansui* (Long Live Mao Zedong Thought) (n.p.: n.p., February 1969), pp. 62–82, trans. in Saich, *The Rise to Power of the Chinese Communist Party,* Document H. 5.

82. We are grateful to Wen Jize and Dai Qing for interviews and materials on the Wang Shiwei affair.

83. Dai Qing, *Wang Shiwei and "Wild Lilies,"* pp. 64–65.

84. Ibid., p. 60.

85. Ibid., p. 61.

86. See Wen Jize, "Douzheng riji" (Diary of Struggle), in *Jiefang ribao,* June 28 and 29, 1942, trans. in Saich, *The Rise to Power of the Chinese Communist Party,* Document G. 18. See also Dai Qing, *Wang Shiwei and "Wild Lilies."*

87. Chen Boda, "Guanyu Wang Shiwei" (Concerning Wang Shiwei), in *Jiefang ribao,* June 14, 1942, p. 4, trans. in Saich, *The Rise to Power of the Chinese Communist Party,* Document G. 17.

88. Dai Qing, *Wang Shiwei and "Wild Lilies,"* pp. 77 and 86. At the end of October 1942, Wang had been charged with being the head of a "Five-member Anti-Party Clique." The others accused were Pan Fang, Zong Zheng, Cheng Quan, and Wang Li. See Yang Shangkun, "The Trotskyite Wang Shiwei's Activities and Liberalism in the Party," originally published in *Party Life* and translated in ibid., pp. 154–164. This speech, delivered to the Political Research Department of the Central Research Institute, claimed that the main crime of the accused was liberalism. As with the other charges against Wang, this was also repudiated by the party in the 1980s.

89. Dai Qing, *Wang Shiwei and "Wild Lilies,"* p. 89. Prior to He Long's admittance, Mao had laid the blame at the feet of Li Kenong.

90. Mao Zedong, "Zai Yan'an wenyi zuotanhui shang de jianghua" (Speech at the Yan'an Forum on Literature and Art), May 2 and 23, 1942. The Chinese text can be found in Liberation Society, ed., *Zhengfeng wenxian* (Rectification Documents) (Harbin: Dongbei shudian, 1948), pp. 249–277. A full English translation and an introduction can be found in Bonnie S. McDougall, *Mao Zedong's "Talks at the Yan'an Conference on Literature and Art": A Translation of the 1943 Text with Commentary* (Ann Arbor: Michigan Papers in Chinese Studies, no. 39, 1980). The speeches were not published until October 19, 1943, perhaps indicating the extent of opposition by the intellectuals within the party to this policy line. The date chosen for publication was the seventh anniversary of the death of the famous Chinese writer Lu Xun. See *Jiefang ribao,* October 19, 1943. To formalize this as party policy, the propaganda bureau of the Central Committee issued a decision on November 7, 1943, outlining the party's policy towards literature and art. See "Zhonggong zhongyang xuanchuanbu guanyu zhixing dang de wenyi zhengce de jueding" (Decision of the Propaganda Bureau of the CCP Central Committee On Carrying Out the Party's Policy on Literature and Art), in The Teaching and Research Group of the Central Party School, ed., *Zhonggong dangshi cankao ziliao* (Reference Materials on CCP History) (Beijing: Renmin chubanshe, 1979), vol. 5, pp. 146–151.

91. For criticism of this viewpoint as applied to Wang Shiwei see Zhou Yang, "Wang

Shiwei's Artistic Views and Our Artistic Views." The Forum also adopted a three point resolution critical of Wang Shiwei that agreed with the denunciation of his thought and activities as Trotskyite. See *Jiefang ribao,* June 20, 1942.

92. Wang Shiwei expressed this view in his article "Zhengzhijia, yishujia" (Politicians, Artists), *Gu yu* (Grain Rain) 1, no. 4, trans. in Dai Qing, *Wang Shiwei and "Wild Lilies,"* pp. 108–111.

93. Interview with Wen Jize, Beijing, July 1988.

94. As Snow was to note much later, "Mao Zedong did not create or command the forces of Japanese imperialism but his understanding of them enabled him to seize leadership and control over the energies of nationalism and patriotic resistance, to win a sovereign victory for social revolution." *Red China Today* (New York: Vintage Books, 1971), p. 69.

3. Three Stories

1. Walter Benjamin, *Illuminations* (New York: Schocken Books, 1969), p. 94.

2. Ibid., p. 102.

3. The term *symbolic capital* is of course Bourdieu's. But there are major differences between the way we use the term. For Bourdieu, symbolic capital is a highly organized and precisely valued set of nonmonetary exchanges. As with economic capital, value is exchanged for value. The relations of people are defined by the exchanges of symbolic capital, and the values of symbolic capital are realized through exchanges. The model is highly rationalistic and parallels that of a market. For us, however, symbolic capital is an endowment, a fund of power on which to draw. Pierre Bourdieu, *Outline of a Theory of Practice* (Cambridge: Cambridge University Press, 1977).

4. Daniel Dennett, "Commandos of the Word," *The Times Higher Education Supplement,* March 27, 1992, pp. 15 and 19.

5. Ibid.

6. Collective individualism contrasts, but is not entirely alternative to, what political scientists such as Olson, Elster, and others refer to as "methodological individualism." See Jon Elster, "Marxism and Methodological Individualism," in Pierre Birnbaum and Jean Leca, eds., *Individualism* (Oxford: The Clarendon Press, 1990), and M. Olson Jr., *The Logic of Collective Action* (Cambridge, Mass.: Harvard University Press, 1965).

7. There were plenty of precedents for Mao's Rectification Campaign, both in the Soviet Union and in the Jiangxi base in the early thirties, though in the latter instance the program was instituted less to establish conformity than to rid the party of presumed GMD spies and others who had insinuated themselves into the party, including Chiang Kai-shek's AB (Anti-Bolshevik) Squads.

8. Any shrewd political leader knows that if an individual's private story varies substantially from the collective one, it will be a false conveyance. Doubt will lurk underneath conviction.

9. Benedict Anderson, *Imagined Communities* (London: Verso, 1983).

10. Mao Zedong, "The Foolish Old Man Who Removed the Mountains," in *Selected*

Works of Mao Tse-tung (Beijing: Foreign Languages Press, 1965), vol. 3, p. 322. Of course in retrospect, one might say that the difference is that God makes quite a difference and the Wise Old Man was right.

11. Once achieved, such powers were regularized and made official in the form of organization codes. The continuing support of the Central Committee was essential, enabling Mao to play by the rules of the game while dominating those who made the rules.

12. Foreword by Richard M. Dorson to Wolfram Eberhard, *Folktales of China* (Chicago: University of Chicago Press, 1973), p. xviii.

13. Benjamin I. Schwartz, *The World of Thought in Ancient China* (Cambridge, Mass.: Harvard University Press, 1985), p. 65.

14. See Max Weber, *Economy and Society: An Outline of Interpretive Sociology,* ed. Guenther Roth and Claus Wittich (New York: Bedminster Press, 1968); and Pierre Bourdieu, *Distinctions: A Social Critique of the Judgement of Taste,* trans. Richard Nice (London: Routledge and Kegan Paul, 1984).

15. For example, Mao begins his Yan'an talks on literature and art as follows: "Comrades! I have invited you to this conference today for the purpose of exchanging opinions with you on the correct relationship between work in literature and art and revolutionary work in general, to obtain the correct development of revolutionary literature and art and better assistance from them in our other revolutionary work, so that we may overthrow our national enemy and accomplish our task of national liberation." Mao Zedong, "Talks at the Yan'an Forum on Literature and Art," in Bonnie S. McDougall, *Mao Zedong's Talks at the Yan'an Conference on Literature and Art: A Translation of the 1943 Text with Commentary* (Ann Arbor: Center for Chinese Studies, Michigan papers in Chinese Studies, no. 39, 1980), p. 57.

16. Repeated questioning by interviewers on this point rarely produced disagreement. When asked "Do you think Mao really believed that his own insights were so superior to others that it constituted a unique gift?" with only one or two exceptions, people said yes. Some thought he was in this regard simplistic. Others believed him much shrewder than some of his associates educated in France or the USSR gave him credit for.

17. For the influence of Comintern agent Maring and Soviet representative Borodin, see respectively Tony Saich, *The Origins of the First United Front in China. The Role of Sneevliet (Alias Maring)* (Leiden: E. J. Brill, 1991), 2 vols., and Lydia Holubnychy, *Michael Borodin and the Chinese Revolution, 1923–1925* (New York: East Asia Institute, Columbia University, 1979).

18. Something of the atmosphere can be found in a curious document purporting to be the memoirs of a mysterious Captain Eugene Pick, "late of the Red Army Intelligence Service in China." The title of Pick's book, which first appeared as a series of articles in the *North-China Daily News and Herald,* is *China in the Grip of the Reds: Sketches of the Extravagant Effort made by Soviet Russia to Set Up and Control a Red Regime in China, with Strong Light upon the Ruthless Character of Borodin and His Agents* (Shanghai: North-China Daily News and Herald, 1927). The book is a virtual who's who of Russian agents, with the Jews among them carefully distinguished from the "real" Russians.

19. Stephen Averill, "The Origins of the Futian Incident," in Tony Saich and Hans J. van de Ven, eds., *New Perspectives on the Chinese Communist Revolution* (Armonk, N.Y.: M. E. Sharpe, 1994).

20. For documentation on the period see Hsiao Tso-liang, *Power Relations with the Chinese Communist Movement, 1930–1934* (Seattle: University of Washington Press, 1961), and Tony Saich, *The Rise to Power of the Chinese Communist Party: Documents and Analysis, 1920–1949* (Armonk, N.Y.: M. E. Sharpe, 1994) (with a contribution by Benjamin Yang).

21. One particular case concerns the fate of He Mengxiong and his supporters, who had opposed Pavel Mif and Wang Ming at the Fourth Plenum (January 1931). The day after bringing their opposition out into the public, they were arrested by the Foreign Settlement Police, handed over to the nationalists, and later executed. The tip-off that brought about their arrest came from their opponents in the CCP.

22. Not so Mao's wife, who received severe wounds and whom he would later leave in favor of Jiang Qing, much to the annoyance of everyone.

23. Interview in Yan'an, 1986.

24. Accounts by Edgar Snow, Agnes Smedley, and others stress his benign presence and charm. A portrait of him is given by two British teachers, husband and wife, who fled Beijing as the Japanese invaded the city and made their way to Yan'an: "We thanked Mao for giving us the honor of calling on us in this way, when he was such a busy man. He replied that he had included us in his New Year round of calls which included the Elders of the Party, like Chairman Lin and Vice-Chairman Li. He was sorry that we had been in Yan'an for just three months before he had time to meet us. He was also sorry that he had no time to prepare answers to our questions; he preferred to have a tea-time chat. He made us talk—in Chinese most of the time— instead of talking himself; about our journey, about teaching the radio boys in Hopei [Hebei], and about our pre-war life in Beijing, about England, about China's future. He gave practically nothing away himself. We were sorry to note that in appearance Mao seemed an effeminate type [sic]. He seemed over-tired too, and kept stroking his half-bald head with one hand as if he was suffering from insomnia. He had, however, a winning kindly smile, a keen sense of humor, and would gaze at one during conversation with steady, thoughtful eyes. He gave us the impression of absolute sincerity, and a deep feeling of responsibility for his position in a critical period of his country's history. There was no blustering cock-sureness in his makeup; hot-headed revolutionary fanaticism was completely absent. He took his leave of us after tea, departing in a closed van, on the outside of which were painted the words, 'GIFT OF THE CHINESE LAUNDRYMEN'S NATIONAL SALVATION ASSOCIATION, NEW YORK.' " Claire and William Band, *Two Years with the Chinese Communists* (New Haven: Yale University Press, 1948), p. 252.

25. As Stuart Schram, the leading Western expert on Mao's life and work, points out, Mao's least noteworthy essays are those where he makes the greatest claims to theory, as for example in his lectures on dialectical materialism, which are wooden, labored, and not very interesting, but over which Mao labored mightily and refused to allow others to lecture on the subject. Stuart Schram, *The Political Thought of Mao Tse-tung* (New York: Praeger, 1974), p. 44.

26. Interview, Changsha, May 1986.

27. Several interviewees remarked on Mao's language "musicality," not in sound but as a total performance, including gestures: "his hands fluttered like birds."

28. Cited in Hayden White, *The Content of the Form* (Baltimore: The Johns Hopkins University Press, 1987), p. 44. See also his *Tropics of Discourse* (Baltimore: The Johns Hopkins University Press, 1978) pp. 56–69.

29. In interviews with surviving Yan'anites, he was described as follows: If Mao was in a group where several people were speaking, he would characteristically listen patiently, letting others speak first. He would listen most particularly to differences in point of view. He would then rearticulate the themes in his own way, giving them fresh and different meanings, raising them above the level of the commonplace, all the while making it appear that the ideas were really those of his associates rather than his own, when in fact the reverse was the case.

30. See Erving Goffman, *Relations in Public* (New York: Basic Books, 1971).

31. Rittenberg, on his arrival in Yan'an in 1946, was struck by the formal, political character of the language. He concluded that many senior leaders, having been illiterate peasants, gained education from the party; "they took readily to the literary sound of propaganda." Sidney Rittenberg and Amanda Bennet, *The Man Who Stayed Behind* (New York: Simon and Schuster, 1993), p. 87.

32. These comments derive from several interviews with Cao Meng in Beijing during May and June 1987. For a good example of her work in English see her book *The Moving Force* (Beijing: Cultural Press, 1950).

33. Mao Zedong, "Talks at the Yan'an Forum on Literature and Art," in Bonnie McDougall, *Mao Zedong's Talks at the Yan'an Conference,* p. 61.

34. Smedley was very aware of what she was doing, right down to the role of storytelling itself. Witness her description of the weaver as storyteller, described in her book *The Great Road* and whom she links to the Taiping rebellion, that revolutionary past which, in the lore, foreshadowed the contemporary struggles of the CCP. The weaver serves as the living connection between the Taiping rebellion (itself part grim reality and part mythic tale) and the communist movement, in which Mao and Zhu De become living legends. In this way she used memory as a literary device to provide contemporary events that were to become an integral part of an interpreted past with an authentic radical inheritance. The weaver weaves a spell, of course, and as she recounts how he used to come to Zhu De's house once a week when he was a child in order to do the family weaving, Smedley herself becomes a storyteller. See Agnes Smedley, *The Great Road* (New York: Monthly Review Press, 1956).

35. See Edgar Snow, *Red Star over China,* (New York: Vintage Books, 1947). The spread of Snow's account in China persuaded many young people to go to Yan'an.

36. This outside validation was given by the "Three S Society," consisting of Edgar Snow, Agnes Smedley, and Anna Louise Strong. One could add others—Jack Beldon, James Bertram, even military figures like Joseph Stilwell and Evans Carlson, and foreign visitors who came to stay, like Dr. George Hatem (Ma Haide), Israel Epstein, and Rewi Alley. See Rewi Alley, *Six Americans in China* (Beijing: Intercul, 1985).

37. While others went off to France, Mao remained at home as a teacher, an organizer, a soldier-scholar-research worker conducting the Hunan investigations. Mao was on the move all the time, gaining wisdom and experience.

38. A number of those interviewed also spoke of their awe of Mao and their appreciation that he would mingle with everyone else. Mao had a capacity for instant intimacy on a momentary basis without incurring obligations.

39. See Franz Michael in collaboration with Chung-li Chang, *The Taiping Rebellion* (Seattle: University of Washington Press, 1966), vol. 1. See also Vincent Y. C. Shih, *The Taiping Ideology* (Seattle: The University of Washington Press, 1967); Rudolf G. Wagner, *Reenacting the Heavenly Vision: The Role of Religion in the Taiping Rebellion* (Berkeley: Institute of East Asian Studies, University of California, 1982); and Philip A. Kuhn, "Origins of the Taiping Vision: Cross-Cultural Dimensions of a Chinese Rebellion," *Comparative Studies in Society and History* 19 (July 1977): 350–366.

40. For an early interpretation of Mao as historian and the events of which his story is composed see Howard Boorman, "Mao Tse-tung as Historian," in Albert Feuerwerker, ed., *History in Communist China* (Cambridge, Mass.: MIT Press, 1968) pp. 306–329.

41. Mao Zedong, "The Chinese Revolution and the Chinese Communist Party," in *Selected Works of Mao Tse-tung* (Beijing: Foreign Languages Press, 1965), vol. 2, p. 306.

42. Prior to the formal founding of the CCP, party branches had been set up in Shanghai, Beijing, Wuhan, Hunan, Canton, Jinan, Japan, and France. For an account of the establishment of the branches in China see Tony Saich, "Through the Past Darkly: Some New Sources on the Founding of the Chinese Communist Party," *International Review of Social History* 30, Part 2 (1985): 167–182.

43. Perhaps the best example of "mirror image" refutation is that of Wang Ming, whose book, *Mao's Betrayal* (Moscow: Progress Publishers, 1979) reverses virtually all of Mao's claims, and charges that Mao falsified history.

44. Mao Zedong, preface to *Souvenirs de la Longue Marche* (Beijing: Foreign Languages Press, 1980).

45. Warren Kuo, *Analytical History of the Chinese Communist Party* (Taibei: Institute of International Relations, 1970), vol. 3, pp. 161–162.

46. No wonder that the Nationalists were so shocked by the accounts of the events by foreigners such as Edgar Snow, whose sympathetic account of the Long March, biography of Mao, and description of life in the Shaan-Gan-Ning Border Area from Mao's headquarters in Bao'an (the main center prior to Yan'an) are recounted in *Red Star over China*. To add insult to injury, the book became an instant classic, both in the United States and to many Chinese. In fact, the book was translated into Chinese before it appeared in English.

47. For a considered view of this idea, see Chalmers Johnson, *Peasant Nationalism and Communist Power: The Emergence of Revolutionary China, 1937–1945* (Stanford: Stanford University Press, 1962).

48. Insofar as the party acts in the name of the people, party members in Yan'an become agents in the overcoming project and in ways impossible as individuals acting on their own. By the same token the party ruled out individual or autonomous acts, such as terrorism, as opportunistic, that is, non-theoretically based.

49. Hayden White, *The Content of the Form,* pp. 9–57.

50. Quoted in Schram, *The Political Thought of Mao Tse-tung,* p. 70.

51. Ibid.

52. David Harvey, *The Condition of Postmodernity* (Oxford: Basil Blackwell, 1989), pp. 201–307.

53. See Jean Baudrillard, *Simulacres et Simulation* (Paris: Galilée, 1981). Yan'an was both a simulacrum and a moral epicenter different from the other border areas partly because this was where the Party Center and Mao were, and also because it was where the techniques for the Rectification Campaign were worked out.

54. Schram, *The Political Thought of Mao Tse-tung,* p. 54.

55. Lucien Bianco, *Origins of the Chinese Revolution 1915–1949* (Stanford: Stanford University Press, 1971), pp. 27–28.

56. The original May 4, 1919, demonstration consisted of several thousand students from thirteen universities and colleges who protested in central Beijing against the turning over of former German occupied Shandong Province to the Japanese at the Paris Peace Conference. The government sent out troops and police, who arrested thirty-two demonstrators. A wave of student strikes broke out, followed by major political strikes all over China. It is the conventional historical break for the intermediate story.

57. "My office was so low that people avoided me. One of my tasks was to register the names of people who came to read newspapers, but to most of them I didn't exist as a human being. Among those who came to read I recognized the names of famous leaders of the renaissance movement, men like Fu SSu-nien, Lo Chia-lun, and others, in whom I was intensely interested. I tried to begin conversations with them on political and cultural subjects, but they were very busy men. They had no time to listen to an assistant librarian speaking southern dialect." Quoted in Snow, *Red Star over China,* p. 176.

58. Mao Zedong, "A Study of Physical Education," in Stuart R. Schram, ed., *Mao's Road to Power: Revolutionary Writings, 1912–1949,* vol. 1, *The Pre-Marxist Period, 1912–1920* (Armonk, N.Y.: M. E. Sharpe, 1992), p. 116.

59. His article "Recruit Large Numbers of Intellectuals," for example, shows both the need for and the suspicion of intellectuals: "We should use various ways and means to recruit all intellectuals who are willing to fight Japan and who are fairly loyal, hardworking and able to endure hardship; we should give them political education and help them to temper themselves in war and work and to serve the army, the government and the masses; and taking each case on its merits, we should admit into the party those who measure up to the requirements of party membership. As for those who do not qualify or do not wish to join the party, we should have good working relations with them and give them guidance in their work with us." Mao Zedong, *Selected Works,* vol. 2, p. 302.

60. For a discussion of the work of Ai Siqi see Joshua A. Fogel, "Ai Siqi: Professional Philosopher and Establishment Intellectual," in Merle Goldman, Timothy C. Cheek, and Carol Lee Hamrin, eds., *China's Intellectuals and the State* (Cambridge, Mass.: Harvard University Press, 1987), pp. 23–41.

61. Mao Zedong, "A Study of Physical Education," in Schram, ed., *Mao's Road to Power,* vol. 1, p. 113.

62. A full translation can be found in M. Henri Day, *Mao Zedong 1919–1927: Documents* (Stockholm: Skrifter utgivna av Föreningen för Orientaliska, Studier no. 14, 1975).

63. See Edgar Snow, *Red Star over China,* pp. 195–197.

64. See Claude Hudelot, *La Longue Marche* (Paris: Archives Gallimard Juillard, 1972) for a compilation of contemporary official descriptions of the Long March. For a reconstruction of the March some fifty years later see Harrison E. Salisbury, *The Long March: The Untold Story* (New York: Harper and Row, 1985).

4. One Line

1. Mao puts it as follows: "As regards the sequence in the movement of man's knowledge, there is always a gradual growth from the knowledge of individual and particular things to the knowledge of things in general." See "On Contradiction," in *Selected Works of Mao Tse-Tung* (Beijing: Foreign Languages Press, 1965), vol. 1, p. 320.

2. See, for example, his "Hunan nongmin yundong kaocha baogao" (Report on an Investigation into the Peasant Movement in Hunan). A full translation can be found in M. Henri Day, *Mao Zedong 1919–1927: Documents* (Stockholm: Skrifter utgivna av Föreningen för Orientaliska, Studier no. 14, 1975).

3. Mao puts it as follows: "Marxists hold that man's social practice alone is the criterion of the truth of his knowledge of the external world." See "On Practice," in *Selected Works,* vol. 1, p. 296.

4. Ibid., p. 297. Mao goes on to say, "In the process of practice, man at first sees only the phenomenal side, the separate aspects, the external relations of things. For instance, some people from outside come to Yan'an on a tour of observation. In the first day or two, they see its topography, streets and houses; they meet many people, attend banquets, evening parties and mass meetings, hear talk of various kinds and read various documents, all these being the phenomena, the separate aspects and the external relations of things. This is called the perceptual stage of cognition, named the stage of sense perceptions and impressions . . . At this stage man cannot as yet form concepts which are deeper, or draw logical conclusions."

5. "On Contradiction," in ibid., p. 320.

6. Stuart R. Schram, *The Political Thought of Mao Tse-Tung* (New York: Praeger, 1974), pp. 135–136. Schram's italics. Schram notes Mao's "extreme voluntarism," a crucial difference from classical Marxism in regard to the problem of "historical necessity."

7. See Leszek Kolakowski, *Main Currents of Marxism* (Oxford: Oxford University Press, 1981), vol. 3.

8. See, for example, "Struggle in the Jinggang Mountains," in *Selected Works,* vol. 1, pp. 73–104.

9. See Mao Zedong, "On Correcting Mistaken Ideas in the Party," in ibid., p. 112.

10. This notion—that Mao was not much of a Marxist—is in general accord with the view of seasoned China scholars such as Schram. His work still represents the most careful and cogent analysis of Mao's writings combined with carefully selected examples. In a

fascinating evaluation of Mao's thought Schram casts doubt on Mao's self-proclaimed "sinification" of Marxism. "He is a very 'Chinese' Marxist, as his preoccupation with the glory of China amply demonstrates. But has he produced a Chinese variant of Marxism— that is, an ideology in which Marxism is not merely clothed in a Chinese dress, but in which the very concepts and methods by which reality is analyzed have somehow become peculiarly Chinese?" It is an interesting question. Similarly one may ask whether there can be a sinified democracy. See Stuart R. Schram, *The Political Thought of Mao Tse-tung,* p. 114.

11. See Frederick C. Teiwes, "Mao and His Lieutenants," in *The Australian Journal of Chinese Affairs* 19 and 20 (1988): 1–81.

12. The Russian case is a good illustration. Development in Tsarist Russia before the revolution, although quite rapid in the period 1895–1913, could hardly be regarded as propitious enough from a classical Marxist perspective to enable a revolutionary transition to socialism. But that hardly stopped Lenin. He literally invented an alternative Marxism that turned the old one on its head. Lenin's emphasis on praxis is a barely disguised pragmatism fitted brilliantly to a Marxist pedigree by the sleight of hand known as dialectics. Establishing as an appropriate orthodoxy what was invented to fit the circumstance is a testimonial to Lenin's dialectical imagination. Its accomplishment was nothing less than to show how the transformation of practical revolutionary experience in a backward country was part of a larger historical necessity. Lenin's ideological doctrine, proclaiming higher truths, provided plenty of space for drastic compromises to fit circumstances. The New Economic Policy was a good example.

13. Throughout Mao's career, despite his emphasis on theory, he always returned to facts and examples. Reframed in a context of logical explanation, he contextualized the instrumental within a more moral frame of meaning.

14. This is also the position taken by Werner Meissner. See his *Philosophy and Politics in China* (Stanford: Stanford University Press, 1990).

15. Ibid., p.185.

16. Ibid., p.186.

17. In a personal interview, Li Rui made the point that what Mao did was combine traditional Chinese thought with Stalin's vulgarization of Marxism. "Mao," he said, "believed that a good emperor comes along only once in five hundred years." Li Rui also said that, in his view, "without the vulgarization of Marxism the revolution could not have succeeded." On the question of how good a Marxist Mao was see Leszek Kolakowski's comments on Mao's "peasant Marxism": "Measured by European standards," says Kolakowski, "the ideological documents of Maoism and especially the theoretical writings of Mao himself appear in fact extremely primitive and clumsy, sometimes even childish; in comparison, even Stalin gives the impression of a powerful theorist." Kolakowski, *Main Currents of Marxism,* vol. 3, p. 494.

18. For a partial treatment of such matters see Guilhem Fabre, *Genèse du pouvoir et de l'opposition en Chine* (Paris: Editions L'Harmattan, 1990). See also David E. Apter, "Discourse as Power: Yan'an and the Chinese Revolution," in Tony Saich and Hans J. van de

Ven, eds., *New Perspectives on the Chinese Communist Revolution* (Armonk, N.Y.: M. E. Sharpe, 1994).

19. See Meissner's fascinating discussion of theory as consummatory disguise, a code for universal meanings that in fact were both highly instrumental and pragmatic and, employed in the factional conflicts within the CCP, produced tactical adaptations to constantly changing and fluid military conditions. Meissner, *Philosophy and Politics in China.*

20. Ibid., pp. 131–187.

21. See Mark Selden, *The Yenan Way in Revolutionary China* (Cambridge, Mass.: Harvard University Press, 1971).

22. Mao Zedong, "The Chinese Revolution and the Chinese Communist Party," in *Selected Works,* vol. 2, pp. 308–309.

23. Ibid., pp. 309–310.

24. Ibid., p. 313.

25. Ibid., p. 317.

26. Ibid., p. 320.

27. Ibid., p. 326.

28. The Whampoa (Huangpu) Military Training Academy was set up in early 1924 on Sun Yat-sen's instructions. It was headed by Chiang Kai-shek, who had undertaken a three-month trip to Soviet Russia that included observation of Red Army training techniques. The Academy combined military training with political instruction. The deputy head of its Political Education Department was Zhou Enlai.

29. Mao Zedong, "The Chinese Revolution and the Chinese Communist Party," in *Selected Works,* vol. 2, p. 331.

30. Two books provided the logical and philosophical underpinnings of the GMD. Both were written by Dai Jitao in order to combat the effectiveness of the communist position. These were *The Philosophical Foundation of Sun Yat-senism* and *The National Revolution and the Guomindang.* Like the communists, the Nationalists claimed the inheritance not only of Sun Yat-sen but also the May Fourth Movement. The books were written in part because the communists inside the GMD were bit by bit dividing it into left and right factions, the left moving closer towards the communists and dominating its auxiliary organizations, labor movements, and literary and intellectual circles. One needs to remember that in 1925 not only were key communists members of the GMD, but also that some members of the CCP Central Committee were also members of the GMD and some of these, like Chen Duxiu (at the time General Secretary of the CCP) were simultaneously members of the GMD Central Committee. Mao Zedong and Zhang Guotao, both founding members of the CCP, were Alternate Members of the GMD Central Committee. Indeed, once the GMD organization had been restructured along the lines laid down by its Soviet advisors, the organization's of the CCP and the GMD were strongly parallell, right down to the dual command system of political and military commissars.

31. Mao Zedong, "On Practice," in *Selected Works,* vol. 1, p. 301.

32. The extent to which Soviet political leaders became embroiled in the China

question is amazing. Even in the first phase of his exile to Alma Ata in 1928, Trotsky fired off tracts on this issue, seeing the need to incorporate the peasants into the revolutionary project but remaining doubtful that China was ready for a proletarian revolution. At the same time, he believed that the bourgeoisie and the neofeudalist landlords were part of the same class mechanism. Hence he also doubted that a bourgeois revolution was likely to succeed. On the whole, he remained pessimistic about the prospects of a radical Chinese revolution altogether. See Harold R. Isaacs, *The Tragedy of the Chinese Revolution*, 2nd rev. ed. (Stanford: Stanford University Press, 1961); and Leo Douw, "The Representation of China's Rural Backwardness, 1932–1937" (Ph.D diss., Leiden University, 1991), pp. 85–95.

33. Quoted in Richard C. Thornton, *The Comintern and the Chinese Communists, 1928–1931* (Seattle: University of Washington Press, 1969), p. 41. Thornton argues that Li Lisan's efforts to concentrate power in his own hands made rural military commanders more independent and concludes that chief among these was Mao.

34. In an interview with an American correspondent in 1946, Mao said, "Judging by the large amount of aid the United States is giving Chiang Kai-shek to enable him to wage a civil war on an unprecedented scale, the policy of the U.S. government is to use the so-called mediation as a smoke screen for strengthening Chiang Kai-shek in every way and suppressing the democratic forces in China through Chiang Kai-shek's policy of slaughter so as to reduce China virtually to a U.S. colony." *Selected Works*, vol. 4, p. 109.

35. See Kamal Sheel, *Peasant Society and Marxist Intellectuals in China* (Princeton: Princeton University Press, 1989), pp. 22–41.

36. On this point, it is interesting to note that the Communist Party of the Soviet Union chose not to look at the Chinese party positions too closely. McLane puts it as follows: "How, for instance, could Communist participation be justified in a revolution which, however proletarian in its origins, was, by 1935, receiving its major impetus from a predominantly agrarian movement? By asserting that the Party in China was conducting a dual effort, and by asserting at the same time, however weak the evidence, that the Party's successes in the urban sector matched those in Kiangsi and the soviets were in any case operating under the 'hegemony of the proletariat,' Moscow could claim orthodoxy for the Chinese Communist movement taken as a whole." Charles B. McLane, *Soviet Policy and the Chinese Communists, 1931–1946* (New York: Columbia University Press, 1958), p. 46.

37. It was precisely this aspect of Marxism that appealed to latter-day western intellectuals and Marxists who in the sixties and seventies came to see themselves as Maoists as opposed to supporters of both social democracy and bureaucratic socialism of the Stalinist variety. These included such diverse groups as the Situationists, the Parti Communiste Marxiste-Léniniste de France, the Gauche Prolétarienne, and a galaxy of intellectuals, including Simone de Beauvoir (whose 1957 book *La Longue Marche* suggests that only China can renovate the old world), Jean-Luc Godard (whose film *La Chinoise* picks up de Beauvoir's theme), and journalist Maria-Antonietta Macciocchi (who, increasingly disenchanted with Stalinism, found her belief in communism reaffirmed by events in China, particularly the Cultural Revolution).

38. See, in particular, Liu Shaoqi's "How to be a Good Communist" and "On Inner

Party Struggle," in Liu Shaoqi, *Selected Works of Liu Shaoqi* (Beijing: Foreign Languages Press, 1984), vol. 1.

39. So writes Christopher Hill of the radical sects in the early phase of the English civil war. Christopher Hill, *The World Turned Upside Down* (London: Penguin Books, 1972), p. 372. Much the same could have been said for Robespierre and those sansculottes who became Babouvistes, Darthians, and other followers of the principle of the Committee on Public Safety. See Francois Furet and Mona Ozouf, *A Critical Dictionary of the French Revolution* (Cambridge, Mass.: Harvard University Press, 1989).

40. See Mao Zedong, "Recruit Large Numbers of Intellectuals," in *Selected Works,* vol. 2, p. 301. Here Mao points out that the CCP must be good at winning over the intellectuals for "without the participation of the intellectuals victory in the revolution is impossible."

41. A remarkable number of those interviewed (including a general in Mao's personal bodyguard, the secretary of the Yan'an City government, and a writer) began in Yan'an as illiterates and from lumpen, if not peasant, origins.

5. The Surviving Yan'anites

1. Rittenberg, in his memoirs, writes that "even decades later, I could recognize people who had been in Yan'an by the expressions they used." Sidney Rittenberg and Amanda Bennett, *The Man Who Stayed Behind* (New York: Simon and Schuster, 1993), p. 86.

2. As one of informants put it, "Kang Sheng had a great deal of support in the beginning. He had the 'Shandong spirit.' People loved to hear him speak. He would go on for hours, with people urging him to take some tea, a bite to eat, and continue. He was inspiring."

3. Shum Kui-Kwong, *The Chinese Communists' Road to Power: The Anti-Japanese National United Front (1935–1945)* (Oxford: Oxford University Press, 1988), p. 233.

4. Information was not entirely internal. There were manifestations of solidarity with Loyalist Spain or various workers' movements abroad.

5. For example, a general who had been political commissar of the Second Front Army under He Long discussed Mao's refusal to cross the Yellow River with Zhang Guotao. The general argued that Mao's refusal was not because of a conflict with Zhang but because Mao did not want to share responsibility with Zhang as this would reduce Mao's freedom to maneuver and possibly weaken his position with the Central Committee.

6. See, for example, Nym Wales in *Red Dust* (Stanford: Stanford University Press, 1952). All those we interviewed in 1986, 1987, 1988, and 1989 not only emphasized rectification, they made it their critical recollection of Yan'an. It is difficult to know how much impact rectification had on them at the time and how much of their emphasis has to be seen in the light of the Cultural Revolution. Many mention the role of Kang Sheng in both contexts, and virtually all treat the so-called Rescue Campaign as a dress rehearsal

for the Cultural Revolution. Almost all of those we interviewed suffered severely during the Cultural Revolution.

7. When they gather together, as the former staff and cadre of Yan'an schools and universities periodically do, they sing the old songs, make windy speeches recalling the old days, propose many toasts, and eat a lot, to the point where theirs is no different from any other "old boy" reunion. There is little passion or any sense of the uniqueness of the original enterprise. We were struck by the shallowness of a reunion we attended of the former students and teachers of the Lu Xun Academy of the Arts.

8. The interviews, taken as a whole, are long enough to make a book by themselves; thus we were forced to be highly selective. Our examples represent a range of Yan'anites —women and men, Red Army soldiers and high-ranking cadres, teachers, artists, Mao's photographer, the original "white haired girl," those involved in writing, publishing, radio, and other such activities. They come from very different social backgrounds—high Mandarinate, gentry, landlord, peasant, poor peasant, worker. They may be compared with the biographical sketches made by Nym Wales in 1939 and by Edgar Snow in *Red Star over China,* as well as other accounts of the period before rectification. Our interviews were conducted during the period 1986–1989. They suffer from the difficulties of translation and the faulty memories of some of the interviewers, as well as the fact that virtually all the interviewees had been "rectified" not once but many times and had suffered lengthy prison sentences or long periods at the May Seventh Cadre Schools during the Cultural Revolution. Yet there are certain continuities between the earlier interviews and ours, despite the passage of years and the vicissitudes of fortune.

9. Mao himself put it very well in a comment he made in 1939 to Edgar Snow: "We are always social revolutionaries; we are never reformists. There are two main objectives in the thesis of the Chinese revolution. The first consists of the realization of the tasks of a national democratic revolution. The other is social revolution. The latter must be achieved, and completely . . . The present 'becoming' of the social revolutionary part in the thesis of the Chinese revolution will turn into its 'being' . . ." See *Red Star over China* (New York: Vintage Books, 1947), p. 508 (original italics omitted).

10. The stories themselves came fluently and without hesitation. Moreover, people had been made to think over their own stories in the light of collective ones many times. Hence their individual stories embody the collective ones, are part of them, and reflect the original conveyance that made for intersubjectivity.

11. How these interviews were conducted has been described in the introduction. Anonymity was promised and is maintained here except where the information was clearly not likely to result in difficulties. Most took place in Beijing, but a good number were in historic places of the revolution—Changsha, Nanchang, Shanghai, Xi'an, Yan'an itself. Sometimes we were given help by members of provincial academies of social sciences, museum directors, and others who had background knowledge of the events that had occurred in their areas. The route of march for these interviews was determined by the short and intermediate stories; we followed events and places back to the founding of the CCP. Each stopping point represented for the interviewees what might be called the Chinese revolutionary equivalent of a Station of the Cross, the entire journey a genuine Via Dolorosa.

12. For example, Kangda, the Anti-Japanese, or Resist Japan, University "graduated" some seventy-thousand students, according to the testimony of a former vice president of the standing committee of the All China Journalists Association.

13. Interview with widow of Lao She, June 1988, Beijing.

14. For example, the *New China Daily* was put out by about twenty-two people, only one of whom had any experience (he had been a journalist in Shanghai and turned out to be a GMD agent).

15. As Wang Kun put it, everyone loved the dramas and became totally engaged by the performances. But for that to happen everything—dress, speech, gestures—had to be exactly correct, true to life, or the magic would disappear and the audience would become preoccupied with errors rather than the flow of the narrative. (Interview with Wang Kun, Beijing, May 1986). Wang Kun is today a distinguished director of a folkloric ballet school. She went to Yan'an at a very young age and became the first "white haired girl" in the Yan'an opera of that name (the first modern Chinese opera, according to some).

16. This was also the rationale given for the unequal food rations. Those who had to "work long hours and make major decisions" received better food; the Central Committee members received a cup of milk a day. Rittenberg and Bennet, *The Man Who Stayed Behind,* p. 86.

17. As an example, our informant recounted a famous case. It concerned a Long March veteran named Wang, an extremely well-known and highly regarded commander who had accomplished great feats of daring and was an outstanding commander of troops. While teaching at Kangda Wang fell in love with a young girl who refused his attentions. One day he chased after her, then took out his pistol and killed her. He was arrested, but there was great debate over what his punishment ought to be. Many thought that Wang was too important to be shot but that he should be sent back to the battlefield. The head of the court wrote to Mao for instructions. Mao replied that because this veteran was a revolutionary, such a serious crime blackened the reputation of the party. Therefore he should be sentenced to death. The rules should be stricter for people like Wang than for ordinary people, said Mao. Capital punishment was the right sentence. Mao asked that his opinion be read in court and made known to the cadres. This was done, and Wang was shot.

18. This person was interviewed on four different occasions. In the later interviews, it became quite clear that prerectification Yan'an was "his" Yan'an. Everything changed after that. During rectification he tried his best to exorcise doubts, but he was unable to do so completely.

19. Eighth Route Army soldiers could pass because of the united front, which had recently been reconsolidated.

20. There are many different estimates of how many people were killed during Kang Sheng's Rescue Campaign. In Xi'an at the provincial Academy of Social Sciences we were told that "only three" were killed, although more committed suicide. A high-ranking party official, Gong Yuzhi, estimated about one hundred. The campaign was most intense in Yan'an and was carried out very lackadaisically elsewhere. It lasted only for a few months (estimates range from three weeks to eleven months).

21. In Boyd Compton, *Mao's China: Party Reform Documents, 1942–44* (Seattle: University of Washington Press, 1952), pp. 9–32.

22. For this reason, Mao said that those who came to Yan'an with letters of introduction were welcome, but that those who came without such letters were also welcome, because the very act of walking to Yan'an with a bedroll on one's back constituted a letter of introduction.

23. For the Hunan investigations see M. Henri Day, *Mao Zedong, 1919–1927: Documents* (Stockholm: Skrifter utgivna av Föreningen för Orientaliska Studier no. 14, 1975), for the essay see *Selected Works of Mao Tse-tung* (Beijing: Foreign Languages Press, 1965), vol. 1, pp. 117–128.

24. During the Long March this person became the expert on local herbs and grasses, on which they had to survive when they crossed the snowy mountains, the grasslands, and the savannah.

25. The twenty-two documents formed the core of study during Rectification. The two books were *Liuda Yiqian* (Before the Sixth Party Congress) and *Liuda Yihou* (After the Sixth Party Congress). These were edited by the Secretariat with Mao having final authority and were used for the study of party history.

26. When asked about Mao's personal life his responses became very guarded. "I worked very closely with Chairman Mao. He was very kind and treated everyone, from generals such as Zhu De to ordinary soldiers, the same. No differences were shown to county or prefecture or local cadres. He was an easygoing person who did not concern himself with small matters. He had big intelligence, not small intelligence. He did not lose his temper. Nor did he show elation or depression. If we lost a battle he might be depressed in his heart, but I could not see that. When we won a battle he did not rejoice. He would hold up an oil lamp and go over the maps pinned on the wall, go over a route or battle lines—win or lose. In cooking for him he mainly ate rice. He particularly liked green chili peppers and pepper powders. He smoked a lot of cigarettes and drank alcohol, but never to excess."

27. Many observers commented on the sexual puritanism prevailing among rank-and-file communists (but from which the highest ranks were exempt). Agnes Smedley, who was particularly interested in the relationship between revolution and sexual liberation, described sexual mores as follows: "One day a visiting cameraman asked me: 'Does the Red Army provide the soldiers with *French letters* to protect them from venereal disease?' It was a question which showed the deep gulf existing between these Red Army men and the men from America. The Red Army was so poor that it lacked money even for the essentials of existence; it had never heard of *French letters*. All Chinese women are married at an early age; a sex life for soldiers would have automatically meant the violation of married women. Violation of women was a criminal offence in the Army, and prostitution was forbidden. When I explained this to the cameraman he looked at me with an expression of horror." See Agnes Smedley, *China Correspondent* (London: Pandora Press, 1984), p. 130.

28. According to a study of Kang Sheng that was never released publicly (it is said that Deng Yingchao objected to it), of 200 students at the Military Communications School, 170 were arrested as "agents." Neither was the Yan'an Guard free from trouble. Some 80 to 90 percent were arrested as GMD agents. Zhong Kan, *Kang Sheng pingzhuan* (A Critical Biography of Kang Sheng) (Beijing: Hongqi chubanshe, 1982), p. 90.

29. See the photographic section in *Red Star over China* between pp. 312 and 313. The interviewee is one of the three in the front row of the third from last photograph.

30. One senior party official who was arrested during the rescue campaign saw it as entirely justifiable. He accepted that there were many spies in Yan'an and that one had to be careful. His own arrest and subsequent release he regarded as evidence of the fact that "the system worked," as he was indeed innocent.

31. Some former ranking officers of the Fourth Front Army remained bitter about Mao's treatment of Zhang Guotao. A good deal of this came out not in interviews with them, but with their widows.

32. In Yan'an there was approximately one woman for every eighteen men.

33. He brought with him his four-by-five plate camera and a large box of Agfa film, which he used very sparingly until it ran out. He also had an Ikoflex and a plentiful supply of 120 film "replenished by the enemy," and a thirty-five-millimeter camera.

34. For this interview we had to be smuggled into the main army base outside Beijing.

35. Epstein went to Yan'an in 1944.

36. See Albert Hirschman's *Exit, Voice, and Loyalty: Responses to Decline in Firms, Organizations, and States* (Cambridge, Mass.: Harvard University Press, 1970).

37. Yan'an was also redolent of the Taipings, the Red Army recapitulating the wanderings of the Taipings, whose revolution was regarded as a prototypical peasant response to imperialism, one that led to the downfall of the Qing Dynasty in the Revolution of 1911. There were other parallels as well. The Taipings were the first to sinify imported western beliefs, a version of Christianity revealed through the agency of the founder. Biblical texts were provided, laying out duties and responsibilities. Signs, insignia, words on paper all became iconographic and emblematic for a social text, a semiotic discourse in which magical interventions occurred. The Taipings also sought to create a political system normatively, structurally, and behaviorally, but no such general configuration prevailed. The antihistory represented by the Taipings was retrieved as part of the cultural mobilization within Yan'an. The point is not to fail again, a theme reiterated in drama, music, poetry, dance, opera. In the process there was created in Yan'an, as with the Taipings, a discourse of signs, insignia, stories, myths, and texts whose interior discourse could be made available to anyone who made the effort to learn it and demonstrate that learning by appropriate behavior and conduct. What Mao Zedong and his lieutenants did was literally to choreograph selected events. By doing so they collectivized individual experiences. In the process individuals conveyed their stories to the collective and by enriching it, provided it with symbolic capital. This was the significance of Yan'an, as compared with other border regions.

38. See Andrew Watson, *Mao Zedong and the Political Economy of the Border Region: A Translation of Mao's Economic and Financial Problems* (Cambridge: Cambridge University Press, 1980).

39. Ibid., p. 197.

40. Here too there is a good deal that is reminiscent of the Taipings, whose texts and writings dealt literally with both the sublime and the concrete aspects of an agrarian utopianism. For example, their land law specified that "the distribution of land is made according to the size of the family, irrespective of sex, with only the number of persons

taken into account. The larger the number, the more land they shall receive; the smaller the number the less land they shall receive. The lands assigned are of various grades of the nine categories. If there are six persons in the family, three shall receive good land, and three shall receive bad land: half good and half bad. All lands under Heaven shall be farmed jointly by the people under Heaven. If the production of food is too small in one place, then move to another where it is more abundant. All lands under Heaven shall be accessible in time of abundance or famine. If there is famine in one area, move the surplus from an area where there is abundance to that area, in order to feed the starving. In this way the people under Heaven shall all enjoy the great happiness given by the Heavenly Father, Supreme Lord and August God. Land shall be farmed by all; rice, eaten by all; clothes, worn by all; money, spent by all. There shall be no inequality, and no person shall be without food or fuel." Taken from a Taiping tract, "The Land Law of the Heavenly Dynasty" (1853) and printed in Jean Chesneaux, Marianne Bastid, and Marie-Claire Bergere, *China from the Opium Wars to the 1911 Revolution* (New York: Pantheon Books, 1976, pp. 123–124.

41. Watson, *Mao Zedong and the Political Economy of the Border Region,* p. 198.

42. Ibid., p. 198.

43. But as far as we can tell from these interviews, there are no direct links between the two periods. The parallel causes that Mao was at pains to emphasize gave Yan'an greater authenticity, a mythic pedigree to match the Marxist one. But it did not seem to matter much to his listeners.

44. See Lowell Dittmer, *Liu Shao-ch'i and the Chinese Cultural Revolution* (Berkeley: University of California Press, 1974), p. 181. This book contrasts the two personalities of Mao and Liu (the latter more technocratic and the former more cosmocratic) and the carefully orchestrated demise of Liu, who is kept in power as a foil to Mao in the Cultural Revolution.

45. It is of interest that after Mao was forced out of Yan'an by the GMD in 1947 he never expressed the slightest interest in going back, even for a short visit. Today Yan'an has become the pilgrimage site of the Chinese revolution. During the Cultural Revolution, vast numbers of Red Guards reenacted the Long March by making their way to Yan'an on foot. After that, Yan'an became a sort of museum, rarely visited until after the events of Tiananmen Square in June 1989, when the government began sending people to Yan'an in order to "promote the Yan'an spirit." They study party history, visit Mao's former residences and caves, and talk with survivors of the period. When asked what she thought of her four-day visit, one young woman replied, "I thought it was very dirty and poor." See Arthur Higbee, *International Herald Tribune,* April 24, 1992.

6. The Terrain on the Ground

1. Mark Selden, *The Yenan Way in Revolutionary China* (Cambridge, Mass.: Harvard University Press, 1971), p. ix.

2. Thomas C. Kuo, *Ch'en Tu-Hsiu (1879–1942) and the Chinese Communist Movement* (South Orange, N.J.: Seton Hall University Press, 1974), p. 13.

3. Shum Kui-Kwong, *The Chinese Communists' Road to Power: The Anti-Japanese*

National United Front, 1935–45 (Oxford: Oxford University Press, 1988), pp. 1–16. See also Chalmers Johnson, *Peasant Nationalism and Communist Power: The Emergence of Revolutionary China, 1937–1945* (Stanford: Stanford University Press, 1962), Donald G. Gillin, "'Peasant Nationalism' in the History of Chinese Communism," in *Journal of Asian Studies* 33 (February 1964), and Selden, *The Yenan Way.*

4. Shum, *The Chinese Communists' Road to Power,* p. 5.

5. Lucien Bianco, "Peasant Responses to CCP Mobilization Policies," in Tony Saich and Hans J. van de Ven, eds., *New Perspectives on the Chinese Communist Revolution* (Armonk, N.Y.: M. E. Sharpe, 1994).

6. A guide will tell you with a sly grin that Mao's air raid shelter was different from the others: Mao's had a secret passage leading to Jiang Qing's cave.

7. Nym Wales, *Inside Red China* (New York: Doubleday, Doran and Company, 1939), p. 75.

8. He Jingzhi was installed as Acting Minister of Culture after the suppression of the protest demonstrations in 1989, only to be removed in 1993 once a more tolerant atmosphere toward the arts was once again proposed.

9. This did not, however, endear it to all its Chinese visitors. Li Ang described Yan'an as "a purely medieval, disagreeable small town" where "Mao Zedong established his Platonic Kingdom. This was not accidental . . . Mao Zedong's backward mind could only find nourishment in this backward, earthen town." Li Ang, *Hongse wutai* (Red Stage) (Chongqing: Minzhong shudian, 1942), p. 139, quoted in John Byron and Robert Pack, *The Claws of the Dragon. Kang Sheng—The Evil Genius behind Mao—And His Legacy of Terror in People's China* (New York: Simon and Schuster, 1992), p. 138.

10. That many lived in caves sounds worse than it was. The caves were cool in winter, easily built, and not difficult to clean. In addition they afforded natural protection from Japanese air raids. While senior leaders could enjoy their own, often spacious caves, the rank and file would live eight to a cave with bunk beds and spartan conditions.

11. Quoted in Selden, *The Yenan Way,* p. 2.

12. Erich Teichman, *Travels of a Consular Officer in North-West China* (Cambridge: Cambridge University Press, 1921), pp. 62–63. A standard account, Teichman is also quoted in Selden and Watson.

13. For example, the extension of the Longhai railroad only reached Xi'an in 1935.

14. Andrew Watson, *Mao Zedong and the Political Economy of the Border Region: A Translation of Mao's Economic and Financial Problems* (Cambridge: Cambridge University Press, 1980), p. 4. The rural economy was characterized by extreme fluctuations. On top of the unpredictability of weather conditions there were other burdens, including the "requisitioning" of foodstuffs by various warlord armies, and roving groups of bandits.

15. See He Hanwei, *Guangxu chunian (1876–1879) Huabei de da hanzai* (The Early Years of Guangxu (1876–1879). The Great Disaster of North China) (Hong Kong: Chinese University of Hong Kong Press, n.d.), p. 124.

16. For a study of this region see Eduard B. Vermeer, *Economic Development in Provincial China: the Central Shaanxi since 1930* (Cambridge: Cambridge University Press, 1988).

17. Previous major droughts had afflicted the area in 1878–1880 and 1898–1900. In the 1927 famine, the harvest was well below normal expectations, and the 1928 harvest

effectively collapsed. The major cause of the famine was drought worsened by bandits and warlord armies operating in the area who took away most of the peasants' grain reserves. Similarly, much of the livestock had been requisitioned for transport, thus making it difficult for food to be brought in from the outside.

18. It is difficult to say just how many died in the famine. Edgar Snow, citing American Red Cross investigators, attributed much of the cause of the famine to the fact that poppy cultivation had been forced on the peasantry, thus aggravating already serious shortages of staple foods. He cites figures of three to five million dead. Snow was shocked by the sight of the dying children. "Corpses frequently disappeared before they could be interred and human flesh was openly sold in some villages." See *Red Star over China* (New York: Vintage Books, 1947), pp. 38 and 39. The economic historian Vermeer has estimated that in Guanzhong alone the population was reduced by some two to three million people. Vermeer, *Economic Development in Provincial China,* pp 28–46.

19. For an interesting account of how such factors shaped the land revolution in the two adjacent subregions of Suide and Yanshu during the CCP's occupation see Pauline Keating, "Two Revolutions: Village Reconstruction and Cooperativization in North Shaanxi, 1934–1945" (Ph.D. diss., Australian National University, 1989).

20. Much interesting information is contained in Hsü Yung-ying, *A Survey of Shensi-Kansu-Ninghsia Border Region* (New York: Institute of Pacific Relations, 1945), 2 vols.

21. Many of these observations are based on Keating, "Two Revolutions."

22. Ibid., pp. 67–68 and 65–66.

23. For an account of rural tax revolts in the subregion before the establishment of the communists see Selden, *The Yenan Way,* pp. 25–26.

24. Keating, "Two Revolutions" p. 72.

25. Wales notes black plague, smallpox, typhoid, and typhus epidemics, while remarking that dysentery and minor diseases were a "sort of habit." Wales, *Inside Red China,* p. 85.

26. See Selden, *The Yenan Way,* pp. 16–17, and Watson, *Mao Zedong and the Political Economy of the Border Region,* p. 6.

27. Wales, *Inside Red China,* p. 85.

28. Reading Mao's major writings during this period, especially on political and economic matters, one is stuck by his capacity for bricolage. See Watson, *Mao Zedong and the Political Economy of the Border Region.*

29. Indeed, it was the combined attacks of the Japanese and the GMD that made Yan'an possible as a simulacrum, the latter by pursuing a blockade rather than prosecuting the war against the external enemy, the former by its ruthlessness. Leys says that Mao Zedong regarded the Japanese invasion with "lucid cynicism" as the key to success. He quotes Mao as saying to an apologetic visiting delegation from the Japan Socialist Party "that they did not need to feel sorry. If the Japanese imperial army had not occupied half of China's territory, the Chinese people would not have united in their struggle and our People's Republic would not have come into existence." See Simon Leys, *Broken Images* (London: Allison and Busby, 1979), p. 54.

30. Edgar Snow saw the communists as similar to the heroic characters in Chinese bandit stories, remarkable for the way they quickly formed a crude, egalitarian working

community in the sanctuary of the Border Region. Snow and others played with the term "red bandits" to emphasize the Robin Hood quality and the moral side of the enterprise.

31. On this see Shum, *The Chinese Communists' Road to Power*, pp. 18–27.

32. Shum suggests that this policy owed its origins to Wang Ming's ideas. Ibid., p. 19. See "Zhongyang gei Manzhou geji dangbu ji quanti dangyuan de xin. Lun Manzhou de zhuangkuang he women dang de renwu" (Letter from the Party Center to Party Organizations at All Levels and All Party Members in Manchuria. On the Situation in Manchuria and Our Party's Tasks), January 28, 1933, in *Douzheng* (Struggle) 18 (June 15, 1933): 1–5; 19 (July 25, 1933): 14–16; and 20 (August 5, 1933): 14–16.

33. "Wei kangRi jiuguo gao quanti tongbao shu" was published in the Paris-based journal *Jiuguo bao* (National Salvation News) and was published in English translation in *Inprecor* 15 (November 30, 1935): 1595–1597. Because the announcement had been submitted to and approved by Dimitrov and Stalin at the Comintern Congress in August, it is commonly referred to as the August First Declaration. According to Wang Ming, he drafted the declaration while convalescing from an illness in June 1935. Wang Ming, *Mao's Betrayal* (Moscow: Progress Publishers, 1979), p. 68.

34. This probably consisted of several formal and informal sessions beginning on December 17. Research Department on Party History of the CCP, *Zhonggong dangshi dashi nianbiao* (Annual Chronology of Major Events in CCP History) (Beijing: Renmin chubanshe, 1987), p. 109. Attending the meeting were Mao Zedong, Zhang Wentian, Zhou Enlai, Bo Gu, Liu Shaoqi, Kai Feng, Deng Fa, Li Weihan, Yang Shangkun, Guo Hongtao, and Zhang Hao (Lin Yuying). Benjamin Yang, *From Revolution to Politics. Chinese Communists on the Long March* (Boulder: Westview Press, 1990), pp. 182–183.

35. "Zhongyang guanyu junshi zhanlüe wenti de jueyi" (Resolution of the Central Committee on Strategic Military Issues), December 23, 1935, in The Secretariat of the CCP Central Committee, ed., *Liuda yilai: Dangnei mimi wenjian* (Since the Sixth Party Congress. Secret Internal Party Documents) (Beijing: Renmin chubanshe, 1952), vol. 2, pp. 286–289. The Central Committee had already sent out a circular on developing guerrilla warfare in the Shaanxi-Gansu area on November 21, 1935. "Zhongyang guanyu fazhan Shaan Gan youji zhanzheng de jueding" (Central Committee Decision on Developing Guerilla Warfare in Shaanxi and Gansu), November 21, 1935, The Central Party Archives, ed., *Zhonggong zhongyang wenjian xuanji* (Selected Documents of the CCP Central Committee) (Beijing: Zhonggong zhongyang dangxiao chubanshe, 1982–1991), vol. 9, pp. 585–586.

36. This was adopted on December 25, 1935 and was drafted by Zhang Wentian. "Zhongyang guanyu muqian zhengzhi xingshi yu dang de renwu jueyi" (Resolution of the Central Committee on the Current Political Situation and the Party's Tasks), December 25, 1935, in The Secretariat of the CCP Central Committee, ed., *Liuda yilai*, vol. 1, pp. 734–735.

37. The shift in policy on rich peasants had been decided at a Politburo meeting on December 6, 1935, when participants passed a resolution drafted by Zhang Wentian. "Zhongyang guanyu gaibian dui funong celüe de jueding" (Central Committee Decision on Revising Policy Towards Rich Peasants), December 6, 1935, in ibid., pp. 729–731.

38. "Zhongyang guanyu dongbeijun gongzuode zhidao yuanze" (The Party's Guiding Principles for Dealing with the Northeast Army), in The Central Party Archives, ed., *Zhonggong zhongyang wenjian xuanji neibu ben,* vol. 10, pp. 33–42.

39. "Tingzhan yihe yizhi kangRi tongdian" (Circular Telegram on Cessation of the War and Unity to Resist Japan), May 5, 1936, signed by Mao Zedong and Zhu De, in The Secretariat of the CCP Central Committee, ed., *Liuda yilai,* vol. 1, p. 762; and "Zhonggong zhongyang zhi Guomindang erzhong quanhui shu" (Letter of the CCP Central Committee to the Second Plenum of the GMD), June 20, 1936, in The Central Party Archives, ed., *Zhonggong zhongyang wenjian xuanji,* vol. 10, pp. 43–46.

40. "Zhongguo gongchandang zhi Zhongguo Guomindang shu" (Letter from the CCP to the Chinese GMD), August 25, 1936, in The Secretariat of the CCP Central Committee, ed., *Liuda yilai,* vol. 1, pp. 773–777.

41. "Zhongyang guanyu kangRi jiuwang yundong de xin xingshi yu minzhu gongheguo de jueyi" (Central Committee Resolution Concerning the New Situation of Resistance to Japan and the National Salvation Movement and the Democratic Republic), September 17, 1936, in ibid., pp. 779–782. The resolution was drafted by Zhang Wentian.

42. Selden, *The Yenan Way,* pp. 105–106.

43. The general secretariat had five members: Zhang Wentian, Mao Zedong, Zhou Enlai, Wang Jiaxiang, and Bo Gu. Wang Jianying, *Zhongguo gongchandang zuzhishi ziliao huibian* (Collection of Materials on the Organizational History of the CCP) (Beijing: Hongqi chubanshe, 1981), pp. 242–243.

44. In September 1937, the GMD agreed to recognition of an area covering twenty-six counties: Yan'an, Yanchuan, Yanchang, Suide, Mizhi, Jiaxian, Qingjian, Wubao, Shenmu, Fugu, Anding, Ansai, Jingbian, Dingbian, Bao'an, Ganquan, Fuxian, Chunhua, Zhengning, Ningxian, Qingyang, Heshui, Zhenyuan, Huaixian, Xunyi, and Yanchi.

45. From Chen Duxiu onwards, much of the internal legitimacy of the CCP and its struggle derived from criticism of the warlords.

46. Selden, *The Yenan Way,* p. 82.

47. The figures for Yanjiachuan are from July 1941; those for Yihe are from February 1942. Chai Shufan, Yu Guangyuan and Peng Ping, *Suide Mizhi tudi wenti chubu yanjiu* (Preliminary Research Into the land Question in Suide and Mizhi) (Beijing: Renmin chubanshe, 1979, originally published 1942), pp. 34–35.

48. Keating, "Two Revolutions," p. 122.

49. The best history of the communist movement in the region before 1935 remains Mark Selden, "The Guerrilla Movement in Northwest China: The Origins of the Shensi-Kansu-Ninghsia Border Region," *The China Quarterly* 28 (October–November 1966): 63–81, and *The China Quarterly* 29 (January–March 1967): 61–81, and Selden, *The Yenan Way,* Chapter 2. For an important official history of the earlier period that links the region's history to the emerging Maoist account of party history see Gao Gang, "Bianqu dang de lishi wenti jiantao" (A Brief Discussion of Historical Questions concerning the Border Region) (Yan'an: Xibeiju, 1942).

50. Selden, *The Yenan Way,* pp. 47–48.

51. See Ren Zhonghe, "Shaan-Gan-Ning bianqu xingzheng quhua yanbian gaishu" (A

General Review of the Evolution of the Administrative Divisions of the Shaan-Gan-Ning Border Region), in *Lishi dang'an* (Historical Archives) 3, no. 31 (1988): 116.

52. The council and administrative system of the Border Region was set out in an outline of May 12, 1937, published in *Zhonghuabao* (New China), May 23, 1937.

53. The two-year election period applied to both the chair of the Border Region Council and the head of the Border Region Court.

54. In 1937 there had also been a Peasant and Workers Department.

55. Selden, *The Yenan Way*, p. 150.

56. Hua Dong, ed., *Shaan-Gan-Ning bianqu quanmao* (A Complete Picture of the Shaan-Gan-Ning Border Region) (Chongqing: n.p., 1940), pp. 17–18.

57. Selden, *The Yenan Way*, p. 172.

58. However, the boundaries of the Border Region continued to fluctuate, and it is difficult to find precise figures. For example, using a different source, Watson writes that in 1941 the 29 counties contained 266 districts with 1,549 townships. Watson, *Mao Zedong and the Political Economy of the Border Region*, p. 12. This was *KangRi shiqi jiefangqu gaikuang* (The General Condition of the Liberated Areas during the Anti-Japanese War) (Beijing: Renmin chubanshe, 1953), p. 7. The number of counties also varied. A report from the people's government from December 23, 1941, added Tongyiyao county in Guanzhong, thus making a total of 30. Yet in October 1942, the government office announced a total of 32. Zizhou was added to the Suide subregion, Wuqi to Sanbian, and Fuxi to Yanshu. Finally in 1943 Tongyiyao and Fuxi were again lost. See Fang Chengxiang and Huang Yaoan, eds., *Shaan-Gan-Ning bianqu gemingshi* (The Revolutionary History of the Shaan-Gan-Ning Border Region) (Xi'an: Shaanxi shifan daxue chubanshe, 1991), p. 611.

59. See, for example, Wang Jiaxiang, "Guanyu sanmin zhuyi yu gongchan zhuyi" (On the Three Principles of the People and Communism), September 25, 1939, in The Secretariat of the CCP Central Committee, ed., *Liuda yilai*, vol. 1, pp. 1061–1067.

60. "Gongchandangren fakanci" (Introduction to the Communist), originally published in *Gongchandangren* (The Communist), October 4, 1939, reprinted in Takeuchi Minoru, ed., *Mao Zedong ji* (Collected Writings of Mao Zedong) (Tokyo: Sōsōsha, 1983), vol. 7, pp. 69–83. "Xinminzhude zhengzhi yu xinminzhude wenhua" (New Democratic Politics and New Democratic Culture) in *Zhongguo wenhua* (Chinese Culture), no. 1, February 1940.

61. Stuart R. Schram, "Mao Tse-tung's Thought to 1949," in John King Fairbank and Albert Feuerwerker, eds., *The Cambridge History of China*, vol. 13, *Republican China 1912–1949, Part 2* (Cambridge: Cambridge University Press, 1986), p. 857.

62. Ibid.

63. As Lyman van Slyke has pointed out, geography was far more important to a base area's success than its social and economic structure. Lyman van Slyke, "The Chinese Communist Movement during the Sino-Japanese War, 1937–1945," in Fairbank and Feuerwerker, ed., *Republican China 1912–1949, Part 2*, p. 652.

64. In January 1938, the Jin-Cha-Ji Border Region was formally established. It was the only base area apart from the Shaan-Gan-Ning to receive recognition from Chiang Kai-shek's government. For an analysis of the Jin-Cha-Ji see Kathleen Hartford, "Step by

Step: Reform, Resistance, and revolution in Chin-Ch'a-Chi Border Region, 1937–1945" (Ph.D. diss., Stanford University, 1980).

65. This idea is developed by Carl A. Dorris in "Peasant Mobilization in North China and the Origins of Yenan Communism," *The China Quarterly* 68 (December 1976): 697–719.

66. See Nie Rongzhen, *KangRi mofan genjudi—Jin Cha Ji bianqu* (A Model Anti-Japanese Base Area—The Jin-Cha-Ji Border Region) (N.p.: Balujun junzheng zazhishe, 1939).

67. "On the Question of Political Power in the Anti-Japanese Bases," March 6, 1940, in *Selected Works of Mao Tse-tung* (Beijing: Foreign Languages Press, 1965), vol. 2, pp. 417–419.

68. "Jin-Cha-Ji bianqu muqian shizheng gangling," in *Jin-Cha-Ji bianqu xingzheng weiyuanhui xianxing faming huiji* (Compilation of Laws in Effect of the Jin-Cha-Ji Border Region Committee) (N.p.: n.p., 1945), pp. 1–5.

69. Here a temporary subregion council was formed on this basis. Lin Boqu, "Shaan-Gan-Ning bianqu sansanzhi de jingyan jiqi yinggai jiuzheng de pianxiang" (The Experience of the Three-Thirds System in the Shaan-Gan-Ning Border Region and Some Erroneous Tendencies that Must Be Corrected), March 25, 1944, in *Zhonggong dangshi ziliao* (Materials on CCP History) 18: 16.

70. Hartford, "Step by Step." In fact, as was stated earlier, after 1937 the rural elite was more attracted to the CCP than was the local peasantry.

71. The opening of the council was presided over by Wang Zhen.

72. Fang and Huang, eds., *Shaan-Gan-Ning bianqu geming shi*, pp. 216–217.

73. Peng Zhen, *Guanyu Jin-Cha-Ji bianqu dangde gongzuo he juti zhengce baogao* (Report on Party Work and Specific Policies in the Jin-Cha-Ji Border Region) (Beijing: Zhonggong zhongyang dangxiao chubanshe, 1981). The report was delivered to the Politburo in September 1941.

74. On this point see Pitman Potter, "Peng Zhen: Evolving Views on Party Organization and Law," in Carol Lee Hamrin and Timothy Cheek, eds., *China's Establishment Intellectuals* (Armonk, N.Y.: M. E. Sharpe, 1986), pp. 27–28.

75. Lin Boqu, "Bianqu sansanzhi de jingyan jiqi yinggai jiuzheng de pianxiang." See Lyman van Slyke, *Enemies and Friends: The United Front in Chinese Communist History* (Stanford: Stanford University Press, 1967), p. 148 for a complete breakdown of the statistics.

76. Fang and Huang, eds., *Shaan-Gan-Ning bianqu gemingshi*, p. 219.

77. Ibid., pp. 219–220.

78. Lin Boqu, "Shaan-Gan-Ning bianqu zhengfu dui bianqu diyijie canyihui de gongzuo baogao" (Work Report of the Shaan-Gan-Ning Border Region Government to the First Council of the Border Region), in Number Three Department of the History Institute of the Chinese Academy of Sciences, ed., *Shaan-Gan-Ning bianqu canyi wenxian wenji* (Selected Materials from the Council of the Shaan-Gan-Ning Border Region) (Beijing: Kexue chubanshe, 1958), pp. 17–18.

79. "Experience and Lesson of the Second Council of the Shaan-Gan-Ning Border Region," January 8, 1942. Fang and Huang, eds., *Shaan-Gan-Ning bianqu gemingshi*, p. 222.

Hsü Yung-ying notes a total number of delegates as 216, *A Survey of the Shensi-Kansu-Ninghsia Border Region*, vol. 1, p. 77.

80. Fang and Huang, eds., *Shaan-Gan-Ning bianqu gemingshi*, p. 224.

81. "Wei chongshi 'sansanzhi' gei gexian de zhishi xin" (A Directive to All Counties in Order to Enrich the "Three-Thirds System").

82. Fang and Huang, eds., *Shaan-Gan-Ning bianqu gemingshi*, p. 225.

83. Ibid., pp. 225–226.

84. This campaign was launched on August 20, 1940, by the Eighth Route Army and was its longest and largest offensive of the anti-Japanese war, lasting until December 5.

85. See Watson, *Mao Zedong and the Political Economy of the Border Region*, p. 17.

86. See Peter Schran, *Guerilla Economy: The Development of the Shensi-Kansu-Ninghsia Border Region, 1937–1945* (New York: State University of New York, 1976), Chapter 7. In 1942, millet prices increased fourteen times over 1941 levels. Selden, *The Yenan Way*, p. 180. In 1941, the commodities index had risen four times in Yan'an; in 1942 it rose fourteen times. The Editorial and Writing Group of the Finance and Economics Departments of the Shaan-Gan-Ning Border Region and the Shaanxi Provincial Archives, ed., *KangRi zhanzheng shiqi Shaan-Gan-Ning bianqu caizheng jingji shiliao zhaibian* (Selected Historical Documents on the Finance and Economics of the Shaan-Gan-Ning Border Region During the Anti-Japanese War) (Shaanxi: Renmin chubanshe, 1981), vol. 5, p. 124.

87. Ibid., vol. 6, pp. 40–41 and 44–45.

88. On the tax measures see Selden, *The Yenan Way*, pp. 181–187.

89. The Finance and Economics Departments of the Shaan-Gan-Ning Border Region and the Shaanxi Provincial Archives, ed., *KangRi zhanzheng shiqi*, vol. 6, pp. 18–19, cited in Chen Yung-fa, "The Blooming Poppy under the Red Sun: The Yan'an Way and the Opium Trade," in Saich and van de Ven, eds., *New Perspectives on the Chinese Communist Revolution*.

90. Chen, "The Blooming Poppy under the Red Sun."

91. For a valuable collection of materials on this campaign see The Editorial Group on the Construction of Political Power in the Shaan-Gan-Ning Border Region, ed., *Shaan-Gan-Ning bianqu de jingbing jianzheng: ziliao xuanji* (Crack Troops and Simple Administration in the Shaan-Gan-Ning Border Region: Selected Materials) (Shandong: Qiushi chubanshe, 1982). The original goal called for a reduction of expenditures of 20 percent. "Bianqu zhengbian weiyuanhui niding bianzheng jihua, suojian tuoli shengchan gongzuo renyuan, jiaqiang qu xiang xiaceng xingzheng jigou" (The Complete Draft Plan of the Border Region Rectification Committee to Reduce Work Personnel Who are Divorced From Production, Strengthen District and Township Lower Level Administrative Organs), *Jiefang ribao*, December 13, 1941, p. 4.

92. "Shaan-Gan-Ning bianqu zhengfu wei shixing jingbing jianzheng gei ge xian de zhishixin" (Directive to All Counties from the Shaan-Gan-Ning Border Region Government on Implementing Crack Troops and Simple Administration) in The Editorial Group on the Construction of Political Power in the Shaan-Gan-Ning Border Region, ed., *Shaan-Gan-Ning bianqu de jingbing jianzheng*, pp. 13–16.

93. See, for example, Mao Zedong, "A Most Important Policy," September 7, 1942, in *Selected Works,* vol. 3, pp. 99–102.

94. "Shaan-Gan-Ning bianqu zhengfu jianzheng zongjie (jielu)" (Summary of Simplifying Adminstration in the Shaan-Gan-Ning Border Region Government [Abstract]), January 7, 1944, in The Editorial group on the Construction of Political Power in the Shaan-Gan-Ning Border Region, ed., *Shaan-Gan-Ning bianqu de jingbing jianzheng,* pp. 154–167. This report to the fourth assembly of the Border Region was originally published in *Jiefang ribao,* February 8, 1944, p. 3. It is important to note that Li, who was very active in the campaign throughout, was a Vice Chairman of the Border Region government and a non-CCP member.

95. These organs included communication stations, sanitary offices, clinics, the Border Region hospital, the medical school, the first and second sanatoriums, the foster care committee, hotels, the food bureau, the tax bureau, the salt bureau, the police school, and the security bureau.

96. Lin Boqu, *Jianzheng wenti* (Problems in the Rectification of Government), p. 13, quoted in Selden, *The Yenan Way,* pp. 215–216.

97. "Zhongyang guanyu kangRi genjudi tudi zhengce de jueding" (Decision of the Central Committee on Land Policy in the Anti-Japanese Base Areas), January 28, 1942, in The Secretariat of the CCP Central Committee, *Kangzhan yilai zhongyao wenjian huiji* (A Collection of Documents Since [the Outbreak of] the Anti-Japanese War) (Yan'an: n.p., 1942), pp. 188–192.

98. The report and associated reference materials were originally delivered to the senior cadres conference held in Yan'an from October 19, 1942, to January 14, 1943. Watson, *Mao Zedong and the Political Economy of the Border Region,* p. 1.

99. Chen, "The Blooming Poppy under the Red Sun." We asked a number of party historians whether there was any truth to the stories that Wang Zhen had been involved in opium production to save the revolution. Most were surprised that we needed to ask the question, as it was to them an "open secret."

100. The first source is The Finance and Economics Departments of the Shaan-Gan-Ning Border Region and the Shaanxi Provincial Archives, eds., vol. 4, p. 68, the second is ibid., vol. 4, p. 50.

7. Yan'an as a Revolutionary Simulacrum

1. See Pierre Bourdieu, *Outline of a Theory of Practice* (Cambridge: Cambridge University Press, 1977).

2. For example Helen Snow, in a written communication to one of the authors, called the Yan'an "mystique" the "'pure and noble' time of the human potential for 'spiritual' power and influence, meaning above and beyond any 'material' factor. Usually only a new religion can create such a mystique and it is true that the socialist revolutionary was a form of religion for the Chinese, the first progressive experience of this type."

3. Vivian Shue, *The Reach of the State: Sketches of the Chinese Body Politic* (Stanford: Stanford University Press, 1988).

4. See especially the discussion of orientational metaphors in George Lakoff and Mark Johnson, *Metaphors We Live By* (Chicago: The University of Chicago Press, 1980), pp. 14–21.

5. Mao called for the party to be made a smelting furnace of communism. See Raymond Wylie, *The Emergence of Maoism: Mao Tse-tung, Ch'en Po-ta, and the Search for Chinese Theory 1935–1945* (Stanford: Stanford University Press, 1980), p. 44.

6. Ibid., pp 59–60.

7. Interviews in Beijing 1986, 1988, and 1989.

8. Among the most important associates of Mao in these endeavors were Zhou Enlai, Liu Shaoqi, Ren Bishi, and Wang Jiaxiang, the latter "inventing" the term "Mao Zedong Thought." According to an interview with Wang Jiaxiang's widow, Mao was suffering from a fit of depression and had taken himself to the hospital at the same moment Wang was recovering from a minor ailment. As they sat next to one another, Wang suggested that Mao's ideas be called "Mao Zedong Thought." According to her, Mao demurred, but later accepted the term. See also Shum Kui-kwong, *The Chinese Communists' Road to Power: The Anti-Japanese National United Front (1935–1945)* (Oxford: Oxford University Press, 1988), p. 221.

9. Jane L. Price, *Cadres, Commanders, and Commissars. The Training of the Chinese Communist Leadership, 1920–45* (Boulder, Colorado: Westview Press, 1976), Chapter 8.

10. Ibid., pp. 12–13. For a discussion of these societies and their links to the early CCP small groups see Hans J. van de Ven, *From Friend to Comrade: The Founding of the Chinese Communist Party, 1920–1927* (Berkeley: University of California Press, 1991).

11. Shanghi University was founded in 1922 with the blessing of the nationalists. For an interesting discussion see Yeh Wen-hsin, *The Alienated Academy: Culture and Politics in Republican China, 1919–1937* (Cambridge, Mass.: Harvard University Press, 1990).

12. Price, *Cadres, Commanders, and Commissars*, p. 112.

13. The first group of Chinese students went to Soviet Russia as early as spring 1921. This was a group of fourteen students from the Foreign Language School in Shanghai. Some one thousand (including those from the GMD) were trained in the twenties and thirties at the Communist University of the Working People of China. From 1925 to 1928, the university was called Sun Yat-sen University of Working People of China. For details, see M. F. Yuriev and A. V. Pantsov, "Comintern, CPSU (B) and Ideological and Organizational Evolution of the Communist Party of China," in R. Ulyanovsky, ed., *Revolutionary Democracy and Communists in the East* (Moscow: Progress Publishers, 1984), pp. 283–333. Yuriev and Pantsov estimate that of 118 top leaders in the CCP during the period before 1949, some 70 percent were trained in the Soviet Union.

14. Mao Zedong, "The May 4th Movement," in *Selected Works of Mao Tse-tung* (Beijing: Foreign Languages Press, 1965), vol. 2, p. 238.

15. Fang Chengxiang and Huang Yaoan, eds., *Shaan-Gan-Ning bianqu gemingshi* (The Revolutionary History of the Shaan-Gan-Ning Border Region) (Xi'an: Shaanxi shifan daxue chubanshe, 1991), p. 100.

16. Mark Selden, *The Yenan Way in Revolutionary China* (Cambridge, Mass.: Harvard University Press, 1971), pp. 20–21.

17. "Zhongyang tonggao nongzi—muqian nongmin yundong zong celüe" (Central Committee Circular Number Nine on the Peasantry—The General Strategy for the Peasant Movement at the Present Time), July 20, 1927, in The Committee for the Collection of Materials on CCP History and the Central Party Archives, ed., *Baqi huiyi* (The August 7 Conference) (Beijing: Zhonggong dangshi ziliao chubanshe, 1986), pp. 84–89, trans. in Tony Saich, *The Rise to Power of the Chinese Communist Party: Documents and Analysis, 1920–1949* (Armonk, N.Y.: M. E. Sharpe, 1994), Document C. 1.

18. Fang and Huang, eds., *Shaan-Gan-Ning bianqu gemingshi,* pp. 100–101.

19. Ibid., p. 103.

20. Ibid., p. 104.

21. Ibid.

22. At the end of 1942, according to Lin Boqu, middle school students totaled 3,300, excluding the military schools. As a part of the Simplified Adminstration program, Lin called for this number to be reduced. Lin Boqu, *Jianzheng wenti* (On The Question of Simplified Administration), p. 13, quoted in Selden, *The Yenan Way,* pp. 215–216.

23. Fang and Huang, eds., *Shaan-Gan-Ning bianqu gemingshi,* p. 102. Subjects in the junior curriculum were Chinese, foreign languages, math, general knowledge, and military training. The senior curriculum added an introduction to social sciences, Chinese and foreign history, Chinese and foreign geography, biology, physics, chemistry, and philosophy.

24. Ibid., pp. 102–103.

25. The most important of the workers' supplementary schools was that at Changxindian. The school was established for the two thousand railway workers stationed there. It had three teachers, all of whom were socialists. Interview with Luo Zhanglong, summer 1988. Luo was one of the founders of the Beijing party organization and an important figure in the communist-led labor movement throughout the twenties. See also "Beijing gongchanzhuyi xiaozu de baogao" (Report of the Beijing Communist Small Group), July 1921, in *Yida qianhou* (Around the Time of the First Party Congress) (Beijing: Renmin chubanshe, 1983), vol. 3, pp. 1–9, trans. in Saich, *The Rise to Power of the Chinese Communist Party,* Document A. 5. This was the report delivered by Zhang Guotao to the First Party Congress.

26. Fang and Huang, eds., *Shaan-Gan-Ning bianqu gemingshi,* p. 106.

27. Ibid., p. 110.

28. When it was initially set up in Yan'an, *Kangda* was situated in the Yan'an Normal School and the old county Yamen inside Yan'an itself.

29. Li Zhimin, "Kangda kangda yuekang yueda" (Kangda Kangda, The More the Resistance the Greater You Are), part one, in *Zhonggong dangshi ziliao* (Materials on CCP History) 7 (1983): pp. 28–29.

30. This was outlined in a letter dated April 26, 1936 from Mao Zedong to Lin Biao.

31. Li Zhimin, "Kangda kangda yuekang yueda," part one, p. 30.

32. In all, Kangda absorbed 609 educated youths of whom 427 graduated to join the CCP.

33. William Whitson, *The Chinese High Command: A History of Communist Military Politics, 1921–1971* (New York: Praeger, 1973), pp. 149, 152–154 (with Chen-hsia Huang).

34. Li Zhimin, "Kangda kangda yuekang yueda," part one, p. 36.

35. Ibid., p. 44.

36. Ibid., p.99.

37. Price, *Cadres, Commanders, and Commissars*, p. 140.

38. Ibid., p. 144.

39. Li Zhimin, "Kangda kangda yuekang yueda," part three, *Zhonggong dangshi ziliao* 11 (1984): 227.

40. Li Liangzhi, "Mao Zedong yu Shaanbei gongxue" (Mao Zedong and the Shaanbei Public School), *Dangshi ziliao zhengji tongxun* (Bulletin on Collected Materials on Party History) 9 (1986): 24.

41. Ibid.

42. Zeng Ruiyan, "Yan'an Zhongguo nuzi daxue shulüe" (An Outline of Yan'an Chinese Women's University), *Zhonggong dangshi ziliao* 23 (1987): 224.

43. Ibid., pp. 224–25 and Luo Lin, "Yan'an Zhongguo nuzi daxue jishi" (A Chronology of the Yan'an Chinese Women's University), *Dangshi yanjiu* (Research on Party History) 1 (1983): 76.

44. Zeng Ruiyan, "Yan'an Zhongguo nuzi daxue shulüe," p. 225 and Luo Lin, "Yan'an Zhongguo nuzi daxue jishi," p. 75.

45. Zeng Ruiyan, "Yan'an Zhongguo nuzi daxue shulüe," p. 226.

46. Luo Lin, "Yan'an Zhongguo nuzi daxue jishi," p. 77.

47. The Youth Cadre School had been set up in May 1940 with Chen Yun as principal.

48. Zhou Yang took over as Principal in April 1943.

49. There was also a Shaan-Gan-Ning Border Region Party School that was set up in Yan'an in July 1937 and was originally under the leadership of Zhu Xumin. In autumn 1942, it was renamed the Northwest Party School and came under the directorship of Xi Zhongxun. It trained lower level cadres for work within the Border Region party and governmental apparatus.

50. "Resolution of the Central Committee of the Chinese Communist Party on the Yenan Cadre School," December 17, 1941, in Boyd Compton, *Mao's China: Party Reform Documents, 1942–44* (Seattle: University of Washington Press, 1952), p. 75.

51. Warren Kuo, *Analytical History of the Chinese Communist Party* (Taibei: Institute for International Relations, 1968), book 4, p. 233.

52. Huang Huoqing, Li Yan, et al., "Huigu Yan'an zhongyang dangxiao de zhengfeng yundong" (A Look Back at the Rectification Movement in the Yan'an Central Party School), in *Yan'an zhongyang dangxiao de zhengfeng xuexi* (Rectification Study at the Yan'an Central Party School) (Beijing: Zhongyang dangxiao chubanshe, 1988), vol. 1, p. 24.

53. Nym Wales, "Historical Notes on China: My Yenan Notebooks," (unpublished manuscript), p. 104.

54. Price, *Cadres, Commanders, and Commissars*, p. 156.

55. Huang Huoqing, Li Yan, et al., "Huigu Yan'an zhongyang dangxiao de zhengfeng yundong," pp. 25–27.

56. The date was chosen to mark the 120th anniversary of Marx's birth.

57. Li Weihan, "Zhongyang yanjiuyuan de yanjiu gongzuo he zhengfeng yundong" (Research Work and the Rectification Campaign at the Central Research Institute), in Wen Jize, Li Yan. et al., eds., *Yan'an zhongyang yanjiuyuan huiyilu* (Memoirs of the Yan'an Central Research Institute) (Jinan: Jinan renmin chubanshe, 1984), p. 6.

58. "Resolution of the Central Committee of the Chinese Communist Party on the Yenan Cadre School," in Compton, *Mao's China,* p. 75.

59. The history department was divided into three groups: modern history, peasant affairs, and nationalities. The department's most important task was to edit and write a General History of China *(Zhongguo tongshi)* as proposed by Mao Zedong and the Central Committee. After volumes one and two had been produced, this work was stopped during rectification.

60. This department focused its research on the period since the May Fourth Movement and studied the various philosophical streams as well as the ideology of the GMD. During rectification this department, together with the politics department, edited the book *The Methodology of the Thought of Marx, Engels, Lenin, and Stalin (Ma En Lie Si sixiang fangfalun).* This became a reference book during rectification and later became one of the twelve books of required reading for cadres.

61. Li was head of both these departments. He was also deputy head of the Central Propaganda Department and was responsible for the work of training cadres. As a result, it was decided that he should take responsibility for both departments.

62. Li Weihan, "Zhongyang yanjiuyuan de yanjiu gongzuo he zhengfeng yundong," pp. 7–9. For the plans of the nine research departments in late 1941 and early 1942 see Wen Jize, Li Yan, et al., eds., *Yan'an zhongyang yanjiuyuan huiyi lu,* pp. 265–291.

63. Mao Zedong, "Xinminzhude zhengzhi yu xinminzhude wenhua," trans. in Saich, *The Rise to Power of the Chinese Communist Party,* Document F. 8. The miscellaneous collection of ideas associated with modernization, and westernization, not to mention Marxism, current in China, especially among May Fourth intellectuals, has been commented on many times. One might say the same for Mao's own views of such matters.

64. Mao Zedong, "Talks at the Yan'an Conference on Literature and Art," in Bonnie S. McDougall, *Mao Zedong's Talks at the Yan'an Conference on Literature and Art: A Translation of the 1943 Text with Commentary* (Ann Arbor: Michigan Papers in Chinese Studies no. 39, 1980), pp. 57–58.

65. With respect to the arts Mao was much influenced by both Lenin and Stalin. Lenin, unlike Krupskaya, his wife, or Trotsky, had extremely conservative views about art. Lenin was influenced by Chernyshevsky, who romanticized folk art, and he liked the Itinerants, or Wanderers, who returned to Russian folk culture for national inspiration. This inspirational, national emphasis on art he combined with strong views about how to use literature and the arts for propaganda purposes, or agitprop. He was opposed in taste and principle to the kind of work that exploded with such force in the Lunacharsky period, and the work of Tatlin, Malevich, Popova, Gonchorova, and Lissisky, as well as poets like Mayakovsky and Yesenin (both of whom committed suicide) and playwrights, architects, and musicians who were interested in revolutionary innovation in the arts. It was precisely this kind of innovation that Lenin saw as a threat to the class unity of a society under socialism

in which the artistic discourse would serve to separate creative work from popular enjoyments.

66. Jonathan Spence, *The Gate of Heavenly Peace: The Chinese and Their Revolution, 1895–1980* (Harmondsworth: Penguin Books, 1982).

67. Mao Zedong, "Xin minzhude zhengzhi yu xinminzhude wenhua," trans. in Saich, *The Rise to Power of the Chinese Communist Party,* Document F. 8.

68. See Merle Goldman, *Literary Dissent in Communist China* (Cambridge, Mass.: Harvard University Press, 1967), pp. 1–17. See also Merle Goldman, ed., *Modern Chinese Literature in the May Fourth Era* (Cambridge, Mass.: Harvard University Press, 1977).

69. Typescript prepared by Mao Dun listing fifty names and their crimes in the Nym Wales Collection, Hoover Institution. With kind permission from Helen Snow.

70. See Kyna Rubin, "Writers' Discontent and Party Response in Yan'an Before 'Wild Lily': The Manchurian Writers and Zhou Yang," *Modern Chinese Literature* 1 (September 1984): 79–193.

71. Ibid., p. 98.

72. Ibid., p. 82.

73. Ibid., p. 84.

74. Ibid., pp. 84–85.

75. Ibid., p. 95.

76. Mao Zedong, "Talks at the Yan'an Conference on Literature and Art," in McDougall, *Mao Zedong's Talks at the Yan'an Conference on Literature and Art,* pp. 60–61.

77. Wang Shiwei, "Statesman—Artist" in Dai Qing, *Wang Shiwei and "Wild Lilies": Rectification and Purges in the Chinese Communist Party 1942–1944* ed. and with an introduction by David E. Apter and Timothy C. Cheek (Armonk, N.Y.: M. E. Sharpe, 1993), pp. 109–110.

78. Ibid., p. 110.

79. Ibid.

80. Mao Zedong, "Reform in Learning, the Party, and Literature," February 1, 1942, in Compton, *Mao's China,* pp. 14–15.

81. See Mao's "Economic and Financial Problems" in Watson, *Mao Zedong and the Political Economy of the Border Region: A Translation of Mao's Economic and Financial Problems* (Cambridge: Cambridge University Press, 1980).

82. It was Liu Shaoqi who put it very well by citing Confucius: "'At fifteen, my mind was bent on learning. At thirty I could think for myself. At forty I was no longer perplexed. At fifty, I knew the degree of Heaven. At sixty, my ear was attuned to the truth. At seventy, I can follow my heart's desire, without transgressing what is right.' Here the feudal philosopher was referring to his own process of self-cultivation; he did not consider himself to have been born a 'sage'." Liu Shaoqi, *Three Essays on Party-Building,* (Beijing: Foreign Languages Press, 1980), p. 8.

83. Mao Zedong, "Concerning Methods of Leadership," in *Selected Works,* vol. 3, p. 119.

84. Mao Zedong, "Xin minzhude zhengzhi yu xin minzhude wenhua," trans. in Saich, *The Rise to Power of the Chinese Communist Party,* Document F. 8.

85. So similar is Mao's notion of class structure to Plato's that one can refer to Mao's

idea of appropriately functioning class as the enlightened gold, the protective silver, and the worthy brass.

8. Exegetical Bonding and the Phenomenology of Confession

1. See Michel Crozier and Erhard Friedberg, *L'acteur et le systéme* (Paris: Éditions du Seuil, 1977), pp. 325–347.

2. Ibid., p. 360.

3. Yang Shangkun, "Activities of the Trotskyite Wang Shiwei and Liberalism in the Party (October 31, 1942)," in Dai Qing, *Wang Shiwei and "Wild Lilies": Rectification and Purges in the Chinese Communist Party, 1942–1944* ed. and with an introduction by David E. Apter and Timothy C. Cheek (Armonk, N.Y.: M. E. Sharpe 1993), p. 162.

4. Liu Shaoqi, "On the Training of the Communist Party Member," delivered August 7, 1939 to the Academy of Marxism-Leninism, translated in Boyd Compton, *Mao's China: Party Reform Documents, 1942–44* (Seattle: University of Washington Press, 1952), p. 122.

5. See Jonathan Spence, *The Memory Palace of Matteo Ricci* (New York: Viking, 1984).

6. As some in Yan'an were moved to say, "Only three things are equal in Yan'an: the sun, the toilets, and the air." Quoted by Li Yaobing in "Wo zai Yan'an zhongyang dangxiao xuexide sannian" (My Three Years of Study at the Yan'an Central Party School), in *Yan'an zhongyang dangxiao de zhengfeng xuexi* (Beijing: Zhonggong zhongyang dangxiao chubanshe, 1988), vol. 1, p. 67.

7. Zhang Ruxin, "Zhongyang yanjiuyuan zhengfeng yilai sixiang gaizao zongjie—zai zhongyang yanjiuyuan zongjie dangfengshide baogao" (Summary Concerning Thought Reform at the Central Research Institute Since Rectification—Report Summarizing the Rectification of Party Style at the Central Research Institute), *Jiefang ribao* (Liberation Daily), October 31, 1942. This same concern was later expressed by the Institute's director, Li Weihan. Li Weihan, "Zhongyang yanjiuyuan de yanjiu gongzuo he zhengfeng yundong" (Research Work and the Rectification Campaign at the Central Research Institute), in Wen Jize, ed., *Yan'an zhongyang yanjiuyuan huiyilu* (Memoirs Concerning the Yan'an Central Research Institute) (Hunan: Zhongguo shehui kexue chubanshe, 1984), p. 13. Li claims that when rectification began, Yan'an was suffering from a wave of "extreme democratization" and "egalitarianism."

8. Huang Huoqing, Li Yan, et al., "Huigu Yan'an zhongyang dangxiao de zhengfeng yundong" (A Look Back at the Rectification Campaign in the Yan'an Central Party School), in *Yan'an zhongyang dangxiao de zhengfeng xuexi*, vol. 1, p. 21.

9. For a critique of this phenomenon and the "leftism" it caused within the party see Liu Shaoqi, "Guanyu guoqu baiqu gongzuo gei zhongyang de yifengxin" (A Letter to the Party Center Concerning Past Work in the White Areas), March 4, 1937, in The Secretariat of the CCP Central Committee (ed.), *Liuda yilai: Dangnei mimi wenjian* (Since the Sixth Party Congress. Secret Internal Party Documents) (Beijing: Renmin chubanshe, 1952), vol. 1, pp. 803–12, trans. in Tony Saich, *The Rise to Power of the Chinese Communist*

Party: Documents and Analysis, 1920–1949 (Armonk, N.Y.: M. E. Sharpe, 1994) (with a contribution by Benjamin Yang), Document E. 22.

10. There is a marvelously deceptive photograph in one of the many editions of Edgar Snow's *Red Star over China* of a child with a book in front of him and the caption "'Even the poorest shall read' was the slogan of the Communist Government Educational Commission in north Shensi [Shaanxi]. These children began early—reading the *ABC of Communism.*" This is, of course, Bukharin's introduction to communism for a lay public, and hardly an ABC in the usual sense of the word. See Edgar Snow, *Red Star over China* (New York: Vintage Books, 1947).

11. For an account of the campaign by Mao to promote the "new party history" see Tony Saich, "Writing or Re-writing Party History? The Construction of a Maoist Party History," in Tony Saich and Hans J. van de Ven, eds., *New Perspectives on the Chinese Communist Revolution* (Armonk, N.Y.: M. E. Sharpe, 1994).

12. Mao Zedong, "The Role of the Chinese Communist Party in the National War," in *Selected Works of Mao Tse-tung* (Beijing: Foreign Languages Press, 1965), vol. 2, pp. 259–260.

13. Mao Zedong, "Reform in Learning, the Party, and Literature," in Compton, *Mao's China*, pp. 21–22.

14. Mao Zedong, "Ruhe yanjiu Zhonggong dangshi" (How to Study CCP History), March 30, 1942, in *Dangshi ziliao zhengji tongxun* (Bulletin on the Collection of Materials on Party History) 1 (1985): 1–8.

15. For a discussion of these terms see David E. Apter, *Choice and the Politics of Allocation* (New Haven: Yale University Press, 1971).

16. "Zhongguo gongchandang zhongyang weiyuanhui guanyu ruogan lishi wenti de jueyi" (Resolution of the CCP Central Committee on Some Historical Questions), in the Secretariat of the CCP Central Committee, ed., *Liuda yilai*, vol. 1, pp. 1179–1200. An English translation can be found in *Selected Works of Mao Tse-Tung* (London: Lawrence and Wishart, 1956), vol. 4, pp. 171–218.

17. Until this time, official party history still credited Wang Ming and his supporters with the Bolshevization of the party—a process that had begun at the Fourth Plenum.

18. Mao Zedong, "Reform Our Studies," in Compton, *Mao's China*, p. 68.

19. Zhang Jingru et al., *Zhonggong dangshi xueshi* (Historiography of CCP History) (Beijing: Renmin daxue chubanshe, 1990), pp. 63–64. It was translated in Chongqing for distribution in GMD areas, in Shanghai for areas where the New Fourth Army was active, and in Moscow for distribution in the Shaan-Gan-Ning and other base areas in North China.

20. See telegram from Wang Jiaxiang and Mao Zedong to Zhou Enlai and Dong Biwu, November 17, 1941, in Documents Research Office of the CCP Central Committee, ed., *Wenxian he yanjiu 1984* (Documents and Research, 1984) (Bejing: Renmin chubanshe, 1985), p. 107.

21. Zhang Jingru et al., *Zhonggong dangshi xueshi*, p. 68.

22. Both were published under the imprimatur of the Secretariat of the CCP Central Committee. *Liuda yiqian. Dang de lishi cailiao* (Before the Sixth Party Congress. Party

Historical Materials) (Bejing: Renmin chubanshe, 1952), and *Liuda yilai: Dangnei mimi wenjian.*

23. Zhao Pu, "'Liuda yilai' he 'Liuda yiqian' liangshu jianjie" (A Short Introduction to the two Books "Since the Sixth Party Congress" and "Before the Sixth Party Congress"), *Dangshi yanjiu* (Research on Party History) 1 (1987), p. 7.

24. Pang Xianzhi, "Guanyu dang de wenxian bianji gongzuo de jige wenti" (On Several Problems in the Editing of Party Documents), *Wenxian he yanjiu* 3 (1986).

25. Mao Zedong, "Ruhe yanjiu Zhonggong dangshi," p. 1.

26. See, for example, *Zhengfeng wenxian* (Harbin: Jiefangshe, 1948). The initial eighteen were announced in an April 3, 1942, circular from the Central Propaganda Bureau and the other four were added on April 16. See "Zhonggong zhongyang xuanchuanbu guanyu zai Yan'an taolun zhongyang guiding ji Mao Zedong tongzhi zhengdun sanfeng baogao de jueding" (Decision of the Propaganda Bureau of the Central Committee on the Discussion in Yan'an on the Decision of the Central Committee and Mao Zedong's Report on Rectification of the Three [Unorthodox] Work-Styles), April 3, 1942, in Liberation Society, ed., *Zhengfeng wenxian*, pp. 1–5, trans. in Compton, *Mao's China*, pp. 1–8.

27. These seven were "Reform in Learning, the Party, and Literature" (February 1, 1942, report to the Central Party School), "In Opposition to Party Formalism" (February 8, 1942), "Second Preface to 'Village Investigations'" (March 17, 1941), "The Reconstruction of Our Studies" (May 5, 1941), "In Opposition to Liberalism" (September 7, 1937), "In Opposition to Several Incorrect Tendencies within the Party" (December 19, 1929), and "Address to the Shaan-Gan-Ning Border Region Assembly" (December 22, 1941).

28. The Yan'an Rectification Campaign Writing Group, ed., *Yan'an zhengfeng yundong jishi* (Chronology of the Yan'an Rectification Movement) (Beijing: Qiushi chubanshe, 1982), p. 10. This was a meeting convened by the Central Organization Department.

29. Ibid., p. 12.

30. "Zhonggong zhongyang ganbu jiaoyubu zhaokai xuexi dangyuan dahui" (The Cadre Education Department of the CCP Central Committee Convenes a Meeting for Party Members), *Xin Zhonghuabao* (New China), May 26, 1939.

31. On June 2, 1939, it was announced that the study movement in the Shaan-Gan-Ning Border Region government had already begun the study of party history, *Xin Zhonghuabao*. On June 6, the Chinese People's Anti-Japanese Military and Political University began study of the *Short Course*. The Yan'an Rectification Campaign Writing Group, ed., *Yan'an Zhengfeng yundong jishi*, p. 16.

32. Zhang Jingru et al., *Zhonggong dangshi xueshi*, pp. 64–65.

33. The Yan'an Rectification Campaign Writing Group, *Yan'an zhengfeng yundong jishi*, p. 41; and The Teaching and Research Department of the Central Party School, *Zhongguo gongchandang shigao* (A Draft History of the CCP) (Beijing: Renmin chubanshe, 1983), vol. 3, p. 145.

34. Mao Zedong, "Fandui zhuguan zhuyi he zongpai zhuyi" (Oppose Subjectivism and Sectarianism), in Documents Research Office of the CCP Control Committee, ed., *Wenxian he yanjiu 1985* (Bejing: Renmin chubanshe, 1986), pp. 1–7.

35. "Zhongyang guanyu gaoji xuexizu de jueding" (Central Committee Decision on

the Senior Study Group), in The Central Party Archives, ed., *Zhonggong zhongyang wenjian xuanji* (Selected Documents of the CCP Central Committee) (Beijing: Zhonggong zhongyang dangxiao chubanshe, 1982–1991), vol. 11, p. 743.

36. This report was important as it called for the Comintern to loosen its direct control over national communist parties. Dimitrov called for problems to be settled on the basis of the concrete conditions and situation in the individual countries.

37. Telegram from Mao Zedong and Wang Jiaxiang to Zhou Enlai, February 21, 1942.

38. "Resolution of the Central Committee of the Chinese Communist Party on the Yenan Cadre School," in Compton, *Mao's China*, pp. 74–79.

39. Mao Zedong, "Rectification of Study, Party Style and the Style of Writing," February 1, 1942, in Compton, *Mao's China*, pp. 9–32, and "Oppose the Party's Eight-Legged Essay [Party Formalism])," in ibid., pp. 33–53.

40. "Guanyu dangxiao zuzhi ji jiaoyu fangzhen de xin guiding" (New Regulations Concerning the Organization of the Party School and Education Policy), February 28, 1942.

41. Together with Lu Dingyi, Peng was also to be responsible for editing a study paper at the Party School.

42. "Guanyu zhongyang dangxiao xuesheng ruxue yu diaodong wenti de guiding" (Regulations Concerning the Question of the Recruitment and Transfer of Students to the Central Party School), March 11, 1942, in *Yan'an zhongyang dangxiao de zhengfeng xuexi*, vol. 1, p. 67.

43. The Northwest Bureau by this time was under the leadership of Gao Gang and provided strong institutional support for Mao Zedong.

44. "Decision of the CCP Central Committee Concerning the Education of Cadres in Service," February 28, 1942, in Compton, *Mao's China*, pp. 80–88.

45. "Zhonggong zhongyang xuanchuanbu guanyu zai quandang jinxing zhengdun sanfeng xuexi yundong de zhishi" (Directive of the Propaganda Bureau of the Central Committee Concerning Implementation of the Rectification Movement of the Three [Unorthodox] Work-Styles Throughout the Party), June 8, 1942, in The Central Party Archives, ed., *Zhonggong zhongyang wenjian xuanji neibuben*, vol. 12, pp. 84–93.

46. John Byron and Robert Pack, *The Claws of the Dragon: Kang Sheng—The Evil Genius Behind Mao—and His Legacy of Terror in People's China* (New York: Simon and Schuster, 1992), pp. 155–157.

47. Ibid., p. 173.

48. Overseeing study groups in the Border Region administration were Ren Bishi (who drafted the resolution on party history) and Gao Gang; study for groups under the Central Committee was overseen by Kang Sheng and Li Fuchun; and the groups under the military system were overseen by Wang Jiaxiang (who invented the term "Mao Zedong Thought") and Chen Yun.

49. "Yan'an yigeyue xuexi yundong de zongjie" (Summary of One Month of Study in Yan'an), *Jiefang ribao*, June 5, 1942.

50. Peng Zhen, "Linghui ershier wenjian de jingshen yu shizhi" (Comprehend the Spirit and Essence of the Twenty-Two Documents), *Jiefang ribao*, May 14, 1942.

51. Huang Huoqing, Li Yan, et al., "Huigu Yan'an zhongyang dangxiao de zhengfeng yundong," vol. 1, pp. 28–29.

52. The Yan'an Rectification Campaign Writing Group (ed.), *Yan'an zhengfeng yundong jishi,* pp. 232–234.

53. Ibid., p. 193. This was decided by the party committee on June 11, 1942.

54. *Jiefang ribao,* May 12, 1943.

55. Zhang Baichun, "Lingdao ganbu yao shishi qiushi, xiang qunzhong xuexi" (Leading Cadres Must Seek Truth From Facts and Learn From the Masses), in *Yan'an zhongyang dangxiao de zhengfeng xuexi,* vol. 1, p. 246.

56. This he did in two speeches: "On the Relations Between the Chinese Communist Party and the Kuomintang from 1924 to 1926," Spring 1943, in *Selected Works of Zhou Enlai* (Beijing: Foreign Languages Press, 1981), vol. 1, pp. 130–143 and "On the Sixth Congress of the Party," April 3–4, 1944, in ibid., pp. 177–210.

57. Zhou Enlai, "Zai Yan'an zhongyang zhengzhiju huiyishang de fayan (jielu)" (Speech at Yan'an Politburo Meeting [Extracts]), in Committee for the Collection of Materials on CCP History and the Central Party Archives, eds., *Zunyi huiyi wenxian* (Documents on the Zunyi Conference) (Beijing: Renmin chubanshe, 1985), pp. 64–65.

58. Zhang Wentian, "Cong Fujian shibian dao Zunyi huiyi" (From the Futian Incident to the Zunyi Conference), in ibid., pp. 78–80.

59. Bo Gu, "Zai zhongyang zhengzhiju huiyishang de fayan (jielu)" (Speech at Politburo Meeting [Extracts]), November 13, 1943, in ibid., p. 103.

60. Bo Gu, "Zai Zhongguo gongchandang diqici quanguo daibiao dahuishang de fayan (jielu)" (Speech at the Seventh Congress of the CCP [Extracts]), May 3, 1945, in ibid., pp. 104–107.

61. See Wang's account of his discussion with Mao Zedong in April 1944. Wang Ming, *Mao's Betrayal* (Moscow: Progress Publishers, 1979), pp. 61–62.

62. The members of the Presidium were Mao Zedong, Zhu De, Liu Shaoqi, Ren Bishi, and Zhou Enlai. See Wang Ming, *Mao's Betrayal,* p. 145.

63. Party History Materials and Research Department of the Central Party Archives, "Yan'an zhengfeng zhong de Wang Ming" (Wang Ming During Yan'an Rectification), *Dangshi tongxun* (Bulletin on Party History) 7 (1987): 11. According to Wang himself, he initially refused to write a statement acknowledging the "Resolution" and repenting his mistakes. Eventually, after discussions with friends, Wang claims that he wrote the letter so that he could preserve his position for a future struggle against Mao Zedong. Wang Ming, *Mao's Betrayal,* p. 145.

64. Liu Shaoqi, "Report on the Revision of the Party Constitution," in Liu Shaoqi, *Three Essays on Party-Building* (Beijing: Foreign Languages Press, 1980), pp. 163–300.

65. For more details, see Timothy C. Cheek, "Textually Speaking: An Assessment of Newly Available Mao Texts," in Roderick MacFarquhar, Timothy Cheek, and Eugene Wu, eds., *The Secret Speeches of Chairman Mao: From the Hundred Flowers to the Great Leap Forward* (Cambridge, Mass.: Harvard Contemporary China Series, no. 6, 1989), pp. 83–86.

66. Gong Yuzhi, "Tong Shi Lamu jiaoshoude tanhua" (A Discussion with Professor Schram), in *Wenxian he yanjiu: 1984 nian huibianben* (Documents and Research: 1984 Selections) (Beijing: Renmin chubanshe, 1986), pp. 243–244.

67. Ibid.

68. Cheek, "Textually Speaking," p. 84.

69. *Mao Zedong xuanji* (n.p.: Jin Cha Ji xinhua shudian, 1944).

70. Both were to play similar roles during the Cultural Revolution, when the inquisitional techniques used in Yan'an were applied en masse, again orchestrated by Kang Sheng. Chen Boda eventually was convicted together with the "Gang of Four"; Kang Sheng died before being brought to trial.

71. See "Abstract of Kang Sheng's Report to a Training Class," August 1943, in Dai Qing, *Wang Shiwei and "Wild Lilies,"* p. 168.

72. Kang Sheng, "Rescue Those Who Have Lost Their Footing," July 15, 1943, in Zhong Kan, *Kang Sheng pingzhuan* (A Critical Biography of Kang Sheng) (Beijing: Hongqi chubanshe, 1982) trans. in Byron and Pack, *The Claws of the Dragon,* p. 179.

73. See, for example, Byron and Pack, *The Claws of the Dragon.*

74. See Zhong Kan, *Kang Sheng pingzhuan.* An account that was clearly prepared to disgrace Kang, this was compiled from materials unearthed during the official investigations conducted into Kang Sheng between 1978 and 1980. The investigation began after Hu Yaobang denounced Kang Sheng by name at the Central Party School. Hu Yaobang, "Guanyu qingsuan Kang Sheng wenti" (Concerning the Issue of the Exposure of Kang Sheng), *Zhongguoren yuekan* (Chinese Monthly) 2 (May 1980): 15–25.

75. It should be noted here that Yu was not even one of the five criticized. Kang simply proclaims that in fact Yu was the sixth member of the group and was its real leader.

76. "Abstract of Kang Sheng's Report to a Training Class," in Dai Qing, *Wang Shiwei and "Wild Lilies,"* p. 174.

77. Ibid., p. 166.

78. The Rescue Campaign was not prosecuted with such vigor in other base areas or behind enemy lines.

79. See his report delivered on March 29, 1944, at a senior cadres' conference in the Northwest Bureau. It is extracted in Warren Kuo, *Analytical History of the Chinese Communist Party* (Taibei: Institute for International Relations, 1968), book 4, p. 421.

80. Paul Ricoeur, *The Symbolism of Evil* (New York: Harper and Row, 1968).

81. Clifford Geertz, "Deep Play: Notes on the Balinese Cockfight," in *The Interpretation of Cultures* (New York: Basic Books, 1973), pp. 412–454.

82. For an excellent discussion of the parodic factor from which the term "parodic negativity" has been adapted, see James A. Boon, "Folly, Bali, and Anthropology or Satire across Cultures," in Edward M. Bruner, ed., *Text, Play, and Story: The Construction and Reconstruction of Self and Society* (Washington, D.C.: The American Ethnological Society, 1983), pp. 156–177.

9. Foucault's Paradox and the Politics of Contending Discourses

1. See James W. Fernandez, *Persuasions and Performances. The Play of Tropes in Culture* (Bloomington: The University of Indiana Press, 1986), p. 43: "While the phenomenological account of a religious experience or any expressive event remains uncertain in nature and perhaps as densely metaphoric as the experience itself, understanding may be sharpened

by scrutinizing the network of associations brought into play in metaphoric predications and performances. Association may be by contiguity or by similarity. Metonym is commonly understood as resting on contiguity in the same frame of experience as the subject and metaphor as resting on similarity, perceived or felt (structural or textual), of experiences in different domains."

2. We use the term "pragmatism" to refer to the notion that there is nothing external to experience, and that meaning is a function of context.

3. See the discussion in Tony Saich, *The Rise to Power of the Chinese Communist Party: Documents and Analysis, 1920–1949* (Armonk, N.Y.: M. E. Sharpe, 1994), introduction; and Hans J. van de Ven, *From Friend to Comrade. The Founding of the Chinese Communist Party, 1920–1927* (Berkeley: University of California Press, 1991), p. 201 and pp. 226–234.

4. See Stuart Schram, *The Political Thought of Mao Tse-tung* (New York: Praeger, 1974). As Schram notes, "The idea that poverty may lead to revolution bears some relationship to Marxism, though Marx singled out the proletariat as the saviour of society not merely because its members were poor but because of the decisive role they played in the productive process." p. 101.

5. See Fernandez, *Persuasions and Performances*, pp. 130–156.

6. See Schram, *The Political Thought of Mao Tse-tung*, p. 71.

7. For an excellent discussion of the effects of education on memory and logical skills see Jack Goody, *The Interface Between the Written and the Oral* (Cambridge: Cambridge University Press, 1987).

8. During this period Mao reenacted a world of enemies and tried to repeat the earlier struggles against revisionism and imperialism; the United States and the Soviet Union replaced the Japanese and the nationalists.

9. It is no accident that virtually every Marxist party in Western Europe converted itself into a social democratic one, accepting market principles and democracy. It is precisely this tendency to "routinize" Marxism in the form of social democracy that communist parties have resisted more than any other. See David E. Apter, "Social Democracy" in Tom Bottomore, ed., *Blackwell's Encyclopedia of the Social Sciences* (Oxford: Blackwell's, 1992).

10. However, there are plenty of other ways in which the party is willing to make changes that would in Mao's time have been utterly unthinkable, such as allowing local stock markets and special economic zones.

11. On this point see Tony Saich, "Much Ado About Nothing: Party Reform in the Eighties," in Gordon White, ed., *The Chinese State in the Era of Economic Reform: The Road to Crisis* (Basingstoke: Macmillan Press, 1991), pp. 149–174.

12. Mao Zedong, "The Chinese Revolution and the Chinese Communist Party," in *Selected Works of Mao Tse-tung* (Beijing: Foreign Languages Press, 1965), vol. 2, pp. 326–327.

13. Mao describes the framework of this transition in his essay "New Democratic Politics and New Democratic Culture."

14. Quoted in Raymond Wylie, *The Emergence of Maoism: Mao Tse-tung, Ch'en Po-ta, and the Search for Chinese Theory, 1935–1945* (Stanford: Stanford University Press, 1980), p. 31.

15. Ibid., p. 41.

16. Perhaps the best discussion of these matters is still Stuart Schram's *The Political Thought of Mao Tse-Tung,* pp. 73–102.

17. Ibid.

18. Bourdieu uses the term "symbolic capital" to refer to precisely calibrated sets of valued qualities that are exchanged in mutually comprehended reciprocities in an exact parallel to monetary or economic exchanges.

19. Plato, *Republic,* trans. and with a commentary by Stephen Halliwell (Warminster: Aris and Phillips, 1988), p. 1.

20. *International Herald Tribune,* April 24, 1992.

21. This should not be taken to imply that the movement of 1989 was of itself a democratic one.

22. It was the Ming Emperors who built the Forbidden City and its high walls, the gates of which open into the square.

23. Tony Saich, "When Worlds Collide: The Beijing People's Movement of 1989," in Tony Saich, ed., *The Chinese People's Movement. Perspectives on Spring 1989* (Armonk, N.Y.: M. E. Sharpe, 1990), pp. 25–49.

24. Lenin's tomb, built of red marble, cubic, if not actually a cube, impacts on the entire space. Indeed, it is so powerful that, despite its small size, it dominates the larger structures around it. The Kremlin wall serves as its backdrop. Indeed, the Kremlin itself, once the place of mystery and terror, has been made more ordinary by the functioning of government, a place of offices, museums, and residences. A similar result has occurred with Zhongnanhai, the area at the western corner of Tiananmen Square where party leaders and top government cadres work and live. The most important difference between these two foci of political power, Beijing and Moscow, is that in the former, Mao's tomb, despite its enormous bulk, does not in fact dominate. Built in a nondescript Stalinist architectural style (with Chinese ornamental characteristics) it fails utterly as a reenactment of Lenin's tomb. It fails too as a reenactment of the tombs of the Ming emperors, which were constructed almost in the shape of a diamond, half above and half below ground, or a double pyramid, one apex towards the sun, the other deep below the earth, so that one must climb up to enter and then go down and down to the tomb at the inverted, or negative, apex, which is perpetually sealed, silent.

25. Initially, Mao lay alone. It was only as the reforms began in the late seventies and early eighties and Deng Xiaoping and his supporters began to revise Mao's legacy stressing the "collective" nature of his thought, that Mao was forced to share his resting place with the other "heroes of the revolution."

26. The monument, the mausoleum, and the Gate of Heavenly Peace might be said to constitute the triangle within the square; together as a design and architecture, they stand for balance, harmony, the cosmos, the sublime. Tiananmen is a formal space, its properties relational, its shape, volume, and form waiting to be filled. A fourth point is just off the square to the rear of Mao's mausoleum and has become a far more significant scene of pilgrimage. This is the largest Kentucky Fried Chicken emporium in the world, with not one but two waxy-looking effigies of Colonel Saunders, rotund, like Mao in his tomb, and almost the same size.

27. Just as Mao's mummy has a waxen quality, more effigy than corpse, so the portrait

is bland, without character, something like a billboard, even a cartoon. All it needs is a painted balloon coming out of its mouth, extended over the pink wall, with one of the quotations from the sacred writings, like "Political power grows out of the barrel of a gun." But since there is no balloon one can attribute whatever thoughts one wants to Chairman Mao.

28. See also Frank Niming, "Learning How to Protest," in Tony Saich, ed., *The Chinese People's Movement*, pp. 83–105.

29. Sometimes the government does learn, as an earlier case study of the conflict between the Hantai Domei and the Japanese government over the airport shows. What the Japanese government learned, among other things, was to negotiate with local officials before making policies affecting particular local areas. However, it took a very long time and many years before such learning occurred. See David E. Apter and Nagayo Sawa, *Against the State. Politics and Social Protest in Japan* (Cambridge, Mass.: Harvard University Press, 1984).

30. See Victor W. Turner, *The Ritual Process* (Chicago: Aldine Publishing Co., 1969), pp. 94–130; and David E. Apter, "Espace public/espace privé" in *Politiques et management public* 5 (September 1987).

31. Terms like simulacrum, spectacle, and magic realism have in the past been used very differently from the way we use them. They have their origins in Marx's notions of the fetishism of commodities and false consciousness, characteristics he regarded as uniquely endemic to capitalism. They have been examined particularly in relation to what has been called "commodification"—the reification of conceptual principles as well as the substitution of artificial worlds for an understanding of the real one, a condition not only of high capitalism but postmodernism. The works of Jean Baudrillard, Guy Dabord, and Frederic Jameson are relevant to this sense of these terms. Our usage is not entirely different, but it is stripped of their implications. What these terms describe is far more applicable to socialist societies than capitalist ones. In no society is commodification more rampant than in socialist society. In those societies magic realism has been carried to its extremes, politically and by design. In any case, one can use the concepts without locking into any particular form of economic or political system.

32. For an interesting discussion of the tradition of student protest in China, see Jeffrey N. Wasserstrom, "Student Protests and the Chinese Tradition, 1919–1989," in Tony Saich, ed., *The Chinese People's Movement*, pp. 3–24.

33. For a review of this period see Tony Saich, "The Reform Decade in China: The Limits to Revolution from Above," in Marta Dassù and Tony Saich, eds., *The Reform Decade in China: From Hope to Dismay* (London: Kegan Paul International, 1992), pp. 10–73.

34. For a full account of the role of the military see Timothy Brook, *Quelling the People: The Military Suppression of the Beijing Democracy Movement* (Oxford: Oxford University Press, 1992).

35. As each anniversary approaches, the authorities step up the guard on the symbolic space, allowing it to be filled only by their own security agents or dancing children singing their love for Tiananmen Square. For the anniversary in 1992, the authorities even banned unsolicited laughter in the square.

36. Adapted from the translation in Geremie Barmé and John Minford, eds., *Seeds of Fire: Chinese Voices of Conscience* (Hong Kong: Far Eastern Economic Affairs, 1986), pp. 256–257.

37. *Guanxi* refers to connections and is understood by all in China as pertaining to the cultivation of beneficial contacts.

38. The need continually to look over their shoulder to judge what their patron is thinking severely hampers the capacity of the "younger" generation of leaders to develop their own independent power bases that can survive their patron's death. This confirms the view that the real power struggle for succession will begin only when the generation of Yan'anites has disappeared entirely from the scene.

39. It is also not simply corruption. The practice has certain rules and patterns of obligation. It is, moreover, rooted in traditional China, but elevated now to become a crucial element in market socialism. And whatever else it is, it is not democratic.

40. This speech was disseminated within the party as Central Document No. 2. The full text can be found in the Hong Kong magazine *Zhengming,* April 1, 1992, pp. 23–27. For a discussion that places the document in the broader context of reform attempts see Tony Saich, "Peaceful Evolution With Chinese Characteristics," in William Joseph, ed., *China Briefing 1992* (Boulder: Westview Press, 1993), pp. 9–34.

41. The most likely way to transform the taken-for-granted quality of a space is by violating its obvious purposefulness. When a street is occupied by militants in Paris, or a public building becomes a fortress, or farmers and militants occupy terrain around an airport and convert it into a mobilization space, that terrain becomes endowed with special meanings. It produces outrage. It challenges the authority of the state. It calls conventional purposes into question.

42. Unfortunately, in politics "experiments" are usually nonretrievable. Nor can leaders back away from the consequences. Hence, given the extraordinary problems of China, it is not so surprising that its leaders back away from political experiment.

43. Karl R. Popper, *The Open Society and Its Enemies* (London: George Routledge and Sons, 1945), vol. 1, pp. 172–173.

44. Without going into the matter, we would reject out of hand the view that modern Taiwan is the alternative that would have taken hold in China.

INDEX

✳

"AB" (Anti-Bolshevik) Squads, 84, 176, 351n7
Academy of Marxian Communism, 229
Academy of Military Affairs, 281
After the Sixth Party Congress, 276, 279, 288, 364n25
Ai Qing, 62
Ai Siqi, 37, 64, 89, 102, 115, 154, 157, 238, 239, 242
All-China Writers' Resistance Association, 250
Alley, Rewi, 311, 354n36
Althusser, Louis, 311
An Ziwen, 241
Anarchism, 17, 74, 101, 119, 128, 132, 151; and Chinese society, 13; and mutualism, 16, 243
Anderson, Benedict, 75
Anglo-French war (1856–1860), 92
Apter, David E., 337n4
Arrow and Target (Shi yu di), 63
Artists: attitude to Yan'an, 171; and Mao, 170, 252–253; in Russian revolution, 247; at Yan'an, 167–171, 246–247, 252–253, 254
Arts, 67, 89, 144, 227, 246–247, 252, 260, 378n65. *See also* Literature; Mao Zedong: on literature and art
August First Declaration (1935), 54, 196, 369n33
August 7 Emergency Conference (1927), 268
Autumn Harvest Uprising, 90, 94, 103, 305

Bai Dongcai, 241
Bakunin, Mikhail, 128
Banditry, 72, 78, 191, 192, 194, 204, 367n14, 368n17; and CCP, 50, 96, 200; and Mao, 79, 121
Barthes, Roland, 22, 114, 337n3
Before the Sixth Party Congress, 276, 364n25
Beijing Opera, 168

Beijing University, 30, 39, 101, 148
Benjamin, Walter, 69, 70
Bernstein, Edouard, 125
Bethune, Norman, 170
Bo Gu, 37, 83, 162, 199, 370n43; and Wang Ming, 56, 286, 287; and Zhang Guotao, 43, 44, 45
Border Region, 226, 228, 273, 282; blockade of, 217, 218; control of, 36. *See also particular border regions*
Borodin, Mikhail, 83, 352n17
Bourdieu, Pierre, 33, 107, 308, 311, 338n15, 351n3, 387n18
Bourgeoisie, 66, 119, 123, 124, 196, 209, 210, 211, 221, 278, 281
Boxer Rebellion, 92, 118, 304
Braun, Otto (Li De), 37, 83, 165, 286
Buddhism, 34, 38, 91, 243
Bukharin, Nicolai, 80, 83, 278, 381n10
Bureaucratism, 133, 220

Cao Meng, 88, 354n32
Capitalism, 92, 97, 117, 128, 129, 132, 138, 152; and communism, 120, 125, 210, 221, 305, 329; comprador, 9, 14, 76, 118, 119, 124; democratic, 330; foreign, 117, 118; international, 304; and modernization, 120; nomenclature, 322, 325; runaway, 30; and socialism, 327, 329
Cave of the 10,000 Buddhas, printing press in, 88, 146, 147, 189, 247
Caves: living in, 26, 159, 166, 173, 227, 239, 302, 367n10; present-day, 187–188, 189; republic of the, 14, 34, 74, 190, 312; visits to, 24, 366n45
CCP. *See* Chinese Communist Party
Central Military Commission, 41, 43, 47, 48, 236, 345n31